REPORTING DISCOURSE, TENSE, AND COGNITION

Related Elsevier Books

BRAS and VIEU (eds.)
Semantic and Pragmatic Issues in Discourse and Dialogue: Experimenting with Current Dynamic Theories

CUTTING
Analysing the Language of Discourse Communities

JASZCZOLT (Ed.)
Discourse, Beliefs and Intentions: Semantic Defaults and Propositional Attitude Ascription

SORACE, HEYCOCK and SHILLCOCK (eds.)
Language Acquisition: Knowledge Representation and Processing

Related Elsevier Book Series

Current Research in the Semantics Pragmatics Interface (CRiSPI)
Series editors: K.M. Jaszczolt and K. Turner

Related Elsevier Journals

Journal of Neurolinguistics
Editors: John Marshall and Michel Paradis

Journal of Pragmatics
Editor: Jacob Mey

Language & Communication
Editors: Roy Harris and Talbot J. Taylor

Language Sciences
Editor: Nigel Love

Lingua
Editors: Johan Rooryck, Neil Smith and Diane Blakemore

On-line journal sample copies available at http://www.elsevier.com/locate/linguistics

For full information about all Elsevier linguistics publications go to:
http://www.socscinet.com/linguistics

REPORTING DISCOURSE, TENSE, AND COGNITION

BY

TOMOKO I SAKITA

*Institute for Language and Culture, Doshisha University
Kyoto, Japan*

2002
Elsevier

Amsterdam – Boston – London – New York – Oxford – Paris
San Diego – San Francisco – Singapore – Sydney – Tokyo

ELSEVIER SCIENCE Ltd
The Boulevard, Langford Lane
Kidlington, Oxford OX5 1GB, UK

© 2002 Elsevier Science Ltd. All rights reserved.

This work is protected under copyright by Elsevier Science, and the following terms and conditions apply to its use:

Photocopying
Single photocopies of single chapters may be made for personal use as allowed by national copyright laws. Permission of the Publisher and payment of a fee is required for all other photocopying, including multiple or systematic copying, copying for advertising or promotional purposes, resale, and all forms of document delivery. Special rates are available for educational institutions that wish to make photocopies for non-profit educational classroom use.

Permissions may be sought directly from Elsevier Science via their homepage (http://www.elsevier.com) by selecting 'Customer support' and then 'Permissions'. Alternatively you can send an e-mail to: permissions@elsevier.co.uk, or fax to: (+44) 1865 853333.

In the USA, users may clear permissions and make payments through the Copyright Clearance Center, Inc., 222 Rosewood Drive, Danvers, MA 01923, USA; phone: (+1) (978) 7508400, fax: (+1) (978) 7504744, and in the UK through the Copyright Licensing Agency Rapid Clearance Service (CLARCS), 90 Tottenham Court Road, London W1P 0LP, UK; phone: (+44) 207 631 5555; fax: (+44) 207 631 5500. Other countries may have a local reprographic rights agency for payments.

Derivative Works
Tables of contents may be reproduced for internal circulation, but permission of Elsevier Science is required for external resale or distribution of such material.
Permission of the Publisher is required for all other derivative works, including compilations and translations.

Electronic Storage or Usage
Permission of the Publisher is required to store or use electronically any material contained in this work, including any chapter or part of a chapter.

Except as outlined above, no part of this work may be reproduced, stored in a retrieval system or transmitted in any form or by any means, electronic, mechanical, photocopying, recording or otherwise, without prior written permission of the Publisher.
Address permissions requests to: Elsevier Science Global Rights Department, at the mail, fax and e-mail addresses noted above.

Notice
No responsibility is assumed by the Publisher for any injury and/or damage to persons or property as a matter of products liability, negligence or otherwise, or from any use or operation of any methods, products, instructions or ideas contained in the material herein. Because of rapid advances in the medical sciences, in particular, independent verification of diagnoses and drug dosages should be made.

First edition 2002

```
British Library Cataloguing in Publication Data

Sakita, Tomoko I.
  Reporting discourse, tense, and cognition
  1.Discourse analysis 2.Grammar, Comparative and general -
  Tense 3.Cognition 4.Sociolinguistics - Methodology
  I.Title
  306.4'4

  ISBN 008044041X
```

Library of Congress Cataloging in Publication Data

Sakita, Tomoko I.
  Reporting discourse, tense, and cognition / by Tomoko I Sakita.--1st ed.
    p. cm.
  Includes bibliographical references and indexes.
  ISBN 0-08-044041-X (alk. paper)
    1. Grammar, Comparative and general--Indirect discourse. 2. Grammar, Comparative and general--Tense. 3. Discourse analysis--Psychological aspects. 4. Language and languages--Style. I. Title.

P301.5.I53 S25 2002
415--dc21
2002068371

ISBN: 0-08-044041-X

∞ The paper used in this publication meets the requirements of ANSI/NISO Z39.48-1992 (Permanence of Paper).
Printed in The Netherlands.

To my parents, Mikiko Sakita and Masahiro Sakita

Contents

Acknowledgments xi

Chapter 1. Introduction
    1.1. Reporting discourse 1
        1.1.1. What is reporting discourse 1
        1.1.2. Significance of reporting discourse 3
        1.1.3. Working questions on reporting discourse 6
        1.1.4. Narrative 7
    1.2. Discourse perspectives 9
        1.2.1. Reporting discourse and context 9
        1.2.2. Discourse analysis 10
    1.3. Overview of chapters 14
    1.4. Data 18

Chapter 2. Review and Problems of Tense-Alternation Theories
    2.0. Overview 19
    2.1. Tense-alternation theories 20
        2.1.1. Traditional theory of HP 20
        2.1.2. Syntactic hypothesis 21
        2.1.3. Timeless present 22
        2.1.4. CHP alternation theory 23
        2.1.5. Clause types and directions of switch 24
        2.1.6. HP in the theory of consciousness 26
    2.2. Problem: *say/said* alternation 27
        2.2.1. *Say* as a special class of reporting verbs 27
        2.2.2. No regularity in *say/said* alternation 28
        2.2.3. Wolfson's hypotheses 29
            2.2.3.1. 'Speech act hypothesis' 29
            2.2.3.2. 'Single speaker continuity hypothesis' 30
            2.2.3.3. 'Third-person story hypothesis' 31
            2.2.3.4. 'Participant distinction hypothesis' 32
            2.2.3.5. 'Outside the tense system hypothesis' 34
            2.2.3.6. 'Relative status hypothesis' 35
        2.2.4. Johnstone's hypothesis 35
            2.2.4.1. New relative status hypothesis 35
            2.2.4.2. Problems with relative status hypothesis 39
    2.3. Conclusions and directions for further research 41

Chapter 3. Cognitive Backgrounds of Tense-Alternation
    3.0. Overview 43
    3.1. Tense and person 44
        3.1.1. Distribution in discourse 44
        3.1.2. Personal deixis and tense forms 50
    3.2. Interpretive processes of reporting 51

viii   Contents

  3.3. Cognitive Recollection Model (CRM)   54
    3.3.1. Construals of perceived events   54
    3.3.2. Construals of remembered events   54
      3.3.2.1. Base   54
      3.3.2.2. Recall of third-person interactions   58
      3.3.2.3. Recall of self-involving interactions   61
  3.4. Psychological involvement   67
  3.5. Self-identity   69
    3.5.1. Levels of narrative   70
    3.5.2. Manipulations of 'footing'   71
    3.5.3. 'Speak for yourself' rule in 'constructed dialogues'   73
    3.5.4. Divided self   74
    3.5.5. Cognitive monitoring theories   75
  3.6. Backgrounds of prevalence of *I says*   76
  3.7. Conclusion   78

Chapter 4. Tense and Attitudinal Contrast
  4.0. Overview   81
  4.1. Searching vs. resultative mode   82
    4.1.1. *Says* vs. *said* in pair   82
    4.1.2. *Says* vs. *said* in a single speaker's speech   85
    4.1.3. *Says, saying, say* vs. *said* in a single speaker's speech   87
    4.1.4. Summary of contrasts   88
  4.2. Conflict vs. conflict-avoidance   89
    4.2.1. *Said* vs. *said* shows conflict; *says* shows watching the situation   89
    4.2.2. *Said* shows challenge; *says* shows step-back   94
    4.2.3. *Said* shows never-intimidated attitude; *says* shows step-back   99
    4.2.4. Summary of contrasts   104
  4.3. Weak vs. strong attitude   106
    4.3.1. Degrees of assuredness in *I don't know*   106
    4.3.2. Degrees of firmness in negation and affirmation   109
    4.3.3. Degrees of upset in exclamation   110
    4.3.4. Summary of contrasts   113
  4.4. Conclusion   116

Chapter 5. Consciousness Flow, Discourse Acts, and Tense
  5.0. Overview   119
  5.1. Discourse organization units   120
  5.2. Consciousness flow in discourse   123
  5.3. Consciousness flow in narrative dialogues   124
    5.3.1. Consciousness flow in exchanges   126
      5.3.1.1. Adjacency pair   126
      5.3.1.2. Three-part exchange   132
    5.3.2. Consciousness flow over a series of remarks   133
      5.3.2.1. In a single speaker's speech   133
      5.3.2.2. Over a series of remarks   141

Contents   ix

	5.3.3.	Consciousness flow in repetition of dialogue-introducers	150
		5.3.3.1. Pre-posing double dialogue-introducers	150
		5.3.3.2. Post-posing dialogue-introducers	151
		5.3.3.3. At restatements	155
	5.4. Conclusion		156

Chapter 6. Tense in Indirect Reporting Discourse
- 6.0. Overview — 159
- 6.1. Treatments of tense in grammar — 160
- 6.2. Pragmatic view — 162
- 6.3. Declerck's hypothesis — 163
- 6.4. Tense in discourse — 165
  - 6.4.1. Prevalence of speaker's viewpoint — 165
  - 6.4.2. Avoidance of the past perfect tense — 170
  - 6.4.3. Discourse functional use of the past perfect tense — 172
  - 6.4.4. Reporting clause as dialogue marker — 174
- 6.5. Conclusion — 181

Chapter 7. Reporting Discourse Style and Function
- 7.0. Overview — 183
- 7.1. General characterizations of reporting discourse style and function — 184
  - 7.1.1. Theoretical backgrounds — 184
  - 7.1.2. Pragmatic studies — 188
- 7.2. Reporting style and structure — 191
  - 7.2.0. Overview — 191
  - 7.2.1. Preliminary study — 191
  - 7.2.2. Experimental study — 193
    - 7.2.2.1. Method — 193
    - 7.2.2.2. Data analysis procedures — 195
    - 7.2.2.3. Results — 195
  - 7.2.3. Backgrounds of structural influence on style choice — 202
  - 7.2.4. Summary — 204
- 7.3. Reporting function and pattern — 205
  - 7.3.0. Overview — 205
  - 7.3.1. Method — 206
  - 7.3.2. Reporting discourse functions — 206
    - 7.3.2.1. Evidentiality — 206
      - 7.3.2.1.1. Disagreement and persuasion — 207
      - 7.3.2.1.2. Response — 210
    - 7.3.2.2. Foreground and background information — 211
      - 7.3.2.2.1. Showing climaxes or punch-lines — 212
      - 7.3.2.2.2. Exemplification and demonstration of emotion — 213
    - 7.3.2.3. Dramatization — 215
      - 7.3.2.3.1. Dramatizing imaginary and future events — 216
      - 7.3.2.3.2. Dramatizing archetypical events — 221

7.3.3. Summary	222
7.4. Correlations between style and function	222
7.4.1. Reporting discourse on continuum	223
7.4.2. Style and function along a continuum	224
7.5. Conclusion	225

Chapter 8. Conclusion

8.1. Summary of chapters	227
8.2. Theoretical implications	231
8.3. Future perspectives	233

Notes	235
Transcription Conventions	257
References	259
Author Index	283
Subject Index	287

Acknowledgments

I first wish to express my greatest respect and deep gratitude to my mentor, Professor Masa-aki Yamanashi, who gave me constant guidance and illuminating comments throughout every stage of my graduate studies at Kyoto University, and afterward. His open-minded academic approach with its broad perspective on human intellect and how it is influenced by environment, and his focus on pragmatics and cognitive linguistics, inspired me to integrate both theoretical and empirical techniques in the interdisciplinary study of human reporting behavior, with special emphasis on discourse and cognition. His tremendous enthusiasm, thoroughness, and insight will continue to influence me throughout my career as a linguist.

I wish to thank my other professors at Kyoto University for their unending patience, guidance, and inspiration. Professor Shinobu Kitayama gave me invaluable instruction and academic guidance especially in the initial stages of my doctoral study. His stimulating influence inspired my study of social and cognitive psychology. Professor Mitsuru Ohki shared perceptive comments on an earlier draft and taught me much about narrative and language structures. Professors Yuji Togo and Toshio Sugiman were supportive and influenced the development of my ideas. Without Professor Carl Becker's constant encouragement, unfailing scholarly guidance and warm assistance for almost fifteen years throughout my undergraduate studies and beyond, I could not have come this far. He spent much time discussing the issues included in this study and providing insights into English discourse, when I was formulating the direction of my analysis. Professor Edward Marx discussed an earlier draft with me and made many helpful editorial suggestions. Each of these scholars contributed significantly to my professional development as I came to write this book and I will forever remain indebted to them. I am also very grateful to my former fellow graduate students for being a constant source of intellectual stimulation.

I wish to take this opportunity to express my appreciation to my professors, colleagues and friends, at the University of Wisconsin at Madison, where I was enrolled in the Master's program in English Linguistics. Professor Cecilia Ford first introduced me to the study of pragmatics and especially to discourse research, and prompted me to pursue the study of linguistics. Professor Jane Zuengler has provided me with an invaluable role model through her approach to language and research, and through her enthusiasm in guiding her students. Her influence both personally and professionally should be evident throughout my work. Professors Charles Scott, Marian Bean, and Peter Schreiber gave me constant support and valuable instruction. My former fellow graduate students William Crawford and Kevin Lesher helped me in gathering data and in working through the initial stages of my analysis. Of my many fellow students, I would like to single out Kevin Lesher for a special mention. I owe him the greatest debt, for his encouragement, intellectual stimulation, and true friendship. He died of cancer during his doctoral work in July 1997. We shared enthusiasm and love for language, and spent most of our time together discussing linguistics. My host parents in Wisconsin, Joy and David Drummond, and MaryJo and Walter Uphoff, gave me constant emotional support and made my research possible. I should also like to thank all those who participated in my data collection in the United States.

I wish to show my great appreciation to professors at University of California, Santa Barbara where I was a visiting scholar in 1999 and 2001. Professors Sandra Thompson and John Du Bois gave me guidance and helpful suggestions on my work. Professor Wallace Chafe has had a formative influence on my ideas about narrative, cognition, and consciousness. I am grateful to him for reading and commenting in detail on my dissertation and encouraging me in my further work. I also sincerely acknowledge that Professor Elizabeth Traugott at Stanford University gave me very fruitful advice and comments on this book.

I am deeply grateful to Professor Koki Komine who first introduced me to the study of language and communication when I was engaged in my undergraduate work, and particularly to Professor Hideki Ariyoshi for his unceasing guidance and constant encouragement for many years. I owe a special debt of gratitude to Professor Katsutoshi Satake for his support, especially in the initial stages of my graduate study.

I also wish to tender a grateful thank-you to Dr. Diane Lehman, of Ann Arbor, Michigan, who reviewed the pre-final manuscript and gave me incisive editorial suggestions and helpful comments. Any remaining shortcomings are, of course, my own responsibility.

Research for this book was partly supported by Research Fellowships of the Japan Society for the Promotion of Science for Young Scientists for the years 1997 through 2000. I remain deeply grateful for the invaluable periods of uninterrupted research time. I have received a Grant-in-Aid for JSPS Fellows from the Japan Ministry of Education, Science, Sports and Culture.

This book originated in my doctoral research completed at Kyoto University in September 1998. Portions of the material contained in this book have been presented at various international conferences, in North America, Finland, France, and Japan, and I am grateful to the audiences who have given me invaluable comments on these earlier versions of this material. Parts of the material presented here have appeared in preliminary forms elsewhere, but they have been extensively revised and rearranged. A portion of chapter 3 (mainly section 3) first appeared as "Tense alternation in English conversational narratives," *Annual Review of English Learning and Teaching* No. 2 (1997), and a preliminary version of chapter 6 as "Tense in indirect reporting discourse in spoken English," No. 1 (1996). Chapter 7 combines extensively revised material from two papers: "Style choice of reporting discourse related to sentence length and complexities," in *Kansai Linguistic Society* 16 (1996), and "Functions of reporting discourse from a discourse analytic perspective," in *Papers in Linguistic Science* No. 1 (1995).

Finally, my parents Mikiko and Masahiro Sakita have always been my most valued source of energy with their constant encouragement. I wish to thank them for their continuing love, their insights, and for helping me see things in perspective. Without their understanding and respect for my work, I could never have completed this book.

1

INTRODUCTION

1.1. REPORTING DISCOURSE

1.1.1. What is reporting discourse

Reporting discourse is an essential part of human language. When people want or need to convey what was communicated in the past or what might be communicated in the future or what is even now being communicated, either by themselves or by others, they use reporting discourse. Without reporting discourse, language would be fatally limited in its potential as a means of communication (e.g., Voloshinov [1929]1986; Bamgbose 1986; Coulmas 1986).

The most fundamental feature of reporting discourse is its reflexivity. People use language to refer to language. They not only report utterances, but also talk about utterances by commenting on, criticizing, or questioning them. This is indeed a fundamental feature that qualifies any sign system as a human language (Coulmas 1986: 2). Accordingly, reporting discourse is defined by its reflexive nature and duplex structure. For instance, Voloshinov ([1929]1986), a pioneer who explored the significance of reporting discourse in its relation to human mind and ideology, defines reporting discourse as "speech within speech, utterance within utterance and, at the same time, speech about speech and utterance about utterance" (p. 115). He emphasizes that two different contexts can appear in an interaction within a single unifying syntactic structure. In his view, the significantly unique nature of reporting discourse is that two distinct stylistic variants of the same dialect can interact within a single sentence.

Reporting discourse is, indeed, universal to all human language. Haberland (1986: 219) points to the universality of reporting discourse in human linguistic action:

Most languages we know of seem to have these devices [reporting discourse] in one form or other, and even languages which are not too well-equipped, somehow seem to make do with whatever devices they have, mostly relying on context features... reported speech *is* a universal of human action.

The vast literature of cross-linguistic surveys of reporting discourse has shown that most languages have reporting discourse in some form. Jakobson (1985: 96) also asserts that reporting discourse, which has the duplex structures of language referring to language, plays a pertinent and indispensable part in the buildup of any human language. Reporting discourse, in its widest sense, is everywhere, and all human verbal communication is, indeed, reporting discourse in its nature. Becker (1984; 1988) claims that every utterance derives from and echoes 'prior text,' in a similar fashion to Bakhtin ([1952-53]1986) who observes that "each utterance is filled with the echoes and reverberations of other utterances to which it is related by the communality of the sphere of speech communication" (p. 91). Bakhtin repeatedly claims in other places that "every conversation is full of transmissions and interpretations of other people's words" ([1975]1981: 338). Kristeva (1986: 37) supports the view that every utterance is in fact a reporting discourse, in that "any text is constructed as a mosaic of quotations; any text is the absorption and transformation of another." Lucy (1993: 11) also notes the significance of the reflexive nature of language. For him, speech is permeated by "reflexive activity as speakers remark on language, report utterances, index and describe aspects of the speech event, invoke conventional names, and guide listeners in the proper interpretation of utterances."

What I am referring to as 'reporting discourse' here has been widely known as 'reported speech.' However, there is no consensus on a single term. Janssen and Wurff (1996: 3) acknowledge that there is "no consensus in the literature on the general terms employed for the various manifestations of the phenomenon of speech-within-speech." Tannen (1986: 311) claims that "the term 'reported speech' is a misnomer," and instead introduces the term 'constructed dialogue,' for the following reason:

Examination of the lines of dialogue represented in storytelling or conversation, and consideration of the powers of human memory, indicate that most of those lines were probably not actually spoken. What is commonly referred to as reported speech or direct quotation in conversation is constructed dialogue, just as surely as is the dialogue created by fiction writers and playwrights.[1]

She stresses that when language produced in one context is repeated in another, it is fundamentally changed even if reported accurately. Thus, language represented as dialogue is, indeed, constructed dialogue, a creation for which the speaker bears full responsibility and credit (1989: 4). Although Tannen's view fits well with the nature of direct reporting discourse, it still does not cover a wide variety of reporting options such as summary reporting or paraphrase that hardly retain the forms of 'dialogue.' My focus upon reporting discourse in this book includes not only the reported part of a duplex construction, but also the human reporting behavior itself in interactions in a wider scope. To achieve a reasonable level of generality, I use the term 'reporting discourse' rather than 'reported speech.' For one thing, it directs our eyes toward the reporting person's discourse in its immediate context, which extracts the reported person's discourse from its original context. For another, it functions as an umbrella term for reported thought, reported perception, reported written discourse, as well as reported spoken discourse, all of which are closely related to each other. It meets what Janssen and Wurff (1996: 4) warn:

> the second word in the term reported speech may be problematic, since it easily leads to the suggestion that reported thought and reported perception are to be sharply differentiated from reported speech. This, however, is an idea we would not support, since both cross-linguistically and intra-systematically, reported speech proper shows many empirical and theoretical connections with reported thought and perception.

Janssen and Wurff, however, compromise with the term 'reported speech,' for "the absence of a viable alternative" (p. 4). I use the term 'reporting discourse' throughout this book in order to maintain a wider perspective. It allows me to view reporting behavior as positive and 'original' activity (McHale: 1978) that is not a mere reproduction of an utterance in the past (Tannen 1986; 1988; 1989).

1.1.2. Significance of reporting discourse

Reporting discourse is significant as a linguistic form on its own in that it both embraces two distinct contexts and verbal forms, and also significantly reflects and encapsulates the systems and nature of communication, social dynamics, and human cognition. An adequate analysis of reporting discourse elucidates essential facts about human beings and their interactions. Reporting discourse illuminates all aspects of verbal communication, because it intrinsically manifests the dialogic nature of language. Bakhtin ([1975]1981) and Voloshinov ([1929]1986) assert that dialogue, which has the polyphonic nature of utterances, is crucial. Voloshinov ([1929]1986: 117) emphasizes that the real unit of language is "not the individual, isolated monologic utterance, but the interaction of at least two utterances—in a word, dialogue." In exploring dialogue, he devotes extensive analysis to reporting discourse, declaring the acute necessity of its investigation to illuminate the dialogic nature of language:

> The productive study of dialogue presupposes, however, a more profound investigation of the forms used in reported speech, since these forms reflect basic and constant tendencies in the active reception of other speakers' speech, and it is this reception, after all, that is fundamental also for dialogue. (Voloshinov [1929]1986: 117)

His perception of reporting discourse as a reflection of the mechanism of the active reception of other speakers' speech originates in his belief in the nonduplicity between speech reception and speech reporting. The framework for human speech reproduction reflects the framework for human speech reception:

> The circumstances under which transmission occurs and the aims it pursues merely contribute to the implementation of what is already lodged in the tendencies of active reception by one's inner-speech consciousness. And these tendencies, for that part, can only develop within the framework of the forms used to report speech in a given language. (Ibid.)

Furthermore, he observes:

> [Standardized] patterns [for reporting speech] and their modifications could have arisen only in accordance with the governing tendencies of speech reception; . . . once these patterns have assumed shape and function in the language, they in turn exert an influence . . . on the tendencies of an evaluative reception that operate within the channel prescribed by the existing forms. (Ibid.: 118)

Therefore, extensive analysis of reporting discourse explicates fundamental issues about the operation of language, mind, and consciousness: the speech reception system, the mode of existence of another's utterance in the recipient's consciousness and its manipulation there, and the processes of orientation the recipient's subsequent speech has undergone (ibid.: 117). Accordingly, what we have in the forms of reporting discourse is "precisely an objective document of this reception" (ibid.). He asserts that such documents provide us with "information about social tendencies in an active reception of other speaker's speech, tendencies that have crystallized into language forms" (ibid.). Since reporting discourse is intrinsically crucial for verbal communication, its operations are crucial in the generative processes of verbal signs. Close analysis of reporting discourse will uncover the mechanism of verbal communication itself.

Reporting discourse is a social product, and thus an analysis of reporting discourse is relevant to the study of social dynamics. According to Voloshinov ([1929]1986: 123), the "conditions of verbal communication, its forms, and its methods of differentiation are dictated by the social and economic prerequisites of a given period. These changing sociolingual conditions are what in fact determines those changes in the forms of reported speech." Following Voloshinov's view, Coulmas (1986: 14) claims that the way people report keenly reflects social dynamics: "it is an undeniable fact that 'the forms of reported speech' differ greatly across languages." There are "significant differences even in areas, which at first sight, one would be tempted to take for universal rather than language specific." He observes that "there are different ways of integrating reported speech into one's own; there are differences as to how reporting devices get grammatically coded; and there are differences concerning the kinds of reported speech that are distinguished in a language" (ibid.).

Moreover, reporting discourse also reflects the operation of complex cognitive processes that comprise perception, storage, recall, and verbalization (Chafe 1977a). In each process, people interpret and organize information, with focalization and subjectivity playing significant roles. The variety of forms of reporting discourse manifests the cognitive operation in such processes. The ways people report also mirror their memory system (e.g., Bartlett 1932; Wade and Clark 1993).

The significance of reporting discourse for humans is also clear from the steady flow of studies of reporting discourse from a variety of perspectives (Coulmas 1986; Besnier 1993; Janssen and Wurff 1996). For instance, ethnographers have investigated the use of reporting discourse as a social tool (e.g., Besnier 1993). Literary theorists have studied the significance of reporting discourse for narratorship (e.g., Feldman et al. 1990). Linguists have focused their attention on the grammatical structure of reporting discourse constructions, exploring issues such as tense and deixis shift in indirect reporting discourse (e.g., Comrie 1986), derivational relationship between indirect and direct reporting style (e.g., Wierzbicka 1974), and grammatical subordination of the quotes to the reporting verbs (Munro 1982). Recent pragmatic approaches considering transactional and interactional functions of language (Brown and Yule 1983) have led some linguists to look at the meaning of reporting discourse in linguistic performance (e.g., Tannen 1988; 1989). This sort of pragmatic consideration follows Voloshinov's ([1929]1986) emphasis on the dynamic relationship between the reporting discourse and the reporting context, since "divorcing the reported speech from the reporting context" (p. 119) obstructs understandings of the dynamics.

1.1.3. Working questions on reporting discourse

This book views reporting discourse as a significant linguistic phenomenon that reflects and at the same time encapsulates the systems and nature of communication, social dynamics, and human cognition. Following this view there are a variety of issues to explore that significantly deepen our insights into the systematic nature of the duplex structures, which ultimately lead to better understanding of human behaviors. For instance, with a stylistic perspective, one might pose the question, "What are the style variations for reporting discourse?" Certainly there are a variety of ways to report. Pragmatic issues follow, such as "What determines reporting style, for example, the choice among direct, indirect, and other intermediate forms?" and "What functions do different reporting discourse forms have?" One may also ask pragmatic questions concerning reporting patterns in dialogues, such as "Are there any sequential patterns of script for using reporting discourse in dialogues?" If we shift our focus to detailed parts of reporting discourse, there are numerous questions concerning feature items in reporting discourse constructions, such as verbs, tenses, the conjunction "that," and deictic elements. For instance, "What determines the choice of reporting verbs?" and "What determines the tense forms of reporting verbs and of reported verbs?" are important questions. When observing ordinary discourse, which is diverse in nature, further questions arise, such as "Does tense have any function other than to reflect temporal relations?" "What is the function of the conjunction 'that'? When is it used and not used?" and "How do deictic elements shift?" On the other hand, shifting our attention to a more macro level issue, we are left with the question: "When and why do people report?" Since reporting discourse is a representation of complex processes including human perceptions and cognitive operations, more cognitively oriented questions may naturally be posed, such as "How do people recall?" "How much subjectivity and objectivity does each reporting reflect?" and "How does a speaker's psychological background affect her/his reporting behavior?" But reporting discourse ultimately raises a more fundamental question of how people perceive events at all.

The present work does not exhaust all these issues, but it keeps them in view from multiple perspectives in exploring reporting discourse. It first focuses on the tense-alternation phenomenon of reporting verbs that has long been set aside as a problematic issue. As reporting discourse is "one of those phenomena whose proper treatment necessarily transcends departmental boundaries" (Coulmas 1986: 1), the present analyses of tense-alternation touch upon varieties of related factors. This book posits a discourse perspective throughout, and approaches the tense-alternation problem by examining factors such as cognition, self-identity, attitude, flow of consciousness, and psychological background. It also examines discourse organization, conversational strategy, and discourse rules. What is significantly related to the problem is narrative organization, since reporting verbs' tense-alternation occurs most frequently in conversational narrative discourse. Second, the book shifts to explore the tense of reported verbs, by introducing a discourse perspective on the issue, which has been treated mostly at the sentential level. The book also examines reporting patterns, styles, and functions.

1.1.4. Narrative

Narrative, especially conversational narrative, is one of the typical forms of discourse that involves reporting discourse. Rather than simply reporting some displaced utterances or thoughts, narrative includes talking about events. In it, reporting discourse is situated in a flow of telling sequential events. Since present research surveys many samples of reporting discourse that appear in narrative, let me briefly characterize what narrative is.

Although there is no universal agreement on the nature of narrative (Banfield 1982; McHale 1983; Genette 1988; Segal 1995), there are some features that inevitably function as its characteristics. First, narrative is generally defined in terms of its inclusion of a sequential order of presentation (e.g., Forster [1927]1963; Labov and Waletzky 1967; Labov 1972a; Chatman 1978; Prince 1982; Rimmon-Kenan 1983; Emott 1997). Labov and Waletzky (1967) claim that a minimal narrative is any sequence of clauses that are temporally ordered with respect to one another, and which contains at least one temporal juncture. Likewise, recent narrative analysts view narrative as "a type of discourse used to describe sequences of events" (Almeida 1995: 159). Almeida (1995: 171) defines the narrative convention, acknowledging Hirschman and Story's (1981) 'narrative time progression,' as follows:

> The Narrative Convention is that unless we (the readers) are given some sign or information to the contrary, we assume that the events of the story occurred in the order in which they are presented in the text.

Emmott (1997: 105) raises Forster's ([1927]1963: 93) well-known examples to define narrative:

(1) The king died, and then the queen died of grief.
(2) Roses are red, violets are blue.

(1) is a narrative, since it contains event sequences, while (2) does not count as narrative, since it describes states rather than actions (Emmott 1997: 105). Second, narrative has two characteristics, the presence of a story and of a storyteller (Scholes and

Kellogg 1966: 4). Accordingly, Smith (1981: 228) defines narrative as "someone telling someone else that something happened." Third, Segal (1995) points out that narrative contains existents (e.g., characters, objects, settings), and events (e.g., happenings, actions). They exist in the same world (Chatman 1978; Pavel 1986) and are "assumed to be temporally and spatially related to one another" (Segal 1995: 13). Schiffrin (1994: 299) points to the agentive role of characters who bring about a particular change in circumstances: "narratives frequently 'tell about' what happened to a human being." Fourth, narrative mode usually assumes 'spatiotemporal displacement' (Chafe 1994). As Toolan (1988: 5) suggests, displacement is "the ability of human language to be used to refer to things or events that are removed, in space or time, from either speaker or addressee." Narrative is the manifestation of such language use, and is an essential way to linguistically represent past experience, whether real or imagined (Traugott and Pratt 1980: 248).

Narrative structure is fairly regular, although differences of situation can cause the same person to tell the same basic story with utterly different kinds of narratives. Schiffrin (1994: 284) claims that narrative is "a discourse unit with a fairly regular structure that is largely independent of how it is embedded in surrounding talk." Labov (1972a) characterizes fully formed oral narrative with the following categorizations:[2]

Abstract	: Summarizing what the story is about.
Orientation	: Setting the scene for the event: who, when, where, what.
Complicating action	: Then what happened?
(Embedded orientation)	: Objective information embedded.
Evaluation	: So what is the point? How is the story interesting?
Result or resolution	: What finally happened.
Coda	: Exit narrative mode and back to the present. "That's it."

Just as reporting discourse is crucially significant to human life, narrative theorists (e.g., Chatman 1978; Genette 1980; Rimmon-Kenan 1983; Bal [1980]1985; Toolan 1988; Georgakopoulou 1997) have asserted that narrative is "inevitably fundamental in human life" (Hymes and Cazden 1980: 131) and is "central to the development of a sense of one's identity and to the (re)constitution and interpretation of personal, social and cultural reality" (Georgakopoulou 1997: 1). Indeed, narrative is one of the best-studied areas in the multidisciplinary discipline of discourse, and has a long tradition beginning with Plato's *Republic* and Aristotle's *Poetics* (Segal 1995: 13).

Reporting discourse is often embedded within narratives and plays a crucial role (e.g., Toolan 1988; Chafe 1994). There, reporting discourse is sequentially ordered: it may appear within a sequence narrating other nonverbal events, or a series of reporting discourse may occupy a long span in narrative discourse. The questions posed above regarding functions and operations of reporting discourse are closely related to whole narrative structure and coherence. The tense-alternation phenomenon of reporting verbs, which is one of the central concerns of this book, is an especially typical feature characteristic of narrative. The elucidation of reporting discourse requires an adequate understanding of narrative; and at the same time, it also provides insights into the nature of narrative.

1.2. DISCOURSE PERSPECTIVES

1.2.1. Reporting discourse and context

According to van Dijk and Kintsch (1983: 32), "studying sentences in isolation may tell us something, but it is also possible that it will mislead us." This book views reporting discourse not as a single sentential construction but as an integrated complex in discourse contexts. As mentioned above, the narrative situation is one of the types of reporting contexts that embrace reporting discourse. Reporting discourse appears in numerous other contexts as well. Contextual information is crucial to the analysis of reporting discourse. Voloshinov ([1929]1986) acutely criticizes the investigators who separate reporting discourse from its context:

> Earlier investigators of the forms of reported speech committed the fundamental error of virtually divorcing the reported speech from the reporting context. That explains why their treatment of these forms is so static and inert (a characterization applicable to the whole field of syntactic study in general). (p. 119)

He claims that the true object of inquiry should be a dynamic interrelationship between the reporting discourse and the reporting context:

> Meanwhile, the true object of inquiry ought to be precisely the *dynamic interrelationship of these two factors, the speech being reported (the other person's speech) and the speech doing the reporting (the author's speech)*. After all, the two actually do exist, function, and take shape only in their interrelation, and not on their own, the one apart from the other. The reported speech and the reporting context are but the terms of a dynamic interrelationship.
> [Emphasis with italics is added] (Ibid.)

Bakhtin ([1975]1981: 340) emphasizes a similar concern that the reporting context crucially influences the meaning of the reporting discourse: "the speech of another, once enclosed in a context, is—no matter how accurately transmitted—always subject to certain semantic changes." He says, "the context embracing another's word is responsible for its dialogizing background, whose influence can be very great" (ibid.). Tannen (1989) supports this view and suggests that reporting discourse is a creative act by a reporter situated in a certain reporting context.

Scholars have seen context as influencing language use, from different points of view. In the past, linguists have viewed the context as a communication situation (e.g., Bloomfield 1933; Pike 1954; Halliday and Hasan 1976), a view which has been also most popularly held by interactional sociolinguists and ethnographers of communication. Narratologists (Labov and Waletzky 1967; Hoey 1979; 1983; Toolan 1988) have attached greatest importance to textual context, asserting that the surrounding text influences the meaning of an individual sentence or clause (Emmott 1997: 79).[3] In both speech act theory and pragmatics, where context is of particular importance, it is viewed primarily as knowledge (e.g., Leech 1983; Levinson 1983; Green 1989). They view context in terms of "what speakers and hearers can be assumed to know (e.g., about social institutions, about others' wants and needs, about the nature of human rationality) and how that knowledge guides the use of language and the interpretation of utterances" (Schiffrin 1994: 365).

Accordingly, when we consider reporting context that embraces reporting discourse, there are numerous factors interacting with each other. It includes not only a textual context and a situational context, but it also includes an intermingled knowledge that the addresser and the addressee possess.[4] Moreover, since reporting discourse is a displaced mode of communication, reporting context includes the reported person's discourse and the situation in which the reported person and event exist. In order to adequately investigate the dynamic interrelationship between reporting discourse and reporting context which Voloshinov ([1929]1986) emphasizes as an object of inquiry, this study takes a discourse analytic approach.

1.2.2. Discourse analysis

In order to take discourse perspectives toward reporting discourse in subsequent chapters, let me further clarify the following essentials at this point: discourse analysis, discourse, data, and genre.

One of the most fundamental aspects of language is that it is dialogic (Bakhtin [1975]1981; [1952-53]1986; Ford 1994).[5] Every utterance has interactional meanings and transactional functions (Brown and Yule 1983) with background contexts. Natural speech does not simply generate grammatical sentences; it matches words and expressions to situational contexts and participants' comprehension. It uses language systems and structures that fit with the situational or contextual information, the participants' cognitive operations, and their communicative goals. To wholly understand such operations of language, 'humanistic approaches' to linguistic analysis, such as those suggested by Tannen (1989), are required: "the scientific study of language must include the close analysis of particular instances of discourse as they naturally occur in human and linguistic context" (p. 196).[6] Likewise, Voloshinov ([1929]1986) claims that a language system can never be understood and explained without simultaneously considering concrete utterances. Linguistic study needs to look at particular instances of language embedded in social interaction. In short, the object of linguistic study is discourse, which is language in use (Brown and Yule 1983; Fasold 1990). The analysis of discourse, as such, "cannot be restricted to the description of linguistic forms independent of the purposes or functions which those forms are designed to serve in human affairs" (Brown and Yule 1983: 1). Such a functional view of language considers discourse as "the realization of functions, i.e., the use of language for social, expressive, and referential purposes"[7] and not merely "a structure, i.e., a unit of language that is larger than the sentence" (Schiffrin 1994: 339).[8]

Discourse analysis is heterogeneous and does not restrict its theories and methods to any unique framework. Georgakopoulou (1997: 29) points out that the basis of discourse analysis is interdisciplinarity, which are indispensable for the multifarious nature of discourse:

> Discourse analysis is not a strictly unified discipline with one or few dominant theories and methods of research; instead, it exhibits a multiplicity of approaches and interdisciplinarities. . . . Interdisciplinary study is indispensable, since it is almost impossible to separate discourse from its uses in the world and in social interactions; as a result, linguistic tools alone are not sufficient for its comprehensive study.

Indeed, because it is hard to separate language from the world it describes, Schiffrin (1994: 419) argues for the interdisciplinary basis of discourse analysis:

> To understand the language of discourse, we need to understand the world in which it resides; and to understand the world in which language resides, we need to go outside of linguistics. When we then return to a linguistic analysis of discourse—to an analysis of utterances as social interaction—I believe that we will find that the benefits of our journey have far outweighed its costs.

Therefore, functionally based discourse analysis includes, as its methods, both quantitative methods drawn from social scientific approaches and more humanistically based interpretive work. It also needs to be combined, or at least associated, with knowledge and information from other related fields. For the study of reporting discourse, such approaches are necessary, as Coulmas (1986) and Voloshinov ([1929]1986) repeatedly claim. This work adopts this view of discourse and of discourse analysis, and thus attempts to explore reporting discourse from multiple viewpoints.

One strict restriction that the present work will adopt is that it should be an 'empirical study' of natural discourse. In that sense, it accepts the assumption of conversation analysis which focuses on the contexts that can be "empirically attested through actual speech or behavior" (Schiffrin 1994: 409). On the other hand, it also renders considerable attention to cognitive operations as backgrounds of reporting discourse and narrative.

Traditional linguistics has mostly been based on the analysis of unnatural language, and has put aside empirically available details of talk. It has idealized situations of language use, as seen in Saussure's ([1922]1966) distinction of 'langue' and 'parole' and in Chomsky's (1965) separation of 'competence' and 'performance.' Under the studies in the traditional framework, basic methodologies have flourished with which linguists invent examples and judge their grammaticality.[9] Chafe (1994: 16-17) criticizes the "ancient tradition" in which "conclusions about language and the mind have been drawn from simpler, though still unnatural examples," since such unnatural data could very easily distort what language is really like:

> It is as if one tried to study birds by building airplanes that were rather like birds in certain ways, and then studied the airplanes, just because they were easier to control than the birds themselves. I suspect that ornithologists have come to understand birds more successfully by examining them as they really are. There is much to be gained from examining language as it really is too. (Chafe 1994: 17)

He insists that the unnaturalness of data is "highly disturbing to anyone who is sensitive to what language is really like" (p. 16). A fuller understanding of language emerges from a constant effort to observe language as it really is. Conversation analysis is one of the disciplines that strictly disallow unnatural data.[10] It focuses on actual occurrences of speech in social interactions (e.g., Sacks 1984; Goodwin and Duranti 1992; Schegloff 1992). As Heritage and Atkinson (1984: 2) assert, "within conversation analysis there is an insistence on the use of materials collected from *naturally occurring* occasions of everyday interaction by means of audio- and video-recording equipment or film." Regrettably, conversation analysis claims that speakers' cognitive states are beyond its scope, and Edwards (1997: 85) even characterizes it as an "*anti*-cognitive enterprise" in that it sets aside cognitive questions: "it avoids attempting to explain talk in terms of the mental states that precede it, generate it, or result from it." However, language production and cognitive operation form a single set and cannot be separated (Yamanashi 1995, 2000). Language represents ways that people view events, persons, actions, and situations in general. Accordingly, reporting discourse and narrative manifest the cognitive operations that a reporter and a narrator go through (e.g., Polkinghorne 1988; Bruner 1990; Chafe 1990; Talmy 1995).[11] A true understanding of language, as van Dijk (1985: 5) claims, is realized not only through empirical observations of natural language, but by integrating empirical approaches with inquiries into cognitive processing of language. In order to participate in meaningful exchange in dialogue, for instance, a speaker needs to understand what has been said by the previous speaker. She/he at the same time holds a cognitive representation of the whole situation. Language analysis should take such cognitive processes into account, but "it requires an integration with a cognitive model of conversational understanding, monitoring, planning, and strategic interaction" (van Dijk 1985: 5). The present work supports the very point van Dijk makes:

> . . . an interdisciplinary approach to discourse cannot be limited to structural analysis of its various levels or dimensions but also needs to pay attention to cognitive processes and to memory representations of discourse. Storage, retrieval, cognitive strategies, memory limitations, and effective organization procedures for information processing become relevant in such an account. (van Dijk 1985: 5)

This study pursues an interdisciplinary discourse analysis, and presents multiple perspectives from which to view reporting discourse and narrative. It attempts to model cognitive processes that are evidenced by speakers' choices among reporting discourse and narrative forms, to examine discourse organizations, and to document reporter's conversational strategic uses of language. It presents both quantitative and qualitative analyses of natural discourse data.

'Natural discourse' in this study includes daily conversations, telephone conversations, dinner-table talks, news reports, interviews, and so on. In addition, the study also analyzes oral discourse elicited in experimental settings. 'Naturally occurring' data often seems to exclude such experimental procedures or interviews (e.g., Psathas 1995: 45), but Edwards (1997: 89) admits that "any interactional phenomenon can be naturalized by treating it as natural." Indeed, such elicited data often renders significant supports and findings when analyzed in combination with naturally occurring data. In the analysis of tense usage and reporting style choice in the latter part of the book, both spontaneous conversational data and experimentally derived data are examined. Just as Emmott (1997: 87) claims, "what is needed is a balanced approach," and not the work of either discipline—experimental work or discourse analysis.

The present research sets its focus on spoken discourse. Speaking and writing are closely related, but differ in several key aspects.[12] Reporting discourse and narrative manifest differences in spoken and written genres. These differences are certainly another significant issue to investigate, as is the question of how spoken and written reporting discourse are related to each other (Coulmas 1986; Chafe 1994).[13] But the present study limits its scope to how reporting discourse behaves in everyday spoken language, in order to concern itself with reporting discourse as a social interactional phenomenon. Indeed, there has been increasing recognition that oral versions of reporting discourse, storytelling, and narrative are more fundamental than their written counterparts (Labov and Waletzky 1967; Polanyi 1981; Rosen 1988; Toolan 1988; Tannen 1989).[14]

In sum, this study follows a set of principles that Schiffrin (1994: 416) proposes for approaching discourse:

1. Analysis of discourse should be empirical, with natural data from a speech community.
2. Discourse is not just a sequence of linguistic units.
3. Discourse is attained through linguistic forms and meanings working with social and cultural meanings and interpretive frameworks.
4. Structures, meanings and actions are interactively achieved.
5. What is said, meant, and done is sequentially situated.
6. Speakers' selection among different linguistic devices is based on: intentions, strategies, meanings and functions, sequential context, properties of discourse mode, social context, cultural framework.

1.3. Overview of Chapters

In this chapter, I have introduced some basic concepts and problems that I will explore throughout the study. The core of my analysis deals with dialogue-introducer tense-alternation phenomena.[15] Focusing on different aspects of reporting, I propose that reporting past experience requires complex processes that include perception, storage, recall, verbalization, and others, with constant interpretations and choices at each stage, in close interaction with cognitive constraint, contextual information, and communicative purposes. Sequentially I observe the cognitive backgrounds of reporting at the recollection stage, the reporter's perception of attitudinal contrast and the reporter's flow of consciousness at the verbalization stage. In this context, dialogue-introducer tense reveals its functions as cognitive, attitudinal, and informational state markers. Finally, I turn to a closely related problem: tense determination of reported verbs, before exploring reporting style, pattern, and function to suggest directions in which future research might head. It may be helpful here to lay out briefly the structure and analysis of each chapter.

Chapter 2 provides an overview of the previous studies of tense-alternation. It first outlines how previous studies have treated tense-alternation in general, from the traditional analysis of the historical present (HP), the syntactic hypothesis, to the conversational historical present (CHP) alternation theory. It then points to the fact that dialogue-introducer tense-switching is not well explained by any of the previous theories. Careful and extensive reexaminations of the previous hypotheses reveal their problems and identify the limitations of the existing frameworks.

The subsequent three chapters present tense-alternation as manifestations of multiple factors in complex reporting processes. As Myhill (1992: 90) claims, in natural discourse, "a variety of different factors affect the choice of which form to use, so that marking in individual cases is determined by a number of factors operating simultaneously." I thus analyze dialogue-introducer tenses as cognitive markers, attitudinal markers, and consciousness stream markers, each pointing to essential phases of reporting discourse.

Chapter 3 explores cognitive backgrounds of reporting discourse tense-alternation, by illustrating speaker's conceptualization of recalled events. It presents Cognitive Recollection Models that particularly incorporate proximity, psychological involvement, and self-identity, as key factors. It claims that when a speaker determines a schema and frames to reconstruct past events, she/he assumes specific vantage points, just as people take different vantage points in perceiving objects in the outer world. I propose that there is, in this process, an inherent asymmetry in a narrator's conceptualization of the third person and of the past self. In reporting third-person interactions, the narrator's choice of tense is related to the degree of psychological ego-involvement in the interactions recalled. In reporting interactions that involve the past self, the ego's identity as narrator is one of the crucial factors for the narrator's manipulation of dialogue-introducer tenses. Theories of narrative, discourse, and psychology emphasize the narrator's self-identity. My theory accounts for the frequency distribution of dialogue-introducer tense variations, which I quantitatively display with discourse data. It shows correlations of dialogue-introducer tense forms with different reported persons, and provides accounts for the correlations.

Chapter 4 turns to the reproduction stage of the interaction, and explores the ways speakers encode their interpretations of events by manipulating dialogue-introducer tense as an attitudinal and informational contrasting device in order to effectively construct narratives. Using numerous examples, I demonstrate that the narrator's mental imagery constructs stories based on her/his interpretation of the event, depending upon her/his purpose in telling the story. Although the tense realization in each story is individualistic and particular to each situation, it still follows certain patterns. Feature analyses of discourse examples lead to some generalizations of systematic contrasts that dialogue-introducers mark. I first look at the discourse of different types of speech acts, and show that what often accompanies tense-contrasts is the attitudinal contrast that the speaker senses from reported speakers. I then focus on stories of conflict that involve the speaker's attitudinal contrast as a significant point of the stories. I show that dialogue-introducer tenses well reflect this power balance and its breakthrough in the situation. Finally, I turn to the cases in which the same speech acts are reported with different dialogue-introducer tenses. These tenses reflect the narrator's interpretation of the speaker's different psyches and attitudes that accompany the utterances.

Chapter 5 explores dialogue-introducers and their tense forms as markers for the speaker's flow of consciousness along with the development of discourse organizations. As a descriptive framework, it begins with a discussion of discourse organization units such as act, move, pair, and exchange. It then briefly characterizes the notion of consciousness. Following this, I argue that the speaker's use of dialogue-introducers is closely correlated with structures of moves and exchanges within conversational organizations, and their tense-shifts follow the speaker's consciousness flow along with the development of such organizations. In discourse examples, I examine move structures and the use of dialogue-introducers that have been considered irregular or difficult to explicate by other frameworks. By presenting Consciousness Stream Models, I illustrate how dialogue-introducer tense-shifts correlate with the discourse organization and the flow of consciousness. I first examine cases of exchange such as adjacency pair and three-part exchange. I next examine the development of a narrative line over a series of remarks. Then I address the repetition of dialogue-introducers in the cases of pre-posing and post-posing dialogue-introducers, and repetition at restatements. The whole analysis covers different directional tense-shifts that previous studies on tense have totally neglected, and demonstrates the significant functions of such tense forms as "I says," "he say," "I saying," that have been considered 'ungrammatical' or 'mistakes.' Dialogue-introducers play significant roles for a narrative to be a coherent whole with a natural flow of consciousness.

Chapter 6 turns to tense determination in indirect reporting discourse, and introduces discourse perspectives on the issue, which has long been considered within the scope of a single sentence. Previous studies have considered tense-alternation as one of the 'performance features' (Wolfson 1982), and have assumed that it occurs only in direct reporting discourse.[16] However, I claim that tense-alternation may appear in indirect reporting discourse. This claim renders a new perspective to the analysis of reported verb tense in indirect reporting discourse. The chapter begins with a brief outline of the previous studies on tense in indirect reporting discourse: the traditional sequence of tenses (SoT) rule that views tense as a purely syntactic phenomenon; and Declerck's hypothesis that incorporates pragmatic and semantic information in the tense theory. Chapter 6 then explores how tense in indirect reporting discourse behaves within the scope of actual language performances, and introduces a discourse perspective that tense in indirect reporting discourse is a discourse functional phenomenon. In naturally spoken discourse, tense in indirect reporting discourse behaves more flexibly than previous studies have assumed. I suggest that speakers often choose to report from their own perspectives in order to keep discourse coherence rather than to keep syntactic integrity within a sentence. By raising discourse examples, I demonstrate the prevalence of the speaker's viewpoint and the discourse functional uses of tense. I show that indirect reporting discourse has tense-alternation, which has long been neglected, and suggest that some reporting clauses behave flexibly as dialogue markers that hardly function as temporal reference points, but rather as hedges, evidential markers, source markers, and personal deictic markers.

Chapter 7 discusses what factors operate to determine reporting style, in order to capture a macro-level picture of reporting discourse that has multiple functions and complex stylistic variations. It first outlines general characterizations of reporting discourse style. By introducing different theoretical backgrounds, it reviews some fundamental and pragmatic differences between direct and indirect styles. To clarify the interwoven factors for style choice, I present two studies with different approaches (quantitative and qualitative) in order to address different factors of style choice. The first study takes an experimental approach to explore how sentence structures affect reporting style. It shows that, as primitive factors, structural complexities and sentence length affect reporting style. The second study uses a discourse analytic approach to explore interactional functions of reporting discourse in linguistic performance. In particular, it discusses the correlations between functions of reporting discourse and discourse patterns and styles. It focuses on the use of reporting discourse as discourse strategic devices related to evidentiality, information grounding, and dramatization. I show reporting discourse as rule-governed, goal-directed and purposeful linguistic action, with each reporting style having a different purpose in communication. My analysis ends with an illustration of function-style correlations as part of a continuum, suggesting the need for its further elaboration and continuing investigation.

Finally, the concluding chapter 8 summarizes the study, discusses its theoretical implications, and suggests directions for further research.

1.4. DATA

This work deals with contemporary 'general' American English. Some of the analysis covers forms that have been considered 'ungrammatical' or 'mistakes' under the prescriptive norms, but they are prevalent facts of discourse in casually spoken general American English. Although speech styles are often influenced by socio-cultural factors, the present study deals with features of reporting discourse that are nonetheless free from dialectical or idiosyncratic usages. Data extracts cited come from published sources, from data corpora of my own and of others (collected mostly in the Middle West and California regions),[17] or from other people's analytic work. Many examples from Wolfson's and Johnstone's studies are reanalyzed in order to demonstrate that they are well explained by the framework presented here. Transcription conventions are listed in the appendix.

2

REVIEW AND PROBLEMS OF TENSE-ALTERNATION THEORIES

2.0. OVERVIEW

Tense marks the temporal properties of the verb. It refers to the time at which the action or state referred to by the verb is asserted to hold (Myhill [1980]1992: 53). The relationship between tense and time has been the subject of much linguistic study, and it is now plain that there is no easily statable relationship between the two (Crystal 1992: 348). One of the features that led Quirk, et al. (1985: 175) to comment that "the association between present tense and present time is strong enough to make the term 'present tense' plausibly appropriate, and at the same time, potentially misleading" is the historical present (HP) tense. It is the use of the present tense to refer to past events. It has been one of the controversial uses of tense, although it has long been recognized as a feature of narrative.

Many grammarians (e.g., Jespersen 1931; Joos 1964; Kiparsky 1968) mentioned the use of HP in conversation. But no distinction had been made between the use of the device in literary and spoken discourse, until Wolfson (1978) focused on the use of HP in narratives which occur in everyday conversational interactions. She referred to this usage of the historical present tense as the conversational historical present (CHP) tense. In contrast to previous analyses of the HP, Wolfson (1979) pointed out that CHP in itself has no significance. Rather, it is the switching between CHP and the past tense which is the relevant feature. More recent discourse-based studies (e.g., Schiffrin 1981; Wolfson 1982; Myhill 1992) have shown that tense-switching occurs systematically in conversational narratives. However, the tense-switching of dialogue-introducers as in the following example has long been set aside as a problematic case:

(1) So I uh—he *said*, "You go over and see X, tell him I sent you—tell him who you are, he'll give you a job here," he *says*, "I can't hire or fire, all I can do is run the place." So I *said*, "All right, where's he at?"

(Wolfson 1979: 178)

Notice that the tenses of reporting verbs alternate between the past and the present regardless of the actual temporal relations of the actions.

There are three separate views on this problem of tense-switching of reporting verbs. First, reporting verbs behave just as general verbs (e.g., Schiffrin 1981; Fludernik 1991). Second, reporting verbs are unique compared to other verbs, hence their behaviors are anomalous (Wolfson 1982). Third, tenses of reporting verbs reflect the status differences of reported speakers (Johnstone 1987). In what follows, I will show that none of these views adequately explains the behavior of reporting verbs. This chapter points to the unsolved problem of tense-switching of reporting dialogue-introducers. It attempts to clarify the controversy surrounding the problem, identifies some limitations of the previous hypotheses, and prepares to search for new perspectives to elucidate the unsolved behaviors of the tense of dialogue-introducers. Since reporting dialogue is one of the prevalent performance features in narratives, it is worthwhile to explicate its systematicity.

I will first introduce the previous analyses of the HP of general English verbs, including traditional theories, syntactic analyses, and recent discourse-based studies. I will then proceed to demonstrate the seemingly unsystematic behaviors of dialogue-introducers, namely, "X say," "X says," "X said" and others. I will examine the hypotheses set forth by Wolfson and Johnstone and note their problems. I will conclude the chapter by suggesting some directions for the problem of tense-switching of dialogue-introducers.

2.1. TENSE-ALTERNATION THEORIES

2.1.1. Traditional theory of HP

Traditional analyses of the HP explain the use of the present tense for events in the past as a way of making events appear to be happening at the very moment of the telling, giving the impression that the speaker imagines that the events are actually happening again. Traditional accounts of the English verb system (e.g., Home 1867; Bain 1879; Brown 1880; Sweet 1892; Jespersen 1929; 1931; Curme 1931; Charleston 1941; Friden 1948; Diver 1963; Joos 1964; Palmer 1965; Leech 1987; Quirk et al.

1972; 1985) suggest that the HP has the function of making a narrative dramatic or vivid. These analyses assume that the HP makes the past more vivid because it moves past events out of their original time frame and into the moment of speaking. Past events come alive with the HP because it is equivalent to a tense which indicates events whose reference time is the moment of speaking. Such explanations often link the use of the HP with the state of the narrator's involvement in the story. Jespersen (1929) refers to the HP as 'dramatic present' which the speaker uses when she/he "forgets all about time, and imagines or recalls what [she/]he is recounting as vividly as if it were now present before [her/]his eyes" (p. 19). Joos (1964) also mentions that "when the speaker gets so deeply involved that he forgets where he is as he speaks, and tends to place himself rather at the scene he is narrating, the actual tense may be used with the exact meaning of the past tense . . ." (p. 125). The use of the HP and the characterization of HP-containing narratives as 'vivid' or 'animated' or 'exciting,' are seen as both cause and effect: narratives are said to contain the HP if they are animated, and also to derive this quality from its presence.

Although the alternation between past and present has been viewed as a popular literary technique, a number of investigators pointed out the colloquial origin of the HP in English (e.g., Jespersen 1924; Visser 1966). This view has been universally held, i.e., in French (Foulet 1920; Buffin 1925; Wartburg [1937]1971), Italian (Ronconi 1942; Ageno 1964), Latin (Emery 1897; Wackernagel 1920; Hoffmann and Szantyr 1963; Grassi 1966), Old Icelandic (Sprenger 1951), and in other languages.

2.1.2. Syntactic hypothesis

In contrast to the traditional analyses, Kiparsky (1968) considers the historical present tense as a kind of neutral tense into which the narrator moves after having established the past time frame through the form of a previous verb. He argues that the use of the HP in earlier stages of Indo-European languages results from a syntactic rule. He considers that the HP functions syntactically as a past tense and that it is semantically indistinguishable from the past tenses. In referring to tense-alternation, he claims that the conversion of an underlying past tense into the present tense in the surface structure must be governed by a syntactic rule, namely "some form of conjunction reduction, which optionally reduces repeated occurrences of the same tense of the present." He explains the reduction in this way: "the sequence ...Past...and...Past... is reduced to ...Past...and...zero... and since it is the present which is the zero tense, the reduced structure ...Past...and...zero... is realized morphologically as ...Past...and...Present..." (p. 33). Paden (1977), following Kiparsky, calls the HP "a neutral tense which behaves like a P [past]."

There are, however, crucial problems with Kiparsky's syntactic hypothesis. First, tense sequences do not always appear as 'past plus present' in the way that he claims. According to Wolfson (1979: 169), "even in Ancient Greek, for example, we have both past plus present and present plus past, a fact which Kiparsky does not consider." Second, as McKay (1974: 247) points out, in relation to Greek, Kiparsky ignores such cases "where a series of historical presents occurs with no alternation of marked forms, just at a critical point in the narrative." Third, since Kiparsky's syntactic hypothesis is an attempt to account for the HP in the literature of ancient languages, it is not certain if his analysis is suitable for modern languages.

2.1.3. Timeless present

Besides the traditional theories of the historical present tense, many linguists have concluded that the English present tense has no semantic component, since it can indicate a variety of reference times. Jespersen (1931) states that it has the meaning of 'general truth,' 'past,' and 'future.' To be more precise Twaddell (1960) claims that it is timeless. He claims:

> [An] unmodified construction conveys the semantic content of the lexical verb alone, with no grammatical meaning beyond that of "verb." It is compatible with any chronological meaning overtly signaled elsewhere in the sentence or situation: future if so signaled by adverbial elements, context or situation; contemporary in proclamations and in explanations accompanying demonstrations; past in the historical present; indefinitely repeatable in stage directions and ritual instructions; immutable and eternal in summaries of a story plot, including headlines. (p. 5)

Crystal (1966) points out that the time reference of the present tense is specified by adverbs:

(2) John begins school *next week*.
(3) Sally leaves for Chicago *tomorrow*.
(4) I was driving down town *yesterday* and all of a sudden this woman starts blowing her horn at me. (p. 6)

Kiparsky (1968) also demonstrates that, in the Indo-European languages included in his analysis, the present is a zero form. Lyons (1977b) also claims that the present tense is semantically unmarked. Herring (1986) has observed that the present tense has a capacity to transform particularized time-bound narration into timeless storytelling.

Wolfson (1979) points out the contradiction between the traditional analysis of the present tense as the HP and the linguistic view that the present tense is timeless. If the present tense has no semantic component, there is no basis for the explanation that the present tense is used as the HP in order to make the audience feel that it is reliving the event with a dramatic effect. She claims that the English present tense is in fact timeless in reference, and that the label 'present' is inaccurate for English, since "this form is not used to refer to present action, except in the sense that it includes the moment of speaking . . ." (p. 179). She not only asserts that the traditional analysts confused tense with time, she further claims that they did not fully understand the very nature and function of the alternation between the HP and the past, which is a discourse phenomenon:

> Interpretations of its function which are in the literature, based as they are on semantic or syntactic analysis, cannot account adequately for the linguistic facts. It is only when CHP is seen, not uniquely as a verb tense, but as part of an alternation set—which must be examined at the level of the discourse, rather than at that of the sentence alone—that we can understand its function: the organization of the narrative.   (Wolfson 1979: 180)

2.1.4. CHP alternation theory

Wolfson (1978; 1979; 1982) made a radical break with traditional understandings of the HP on four points. First, she claims that the function of this tense and the rules which condition its use depend on the type of narratives which contain the HP. Traditionally, it had been assumed that the usage of the HP is the same regardless of genre. Wolfson restricted her study to the use of the HP specifically in the genre of conversational narratives in modern American English. She refers to this usage of the HP as the conversational historical present (CHP).[1] She claims that the CHP always alternates with the past tense,[2] and in this sense the usage of this tense is genre-specific (Wolfson 1978: 218). Georgakopoulou and Goutsos (1997: 109) confirm that the actual choices of tense forms depend on the text's genre. Literary narration and oral stories show different uses of the narrative present, which is in line with the recent view that written and spoken discourse are different genres (e.g., Coulmas 1981; Tannen 1982a; Brazil 1995).

Second, Wolfson demonstrates that the traditional interpretation that the CHP dramatizes certain acts does not fit with the empirical facts that much of the most important action is recounted in the past tense (Wolfson 1978: 219). If the CHP were the significant feature as traditional theorists had claimed, then the tense should switch from the past to the CHP in recounting the dramatic action, and all the rest should stay in the past tense. But this is not the case. Thus the function of the CHP is not simply to report events as if they were happening now, as traditional analysts had viewed the function of the HP.

Third, Wolfson argues that what is communicatively significant is not the occurrence of the CHP itself, but the switch between the CHP and the past. When a speaker changes from the past to the CHP or from the CHP to the past, the switch operates to partition off important events or points in the story from one another. The direction of the tense-switch is said to be irrelevant: a switch either from the past to the HP or from the HP to the past organizes the story into chronological segments (1979: 174) and focuses on the event seen by the narrator as most important (1978: 222). Later, Hoey (1979), Polanyi and Scha (1983), and Sinclair (1988) showed that tense-shifts work as segmentation signals in non-narrative discourse as well, although the actual use of tense varies depending on the text types.

Fourth, Wolfson (1978) shows that the speech situation in which the narrative occurs has a strong influence upon whether or not CHP alternation occurs. She raises situational factors such as the degree of interaction in the story, the topic of the story, the similarity of attitude between the speaker and the audience, the time elapsed between the event and its telling, and the type of speech events. Social factors, such as sex, age, ethnicity, intimacy, occupation, and relative status also greatly influence the probability of CHP alternation.

Wolfson (1978) claims that CHP alternation is one of the performance features contained in a performed story, as well as dialogue, asides, expressive sounds, repetition, sound effects, and motions and gestures.[3] In exploring the functions of CHP alternation, she refers to important discourse notions such as code-switching (Hymes 1975), evaluative device (Labov 1972b), footing (Goffman 1974; 1981a), and topic discontinuity (Silva-Corvalán 1983).

2.1.5. Clause types and directions of switch

Since Wolfson's proposal of CHP alternation theory, more observations have been presented for characterization of tense-alternation phenomena. Schiffrin (1981) conducted a quantitative analysis to solve the controversies on the use and the functions of HP in narrative. She presents two arguments on the use of the HP.

First, there is a close correlation of narrative clause types and occurrence of switch. The HP does not occur at the beginning or end of a narrative but rather in the middle, after the scene has been set with past-tense forms. In this sense, Schiffrin supports Kiparsky (1968) in claiming that HP is a neutralization of an underlying past tense. She points out that the use of the HP is almost completely restricted to 'complicating action' clauses (Labov 1972b), the clauses in which the central events are related in chronological order (Schiffrin 1981: 51). She claims that it is only in these complicating action clauses that the actual temporal reference is clear and does not need to be encoded in the verbs. Even among complicating action clauses, there is a tendency for the HP to occur more in the middle of a narrative. In Table 1, I have summarized correlations of narrative clause types and possible occurrences of the HP, following Myhill (1992: 62-69).[4]

Table 1: HP and Narrative Clause Types

TYPE	DESCRIPTION	ASPECTS	HP
Abstract	summarizes narrative	anterior	Past Habitual present *HP *Past perfect
Orientation	objectively sets scene	stative progressive habitual	HP very rare
Complicating action Restricted clause Narrative clause	gives story line	sequenced	HP often
Embedded orientation	gives objective information	stative progressive	HP very rare
Evaluation External Embedded	subjectively comments	stative sequenced progressive habitual anterior	*HP
Coda	finishes the story	anterior	*HP

(N.B. The symbol * indicates that the tense does not occur.)

Second, Schiffrin agrees with Wolfson that switches in tense may signal breaks in events, though she points out the need for a clearer understanding of what constitutes an 'event' (1981: 53). However, she claims that only switches from the HP have this function (p. 56).[5] When a switch goes from the past to the HP, the function of the HP is 'evaluative,' serving to underscore the unusual or surprising events which give the story its point (p. 59). In this respect, she supports the traditional account. She claims that the HP is used mainly in the climax and in the buildup to the climax. She concludes that the HP brings the past event into the moment of speaking and illustrates it more vividly.

2.1.6. HP in the theory of consciousness

Chafe (1994) characterizes the HP in his theory of consciousness in line with the traditional theory of the HP. Chafe distinguishes the two modes of speaking in conversation: the Immediate Mode (IM) and the Displaced Mode (DM). Speakers activate extroverted consciousness in the IM, while they activate introverted consciousness with the DM. Speakers take the IM when they directly perceive events and states in the outside world that surrounds the conscious self. On the other hand, speakers take the DM when they remember what was present in a distal extroverted consciousness or when they imagine what might be present in such consciousness. Narrative behavior requires speakers to take the DM. Chafe (1994: 208) argues that the HP and direct reporting discourse are devices for speakers in the DM to pretend to be representing experiences that are closer to those of an extroverted consciousness. In this sense, his characterization of the HP is similar to that of traditional theories. He emphasizes immediacy as the effect of the HP, in that "The effect is to present the event or state as if its time coincided with that of the representing consciousness. . . . The historical present is a limited pretense that a remembered idea is an idea being perceived, acted on, and evaluated at the time of the representing" (p. 208).[6]

Chafe (1994) comments on the importance of distinguishing what the historical present is and what speakers do with it. "To say that speakers sometimes make the displaced mode more like the immediate mode in this way is not to account for the circumstances under which they employ this option" (p. 209). For this problem of the actual use of the HP, he accepts Schiffrin's (1981) view of the HP. Regarding tense-switching to the HP, he concludes:

> Evidently conversational narrators have a tendency to slip into the historical present at points in their talk where there is some reason for a remembered event or state to be expressed in a way that more closely resembles the immediate mode, a strategy likely to be most appropriate at, or shortly before, the climax of a narrative. (Chafe 1994: 210)

However, he does not go into detail to explain tense-switching which Wolfson (1982) and others have claimed to have nothing to do with the climax or vividness of the reported events. As for what leads to tense-alternation, he simply comments that the "use of the past tense to establish displaced immediacy is more effective than an extended use of the historical present" (Chafe 1994: 236).

2.2. PROBLEM: *SAY/SAID* ALTERNATION

2.2.1. *Say* as a special class of reporting verbs

In a study of the use of the conversational historical present (CHP) tense in American English narrative, Wolfson (1979; 1982) claims that only one verb, namely "say" in introductions of reporting discourse does not follow the past/CHP alternation rules. The alternation between "say" and "said" does not function the same way as do past/CHP alternations in all other places. This is quite a large problem, since 35% of all the verbs in Wolfson's corpus for the study of CHP alternation are uses of "say" or "said":

> The last point to be taken up in this chapter concerns the alternation between the verbs "say" and "said." Here there is a very serious problem in the analysis since many, indeed most of the switches between the two verb forms appear to be unmotivated. (Wolfson 1982: 50)

She finds no way to explain "say"/"said" alternation, though she tries a number of hypotheses.

Schiffrin (1981) admits that one of the HP's "more perplexing uses" is "with verbs of saying and direct quotes" (p. 58). But she does not discuss the operation and motivation for dialogue-introducers' past/CHP alternation, implicitly assuming that tense choices of dialogue-introducers function the same way as do tense choices of other general verbs (Johnstone 1987: 36), which is inadequate. She merely shows that since the present tense with a verb of saying makes the reported material more immediate, the HP occurs more frequently with direct than with indirect reporting discourse.

Johnstone (1987) supports Wolfson's claim that tense choice for dialogue-introducers is different in some ways from tense choice elsewhere. She points out that in stories, verbs like "say" or "go" do not carry the kind of lexical meaning that other verbs do. Precisely, unlike verbs like "yell," "shout," and "whisper," verbs like "say" and "go" "do not carry any information about the exact nature of the verbal event, beyond the fact that it was verbal" (p. 42). She characterizes them as semantically neutral place markers. Quirk, et al. (1985) also mention that the verbs of communication behave very differently from all other verbs, in terms of the present tense referring to the past.[7]

2.2.2. No regularity in *say/said* alternation

Wolfson (1982) claims that the general tense-alternation rule works for the verb "say" in coordinate sentences in which the verbs of speaking follow the verbs of motion. But when it comes to the tense-alternations among the verbs of speaking only, she admits that the tense-alternation rule does not work for most cases. Although she claims that she tested a number of hypotheses for the function of the "say"/"said" alternation, she does not provide any explanations for her hypotheses.

Wolfson's past/CHP alternation rule postulates that the switch in form serves to separate different events or to focus attention on a turning point in the story. Wolfson hypothesizes that one of the rules, namely tense-agreement in coordinate sentences, applies to verbs of speaking. She calls this particular case "the rule of tense-agreement for action-speech" (Wolfson 1979: 177). For example, in (5), in which the verb of motion and the verb of speaking are both part of the same event, the tense remains constant. The same is true for (6), in which it is more obvious that the motion and the speaking are in the same speech event, since the second pronoun is deleted:

(5) So she comes back and she *says*, "Mr. X will give you 15 minutes on Friday."
(6) And then she comes in and *says*, "You didn't do this and you didn't do that." (Wolfson 1979: 177)

On the contrary, in (7) and (8), the tense-agreement is broken since the verb "say" introduces a comment which represents a turning point in the story:

(7) Then he goes to the cupboard and he opens it up and he *said*, "Too bad, you can't have any brandy . . ." (Ibid.: 177)
(8) We get up to the place, we have our lunch, we get back in the boat and I *said* to Bud, "I think the wind died." (Ibid.: 173)

As far as seen in coordinate sentences like these, the CHP alternation rule appears to work for the verb of speaking "say," in the same way as for all the other verbs. However, it is only in this particular case that the general tense-alternation rule works for the verb "say." Fludernik (1991: 391-92), admitting the "vexed problem of *says/said* alternation" in her discussion of tense-switching, agrees with Wolfson upon the tense-switching in an 'action plus saying' unit, but leaves other cases unmentioned.

Having considered a number of possibilities, Wolfson's conclusion was that there is no regularity in "say"/"said" alternation. She gives a reason for the lack of regularity in the behavior of the verb of speaking, by referring to the linguistic phenomenon of the loss of significance through overuse. She points out that "say" is the most frequent of all verbs in stories, and thus it is very likely that it has lost its distinctive meaning:

> Thus, after a great deal of very careful analysis, I am forced to say that this one lexical item is an anomaly. The only explanation for this extremely common and highly unstable alternation between "say" and "said" has to do with the fact that it is so common. The verb "say" is both the only lexical item which shows such instability and the most frequent of all verbs in stories. This single lexical item accounts for approximately 35% of all verbs in stories whether in past tense or in historical present tense. If we count only those verbs in stories which are in CHP, including "say," the figure is still just under 35% for "say." The verb is pervasive in all reportings of direct speech. The loss of significance through overuse is a well-known linguistic phenomenon,[8] and it may be at work here; the "say/said" alternation may have lost its significance and distinctive meaning. (Wolfson 1982: 52)

2.2.3. Wolfson's hypotheses

Wolfson claims that before she concluded that the tense-alternation of dialogue-introducers is an anomaly, she tested numerous hypotheses. However, since she did not provide any explanation for the hypotheses, it is not clear what the problems are. Indeed, Johnstone (1987) reexamined and reevaluated one of the hypotheses that Wolfson merely had claimed wrong without explanation. In the following section, I shall examine possible hypotheses that Wolfson abandoned summarily in her work, and show problems for each hypothesis. (Although I will cite many examples from Wolfson's work, she did not use them to explain these hypotheses but used them for other purposes in her paper.)

2.2.3.1. 'Speech act hypothesis'

Based upon the general tense-alternation rule of event separation, we can assume that the choice of tense might correlate with the type of pattern involved in the dialogue being presented. Wolfson hypothesized that in two-persons interactions, if the speech acts being reported for two participants in a story were parallel (e.g., insult-insult) then the tense would remain constant, while if they were asymmetrical, there would be a switch in tense. However, there are examples that do not conform to this hypothesis:

(9) and this jeep wheels up and it's this real hard-ass Lieutenant Mead and he hops out and he *says* "MALONE WHERE IN THE FUCK HAVE YOU BEEN?" [performing a tough voice] I *said* "Mead" a lieutenant you know I *said* "MEAD WHERE IN THE FUCK HAVE YOU BEEN?" [performing the same tough voice] [Quotation marks are added][9] (Johnstone 1987: 41)

(10) Wait! Listen! So I look up and I see Kenny, who is a very good sailor, Marion, who swims well, and my Mom in the dingy. And they *say*, "All right, look, we'll meet you at shore." And Kenny *said*, "All right, I'll go back with it." So they . . . (Wolfson 1982: 46)

In (9), the speakers "he" and "I" perform the same speech act, indeed their utterances are identical. But the tenses for the dialogue-introducers are different. Likewise, in (10), the two speakers "they" and Kenny perform the same speech act: wrapping up the conversation, greeting, and promising to see the speaker "I" later. But they use different tenses for their dialogue-introducers. Like these, there are many cases in which "say" and "said" alternate in a way that cannot be explained by the separation of speech acts.

2.2.3.2. 'Single speaker continuity hypothesis'

Tense determination may relate to distinctions among participants in the story.[10] Let us assume that as long as one speaker keeps talking, the tense used to introduce her/his speech stays the same. For example, in the following, "said" is used constantly for the speaker "she":

(11) Anyway she *said*, it's gonna be better, he's gonna walk better, he's gonna feel better, his knee's not gonna hurt, we've seen it over an' over. An' I kept a:sking her ya know, are you su:re. She *said*, well w- ya know she *didn't say*, Yes your Dad. Well, but she *said*, when you see hi:m n.hh so I- what I wanna do with my Mom is go back to her 'n tell her ya know, I checked this ou:t an' I'm convinced. (VK)

But the constant use of the same tense for the same speaker does not apply in all cases. In the following, tense switches between "says" and "said" while reporting the speeches of the same speaker. "He" in (12) is reported with both "says" and "said," and so is "I" in (13):

(12) Anyway, we went to the Smith's [sic] house after dinner and Mr. Smith very nicely *says,* "Would you like some brandy?" So I *said,* "Yes, I will have some brandy." So he *says,* "We have some very nice brandy." He adds that. Then he goes to this cupboard and he opens it up and he *said,* "Too bad, you can't have any brandy 'cause I can't find any brandy snifters." . . . So he *says,* "Well, if that's the case," he *said,* "I will find you some other glasses." (Wolfson 1982: 51)

(13) So he *says,* "All right, put your right hand up." So I *said,* "What the hell, right hand, left hand," I *says,* "I don't know what the hell to do with any of them—either hand." (Ibid.)

These two cases show that even when a narrator keeps reporting a single speaker's continuous speech, she/he may still switch tenses.

2.2.3.3. 'Third-person story hypothesis'

Some narratives involve the first person as a participant, while others involve only a third-person participant. The first person's presence or absence may affect the tense forms. Wolfson hypothesized that in third-person stories, in which the storyteller is not one of the characters talking, only the past-tense form "said" is used. The following example shows such a case:

(14) So she couldn't get up she *said,* she, it was a—so she crawled to the door and then finally one of the women came and rang the bell and she *said* to 'em, "I'm on the floor, I fell and I can't get up." So Nancy *said,* "Well, open the door," and she *said,* "I can't reach the knob," she *said,* "I'm really hurtin." She *said,* "I can't pick myself up." She *said,* "My God, what d'ja do?" She *said,* "I don't know, I fell down the steps." So she *said,* "Well, can't you roll over on your other side?" and she *said,* "Honest to goodness I can't do anything," she *said,* "can't you come in?" She *said,* "Well, how am I gonna get in?" She *said,* "Well, try the kitchen window, that's, that's open." She *said,* "Tell Jane," who's a little tiny thing—she's only about four feet ten—she *said,* "Tell—can you hike Jane up and get her—go in the garage and you'll find a stool or something for her to get on and then hike her through the kitchen window." . . . (Wolfson 1982: 94)

Here, two third-person participants are both introduced with "said." But Wolfson's hypothesis is contradicted by the following case of a third-person story in which interactions by two persons "he" and "she" are reported:

(15) So he *says* to my wife, he *says*, "Well, what would you bid?" So she *says*, "It's stupid for me to talk," she *says*, "You got a bid for thirty-three, thirty-four," she *says*. "Why should I even talk to you? It ain't gonna be anywheres near." So he *says* to her, he *says*, "Well," he *says*, "the person at thirty-four backed out." So she *says*, "Oh, yeah?" He *says*, "Yeah," he *says*, "What would you bid?" So she *says*, "Twenty-eight." He *says*, "Oh," he *says*, "No, that she'll never go for." So she *says*, "Okay, that's my bid, Mr. Smith. You want it, fine; you don't, fine." (Ibid.: 26)

In this case, only "says" is used for both third-person participants, contrary to (14). There are also cases in which both "says" and "said" are used for the same third person's continuous speech:

(16) . . . he comes running down the aisle, screaming at the airline hostess, "Does this plane go to Madrid?" and she finally *said*, "Yes," so she *says*, "Sit down," you know, so he finally went in the back and sat down.
(Ibid.: 51)

2.2.3.4. *'Participant distinction hypothesis'*

Wolfson has another hypothesis concerning participant distinction that different dialogue-introducer tenses are used to keep apart different participants. This simply assumes that a narrator always uses "said" for one participant, while she/he always uses "says" for the other. In particular, in stories with dialogues between a first person and third persons, the contrast in forms might be used to distinguish participants in the dialogue. In the following, "says" is used for introducing the third person's dialogue, while "said" is used for the first person:

(17) I was at the shopping center the other day so I met, I met Gary there and I asked him what he's doin', he's goin' to school, and this, that and the other, and he *says*, "Come on down, I want to play some pool with you." So I *said*, "All right."
. . . .
So he—you know, when we started off, he takes this cue stick that he put together there, and he puts it on the side and he takes one of those solid cue sticks. I *said*, "What are you doing that for?" He *says*, "Can't use this on the break." He *says*, "This is only for delicate shots." (Ibid.: 43-44)

The following case includes the verb "go" as a dialogue-introducing verb, and tense-switching is used likewise: "said" is used for the first person, while "goes" is used for the third person:

> (18) so I *said* to the waitress that'd been waiting on our table all morning. I *said* "could I buy a couple ashtrays?" and she'd been so nice, I didn't want to rip one off you know [laughs] she *goes* . . . "honey you don't buy ashtrays in Vegas," and she *goes* "stay right there I'll be back."
> (Johnstone 1987: 40)

However, there are numerous instances in which this hypothesis does not work. First, there are cases in which both "says" and "said" are used with the first and third person subjects:

> (19) . . . And I'm standing in line for like two and a half hours to get gas, and I get up there—just as I get to the pups, the guy *says*, "You only gettin' two dollars worth of gas." So I get a little tense in the first place because it cost me three dollars worth of gas just to get up to the gas pups. [laugh]
> . . . .
> And I *said*, "Mister, you're not gonna get any gas in front of me." And he *said*, "Get out of my way kid, or I'm gonna hit you." That's what he *said* to me.
> . . . .
> All of a sudden there was a reputation to defend, 'cause a old lady *says*, "There, that a boy, kid, hit him!" And I *says*, "Pal, you can hit me, but if I fall, I promise you I'm gonna fall on you." So he went and he got his gas can and he went down the road. (Wolfson 1982: 38-39)

Second, there are cases in which the narrator gets only "said," while the third person gets both "says" and "said":

> (20) I didn' notice it b't there's a woman in my class who's a nurse 'n. hh she *said* to me she *said*, didju notice he has a ha:ndicap en I *said* wha:t. You know I *said* I don't see anything wrong with im, she *says* his ha:nds.
> (TG: 8)

> (21) So I uh—he *said*, "You go over and see X, tell him I sent you—tell him who you are, he'll give you a job here," he *says*, "I can't hire or fire, all I can do is run the place." So I *said*, "All right, where's he at?" (=1)

Conversely, there are cases in which the third person gets "says," while the first person gets both "says" and "said":

(22) So he *says*, "All right, put your right hand up." So I *said*, "What the hell, right hand, left hand," I *says*, "I don't know what the hell to do with any of them—either hand." (=13)

(23) And he *says*, "Quick! Quick! Towels!" I *said*, "What do you mean, towels?"—"Nana fell in!" I *says*, "Kenny, let me. . ." (Wolfson 1982: 47)

I have not found many examples of the case in which the third person gets only "said" while the first person gets both "say(s)" and "said." Fourth, there are other cases in which "say(s)" and "said" are used freely. For instance, the following example contains three participants, and "said" is used for the third person "she" and the first person "I," while another third person "he" gets "says":

(24) My girlfriend called and she *said*, "Do you want to go to the movies?" So I *said*, "Fine." So Larry *says*, "Good, go," you know, he was doing paper work, he *says*, "Go." (Ibid.: 51)

In the following, "says" is used throughout, and tense is not used to separate the first and the third person:

(25) . . . he *says*, "Settlement's no good. She's got us for forty-five days." In October she wanted to settle. So I *says*, "Okay, I'll try to get January and I'll play around with that." So I walk in and I sign a check for twenty-eight hundred dollars and I *says* to him, I *says*, "Now," I *says*, "take this back to her." So he picked up the agreement—all of a sudden he looks at the agreement. He *says*, "Well," he *says*, "This uh date was changed." I *says*, "That's right. Settlement." I *says*, "Now you take it and show her the check. She wants to play around fine. Deal's off!" (Ibid.: 26-27)

2.2.3.5. 'Outside the tense system hypothesis'

There is a possibility that the reporting verb "say" is outside the usual tense system, since "says" is frequently used not only for the third person but also for the first person such as in "I says," as we saw in (22)(23)(25). Wolfson denies this consideration, however, claiming that there are numerous examples of other verbs in which the third-person singular morpheme -*s* co-occurs with a first-person pronoun.[11]

2.2.3.6. *'Relative status hypothesis'*

We may consider that tense choices in dialogue-introducers have to do with differences in the relative status of the reported speakers. Wolfson rejects this hypothesis because the same speaker in the same dialogue is sometimes introduced both ways, with the past and with the CHP, as we have seen in many of the examples above. Later Johnstone reexplored this possibility. Let us look at Johnstone's relative status hypothesis in detail in the following section, and show some limitations to it.

2.2.4. Johnstone's hypothesis

2.2.4.1. *New relative status hypothesis*

Johnstone (1987) reevaluates one of Wolfson's rejected hypotheses, the relative status hypothesis. Wolfson rejected it simply because the same speaker in the same dialogue can be introduced with the past for one utterance and with the HP for another. However, Johnstone claims that this reasoning is insufficient, raising two points. First, storytellers do not simply capture a static social fact about relative status in their stories, but they construct relations between speakers which are more fluid, and may evolve in the course of the reported talk. So the status hypothesis should be seen in a more fluid and more individual way. Second, once a storyteller's audience gets to a certain point, the teller does not need to keep making the point. A storyteller may mark status relations once or twice and then not keep marking them, until they change. Thus, while there is a general pattern that is repeated in many stories, it is necessary to look at individual stories to understand particular choices. She bases these claims on Becker's (1984; 1988) 'linguistics of particularity' as a theoretical framework.

After having conducted a quantitative study and microanalysis of a corpus of narratives in which storytellers had recreated conversations with figures of authority, Johnstone concluded that speakers use tense-alternation to mark differences between authority and nonauthority figures. She hypothesized that tellers use the past tense (e.g., "said"; "was going") for introducing the speech of nonauthority figures, while the HP (e.g., "says"; "goes") for the speech of authority figures. She raises the following example of this general pattern:

(26) and then I *said* "what's the problem here?" he *says* "well ma'am . . . ah . . . you didn't stop for that stop sign back there" I *said* "WHAT . . ." I mean I was mad I *said* "WHAT" and he *says* . . . he *says* "it's the In-" he just starts off rattling "it's the Indi- Indiana State Law you must come to a complete

stop . . . before the stop sign da da da da" I *said* "I did" I *said* "there's a crosswalk there and the thing's before that" I *said* "where were you sitting anyway" [laughs] he *says* "I was right in that parking lot by the church" and that parking lot's right back here [indicating on table] you can't even see the stop sign I *said* "I'm sorry" I *said* "you didn't see me" he *said* "it's the Indiana State Law da da da da da" (Johnstone 1987: 34)

The context is that a young woman is describing a conversation she had with a police officer who stopped her on the road when she was a new driver. Here the storyteller's speech is introduced in the past, while the policeman's speech is introduced with the HP, except for the last instance, which she claims as an individual variation (I will mention this point later). The same pattern also applies to "go" and zero-introducer (which I represent with the mark [ø] in examples):

(27) so I *said* to the waitress that'd been waiting on our table all morning. I *said* "could I buy a couple ashtrays?" and she'd been so nice, I didn't want to rip one off you know [laughs] she *goes* . . . "honey you don't buy ashtrays in Vegas," and she *goes* "stay right there I'll be back." (=18)

(28) Misses Czinski's got her housecoat on and down the lawn by then . . . you know [ø] "what's going on here Carol?" [raised pitch] [Jim: laughs] I *said* "it's okay" I *said* "this . . . this guy *says* he saw something and he can't even see it from where he's parked anyway" [laughs]
. . . .
and Misses Czinski's out there [ø] "Carol is there any problem?" I *said* "no . . . no" (Johnstone 1987: 40-41)

In (27), Johnstone claims that the waitress is the authority figure since she is a waitress in a casino in Las Vegas while the storyteller makes a somewhat embarrassing request of the waitress. In (28), the authority is an older neighbor, a member of the teller's parents' or grandparents' generation. Johnstone treats the zero-introducer as present tense in opposition to the past tense. The examples so far had cases in which tellers are the nonauthority figure. Johnstone raises the next one as the case in which the teller is the authority figure:

(29) she called back on Sunday night she *said* "uh . . . car won't start" [laughs] I *says* "what do you mean the car won't start?" (Ibid.: 40)

Here the storyteller is an auto mechanic and garage owner, middle-aged. He tells about an episode about his wife who has gone into town for a meeting and called to find out what to do when the car fails to start. The HP is used for the authority figure "I" and the past is used for the nonauthority figure "she."

Johnstone gives three explanations for the status hypothesis for tense choice for dialogue-introducers. First, storytellers use the HP as an evaluative device in narrative, which fits well with Schiffrin's (1981) claim. Narrative stories need to have a point (Labov 1972b; Polanyi 1979), which makes it worth telling and worth listening to. A speaker points up the tellability of a story by means of evaluative devices, and one such device is the use of the HP. For stories that include interactions with authorities, what makes the events tellable stories is the presence of authorities. So it is the authority who gets the marked form, the nonpast form for a past event (Johnstone 1987: 43). Second, storytellers use tense choices for tracking shifts in 'footing,' which Goffman (1981a: 128) defines as "the alignment we take up to ourselves and the others present as expressed in the way we manage the production or reception of an utterance." One of the devices that storytellers use to manage their footings is their choice of tense in dialogue-introducers. The different tenses of dialogue-introducers indicate that the two characters in the story are on unequal footings. Nonauthorities are presented with "said" since they tend to be presented as having spoken more carefully, more in accordance with prescriptive norms, while authorities are introduced with "says" or "goes" since they can afford to be more colloquial and slightly incorrect. The third explanation is related to 'authorship' (Goffman 1981a).[12] Storytellers generally need to give speakers in their stories authorial voices, while at the same time maintaining their (tellers') own authorial voices. But authority figures are often not entirely the authors of their own words in Goffman's sense. Authority figures' words are not a verbatim citation of anyone's real words, but they are conventionalized version of the public, formulaic language:

> There are thus two senses in which authority figures in stories are not the authors of their words. In the first place, it is the teller who is the author of the story, and in the second place, it is the public that is presented as the real author of the words authority figures speak. In other words, authority stories involve conventionalized public authorship embedded in the individual authorship of the teller.   (Johnstone 1987: 49)

From this, Johnstone further claims that the public language of authority figures is timeless and universal. Therefore their words are introduced with the simple present, which is timeless and universalizing in English. In contrast, when the authority figures are not presented as speaking with the voice of public authority, but are rather presented as individual authors, their talk is keyed in the same way as that of the nonauthority, and there is no tense-shift.

Johnstone gives some reasons for the cases in which tense-shifting does not occur. First, she claims that one's alignment with respect to others changes in the course of interaction, and these changes must be encoded in the story. She refers back to the final interchange of example (26):

(30) I *said* "I'm sorry" I *said* "you didn't see me" he *said* "it's the Indiana State Law da da da da da" (from 26)

Here, the policeman is presented as having quoted verbatim a legal text, as he was once before. As far as he sticks to the authoritative status, he is introduced with "says." Once he starts talking carefully, he is introduced with "said," as already explained above that "said" introduces words spoken more carefully in accordance with prescriptive norms, which is usually characteristic of nonauthority figures. Second, some storytellers simply do not choose this cue out of the range of strategies they have available for marking footing. Third, teenagers cannot manipulate footings effectively in their retelling. For instance, the following is told by a 14-year-old boy:

(31) that guy *goes* "what are you guys doing on the private property?" and we *go* "there's other people back there fishing" I *say*—and he *goes* . . . "well get in here, I'm going to call your parents" so we *go* . . . "uhohh" [laughs]
(Johnstone 1987: 46)

Johnstone claims that the lack of tense-shift here reflects the boy's inability to manipulate footings. Fourth, the occurrence or non-occurrence of tense-shifting depends entirely on individual situations, but for good reasons. For instance, in the next example, the storyteller who had an accident and was arrested for drunk driving, interacts with a nurse at the police station. The teller suddenly stops using tense-alternations:

(32) and the nurse . . . there was this lady . . . *goes* "you sure you don't want to be checked out?" and I *go* "HELL YES I want to be checked out"
(Ibid.)

Johnstone claims that this is a crucial point in the story, so the last line is doubly marked for importance, by means of the evaluative HP, and also by not introducing his speech with the normal past tense.

Fludernik (1991: 392) agrees with Johnstone's (1987) relative status hypothesis, in which the "says"/"said" alternation makes subtle comments about the status of participants in relation to the 'point' of the story. Regarding the exceptional cases to the hypothesis, she claims that "influence from stories told exclusively in the present tense and from jokes has helped to blur the dynamics of "said"/"says" alternation so that continuous series of "says I," "says he" are quite common."¹³

2.2.4.2. Problems with relative status hypothesis

I find problems with Johnstone's hypothesis, which need to be overcome in order to validate it. First, Johnstone has only dealt with stories that, she claims, include authority and nonauthority figures. Although she mentions that the study has implications for other kinds of stories as well (Johnstone 1987: 50), she has not demonstrated how it applies to other kinds of stories. In interactions among friends, in which there is hardly any distinction between authority and nonauthority, there still occur tense-switchings. In the following example, three participants are friends, and there's no distinction between authority and nonauthority, but the dialogue-introducers still switch tenses:

(33) I know it wasn't nice, it sure was funny. hhh hhh So finally he *said*, "You talk to Terry, I'm goin' to the bathroom," hhh so he disappeared to the bathroom, an' I *said*, "Well let's (0.3) see how far this can go." I *said*, "Terry, You wanna step outside for a few minutes?" hhh She *goes*, "That's great." So we ran outside, . . . (HK)

Second, Johnstone has not provided clear definitions of 'authority' and 'nonauthority.' She raises examples of authorities such as police officers, older neighbors or parents' friends, parents, emergency-room nurses, merchants, military superiors, auto mechanic as opposed to his wife, but she does not show how we can judge authority versus nonauthority.

Third, there are many examples in which the tenses used for authority and nonauthority figures are opposite to her claim. For instance, in the following story about boating, Kenny who is apparently an authority in boating is introduced with "said":

(34) Wait! Listen! So I look up and I see Kenny, who is a very good sailor, Marion, who swims well, and my Mom in the dingy. And they *say*, "All right, look, we'll meet you at shore." And Kenny *said*, "All right, I'll go back with it." So they . . . (=10)

Although she gives explanations for such cases in her data, some are still questionable and unsatisfactory. She explained the exceptional case (30) by saying that, because the policeman quoted verbatim a legal text and was talking carefully, he is introduced with "said" which is used for carefully spoken words in accordance with prescriptive norms. However, it contradicts the fact that the verbatim legal text should be of a timeless universal nature, which should logically be introduced with the timeless "says" according to her theory. Moreover, this policeman made almost the same utterance earlier as quoted in (26), and that was a more precise verbatim than this line. If Johnstone claims that the reason for the narrator's using the past tense for the policeman in (30) is the carefulness of the speech, then the policeman's former utterance which was more precisely and carefully spoken should be introduced in the past tense, too. But this is not the case.

Fourth, Johnstone's hypothesis fails to explain tense-alternation in a single speaker's continuous utterances, as we already saw in (12) and (21), and as we can observe in the following:

(35) So, Willie Dixon heard me sitting in with them and after I was finished, he came over and *says*, he *says*, "My God, I never heard a woman sing the blues before like you sing the blues." He *saying*, "that's what the world needs today, a woman to sing the blues." He *say*, "We got plenty of mens out here singing." He *said*, "But we don't have no women, you know." He *said*, "That's why we need a woman to sing like you sing and to sing the blues." (EJ 1992. 3: 111)[14]

Here, Willie Dixon is a famous singer, who made this storyteller become a singer. Thus, he is in an authoritative position as opposed to the teller. To introduce his speech, the tense switches between "says," "saying," "say," and "said." Johnstone's hypothesis is hardly applicable to such cases.

Finally, the most crucial question may be whether Americans take the distinction between authority and nonauthority as such an important concept in their perception of human relationships, important enough so that they unconsciously change their verbal behavior to reflect such distinctions.

I would suggest that we need a more general theory than Johnstone's, that will cover a wider range of human interactions, which at the same time will allow individuality and particularity.

2.3. CONCLUSIONS AND DIRECTIONS FOR FURTHER RESEARCH

Tense-switching of the reporting verb "say" is a significant performance feature in conversational narratives that often accompany direct reporting discourse. Because it does not fit in the framework of general tense-alternation theory, it has long been set aside as a problematic case. This chapter reviewed the problem of the tense-switching of reporting dialogue-introducers, and examined existing hypotheses. After summarizing Wolfson's viewpoint that "say" is an exceptional case with its unique character in narrative, I reexamined the hypotheses that Wolfson simply mentioned in her work. This is a necessary step for leading our focus in the right direction, since it was by reevaluating one of the Wolfson's rejected hypotheses that Johnstone presented her relative status hypothesis. I agree with Johnstone's attitude that we need to accept individuality and particularity in considering discourse data, since all conversational narrative has different contextual information in each instance. But we see in her hypothesis a fatal problem that exceeds the particularity: lack of consistency in characterizations of a sense of authority.

As a possible direction for further research on this problem, I suggest that discourse-based approaches are plausible. Traditional analyses of the historical present, which are highly subjective, did not attempt to specify the particular circumstances in which the speaker chooses to make events more 'vivid.' Syntactic studies of tense systems still deny the existence of tense-switching, as Hornstein (1990: 199) says: "in the course of a narrative one cannot move back and forth between the past tense and the historical present. Once one switches, the present tense must be maintained." Formal semantic studies are also blind to discourse realities, as Parsons (1990: 257) claims that the appropriate tense for reports is the preterit, the present tense being more usually reserved for "gnomic" or generic uses. From adequate empirical data that shows the prevalence of tense-switching, I have to say that such comments are based on studies that neglect empirical facts in discourse. Recent researchers started discourse-based studies, arguing that a complete picture of tense-marking can be obtained through the use of discourse data. They have shown that tense-switching in general obviously has discourse functions which appear systematically in a particular surrounding context, one which establishes that the speaker is telling a story. By discourse analysis which considers context and quantitative data, we can make the description of the use of the HP substantive. But as I have shown, the behavior of reporting verbs has not been fully explained yet.

We may think of the dialogue-introducer tenses as reflecting the interpersonal relationships of reporters and reportees, as Johnstone's status hypothesis suggests. But we still need to remember that reporting as well as narrating is a complicated information processing behavior (Chafe 1977a), thus the surface reporting form is a reflection of numerous factors interacting simultaneously (Sakita 1996a). In addition, tense also has such multifarious characters. As Myhill (1992: 90) claims about future-tense forms, in the great majority of cases, a variety of different factors affect the choice of which form to use, so that marking in individual cases is determined by a number of factors operating simultaneously. In this regard, the hypotheses to which I presented counter examples should not be disregarded too soon as Wolfson did in her work. Each single hypothesis may work context-dependently or in combination with other factors. The next step is to work on the issue systematically with both qualitative and quantitative approaches.

I will examine the phenomena as a reflection of interoperations of functions of language and reporters' cognition and consciousness. In chapter 3, I will first examine reporters' cognition, considering tense-alternation as closely related phenomena to reporters' ways of viewing reported participants. I will, in a sense, reevaluate Wolfson's participant distinction hypothesis, although I will consider it not as a functional or deliberate device but as a reflection of reporters' natural cognitive operations. It is also partly related to the third-person story hypothesis, in that the reporter's participation or non-participation in the reported event influences the construals of reported events. On the contrary, in chapter 4, I will consider more deeply the function of dialogue-introducer tense as a conversational strategic device, namely, to contrast reported speaker's attitudes. I will discuss how such a function more generally contextualizes Johnstone's relative status hypothesis. In chapter 5, I will discuss the use of dialogue-introducers and their tenses as reflection of a speaker's flow of consciousness along with discourse organizations. I will explore the notion of continuity and discontinuity that arose from the single speaker continuity hypothesis, and examine discourse organization that is related to the speech act hypothesis. Since previous philological approaches such as semantics, syntax, and pragmatics have not yet provided an answer to the question of dialogue-introducer tense-alternation, I will attempt to take a different view of the issue from previous studies, while incorporating some of their essentials into my analyses.

3

COGNITIVE BACKGROUNDS OF TENSE-ALTERNATION

3.0. OVERVIEW

Narrative psychologists characterize narrative as the basic mode of human understanding (Edwards 1997: 268). In narrative psychology, Bruner (1990: 35) considers narrative not merely as a kind of discourse, but as a mode of thought and action describable in terms that can be related to cognitive plans and representations.[1] Chafe (1990: 79), a linguist, mentions that narratives are "overt manifestations of the mind in action." They are "windows to both the content of the mind and its ongoing operations." When we study narratives, we should consider that, as Edwards (1997: 271) puts it, narratives reflect the nature of people's perspectives on events, how people see things.

When we report or narrate past events, we first consciously or subconsciously recollect past events stored in our memory, in order to reconstruct them for the purpose of conveying them to our present audience. Since narrating behavior is based on recollecting activity, the ways we recollect influence the ways we narrate. I assume that linguistic phenomena accompanying reporting behavior reflect the modes of our cognitive recollection. Previous studies on dialogue-introducer tense-alternation overlooked considerations of the cognitive backgrounds of reporting behaviors. This chapter shows that stylistic choices of narrative reporting discourse in natural conversations reflect the speakers' cognitive operations of conceptualizing experience. Tense-alternation phenomena of reporting verbs, which have long been at issue but never been correctly explained, indeed reflect how a speaker perceives the past scenes that existed in her/his memory and are now being recollected. This chapter aims to reveal and account for the systematic nature of tense-alternation in reporting discourse, by exploring recall and conceptualization of past events.

I will first present my observations of tense usage for different personal deixis, with a quantitative analysis of tense-switching in conversational narrative discourse. It suggests that our perception of personal deictic relations is closely related to narrative tense forms. To account for the distribution, I will next present a Cognitive Recollection Model that illustrates a speaker's recollection of different interactional settings, incorporating her/his psychological distance from the observed participants and perception of the relationships among them. The first model illustrates interactions among third-person interlocutors. It relates choice of tense ("says" vs. "said") to the degree of the speaker's psychological involvement in the recalled interactions. The second model illustrates the interactions that involve the past self. In this case, choice of tense is further regulated to protect the ego's self-identity as narrator in relation to the present audience.[2] I will discuss the ego's self-identity as one of the crucial factors for the narrator's manipulation of dialogue-introducers' tense forms. I will refer to discourse rules (Schiffrin 1993) especially in 'constructed dialogues' (Tannen 1989), levels of narrative (Labov and Waletzky 1967; Hopper 1979; Hopper and Thompson 1980; McNeill 1992), and manipulation of 'footing' (Goffman 1981a). My claims about self-identity also concur with cognitive monitoring theories in psychology (Flavell 1978; Koyazu 1985). Finally, I will point out that tense-alternation is a product of the interaction of multiple factors in the complex processes of reporting. Some remaining problems will be explored in the further chapters.

3.1. TENSE AND PERSON

In chapter 2, I examined one of Wolfson's rejected hypotheses: the participant distinction hypothesis, which assumes that different tenses are used to distinguish different participants. One possibility that I considered was whether different tense forms contrast first person and third person. There were many counter-examples against this hypothesis, which seemed to be a good reason for Wolfson to reject it. However, in further observation of conversational narratives, I have found numerous cases that still conform to this hypothesis. More precisely, my quantitative analysis shows that "says" is often used for introducing the third person's dialogue, while "said" tends to be used for the first person. Indeed, such cases appear frequently enough to merit further examination.

3.1.1. Distribution in discourse

Let us consider the frequency distribution of tense forms for different reported persons in discourse. The surveyed discourse data includes transcriptions of audiotaped casual spoken American English, and sample discourse of the same type which appeared in previous studies, yielding 105 narrative excerpts that included direct reporting discourse, chosen from all the discourse data compiled.

Table 1 shows which of past tense (PST), present tense (PRE), present tense in 'third-person singular present' form (PRE-*s*), and others are used to introduce dialogues by first person, third person, third-person plural (e.g., "they"), and first-person plural (e.g., "we").[3] Table 2 shows the ratio of frequency distribution for each person group shown in Table 1.

Table 1: Tense with First and Third Person

	1st person	3rd person	3rd person pl.	1st person pl.
[PST]	104	86	9	0
[PRE]	12	9	5	4
[PRE-*s*]	21	129	0	0
others	12	32	9	2
TOTAL	149	256	23	6

Table 2: Ratio of Past and Present Tense

	1st person	3rd person	3rd person pl.	1st person pl.
[PST]	69.8%	33.6%	39.1%	0.0%
[PRE]	8.1%	3.5%	21.7%	66.7%
[PRE-*s*]	14.1%	50.4%	0.0%	0.0%
others	8.1%	12.5%	39.1%	33.3%

The result shows the frequency of different uses of reporting verb tenses for first person and third person. For reporting third-person utterances, the present tense is used for 53.9%, including 3.5% for the present and 50.4% for the present in 'third-person singular' form, and the past tense is used for 33.6%. For reporting first-person utterances, mainly the past tense is used. It occupies 69.8% of all the dialogue-introducers that are used for the first person. In addition, the present tense is used for 22.2%,

46 *Reporting Discourse, Tense, and Cognition*

including 8.1% for the present and 14.1% for the present in 'third-person singular' form. This indicates that the use of a present tense verb is restricted in introducing first-person dialogues, compared with introducing third-person dialogues.

This difference is clearer when we focus our attention on the reporting verb "say." Table 3 shows the frequency distribution of the tense variation of "say." It shows which of "said," "say," "says," past-tense "saying" (e.g., "was saying"), and present-tense "saying" (e.g., "is saying") are used to introduce dialogues by first person, third person, third-person plural (e.g., "they"), and first-person plural (e.g., "we"). Table 4 shows the ratio of frequency distribution for first and third person shown in Table 3.

Table 3: Use of *Say* with First and Third Person

		1st person	3rd person	3rd person pl.	1st person pl.
[PST]	*said*	94	77	8	0
	saying	0	2	0	0
[PRE]	*say*	6	7	1	0
	says	21	97	0	0
	saying	2	3	0	0

Table 4: Ratio of *Say* in Past and Present Tense

		1st person		3rd person	
[PST]	*said*	(*I said*)	76.4%	(*she/he said*)	41.4%
	others		0.0%		1.1%
[PRE]	*say*	(*I say*)	4.9%	(*she/he say*)	3.8%
	says	(*I says*)	17.1%	(*she/he says*)	52.2%
	others		1.6%		1.6%

Table 4 confirms the different uses of reporting verb tenses for first person and third person limited to the use of "say." For reporting third-person utterances, "says" is used for 52.2%, and "said" is used for 41.4%. For reporting first-person utterances, "I said" is used primarily. It occupies 76.4% of all the dialogue-introducers used for first person. In addition, "I says" is used for 17.1%, and "I say" for 4.9%. This indicates that the use of the present tense for "say" is limited when introducing first-person dialogues.

Even in the cases in which present-tense forms are used for first persons, "I says" and "I say" are often supplemented by "I said" immediately after the reported phrases. The following examples show such cases (with corresponding pairs of reporting phrases underlined):

(1) We went to clean the drain in the sn- in the snowstorm. This was right after the war. So, w- we- it was- my feet were wet. We were riding in the truck. In a car. <u>I say</u>, "Hey Joe." <u>I said</u>- I took my stockin's off, and my shoes.
(Schiffrin 1987: 192)

(2) and I *said* "what's the problem" and he *says* "well misses um . . . I saw back down there by the high school I think you were going a little FAST there it's a thirty-mile-an-hour zone you know" and <u>I says</u> "yeah I know" <u>I said</u> "ah I know" . . .
[Quotation marks are added (hereafter)] (Johnstone 1987: 41)

(3) So I felt him lean over the bed. And I- I start laughin'. <u>I says</u>, "Oh you s-" excuse the expression <u>I said</u>, "Oh you son of a bitch," right, And he came, he kissed me. When he kissed me I felt his beard. And I'm pushin' I'*m saying*, "Ooh, my God! It isn't you!" And I'm pushin' with all my might, right? I'*m saying*, "Oh my God! Who is he?" y'know. And I PUSH. And I'm- uh uh I try to scream and I was too scared. (Schiffrin 1981: 59)

In (1), after "I say, 'Hey Joe,'" the reporting phrase is repeated as "I said." In (2), "I says, 'yeah I know'" is repaired by "I said, 'ah I know.'" In (3), in the first line, after starting to report with "I says," the narrator inserts an excuse for a bad expression. She resumes her report with "I said." These examples imply that present forms are not normally used with first person. Let us compare these examples with the following cases that also contain repeated dialogue-introducers:

48 *Reporting Discourse, Tense, and Cognition*

(4) so I *said* to the waitress that'd been waiting on our table all morning. I *said* "could I buy a couple ashtrays?" and she'd been so nice, I didn't want to rip one off you know [laughs] she *goes* . . . "honey you don't buy ashtrays in Vegas," and she *goes* "stay right there I'll be back."

(Johnstone 1987: 40)

(5) and this jeep wheels up and it's this real hard-ass Lieutenant Mead and he hops out and he *says* "MALONE WHERE IN THE FUCK HAVE YOU BEEN?" [performing a tough voice] I *said* "Mead" a lieutenant you know I *said* "MEAD WHERE IN THE FUCK HAVE YOU BEEN?" [performing the same tough voice]

(Ibid.: 41)

(6) and then I *said* "what's the problem here?" he *says* "well ma'am . . . ah . . . you didn't stop for that stop sign back there" I *said* "WHAT . . ." I mean I was mad I *said* "WHAT" . . .   (Ibid.: 34)

In these cases, a reporting phrase is repeated after the insertion of a short situational explanation that comes after the first reporting phrase. The dialogue-introducer "I said" is followed by another "I said." Consider the following examples:

(7) Misses Czinski's got her housecoat on and down the lawn by then . . . you know [ø] "what's going on here Carol?" [raised pitch] [Jim: laughs] I *said* "it's okay" I *said* "this . . . this guy says he saw something and he can't even see it from where he's parked anyway" [laughs] . . .   (Ibid.: 40)

(8) I *said* "wo::wuhh huhh!" hhh I *said* "theh go," I *said* "there's- there's three courses a'ready thet uh(hh)hhhff"   (TG: 9)

(9) *Like* "wu—hh Didju n- Didju know what he wz talking about didju know wh't structural paralysis was" I *said* "no" I *said* "but we're supposetuh know what it is (fawuh-) hh yihknow fuh tihday's class."   (TG: 10)

(10) there wz anothuh girl walking around she *says* hhh "uh-dihyou know where the science building is" 'n I *said*- "well" I *said*- "yihknow, the guard jus' told me thet this wz the bui:lding." So she *seh*- hh "are you goin here fer 'n-hh fer en in:dian class by any chance" 'n I *said* "yes" hh So I *said* "c'mon we'll fi:nd it tuhgethuh"   (TG: 17-18)

In these examples, the reporting phrase is repeated after a short dialogue. Whether the second dialogue-introducer follows the insertion of a situational explanation (4-6) or follows a short dialogue (7-10), we see that when the speakers repeat the reporting phrases after the use of "I said," they use the same past-tense form "I said." In (1)(2)(3), narrators shifted to the past-tense form "I said" after their first use of the present forms "I says" or "I say" when repeating the reporting phrases. All these examples suggest that the present forms "I says" and "I say" tend to be supplemented by the past form "I said" immediately afterwards but not vice versa: it is rare that tense shifts from the past to the present for introducing first-person dialogues.

It is interesting to see that typically in third-person reporting, the present-tense reporting phrase is supplemented by another present-tense reporting phrase, as in the following:

(11) My girlfriend called and she *said*, "Do you want to go to the movies?" So I *said*, "Fine." So Larry *says*, "Good, go," you know, he was doing paper work, he *says*, "Go." (Wolfson 1982: 51)

Here the narrator inserts a situational explanation after the first reporting phrase "Larry says." The repeated reporting phrase is in the same present-tense form, "he says." In the following examples, a reporter repeats reporting phrases with present-tense verbs again and again:

(12) Jumps up and down, on the bed, and *says*, after he *says*, "Wake up." Sam *says*, "Bobby and Peter," and *says*, "You're acting dead, wake up." And *says*, "Do it again." (Johnston 1985: 85)

(13) N: nNo:, it's awr- it's a'right, jist'nna couple places b't I c'n cover it u:p,=
But he *goes*, (.) he:- he *goes* yih 'av a rilly mild case he *goes*,
H: Of wha:t.
N: Yih sh-
N: A:cne-e,= (HG)

In the following examples, the past-tense reporting phrase is supplemented by the present-tense reporting phrase:

(14) I *said*, "Did he get fresh?" She *said*, "No!" She *says*, "But he's different!" She *says*, "I'm not used t' Gentile boys!" That cured her! She'd never go out with one again. (Schiffrin 1990: 250-51)

(15) An' I didn' wanna say-eh: A:deline *said* she a'ways wanted uh see it so .hnhh I never *said* anything but- uh: Claude *said* today he *says* wasn' that the dirtiest place? (Edwards 1997: 147)

In (14), "she said, 'No'" is followed by "she says." In (15), after "Claude said today," the reporting phrase "he says" is added. For third-person stories, this phenomenon is rare, where the present-tense form ("X says") is followed by the past-tense form ("X said"). This is a significant difference from first-person stories.

Table 2 and Table 4 raise another important point. For the first person, a present-tense verb in 'third-person singular present' form is used more frequently than a simple present-tense verb. Namely, the 'ungrammatical' form "I says" is more frequently used than the 'grammatical' form "I say." One may assume that the 'third-person singular present' form may have lost its significance for some reason and has become used for introducing non-third person dialogues. However, this is unlikely, since the 'third-person singular present' form is used irregularly only for the first person, and not for third-person plural or first-person plural.

3.1.2. Personal deixis and tense forms

The frequency distribution above shows a significant correlation between the first/third person distinction and past/present tense forms. Fleischman (1990: 83) mentions her similar assumption that in personal experience narratives, the present tense correlates overwhelmingly with persons other than the first person, and commonly with third-person subjects, although she does not show any concrete study to support her observation but one example. She also points out the issue of "I says," following Casparis (1975) and Bellos (1980), in asserting that "'say' can occur with the first person, but interestingly it is always 'I says,' or more commonly 'says I' (with pragmatically marked word order), never 'I say.'" She assumes that the past/present alternation serves "to contrast situations associated with the narrator, rendered almost consistently in the P [past], with those of his third-person interlocutors, in the PR [present]" (p. 84). She further suggests that such person-tense correlation is universal: "narrators across languages tend to avoid reporting their own actions—and even more so introducing their own speech—in the PR [present] tense." Her claim concurs with the result of my survey, but the present data show that the empirical fact is not so clear-cut. It shows that first persons are introduced mostly with the past tense, and next with "says," but there are still cases of "I say," although very few. Third persons are most often introduced with the present tense, but also often with the past.

When claiming universal correlations of tense forms and personal deixis, Fleischman admits that "it is not entirely clear why this is the case" (1990: 84). I would argue that the correlations reflect narrators' different construals of different persons in the process of recollection, which would explain the empirical facts that do not

Cognitive Backgrounds of Tense-Alternation 51

merely follow a distinct correlation between past/present tenses and first/third persons but are more complicated. Personal deixis plays a cognitively significant role in narratives, as one of the three deictic components of the situation—temporal, spatial, and personal (Bühler 1982).[4] Narrators' modes of recalling events are closely correlated with personal distinctions, and such recollection modes are reflected in tense forms in narratives. Before modeling recollection modes in accordance with personal distinction, I shall briefly characterize the interpretive processes of reporting.

3.2. INTERPRETIVE PROCESSES OF REPORTING

Using a simple model (Figure 1), Chafe (1977a: 216) illustrates how we process information for reporting past experiences. We have a 'stimulus' which is the physical input to our sense organs when we first experience the incident we later tell about. It enters 'consciousness,' which represents our phenomenological awareness of the experience in question, through 'perception.' Some of what has been in consciousness passes into memory.[5] What is in consciousness is knowledge that is activated or 'lit up' at any particular time, while what is in memory is inactive or not lit up at the moment, but is still 'present' in some fashion in the mind (ibid.: 218). Information can be 'recalled' or reactivated from the memory to consciousness.

Figure 1: Information Processing of Past Experience (Chafe 1977a: 216)

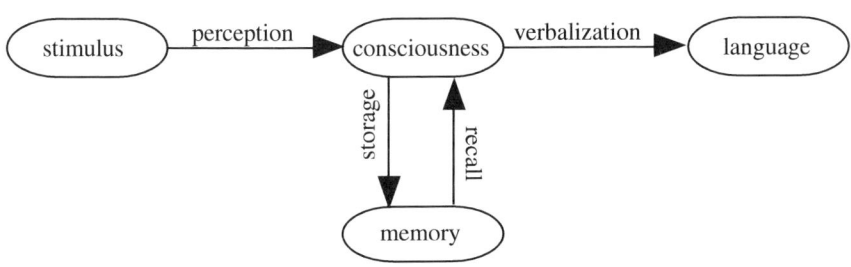

Chafe claims that perception is interpretive (Hochberg 1964), in the sense that what enters consciousness is not a faithful replica of the stimulus but rather an interpretation of it. He emphasizes that both perception and verbalization are interpretive. As people speak they are constantly making choices about the best way to express what they are thinking of. I assume that the same applies to the process from recall to verbalization. Recall is an interpretive process just as perception is, and it is a reconstruction process from a specific viewpoint. Before verbalizing remembered events, speakers fix in their minds a schema (Bartlett 1932) and a frame (Goffman 1974; Fillmore 1975a; Minsky 1975) to reconstruct the events (Chafe 1977b; Tannen 1993).[6] In such a schema, they interpretively reconstruct the events. Tannen (1986: 313) argues that speakers listen for meaning and, when recalling what was said, they reconstruct it into words, much as Bartlett (1932) discovered that memory for objects and events is constructive. This idea is reflected in her characterization of reporting discourse as 'constructed dialogue' (Tannen 1989).

Similarly, narratives are "reconstructions and reconstitutions of past events cast in a particular perspective that fits into the narrative's context of occurrence" (Georgakopoulou 1997: 3). To more precisely characterize the reconstruction process in narratives, namely 'narrativization,' Fleischman (1990: 96) proposes a two-step process consisting of cognitive and linguistic operations. The first operation is an "unconscious segmentation of the seamless experiential continuum into cognitive units that we call 'events.'"[7] The second operation is the linguistic encoding of the events as a sequence of predicates of various types. It is "linearization and perspectivization, the goal of which is to impose a particular order and coherence on the events and to render their configuration meaningful." The narrativization process is interpretive, as she claims that it is an individual, subjective act: "experience is passed through the filter of a focalizing consciousness whose point of view the story will reflect. No two narrators will configure an experience, or evaluate its component elements, in precisely the same way."

As we can see in Figure 1, before verbalization, there are two inputs into consciousness: perception and recall. Both are crucial interpretive stages. I assume that direct perception and recall share parallel characteristics of viewing events interpretively and egocentrically. Chafe (1994: 197) describes how the environment, which contains perceived events and states in the outside world that surrounds the conscious self, enters consciousness and becomes verbalized as language. He distinguishes two inputs into consciousness in Figure 2: one in the process of speaking about immediate events (Figure 2[a]); the other in the process of reporting past events (Figure 2[b]). In the immediate speaking process, people are speaking in an immediate mode, in which events are perceived, acted on and evaluated by consciousness at the time and place of the story's telling. In the process of reporting, on the other hand, people are speaking in a displaced mode, in which the consciousness is focused on events remembered or imagined, that is, events which are displaced in time and space. The displaced mode (Figure 2[b]) corresponds to the reporting process illustrated in Figure 1.

Cognitive Backgrounds of Tense-Alternation 53

Figure 2(a): Speaking in the Immediate Mode (Chafe 1994: 197)

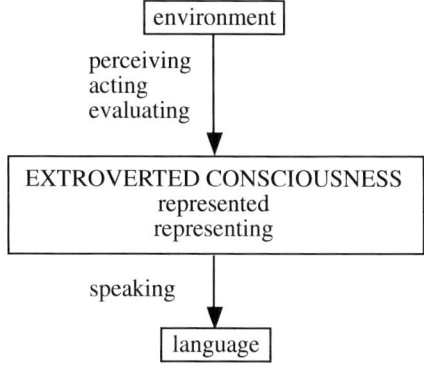

Figure 2(b): Speaking in the Displaced Mode (Chafe 1994: 199)

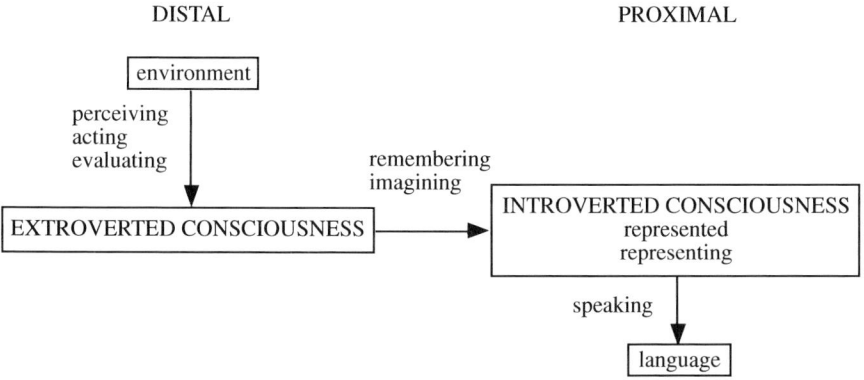

In the displaced mode of reporting, input into introverted consciousness comes not from directly perceiving, acting on, or evaluating the immediate environment, but through the process of remembering what was present in a distal extroverted consciousness, or alternatively through the process of imagining what might be present in such a consciousness.

Cognitive linguists have modeled the ways a speaker interpretively perceives events. For instance, to illustrate someone's perception of events, Langacker (1990) claims that people take specific vantage points. He describes how such cognitive operations result in different language forms. I assume that when a speaker recalls (or remembers; or imagines) past events in the displaced mode, she/he takes specific van-

54 *Reporting Discourse, Tense, and Cognition*

tage points toward the remembered events, which lead to different ways of reporting.[8] Following Langacker's model of the direct perception of events, I will model how people envision past interactional events during the recall process in the next section.[9]

3.3. COGNITIVE RECOLLECTION MODEL (CRM)

3.3.1. Construals of perceived events

To illustrate human cognition of events, Langacker (1990) presented a 'stage model' and metaphorically described the relation of the speaker to the perceived events. 'Stage' in his term included spatial and temporal settings. The speaker, or the conceptualizer, construes the events happening on stage, and for expressive purposes, portrays it using language. Langacker (1990: 7) made a diagram of this viewing arrangement (Figure 3). V is the viewer, P is the perceived object, and the dashed arrow stands for the perceptual relationship between them. The box labeled PF represents the full expanse of the viewer's perceptual field, while OS is the onstage region (also referred to as the objective scene) which is characterized as the general locus of viewing attention. Heavy lines indicate profiling.

Figure 3: Viewing Arrangements (Langacker 1990: 7)

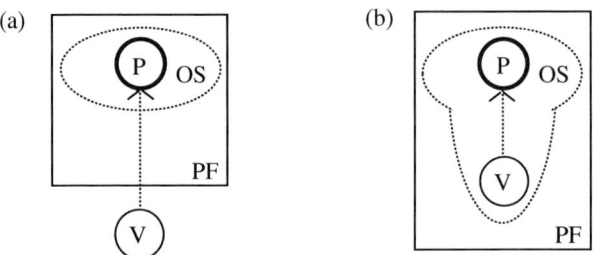

3.3.2. Construals of remembered events

3.3.2.1. Base

Langacker's stage model basically represents a speaker's conceptualizations and subjectification. I hypothesize that a speaker perceives past events in a similar fashion, i.e., viewing past events onstage and shifting vantage points. I shall borrow Langacker's approach to the perceptual relationship between the speaker and the per-

Cognitive Backgrounds of Tense-Alternation 55

ceived object, to illustrate how the reporting speaker envisions the reported speaker in recollecting past interactional events. In Figure 4, I have diagramed the speaker's mental image recalling past speech events between two persons. This is my basic recollection model. In recalling past interactional speech events, the narrator's present ego (E) envisions the speakers (S_1; S_2) in the onstage region (OS) in the mental field of recollection (MF), which represents the recollected past temporal and spatial sphere. The onstage region is the focus of attention where the recalled speakers are salient among other persons and objects that are also in the mental field of recollection but not focused on directly. The arrow from each speaker represents utterances to be reported.

Figure 4: Base Models for Recall of Past Interactional Events

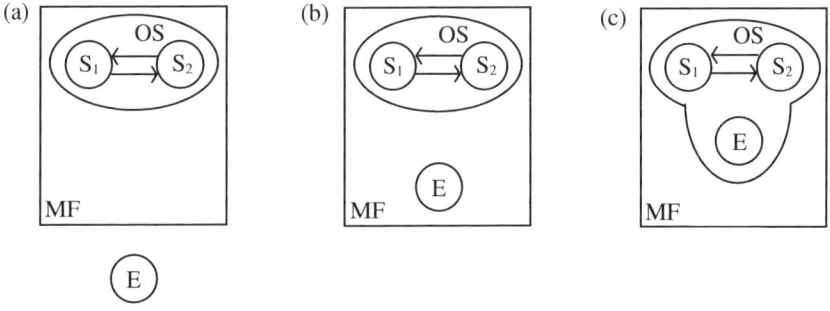

The present ego takes different vantage points, varying its distance to each speaker. The ego may stay at a distance from the mental field of recollection (MF) as in Figure 4(a), or move into the MF and view the interacting events in a more involved way as in Figures 4(b) and 4(c). The ego's entrance into the stage in Figure 4(c) indicates that the ego is not only involved in the observation but also imagines that it is experiencing the target event directly as a participant in the event. Many factors affect which vantage point or perspective a speaker takes toward the perceived event, as Bal ([1980]1985) suggests. I find that one of the most influential factors in conversational narratives or reportings is the speaker's psychological involvement in the recalled events. This involvement is the internal, emotional connection an individual feels binding him/her to other people and to places, things, activities, ideas, memories, and words (Chafe 1985b; Tannen 1989).[10]

The different recollection modes represented by Figures 4(a), 4(b), and 4(c) result in the different reporting styles in reproduction. The distal conception mode in Figure 4(a) illustrates the recollection mode that leads to indirect reporting styles (ID), while the proximal conception modes in Figures 4(b) and 4(c) lead to direct reporting styles (D) in reproduction.[11] In the following excerpt, in which speaker A tells speaker B about a newspaper agony column, A uses both indirect and direct styles:

(16) A: =this fifteen-year-old girl *wro:te* thet (h)er mother doesn' let'er wear nail polish er short sker:ts er do any a' this stuff,=
B: Ri:ght.
A: =hh en sh-she jis:t doesn't trus' me:: en she doesn't think I'm mature'r any'v this, hhhhhhhh
B: Uh hu:h
A: Abbey *says* hh we::ll, hh you haftih give yer mother chance ttuh(r) (.) to: u (.) realize thet she: hh hass- thet she c'n respectchu'n that c'n only be by you acting matu:re. hh en not c'mplaining about the way she- m-yihkno:w=   (HG)

In the introductory remark, A uses an indirect style. In the second and the third remarks, she quotes a fifteen-year-old girl and Abbey. (The second quote is the 'zero-quotation' without any reporting phrase.) Speaker A uses an indirect style to introduce the story setting, whereas in reporting the content, A uses a direct style. The shift in narrative style follows the shift in conceptual style. The speaker first takes a bird's-eye view of the setting, then goes into the detailed part which is the essence of the story. Since A is feeling strong resentment to Abbey's answer to the fifteen-year-old girl's claim about her mother, she is emotionally involved in this interaction. Depending on the degree of the ego's psychological involvement in each part of the recalled episode, the narrator uses direct or indirect reporting style in reproducing the speech event.

The following excerpt also contains both direct and indirect styles:

(17) M: Called 'er 'n I t- well actchilly I *told* 'er thet my best friend hed gotten (.) the measles.
(0.4)
M: Sh' s- "Oh that's TE:rrible. W'l you better stay in an re:st." So I *said* "Yeah I sure better."
( ): hhh
M: I didn't tell her I wz sick I jus' *said* my best friend // had the mea:sles.=
( ): hunh
( ): =HHH=
S: =Djiju tell'er you 'ad sympathih- sympathy pai//ns for'm?
(SN: 27)

The first line sets the context that the narrator M telephoned someone (suppose it is G) and told her that her best friend had gotten the measles. Her second remark is the point that she wants to make in this episode, namely, G's reaction to it. This is an 'evaluative point' in Labov's (1972a) sense. After presenting this dialogue, M and S start to talk about the dialogue. This is, so to speak, meta-talk about the dialogue. We see that the speaker first takes a bird's-eye view of the setting, then goes into the detailed part which is the essence of the story. After that, they start discussing the conversation when they stand apart from the episode and search it for meaning. When M recalls the most crucial part of the episode, she uses a direct style. When she adopts the bird's-eye view of the setting, or a meta-level-view of the talk, she is more distanced from the episode. With such viewing arrangements, she uses indirect style.

The following excerpt demonstrates a similar shift from indirect to direct style:

(18) S: Barbara was stra:nge
 M: Very o:dd. She usetuh to call herself a prostitute 'n I useteh- (0.4) ask 'er if she wz gitting any more money than I was doing it. An' she *said-* we'd compare notes yihknow. (SN: 30)

M wants to talk about an episode showing how Barbara was strange, in answer to S's remark, "Barbara was strange." At first, when M sets the context, she uses indirect style. She shifts to direct style to report Barbara's remark which made her feel that Barbara was strange. Establishing context, M stands off from the episode. It is natural that she has more emotional involvement when M recalls the most crucial part of the episode with which she wants to convey her surprise, funny feeling and puzzlement.

A correlation between reporting style and degree of psychological involvement fits well with observations by some researchers that direct speech is a way of expressing involvement (e.g., Chafe 1982; 1994; Li 1986; Tannen 1989). Indeed, in every part of reporting events and of narrative storytelling, speakers' point of view, psychological involvement, and psychological distance are interwoven. Lanser (1981: 202) claims that it is virtually impossible for a narrator to tell a story without communicating, either explicitly or more often implicitly through a variety of means, some degree of distance or affinity, detachment from or involvement with the various subjects (events, objects, places, and especially personae) which constitute the story world. I assume that it is neither a deliberate nor intentional use of language, but rather a natural reflection of cognitive recollection modes. In reporting, such cognitive distanciation or 'focalization' (Genette 1980), which results from the degree of psychological involvement in the recalled event, appears in reporting style and is well reflected in dialogue-introducer tenses.

58 Reporting Discourse, Tense, and Cognition

3.3.2.2. Recall of third-person interactions

In viewing each interaction, the ego focuses on each speaker. Suppose the ego recollects the interaction between third-person speakers (H) and (S) from outside of the mental field of recollection (MF). Figures 5(a) and 5(b) show the ego noticing each person at a distance. The dark arrow extending from the ego (E) represents the viewing intention or the recollecting will of the present ego as narrator. This dark arrow thus represents the ego's mental path toward the recollected person or object, rather than representing the direct perceptual relationship between the viewer and the perceived object, the relationship which Langacker represented with the dashed arrow in Figure 3. The recollection modes illustrated in Figures 5(a) and 5(b) lead to indirect reporting styles (ID). In indirect style, the ego holds an objective view of the reported events. It maintains a bird's-eye view of the interactional events occurring in the mental field of recollection.

Figure 5: Recall of Third-Person Interactions in Distal Conception Mode

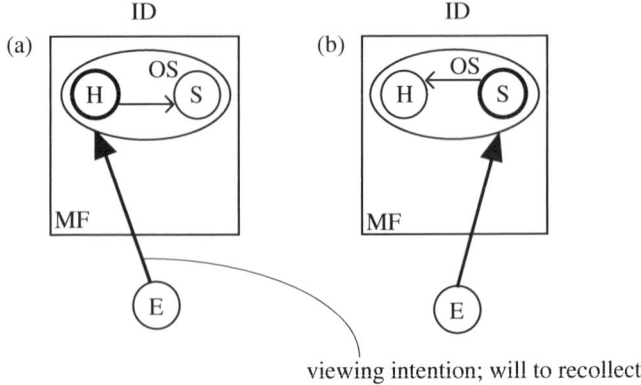

viewing intention; will to recollect

On the other hand, in direct style (D), the ego views each speaker from within the mental field of recollection. The ego may stay off stage as shown in Figures 6(a) and 6(b), or move on stage as shown in Figures 6(c) and 6(d), and experience the interaction in a more involved way. The dotted arrow from the third-person speaker to the ego shows that the ego feels as if the ego itself is hearing the same speech that is uttered toward the third-person interlocutor. When the ego stands off stage as in Figures 6(a) and 6(b), the dialogue-introducer tense that the speaker will choose in later reproduction is the past ("he said"; "she said"). When the ego goes on stage and experiences the interactions in a more involved way as in Figures 6(c) and 6(d), the present tense will be chosen ("he says"; "she says").[12] In the former cases, although

Cognitive Backgrounds of Tense-Alternation 59

Figure 6: Recall of Third-Person Interactions in Proximal Conception Mode

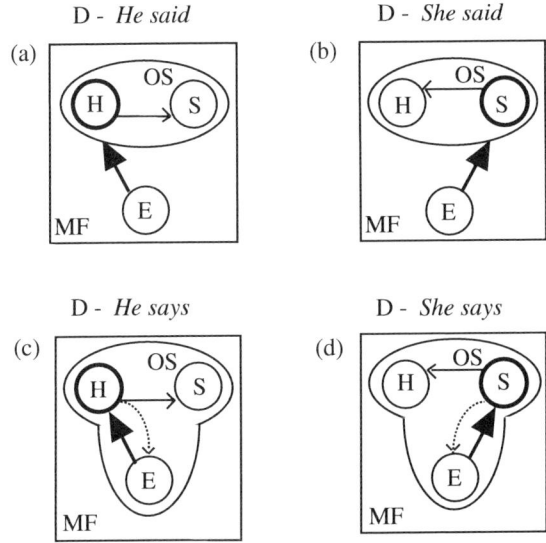

the ego steps into the temporal and spatial sphere of the narrated persons, it still keeps distance from the observed speech events. The ego is not psychologically involved in the recalled interactions as a participant. In the latter cases, by contrast, the ego is psychologically involved in the interactional events in the narrated spheres.

Let us compare examples that contrast the different degrees of psychological involvement and distance from reported events. The following excerpts use a direct style. In (19), the narrator tells the story of an emergency when a woman who fell on the floor could not get out of her house. The woman asks another woman named Nancy to help her. In (20), a man who made a very good deal on the purchase of a new house relates the story of the negotiation between his wife and the real estate agent.

(19) So she couldn't get up she *said*, she, it was a—so she crawled to the door and then finally one of the women came and rang the bell and she *said* to 'em, "I'm on the floor, I fell and I can't get up." So Nancy *said*, "Well, open the door," and she *said*, "I can't reach the knob," she *said*, "I'm really hurtin." She *said*, "I can't pick myself up." She *said*, "My God, what d'ja

do?" She *said*, "I don't know, I fell down the steps." So she *said*, "Well, can't you roll over on your other side?" and she *said*, "Honest to goodness I can't do anything," she *said*, "can't you come in?" She *said*, "Well, how am I gonna get in?" She *said*, "Well, try the kitchen window, that's, that's open." She *said*, "Tell Jane," who's a little tiny thing—she's only about four feet ten—she *said*, "Tell—can you hike Jane up and get her—go in the garage and you'll find a stool or something for her to get on and then hike her through the kitchen window." . . . (Wolfson 1982: 94)

(20) So he *says* to my wife, he *says*, "Well, what would you bid?" So she *says*, "It's stupid for me to talk," she *says*, "You got a bid for thirty-three, thirty-four," she *says*. "Why should I even talk to you? It ain't gonna be anywheres near." So he *says* to her, he *says*, "Well," he *says*, "the person at thirty-four backed out." So she *says*, "Oh, yeah?" He *says*, "Yeah," he *says*, "What would you bid?" So she *says*, "Twenty-eight." He *says*, "Oh," he *says*, "No, that she'll never go for." So she *says*, "Okay, that's my bid, Mr. Smith. You want it, fine; you don't, fine." (Ibid.: 26)

These excerpts represent important parts of the stories, and thus both narrators employ direct reporting styles. We can see that past tenses are used for the reporting discourse in (19), while present tenses are used for the reporting discourse in (20). Does this mean, as traditional theorists would put it, that the narrator chose the historical present tense in (20) because he imagined the negotiation happening again, whereas the narrator of (19) did not? I would rather see the differences as a manifestation of the different degrees of the narrators' psychological involvement in the reported events. When the accident in (19) happened, the narrator was not present. She only heard the story through a friend. The narrator thinks that this is such an exciting story that she reports it in full detail. But she was not involved in the episode. On the other hand, in (20), the narrator was present when his wife was having the negotiation. The narrator had even told his wife every word that she would have to say in negotiation. The narrator's psyche is deeply involved in this episode. Both (19) and (20) contain the excitement and liveliness that are the features of direct style, but they reflect different cognitive modes that the narrators hold in recalling each episode. When a narrator recalls an episode in which she/he has more psychological involvement, she/he activates her/his memory as in Figures 6 (c) and (d); with less psychological involvement, a narrator activates the memory as illustrated in Figures 6 (a) and (b). In third-person stories, tense alternates between "she/he says" and "she/he said," or remains "she/he says" or "she/he said," according to the degree of the narrator's psychological involvement.

3.3.2.3. Recall of self-involving interactions

Now, let us consider interactions that involve the narrator's past self ("I"). In contrast to (19) and (20) that exclusively involved reports of third-person interactions, the following example includes reports of interactions between a third-person speaker and the narrator's past self. It is an excerpt of a casual conversation between two female college students:

(21) I didn' notice it but there's a woman in my class who's a nurse. She *said* to me she *said*, "did you notice he has a ha:ndicap," and I *said*, "wha:t." You know I *said*, "I don't see anything wrong with him," she *says*, "his ha:nds." So the next class! for an hour and fifteen minutes I sat there and I watched his ha:nds! (TG: 8)

I propose that the mode of construal of self-involving interactions is significantly different from the mode of construal of third-person interactions. When the ego recollects the interaction of its past self with others, the vantage point that the ego establishes is closer to its past self than the narrator did in keeping the same distance to all the participants in Figures 4, 5 and 6. When the ego recalls its past interaction with others, it assumes a special vantage point to view the participants as shown in Figure 7. The ego stands closer to the past self rather than keeping the same distance from all the participants as in viewing the interactions among third persons. It shows the ego's closer psychological distance to the past self (I) than to the third-person interlocutor (S).

Figure 7: Base Model for Recall of Self-Involving Interactions

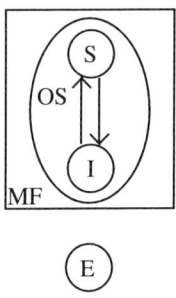

Gergen and Gergen (1983: 255) argue that individuals use narratives to reflexively reconstruct a sense of self. "The fact that people believe they possess identities fundamentally depends on their capacity to relate fragmentary occurrences across temporal boundaries." Although I will later argue that the ego does not identify itself with the past self, I still believe that the present ego and the past self are points on a temporal continuum. The ego naturally fixes vantage points closer to the past self than to the third-person interlocutors.

In recalling a third person who is speaking to the past self (I), the ego views the third person partly through the eyes of the past self. In other words, the present ego (E) perceives the speech by a third person (S) through the perception of the past self (I). The ego may keep maximal distance from the interlocutor as shown in Figure 8(a). The ego may move into the mental field of recollection as in Figure 8(b), or move on stage as in Figure 8(c) where the ego is assimilated to its past self. In the last case, the ego views the third person's speech as if she/he is directly experiencing it. The latter two cases model recollections which result in direct reporting styles (D). It is only in the last case, in which the ego recalls an interaction as if experiencing the interaction itself, that the present-tense verb "says" will be used in introducing the interlocution. The recollection mode illustrated in Figure 8(b) will lead to the narrator's use of "she said," while Figure 8(c) will lead to the use of "she says."

Figure 8: Recall of Third Person in Self-Involving Interactions

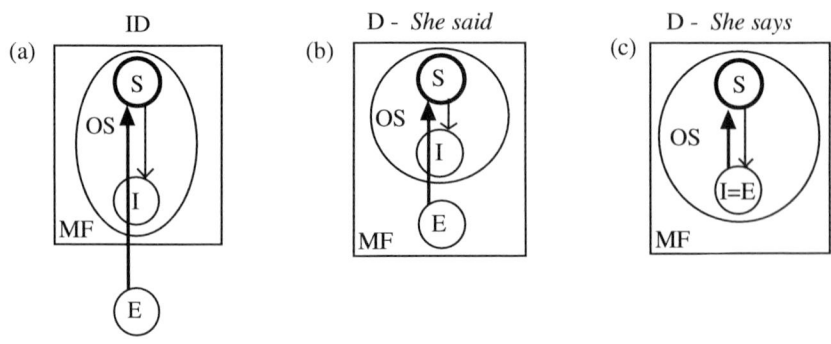

The following example illustrates the transition between (b) and (c) modes. Zelda has been telling Debby about her daughter's first summer away from home:

(22) Zelda: Well right now she *says*, "I'm so: lonely." She *said*, "Everyone went on the boardwalk." And she's ti:red. She- just got a job: oh I didn't tell you!
Debby: Oh no!
Zelda: She got- she- she had applied eh: for a job at the drugstore, as a counter girl? Y'know [lunch] eonette? As a waitress.=
Debby: [Y e h.]

Cognitive Backgrounds of Tense-Alternation 63

Zelda: And they called Sunday. So she's workin', [she's been] working,=
Debby: Oh [great !]
Zelda: =and she *says*, "I'm so tired!" (Schiffrin 1987: 269-70)

To the narrator, her daughter's claims "I'm so: lonely" and "I'm so tired!" are both emotionally appealing as a mother. In contrast, the daughter's remark "Everyone went on the boardwalk" is background supporting information for her loneliness. The narrator herself is not as psychologically involved in this remark as in the other two claims. The narrator introduces her daughter's emotionally appealing remarks with "she says," while she introduces the less appealing remark with "she said."

Alternatively, contrasting with the involvement shown in Figure 8, in perceiving the past self, the ego may also stay out of the mental field of recollection and view the past self at a distance (Figure 9[a]). The ego may view the self from within the mental field of recollection (Figure 9[b]) or go on stage (Figure 9[c]).

Figure 9: Recall of Past Self in Self-Involving Interactions

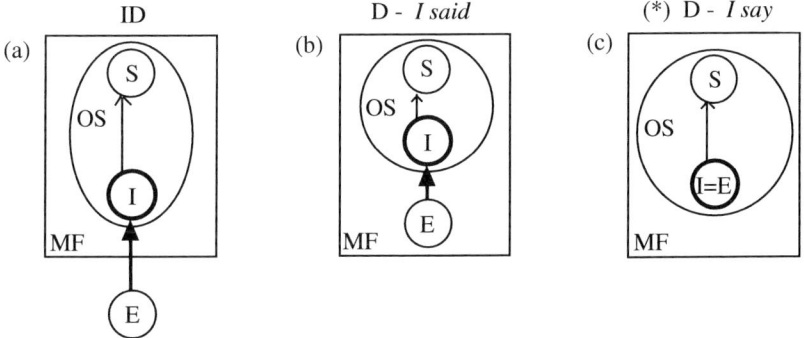

Following the logic applied above through Figures 5 and 8, the recollection mode illustrated in Figure 9(a) would result in the use of indirect style (ID), Figure 9(b) in the use of direct style (D) with "I said," while Figure 9(c) would result in the use of "I say." But, notice that the case in Figure 9(c) is unlikely (as indicated by the symbol *). Here, the past self and the present ego overlap, as was the case in Figure 8(c). In Figure 9(c), however, the dark arrow that represented the ego's viewing intention disappears. It shows that, in this mode, the ego can hardly maintain the narrator's intention and willingness to view the past event. It leads the ego to lose its identity as narrator. This causes the collapse of the present ego's self-identity. It can no longer maintain its identity as narrator in relation to the present audience. In other cases in which the ego entered the stage (Figures 6[c]; 6[d]; 8[c]), the ego was able to experience the interaction in a more involved way while still maintaining its viewing intention shown by the dark arrow in the models. Only here, in Figure 9(c), viewing the past self by entering the stage causes a problem.

In viewing third-person speakers in proximal conception styles, the narrator has a choice of Figure 8 (b) or (c) modes; in viewing the past self, she/he does not have the same choice. Such asymmetry in recollection modes for the third person and the first person explains a crucial part of tense-alternations. It is related to the fact that the present-tense verb is rarely used to introduce the speech of the first person, in the forms "I say,"[13] while the timeless present form is often used for third persons. In the following, the past tense is used for the first person while the present tense is used for the third person, although both utter almost the same phrase:

(23) and this jeep wheels up and it's this real hard-ass Lieutenant Mead and he hops out and he *says* "MALONE WHERE IN THE FUCK HAVE YOU BEEN?" [performing a tough voice] I *said* "Mead" a lieutenant you know I *said* "MEAD WHERE IN THE FUCK HAVE YOU BEEN?" [performing the same tough voice]
(=5)

The narrator Malone is relating how he blamed his boss Mead for not coming sooner to rescue him in a desert. In this emotionally heightened event, the narrator first uses "he says" which reflects his psychological involvement in the interaction. Malone's last remark to Mead has an ironical effect by repeating the exact same words uttered by Mead. It is more crucial in this episode, and Malone, as narrator, is deeply involved in describing his past self. But he does not use the present tense for his own remark. I suppose this is because the Figure 9(c) recollection mode is not a possible choice in his cognitive operation. A similar contrast is seen in the following:

(24) I was at the shopping center the other day so I met, I met Gary there and I *asked* him what he's doin', he's goin' to school, and this, that and the other, and he *says*, "Come on down, I want to play some pool with you." So I *said*, "All right."
. . . .
so he—you know, when we started off, he takes this cue stick that he put together there, and he puts it on the side and he takes one of those solid cue sticks. I *said*, "What are you doing that for?" He *says*, "Can't use this on the break." He *says*, "This is only for delicate shots."

(Wolfson 1982: 43-44)

The tense asymmetry between the first person and the third person also applies to other reporting verbs:

(25) so I *said* to the waitress that'd been waiting on our table all morning. I *said* "could I buy a couple ashtrays?" and she'd been so nice, I didn't want to rip one off you know [laughs] she *goes* . . . "honey you don't buy ashtrays in Vegas," and she *goes* "stay right there I'll be back." (=4)

(26) He *says*, "Son, you, can you come home?" I *was like*, "Yeah, but what's wrong?" He *says*, "Well, your mother's leaving me." And I was, I just, my jaw just dropped. I fell to my knees. I *was like*, "What's going on?" I *was like*, "Why, why?" (Ferrara and Bell 1995: 284)

Example (25) contrasts "I said" and "she goes"; example (26) contrasts "I was like" and "he says."

According to the cognitive models for recall that I presented above, there are two basic combinations of tenses in the stories that involve both the third person and the first person. When a narrator is psychologically involved in narrated events, the likely tense-alternation is between "I said" and "she/he says." When a narrator feels less psychological involvement in recalled episodes, the tense choice is "I said" and "she/he said." Let us examine contextual information to make correlations between tense forms and a narrator's involvement in recalled events. In the following excerpt, a narrator recalls how a classmate told her that their teacher has a handicap. The narrator uses the past-tense verb "said" to indicate her own remark, while both "said" and "says" are used to introduce utterances by her classmate:

(27) I didn' notice it but there's a woman in my class who's a nurse. She *said* to me she *said*, "did you notice he has a ha:ndicap," and I *said*, "wha:t." You know I *said*, "I don't see anything wrong with him," she *says*, "his ha:nds." So the next class! for an hour and fifteen minutes I sat there and I watched his ha:nds! (=21)

The narrator uses the past tense ("she said") to introduce the first utterance of the classmate ("did you notice he has a ha:ndicap"). She continues to use the past tense ("I said") for the following two utterances of her own. She uses the present tense ("she says") only for the last remark made by her classmate. This tense-shift is accompanied by a shift in the narrator's involvement in the interlocution. Initially, the narrator does not pay very much attention to her classmate. When the classmate starts talking to her about their teacher's handicap, she does not take her seriously. This is indicated by her next remark, "I don't see anything wrong with him." She does not believe her classmate. But when she hears "his ha:nds," these words have a strong impact on her, and she ends up watching her teacher's hands all through the next class. At the climax when the narrator experiences an emotional heightening, the present tense is used for the reporting verb.

The following example confirms how the use of the present tense coincides with the heightening of the narrator's excitement and involvement in the episode. This is an excerpt from a telephone conversation between two male college students. A man is describing how he ruined a date of his roommate with his girlfriend Terry.

(28) I know it wasn't nice, it sure was funny. So finally he *said*, "You talk to Terry, I'm goin' to the bathroom," so he disappeared to the bathroom, an' I *said*, "well let's see how far this can go." I *said*, "Terry, You wanna step outside for a few minutes?" She *goes*, "that's great." So we ran outside, and we hid telling our other roommate to tell him that we were outside in the front talking. (HK)

The man first mentions how he enjoyed teasing his roommate, at which the roommate got angry and went out into the bathroom. The man further attempted to tease the roommate. He suggested that he and Terry hide themselves together. The crucial point in this episode is that Terry, who is the girlfriend of the narrator's roommate, joined in teasing him. The narrator uses the past tense ("I said"; "he said") to indicate his utterances and his roommate's. He uses the present tense ("she goes") only for Terry's words "that's great." Terry's agreement indicates that it was really funny (so she enjoyed it) and even works to justify his teasing the roommate. The narrator becomes emotionally heightened at this point, and here he switches to the present tense. The narrator's involvement appears also in the use of the verb "go." Li (1986) points out that when a speaker is highly involved in the event that she/he is recounting, she/he uses "direct quotes exclusively, often with 'go' as the verb of saying" (p. 41). In (28), Terry's last remark accompanies the verb "go" as well as the timeless present tense, both of which suggest the narrator's involvement in the remark.

The next example manifests a similar operation of tense-switching between "I said" and "he says." In contrast to the above examples, the tense shifts back to "he said" at the end:

(29) and then I *said* "what's the problem here?" he *says* "well ma'am . . . ah . . . you didn't stop for that stop sign back there" I *said* "WHAT . . ." I mean I was mad I *said* "WHAT" and he *says* . . . he *says* "it's the In-" he just starts off rattling "it's the Indi- Indiana State Law you must come to a complete

stop . . . before the stop sign da da da da" I *said* "I did" I *said* "there's a crosswalk there and the thing's before that" I *said* "where were you sitting anyway" [laughs] he *says* "I was right in that parking lot by the church" and that parking lot's right back here [indicating on table] you can't even see the stop sign I *said* "I'm sorry" I *said* "you didn't see me" he *said* "it's the Indiana State Law da da da da da" (Johnstone 1987: 34)

In this context, a young woman is describing a conversation she had with a police officer who stopped her on the road when she was a new driver. From the beginning the narrator shows excitement and anger toward the police officer who unreasonably accused her of a traffic violation. Toward the end, she justifies her behavior. Her remark, "you didn't see me," is a turning point as she finally claims that the police officer had not seen her. The woman secured her innocence. The narrator calms down at this point, and relates how, in the end, all the police officer could do was to repeat the formulaic legal dialogue. Only here the narrator uses the past tense ("he said") for the police officer. This indicates that she steps back from her emotional involvement in the recalled interactions.

3.4. PSYCHOLOGICAL INVOLVEMENT

I have shown that the way a speaker establishes specific vantage points in remembering past events, which uses an inherent asymmetry of conceptualization of the first and third person is an influential cognitive operation for dialogue-introducer tense-switching. For such a cognitive operation, I have raised psychological involvement as a key factor that influences a speaker's establishment of a specific vantage point in viewing past interactional events. I have defined psychological involvement as an internal emotional connection individuals feel which binds them to other people as well as to places, things, activities, ideas, memories, and words (Chafe 1985b; Tannen 1989). In the present case, a speaker feels psychological engagement or involvement with the interactional speech events that are being recalled.

Let me summarize how psychological involvement accompanying tense-switching appears in the empirical data above. When a speaker is psychologically involved, generally, the following features are observed. First, the speaker moves into the content from the contextual background, and she/he gives detailed descriptions of events. Second, she/he feels that the story is so exciting that it is worth reporting in full detail. The narrator's psyche is deeply involved in the episode, and the narrative contains the excitement and liveliness evidenced by a direct reporting style. Third, the speaker recalls the essence of the story, which is the point that she/he wants to make in the episode, often an 'evaluative point,' the most crucial part of the episode.

By contrast, when a speaker is not psychologically involved, the following features are observed. First, a speaker often uses indirect style when she/he first introduces the story setting. When establishing the contextual background, she/he holds a bird's-eye view of the setting, or of whole interactional events in the mental field of recollection. Second, a speaker uses indirect style to talk about the dialogue. For this 'meta-talk' about the dialogue, she/he stands apart from the episode to take a meta-level-view of the whole interaction. This is also true when she/he uses a searching mode on the episode to examine the content of the past speech. In these cases, the ego maintains an objective view of the reported events, keeping distance from them.

Psychological involvement has a gradient. There is no fixed level which distinguishes 'more psychological involvement' from 'less involvement.' It is of a subjective and relative nature. In this chapter, I discussed some cases that exemplified the contrast between more and less involvement. First, it is often necessary for the speaker herself/himself to have been directly involved in the recalled interactions as a participant. This is in contrast to a story that the speaker heard through somebody else. Second, more involvement accompanies heightened emotion. In the examples in this chapter, we saw some clear cases that exemplify emotional heightening. For instance, a speaker feels strong sympathy and resentment to the reported persons (example 16). A speaker wants to convey her/his surprise, funny feeling, and puzzlement (example 18). The report involves irony with a distinct voice quality (example 23). A speaker is strongly affected by the words, in contrast to the words which she/he does not take seriously (example 27). It is often a climax when the narrator experiences an emotional heightening. In a series of recalled speech interactions, the remark works to support the speaker's point, or works as a turning point in the episode (example 28). The speaker shows excitement and anger in negotiation (example 29). Direct style with more psychological involvement accompanies the salient voice quality, whereas less involvement accompanies the calm voice with downward intonation. A calm voice indicates that the speaker steps back from her/his emotional involvement in the recalled interactions.

I have related how psychological involvement reflects a speaker's psychological distance from recalled events or participants in the events. The speaker's psychological involvement in the events leads to proximal conception style, while lack of involvement leads to distal conception style. Proximal conception style results in direct style, in which more information is provided and the information is more detailed than in the indirect style that results from distal conception style. In Labov and Waletzky's (1967) sense, distal conception style leads to summarization and reproduction of basic story lines. Proximal conception style, on the other hand, frequently features elaborative elements (details of specific and general statements) that make a story more alive and interesting, as Kernan (1977) points out. In proximal conception style, a speaker may further take different viewing arrangements depending on degrees of psychological involvement. They lead to different tense forms. When a speaker is more deeply involved in the episode, she/he moves on stage in the past temporal and spatial field. In this case, she/he is not only involved in the observation but is also imagining that she/he is experiencing the target event directly as a participant in the event. In such a case, the tense form of a dialogue-introducer is the present.

3.5. SELF-IDENTITY

I have illustrated the cognitive backgrounds of the observed discourse fact that both the present and the past tense are used to report a third person's speech, while the present tense is rarely used for the first person.[14] The use of different tenses for different persons is attributable to the inherent asymmetry of a narrator's conceptualization of the first and the third persons in remembering past events. In quoting a third person's speech, a narrator chooses dialogue-introducer tense from the present and the past, according to her/his own psychological involvement in the episodes. On the other hand, a narrator primarily uses the past-tense form "I said" for her/his own past remarks. Such an asymmetrical conceptualization, I have argued, is induced by the necessity of preserving a speaker's self-identity as narrator. The narrating ego maintains its self-identity as narrator who holds the viewing intention or the will to recollect. There is a restriction on the ego's conceptualizing itself as overlapping the past self when it reports its own past speech. Therefore, the recollection mode in Figure 9(c) is unlikely to happen.

A narrator's self-identity, indeed, has been widely claimed to play a central role in conceptualization. Clark (1973), Fillmore (1975b), Bühler (1982), Zubin and Hewitt (1995), and others have emphasized that "there is a unified conceptual centering of events underlying the linguistic fact," and it is "an egocentric modeling of reality in which the 'here,' 'now' and 'I' of the speaker (and secondarily, of the addressee) have priority over other elements of the speech situation" (Zubin and Hewitt 1995: 129). Shotter (1989: 137) also claims that "one's own *self* . . . exists somewhere inside one, as something unique and distinct from all else that there is" and it is "its substantial existence, which guarantees one's personal identity." The ego as narrator needs to exist distinctly from the other existents including the past self in the narrated world.

Here I shall further discuss the significance of narrator's self-identity in narratives, referring to theories of narrative and discourse, morphological facts of pronouns, and psychology. The particular notions are levels of narrative; manipulation of 'footing'; discourse rules in 'constructed dialogues'; pronominal uses for divided self; and cognitive monitoring theories.

3.5.1. Levels of narrative

Manipulating levels of narrative (Labov and Waletzky 1967; Hopper 1979; McNeill 1992) is an important requirement of the role of the narrator for successful narration. Narrative structure has three levels: narrative, metanarrative, and paranarrative (McNeill 1992: 185-88). The narrative level consists of references to events from the world of the story proper that are sequenced in their actual order. It follows a story plot line. The metanarrative level consists of clauses that present the story about the story. Metanarrative clauses are not constrained by the actual order of events. At the metanarrative level, a narrator manipulates the story as a unit, objectifies it, and comments on it as an event in itself. The paranarrative level consists of references to the narrating behavior itself, and the emphasis is on the relationship of narrator to listener. Narrators step out of the official narrator role, and speak for themselves, as their own personality. McNeill illustrates each of these levels in the following excerpt:

(30) um have you seen any of the uh Bugs Bunny cartoons? [PARA]
    (Listener: yeah like)
    right, ok, this one actually wasn't a Bugs Bunny cartoon. [META]
    it was one of the- the series [META]
    (Listener: oh, ok)
    and it had Tweety Bird and Sylvester [META]
    (Listener: alright {laughs})
    so so so you know [PARA]
    (Listener: the car right?)
    right uh huh [PARA]
    (Listener: ok)
    and uh the first scene you see is uh [META]
    this this window with Birdwatcher's Society underneath it [NARA]
    and there's Sylvester peeking around the window [NARA]
                             (McNeill 1992: 186)

We can observe that narrative storytelling involves frequent shifts of levels. Both speaker and listener necessarily have to trace such switching between the levels. In this McNeill's excerpt, the narrator is starting to tell a third-person story. In this type of case, the narrator may appear only at the metanarrative and paranarrative levels. In a self-involving story, on the other hand, the narrator's past self may appear as a story participant at the narrative level as well:

(31) I know it wasn't nice, it sure was funny. So finally he *said*, "You talk to Terry, I'm goin' to the bathroom," so he disappeared to the bathroom, an' I *said*, "well let's see how far this can go." I *said*, "Terry, You wanna step outside for a few minutes?" She *goes*, "that's great." So we ran outside, and we hid telling our other roommate to tell him that we were outside in the front talking. (=28)

In this excerpt, two first persons appear as "I" that refer to the self at different levels. The first "I" is in the remark "I know it wasn't nice, it sure was funny" which is a comment on the story at the metanarrative level. Another first person "I" is in other action clauses at the narrative level: in "I said . . ." as well as in "So we ran outside, and we hid . . ." in the form of first-person plural.[15] Thus, in the telling of a self-involving story, the narrator needs to distinguish two selves: the present self as narrator and the past self as protagonist, while she/he switches back and forth between the present world and the storyworld. In all such processes, the narrator's self-identity is anchored in the present world, and the story is told from her/his point of view.

The multiple functions of self and the levels of narrative are crucially integrated in narrative storytelling. Since storytelling is an egocentrical behavior (Zubin and Hewitt 1995) that comprises a narrator's interpretations and intentions, the narrator's self is always there, even when it is backgrounded at a narrative level. The Cognitive Recollection Model that I presented reflects this protection of the ego's self-identity as narrator in relation to the present audience. Contrast of tense forms, in that sense, is a projection of the firm base of a narrator's self-identity. A narrator needs to reserve such present-tense expressions as "I say" for expressing her/his own ego as narrator in relation to the audience in the present world.

3.5.2. Manipulations of 'footing'

The ego's maintenance of self-identity as narrator is also closely related to the manipulation of 'footing' which Goffman (1981a: 128) characterizes as "participant's alignment, or set, or stance, or posture, or projected self." Explaining aspects of footing, Goffman (1981a: 144-45) claims that storytellers, especially of personal narratives, present themselves with three aspects of self: author, principal and figure. 'Author' is the aspect of self which is responsible for the content of talk when they quote their prior words. 'Figure' is the aspect of self which is displayed through talk. It is (the main) character in the story, someone who belongs to the world that is spoken about. 'Principal' is the aspect of self whose position is established by the words that are spoken, someone whose beliefs and views have been encoded in the story, someone who is committed to what the words say. In addition, the narrator is in the conversational world as the 'animator' who is a talking machine, the person who produces talk. The complex of the relations between these aspects of self determines a participation framework in discourse. In this regard, the present self and the narrated past self are different aspects of self that a speaker holds in conversational narratives. In the course of a narrative a speaker constantly changes her/his footing, while shifting levels of narratives as discussed above:

> A change in footing implies a change in the alignment we take up to ourselves and the others present as expressed in the way we manage the production or reception of an utterance. A change in our footing is another way of talking about a change in our frame for events. . . . participants over the course of their speaking constantly change their footing, these changes being a persistent feature of natural talk. (Goffman 1981a: 128)

Regarding the first person "I" in reporting self-involving interactions, Goffman (1981a) distinguishes the reporting self and the reported self as totally different footings. In support of Hockett's (1963: 11) point of unrestricted displacement in time and place, he claims that the "I" as the present self and the "I" as the past self are distinct aspects of self as separate animators:

> The "I" in "I said shut the window" is linked to us—the person present—merely through biographical continuity, something that much or little can be made of, and nothing more immediate than that. In which case, two animators can be said to be involved: the one who is physically animating the sounds that are heard, and an embedded animator, a figure in a statement who is present only in a world that is being told about, not in the world in which the current telling takes place. (Goffman 1981a: 149)

Goffman further emphasizes that the speaker's shift between the current self and the past self is a change of footing, claiming that the significance of production format is closely connected to the embedding function of talk:

> For obviously, when we shift from saying something ourselves to reporting what someone else said, we are changing our footing. And so, too, when we shift from reporting our current feelings, the feelings of the "addressing self," to the feelings we once had but no longer espouse. (Indeed, a code switch sometimes functions as a mark of this shift.) (Ibid.: 151)

Especially in reporting self-involving interactions, a narrator needs to play different roles for different aspects of footing. Both the narrating self and the narrated self are inevitably present and must be clearly distinguished. Under the shift of footing between the narrating ego and the past self lies the speaker's intrinsic identity as speaking self, since storytelling is a creation of an egocentric world around the present self. Such manipulations of footing in a speaker's egocentric modeling of the world are in accordance with the speaker's recollection mode which I illustrated in Figure 9 with the Cognitive Recollection Model. In recalling self-involving interactions the present ego does not view the past self in a way that abandons its recollection will, which may obscure the narrator's self-identity as a central self. Thus, tense realization in narratives shifts in consequence of the narrator's securing her/his self-identity.[16]

3.5.3. 'Speak for yourself' rule in 'constructed dialogues'

In accordance with the discussions so far on self-identity, but shifting to a more functional view, let me point to the effect of applying one of the discourse rules on self to reporting context. Schiffrin (1993), in a study of discourse phenomena of speaking for another, points out that participation frameworks and 'identity displays' are related to 'interactive frames' (Tannen and Wallat 1993) through which utterances are interpreted (p. 233).[17] In carrying out a conversation, a speaker and a hearer need to define how they are related to their utterances as well as to one another. She argues that when we engage in conversation we follow the 'speak for yourself' rule that "the person who has something to say is the one who can and should say it" (ibid.).[18] The rule reflects a tacit agreement between the self and the other to protect the other in exchange for protection of oneself (Goffman 1967a; 1967b).[19] As one indication of the strength of this rule, she claims that using reporting discourse is one of the contexts in which a speaker needs to display the deictic shift from the current situation:

> if we do speak for another, e.g., if we report another's words as 'constructed dialogue' (Tannen 1989), we are required to use a wide array of devices (grammatical and/or paralinguistic) to show displacement in person, space, and time from the 'I,' 'here,' and 'now' of the current situation.
> (Schiffrin 1993: 233)

In reporting discourse, the present speaker, who is a reporter or a narrator, needs to clearly mark that it is not the present speaker herself/himself who is responsible for the message's content, but that there is an original speaker for the message. In Goffman's (1981a) sense, the present speaker produces a message while another person (the source) is responsible for its content, so the present speaker is acting as the animator for another person who is in a principal role.

Schiffrin's claim about reporting discourse mainly focuses on cases in which one person speaks for another, but it also has a significant effect on a reporting context of a person reporting her/his own interaction. It rationalizes the tense choices that the narrating ego tends to make: the past tense ("said") to report the past self but the present tense ("says") to report a third person. When the ego speaks for a third person, the ego can easily show that it is a constructed dialogue: first by grammatically indicating the third person's name or pronoun as an agent in a reporting phrase (e.g., "Joy says"; "he says"); second by paralinguistic means, e.g., adopting the reported person's voice which is different from the voice of its own. The audience immediately knows that the narrator speaks for someone else. On the contrary, when reporting a speech of the past self, it is not as easy a thing to show that it is a constructed dialogue. The pronoun "I" in fact refers both to the present and the past self; the paralinguistic features are likely to apply both to the present and the past self. What the ego can use as an indication of constructed dialogue, then, is grammatical means. For that purpose, dialogue-introducer tense effectively contrasts the present self and the past self by using the corresponding tense forms. It serves as one of the devices to show displacement in person, space, and time from the 'I,' 'here,' and 'now' of the current situation. It is, in accordance with Schiffrin's 'speak for yourself' rule, the ego's way of protecting the identity of the past self, by letting the past self speak. In the other direction, it profiles the ego's boundary in time axis, and consequently protects its own identity as narrator.

3.5.4. Divided self

In the same line of argument with Schiffrin, another view to support the distinction of the present self and the past self is Haiman's (1995) notion of 'divided self.' Haiman argues, in his study of reflexive pronouns, that 'the self,' as a common noun and as a separate reflexive pronoun in English, is a grammatical symptom of a mind/body dualism, or even a divided or alienated self.[20] As one example of this alienation or estrangement in language, he comments that "speakers uttering quotes may be alienated from the words they repeat, words which were originally spoken by another person, or they may feel estranged from that person" (p. 214). For this purpose, speakers "may indicate that they are, literally, playacting (Wierzbicka 1974) by using framing devices like 'I quote' or a heavy pause, or by ostentatious mimicry of another person's speech mannerisms" (Haiman 1995: 214). My argument is again that it is easy to alienate another person from the self in reporting a third-person speech, but it is not as easy to alienate the past self from the present self linguistically and paralinguistically in reporting own's past speech, because they are parts of a continuity of the self across the temporal axis.

Haiman claims that the English language has developed, in its grammar, a pronoun system for the self-alienation of mind-body dualism, namely the distinct uses of "me" and "myself" in object positions (1995: 229). For instance, the following sentences show the contrast of "me" and "myself":

(32) (a) I'm in charge of myself.
(b) I'm in charge of me.

In (a) the use of the word "self" signals 'sameness of reference,' while in (b), the subject/speaker "I" is treating the object "me" as an entirely separate entity.[21] In contrast, the alienation between the narrating self and the narrated self has not been grammatically encoded in English pronoun uses. The separation of the narrating self and the narrated self is, nevertheless, an important self-alienation as well. Sociologists, Riesman (1950: 44) and others (e.g., Trilling 1972; LeJeune 1980; Elias 1982; Tuan 1982), have shown that in diary-keeping and autobiographies, self-alienation or self-separation evidently exists "between the behaving and the scrutinizing self," between protagonist and narrator. For such self-alienation, I assume, speakers distinctly use the two forms "I said" and "I say" in referring to the past self and the narrating self respectively. In this way, the narrating ego avoids mingling two distinct aspects of self. The ego secures self-identity by contrasting the present self and the past self, not with morphology but with tense markers.

3.5.5. Cognitive monitoring theories

As a final claim in support of the significance of a speaker's self-identity and of the separation of the present and the past self, I briefly draw upon cognitive monitoring theories in psychology. Self-identity is a very important part of human mentality. People need to protect self-identity, in one way to make a distinction between the self and the others, in another way to make a distinction between the present self and the past self. Psychological studies have revealed the importance of identity of the present self against the past self (Koyazu 1985: 16). As an extreme case, the loss of temporal ordering of the present and the past causes 'ecmnesia' which is a serious disorder of memory. Ecmnesia is hypermnesia that accompanies memory hallucination (Yasunaga 1984; Hamada 1993; Nakata 1993). Past episodes overflow into the mind too vividly, and the person becomes obsessed by delusions that she/he is actually experiencing past events at the present moment. The person confuses the present and the past temporal spheres. It often results in symptoms of somnambulism.

Under normal circumstances, people have a cognitive monitoring ability or cognitive regulation ability. A human being naturally monitors her/his own behavior and thought, and controls the self so as to achieve accuracy, continuity, coherence, and normality. With this monitoring ability, a human separates and identifies the present and the past self. Flavell (1978) points out that the cognitive monitoring and regulating ability develops at the period when a child develops the ability to view everything, including the self, objectively. Accordingly, people have metacognitive experience, which is a conscious, evaluative, cognitive, and emotional experience that accompanies intellectual behaviors (thinking and behavior) (Flavell 1979), and leads to the distinction between the observing self and the observed self (Koyazu 1985).

These psychological considerations support my present claim regarding self-identity and self-separation. A speaker, under normal circumstances, self-monitors her/his behavior and thought, so that she/he does not confuse temporal relations. A speaker identifies with the present self against the past self who is in another temporal sphere.

3.6. BACKGROUNDS OF PREVALENCE OF *I SAYS*

In natural conversational discourse, a speaker may still use the present tense to report a dialogue by her/his past self. In such cases, "I says" is more frequently used. This seems like an exception to my Cognitive Recollection Models since I postulated that there is basically no cognitive background for introducing the first person in the timeless present tense. Johnstone (1987) points out teenagers' frequent use of "I says," and views it as their inability to manipulate tenses. She interprets such cases as exceptions to her status hypothesis. Rather than treating such usage as exceptional, or attributing it to an inability to manipulate tenses, the present theory suggests that it is a reasonable deviance of the Cognitive Recollection Models.

The ego may view the past self as if it were a third person, thus taking the viewing arrangements for third-person interactions (Figures 5 and 6) rather than those for self-involving interactions (Figures 8 and 9). It leads to the practice in which the narrator uses "I says" rather than "I say" to report her/his past self. Such usage of "I says" often appears in rapid and casual conversations. It arises when a narrator, deeply involved in rapid turn-taking interactions between a third person and the past self, views both participants as third persons in a parallel way. This way of accounting for "I says" conforms well to the present theory which incorporates the self-identity of the narrating ego. While using the timeless tense for the past self at the emotional heightening, the narrator can reserve an expression such as "I say" for the narrator's ego. As we saw in Tables 1 through 4, in my corpus, out of 29 instances of the use of timeless present form with the verb "say" for reporting the speech of the first person, "I say" was used in only six instances (20.7%) in contrast to "I says"

(72.4%). It agrees with the narrative restriction to protect the narrator's self-identity discussed above.

Viewing the self in the third person is not uncommon in the English language. Haiman (1995: 220) points out that English speakers often use third-person construals in viewing the first person. He raises the phenomenon of the divided speaker talking about herself/himself in the third person. He comments that such usage is affected by some popular usages such as: public figures who refer to themselves by name; writers who refer to themselves as "the author"; announcers who waggishly refer to themselves as "yours truly"; obsequious letter writers of Addisonian English who refer to themselves as "your humble and obedient servant"; and parents who adopt their child's perspective in referring to themselves as "mom" and "dad." The last factor, parents' talk, may be the most influential on the young speakers' frequent use of "I says" by representing the self as third person. Parents often refer to themselves as third persons in speaking to their children. For instance, in the following, parents refer to themselves as third persons:

(33) (a) father : Come to daddy. (= Come to me.)
    (b) mother : Mom loves you. (= I love you.)
    (c) child : Why do I have to do that?
        mother : Because Mom says it. (= Because I say it.)

In (c), the mother responds to her child by saying "Because Mom says it," instead of saying "Because I say it." In addition, in children's cartoons (e.g., *Calvin and Hobbes*; *Garfield*), the word "says" has attained a firm status. It is sometimes written as "sez" instead, and is given a status as one word form. Children acquire the word not as a "say" plus 'third-person singular present' marker -*s*, but as a single word "sez."

In sum, there are three choices of dialogue-introducer tense forms for the first-person pronoun "I": "I said," "I says," and "I say." The past form "I said" is the unmarked choice for the past self, and is most prevalent. The third-person form "I says" is the marked case which may be used by adopting a third-person viewing arrangement. It may be a good example of cognitive and functional reshaping of grammar, since "I says" is ungrammatical under traditional English grammar. In addition, there are a few instances of the form "I say." It is rare since the simple present-tense form is basically reserved for the narrating ego to secure its identity. The still available choice of "I say," however, is a functional choice, which I will explore in detail in chapter 5. There I will also show that the use of "I says" is not only a cognitive manifestation but also a realization of a functional use of tense. I will argue that

"I say" and "I says" have different functions. Indeed, there are many factors interwoven in the surface manifestation of the forms of reporting verbs.[22]

3.7. CONCLUSION

I have explored the cognitive operation at work for dialogue-introducer tense-switching in conversational narratives. It supports my observation that both the present and the past tense are used to report speeches in third-person interactions, while the past tense is primarily used to report speeches of the first person in self-involving interactions. This is due to the inherent asymmetry of a narrator's conceptualization of the first and the third person in remembering past events. Table 5 summarizes factors for tense forms that I have shown in this chapter.

Table 5: Factors for Tense Forms

3rd persons	— psychological involvement	— *she says / she said*
1st persons	— psychological involvement, identity, 3rd person construals	— *I said* (optional use of *I says*)
all persons	— functional alternations	

(Sakita 1997a)

To quote third-person speeches, narrators choose reporting verb tenses from the present and the past, according to their psychological involvement in the recalled episodes. On the other hand, narrators mainly use the past-tense form "I said" for their own remarks. Narrators need to reserve such expressions as "I say" for expressing their own egos as narrator in relation to the audience at the metanarrative and paranarrative levels. The choice of tense forms is regulated to protect the ego's self-identity as narrator in relation to the present audience. The timeless present form "I says" is an optional choice when the narrator takes third-person construals. In addition to the asymmetrical construals for the first person and the third person, functional factors affect the tense forms in the verbalization stage, as I will discuss in subsequent chapters.

The Cognitive Recollection Model has at its base a narrator's vantage points in viewing recalled events and participants, which are closely connected to the degrees of a narrator's self-distancing from the narrated events. The model thus concurs with traditional theories concerning the historical present tense: immediacy, eyewitness effect, and past-more-vivid effect. Georgakopoulou and Goutsos (1997) comment on the proximity expressed by tense-switching:[23]

> Combined with the characters' animation of voices, tense shifts function as a means of abolishing the distance between the past taleworld and the immediate situation of telling. Conveying this sense of proximity has significant implications for the relation between teller and listeners: the teller is presented as recording the experiences as if they were happening at the moment of their telling and, by implication, the listeners become 'eyewitnesses' of the events. (p. 140)

The present model covers the essential notion of proximity that underlies the use of the historical present tense, "which owes its expressive function to its shift from the distant and reminiscing mode of the past tense to the proximal visualizing mode of the here and now of storytelling" (ibid.: 142). The signaling of proximity between teller, tale, and audience results in displays of subjectivity (ibid.).

There are, however, some crucial differences between the Cognitive Recollection Model and the traditional theory of the HP. First, the Cognitive Recollection Model suggests that tense determination is rather the natural realization of the restriction of human cognition in viewing human interactions in the past sphere. At base, there is the reporter's cognitive system. In addition, tense reflects the reporter's rhetorical configuration, which is to be modeled in the next chapter as part of the strategic and functional uses of tenses. Such functional uses in the reproduction stage may override the choice made in the recollection stage. Second, the traditional account has no way to account for the different tenses used for different persons. The present model shows the basis for the fact that while reporters may choose to use timeless introducers for third persons, their use is restrained in referring to first persons. Third, there has been minimal acknowledgment of the significant role played by tense-aspect categories of verbs in the linguistic encoding of points of view (Fleischman 1990: 216). The present model sheds light on the different tense forms as reflections of a speaker's vantage points or stances toward reported events, and not merely as rhetorical devices for an effect of immediacy.

The present theory pointed to self-identity and self-separation as essential factors of dialogue-introducer tense-determination. On the surface, tense-switching seems to functionally contrast the first person and the third person, as once hypothesized by Wolfson (1982) and Fleischman (1990). As I have shown, tense does not actually work by contrasting the third person and the first person. Rather, the surface manifestation of contrast is actually a consequence of asymmetrical construals between the first and the third person, and the contrast between the present self and the past self in securing the self-identity of the narrator who possesses the will to recollect and to narrate. As Haiman (1995: 230) acknowledges, "one cannot contrast things that are too different from each other: contrast is only possible between entities which are both formally and conceptually on a par." The intra-contrast of self emerges in the discourse facts of tense-switching, as consequences of both cognitive and functional operations. I showed the contrast by modeling different viewing arrangements for the reported situations with first-person involvement and for those exclusively involving third-person interactions.

Finally, my analysis of cognitive backgrounds of tense choice captures only one phase of the complex process of reporting. Recall the illustration of the reporting processes presented in Figure 1. From multiple stages within the reporting process that include perception, storage, recall, and verbalization, I focused my attention on the conceptualization of past events during the recall process in this chapter. Other factors also influence tense choice. For instance, recalled information will interact with functional, interactional, and socio-cultural factors in verbalization, which is another interpretive stage. In the next chapter, I will view tense-alternation as one of the speakers' strategic devices, and will show how tense works functionally to reflect attitudinal factors.

4

TENSE AND ATTITUDINAL CONTRAST

4.0. OVERVIEW

The process involved in turning thoughts into words is in the nature of interpretation of the thoughts. Talking about something recalled from memory is a creative activity, since the talker at many points makes choices reflecting a specific interpretation of her/his underlying thoughts (Chafe 1994). In this process, the speaker conveys mental imagery, which is her/his interpretation of the events, to the audience so that the audience receives comparable mental imagery to that which the speaker herself/himself holds. The speaker utilizes imitation of voices and gestures for this purpose. Choices of dialogue-introducers and their tense forms, I claim, also function the same way, and they reflect how the speaker interprets the factual events and in what way she/he guides the development of the audience's mental imagery in accordance with hers/his. In this sense, dialogue-introducer forms function in a similar way to the function of the modifiers that Chafe (1977a: 233) illustrated.[1] In this chapter, I will show how speakers encode their interpretations of events by manipulating dialogue-introducers as an attitudinal and informational contrasting device in order to effectively construct narratives.

Speech interactions are one of the crucial parts in the story, frequently serving as internal evaluative devices. In narrating interactional speech events, speakers attempt to reconstruct the events as a coherent series of interactions, through which they communicate to the audience their attitude and evaluation of the events. For this purpose, dialogue-introducer tense-alternation systematically functions as one of the speakers' information presenting strategies. The Cognitive Recollection Model (CRM) illustrated in chapter 3 accounted only for the interactional speech relations among the narrator and third persons. It represented how speakers view past events and their participants in the recall process, as a preset background stage for reporting discourse. In this chapter, I will shift my attention to the reproduction and presentation of recalled events, and will examine interactive purposes and strategic motivations that accompany reporting discourse. Some are compatible with CRM, but others contradict it and therefore require more communication-based arguments.

When telling stories that contain interactional speech events in the past, a speaker does not simply report the speech events as a linear enumeration of neutral information. Rather, the speaker expresses human relations, the participants' psychological states, her/his empathy to the participants, and other pragmatic information. A speaker also includes each event's relation to the story's theme, such as whether it is central or background information. A speaker encodes her/his judgments of the nature and type of reported information into her/his reports. Tense-alternation between past and present ("said" vs. "says") functions as a speaker's strategic device which effectively conveys these delicate but crucial aspects of the speech events in a flow of information.

In what follows, I will show that tense-alternation is a speaker's strategic device that encodes informational and attitudinal contrasts of reported information in discourse, i.e., a speaker's attitude (e.g., empathy to participants and to speech events), and contextual information (e.g., human relations, participants' psychological states). First, I will look at the basic contrast of the searching mode versus the resultative mode that accompanies tense-contrast. Next I will examine narrative stories that involve conflict situations. I will show that in such situations, tense forms contrast conflicting attitude versus conflict-avoidance. Third, I will more broadly contextualize how tense-contrast correlates with attitudinal contrast. I will show that the present tense and the past tense contrast weak versus strong attitudes, reflecting degrees of certainty and assuredness, and of emotional upset.

4.1. SEARCHING VS. RESULTATIVE MODE

4.1.1. *Says* vs. *said* in pair

There are many cases in discourse, in which "says" and "said" are paired rather systematically in accordance with some contrasting speech acts such as question vs. answer, and offer vs. acceptance. Consider the following example (reporting verbs are italicized):

(1) there's no way tuh get in the building the firs' da:y. hh Jack dropped me off et schoo:l, e-en::d, there wz a ha-et-there wz a hole in the wall in the back a' the building en, eh-there wz anothuh girl walking around she *says* hhh uh-dihyou know where the science building is 'n I *said*- well I *said*- yih-know, the guard jus' told me thet this wz the bui:lding. So she *seh*- hh are you goin here fer 'n-hh fer en in:dian class by any chance 'n I *said* yes hh So I *said* c'mon we'll fi:nd it tuhgethuh en we craw::led through the hole in

the wa::ll, hmhhh tch! We wou:nd up among paint ca:ns en:d hh an:::d yihknow stucco floo:r, en' hhh   (TG: 17-18)

In this narrative, the narrator includes direct quotations of speech interactions between herself and another girl. There are two question-and-answer pairs. In the first pair, the speaker uses "says" for a question and "said" for an answer. In the second pair, the speaker uses "say" for a question and "said" for an answer. In the rest of the narrative, the speaker consistently uses the past tense.

The next example shows a similar pattern of tense usage for question vs. answer:

(2) Misses Czinski's got her housecoat on and down the lawn by then . . . you know [ø] "what's going on here Carol?" [raised pitch] [Jim: laughs] I *said* "it's okay" I *said* "this . . . this guy says he saw something and he can't even see it from where he's parked anyway" [laughs]
. . . .
and Misses Czinski's out there [ø] "Carol is there any problem?" [raised pitch] I said "no . . . no"   (Johnstone 1987: 40-41)

The speaker uses zero-quotation form (ø) for questions and "said" for answers in two pairs of question vs. answer.

The next example also contains paired switching of tenses, but not for question and answer:

(3) Well, my sister, as she was growing up and going to college, I was on the road, out singing "Just One Look" and doing my thing with my own band, and then I went to live in England. And when she graduated from college, my gift to her was a trip, round trip, to London, and there she saw me doing what I do. And I had offers from Apple Records and I was producing and writing and I was an artist signed to them. And she *says*, "You know, one of these days I'm going to write your life story." I *said*, "Well, great. Go ahead." And sure enough, down through the years, she came to Vegas, where I live now, and she *says*, "I got the idea. And I'm going to write it about your life story, and that way we can work together and you don't have to be away from home so much. You can be with us." I *said*, "Well, go ahead." And she called it "Mama, I Want to Sing." And I've played the role of my own moms [*sic*], and her and her husband wrote it, directed it and produced it.   (EJ 1995. 8: 16)

The narrator is telling how she came to work in musicals. She quotes two dialogues between her sister and herself in the narrative. She introduces her sister's remarks with "she says," and her own remarks with "I said." In the rest of the narrative, she constantly uses the past tense. Here the sister's remarks are not questions as were the cases in (1) and (2), but they indicate the onset of dialogues and are uttered in expectation of receiving some form of answer from the interlocutor.

Let me compare the information in paired quotes in all three cases. In (1), the first quote is by a girl who is asking the narrator the way. The narrator gives an answer to the question. She prefaces her answer with "well," suggesting that she is not giving the direct answer to the question, but does hold the answer in some form that she can offer. This use of "well" indicates that the ideational options offered by questions are not precisely followed in the content of answers (Schiffrin 1987). She then tells the girl a piece of information on the building in the form that she can precisely offer, namely in the form of a report. In the second pair of question and answer, the girl further asks her a question in the hope that the narrator is attending the same Indian class in the building. In these dialogues, what the narrator is showing is not only the contrast of question versus answer, but also the attitudinal contrast. One searches for help and hopes to ally, while another offers information, help, and alliance. The one who is asking is the one who is in search, while the one who answers shows a clear and positive attitude. The dialogue-introducers with "say(s)" and "said," I assume, are used contrastively for them. In (2), Misses Czinski comes down the lawn asking a question ("what's going on here Carol?"). She has no idea what is happening between Carol and a man, but is worried since the man is a police officer. She is trying to grasp the situation. Carol, the narrator, says "it's okay" to negate Misses Czinski's worry. Then she gives some explanation for what is happening between herself and the police officer, followed by her claim of innocence in the form of reproaching the police officer. In the second part, which is another situation, Misses Czinski again asks Carol a similar question ("Carol is there any problem?"). The narrator simply negates any problem by double negation. Here the one who asks a question is in a 'searching mode,' and is introduced with zero-quotation form (ø).[2] Contrastively, the one who gives information or explanation is introduced with "said." Dialogues in (3) are not in the form of question and answer, but in the form of suggestion and promotion, which again is contrastively introduced with the present- and the past-tense verbs. The first remark by the narrator's sister, "You know, one of these days I'm going to write your life story," indicates a perspective towards the future and a hope, to which the narrator gives a positive response. The sister's remark includes an implicit question to the narrator, meaning, "What do you think?" or "Do you agree with me?" since her future plan involves the narrator. The use of "well" as a preface for the response shows that the narrator is in a position to give an evaluation of the preceding remark (Schiffrin 1987: 124). The same is true for the sister's second remark "I got the idea. And I'm going to write it about your life story, and that way we can work together and you don't have to be away from home so much. You can be with us." She requests the narrator's participation in her future plan, thus implicitly searching whether the narrator agrees to it or not. Then the narrator gives a positive response, "Well, go ahead." Although explicit levels of searching vary from (1) to (3), they are all in the searching mode to some extent. By contrast, the quotes in answers are all with more assured attitudes, and contain some clear and decisive features in the dialogues. Such a contrast of attitudes accompanies tense-contrast of present and past.

The dialogue features in each example are summarized in the following:

(1)' she *says*: {Q, search for help}
  vs. I *said*:   {A, TI}   I *said*: {offering information}
 she *say*: {Q, hope, search for alliance}
  vs. I *said*: {A, affirmation}   I *said*: {invitation, positiveness,
             optimism}
             (Q=question; A=answer; TI=turn initiator)[3]

(2)' Misses Czinski [ø]:{Q, no idea, search}
  vs. I *said*: {A, negation} I *said*: {explanation, claim, reproach}
 Misses Czinski [ø]:{Q, no idea, search}
  vs. I *said*: {A, insist of negation}

(3)' she *says*: {future perspective}
  vs. I *said*: {TI, evaluation, clear agreement, promotion}
 she *says*: {idea, future perspective, hope, offer}
  vs. I *said*: {TI, evaluation, promotion}

In these cases, timeless present forms such as "says," "say," and "ø" are used correspondingly for searching attitudes and "said" is used for more assured attitudes. The examples shown here also conform to CRM, in that the third persons are introduced with present-tense forms while the first persons are constantly introduced with past-tense forms. In order to examine whether what I have shown now is working independently of CRM, let me discuss a similar use of tense-contrast independent of personal distinctions.

4.1.2. *Says* vs. *said* in a single speaker's speech

The following excerpt shows a narrator's dialogues with Mr. Smith. The narrator only speaks once, and the rest is the remarks by Mr. Smith:

86   Reporting Discourse, Tense, and Cognition

> (4)   Anyway, we went to the Smith's [sic] house after dinner and Mr. Smith very nicely *says*, "Would you like some brandy?" So I *said*, "Yes, I will have some brandy." So he *says*, "We have some very nice brandy." He adds that. Then he goes to this cupboard and he opens it up and he *said*, "Too bad, you can't have any brandy 'cause I can't find any brandy snifters." . . . So he *says*, "Well, if that's the case," he *said*, "I will find you some other glasses."
> (Wolfson 1982: 51)

The first utterance by Mr. Smith is an offer of some brandy, to which the narrator gives a clear answer of acceptance. This pair of question and answer accompanies tense-switching from "says" to "said" following the pattern discussed above. The next remark of Mr. Smith, "We have some very nice brandy," is added to this dialogue, and is a light confirmation. It is led by a dialogue-introducer in the present tense. The next remark by Mr. Smith, "Too bad, you can't have any brandy 'cause I can't find any brandy snifters," is a result of the searching move expressed in "Then he goes to this cupboard and he opens it up." Although the searching move is not in the form of a verbalized quotation in this pair of information, this also displays tense-switching from present to past along with the informational contrast of search versus result. The last remark by Mr. Smith, "Well, if that's the case, I will find you some other glasses," is divided into two parts in quotes. The former part, "Well, if that's the case," is the start of a mental or inner search for an alternative way to serve brandy, since he could not find any brandy snifters. The latter part, "I will find you some other glasses" is a response to his mental search, and it is his decision. The former remark in a searching mode is introduced with "he says," while the latter resultative part is led by "he said."

The dialogues in the excerpt proceed as in the following:

> (4)'   Mr. Smith . . . *says*: {Q, offer}
>   vs. I *said*: {A, acceptance, clearness}
>   ad. he *says*: {addition}
>   he goes . . . and he opens . . . : {new move, search}
>   vs. he *said*: {result of search, apology, factual}
>   he *says*:   {search, supposition}
>   vs. he *said*: {decision}

We can see a correlation of the tense-contrast with the informational and attitudinal contrast. In this example, the tense-switching still seems to work in accordance with CRM in terms of personal distinctions in that the third person is introduced both in the present and the past tense, and the first person is introduced in the past tense. But in some cases it is hard to relate the tense-shift to varying degrees of psychological involvement. For instance, in the last supposition-decision pair in (4), it is odd to assume that the speaker is more involved with Mr. Smith's suppositional remark than with the concluding remark. I suggest that such tense-alternation between the present and the past is motivated by the attitudinal and informational contrast rather than by varying degrees of psychological involvement.

4.1.3. *Says, saying, say* vs. *said* in a single speaker's speech

We have seen examples in which informational contrasts accompany simple pairings of onset and coda. I shall now examine the case in which the attitudinal shift is seen in a longer span of dialogues. The following is an excerpt from an interview of a female singer, Koko Taylor:

(5) (Interviewer: How did you get together with Willie Dixon and record?) Well, Willie Dixon heard me sitting in and this was for my own enjoyment. This was something that I just wanted to do because I loved singing, you know. And this after I left Memphis and moved to Chicago. All of these people was there that I had been listening to on records, you know, Muddy Waters and Howlin' Wolf and all these people. So, Willie Dixon heard me sitting in with them and after I was finished, he came over and *says*, he *says*, "My God, I never heard a woman sing the blues before like you sing the blues." He *saying*, "that's what the world needs today, a woman to sing the blues." He *say*, "We got plenty of mens out here singing." He *said*, "But we don't have no women, you know." He *said*, "That's why we need a woman to sing like you sing and to sing the blues."

(EJ 1992. 3: 111-12)

The narrative proceeds in the past tense until the speaker quotes Willie Dixon, where she uses the present-tense dialogue-introducer ("he says"). From this point, dialogue-introducer tense shifts from "says," "saying," "say," to "said," for introducing a series of utterances by one person, Dixon. The dialogues in the narrative proceed as follows:

(5)' he came over and *says*, he *says*: {surprise, statement}
 He *saying*: {idea, ideal}
 He *say*: {factual}   } {search}
 He *said*: {negation, factual, problem presentation}
 He *said*: {conclusion, determination}

The first remark starting with "My God" expresses Dixon's surprise at seeing a woman singing the blues. Subsequently, Dixon's remarks show his growing excitement, until he reaches his own conclusion that "we need a woman to sing like you sing and to sing the blues." As the first remark is an onset for his excitement, the last remark is a coda that wraps up his emotional burst. As shown by his last remark "That's why," the three comments between the first and the last form an analysis of Dixon's worldview and the reasoning for his determination, namely to promote Taylor as a singer. This series of quotes follows Dixon's progression from a cue, shifting into a searching mode, and reaching a conclusion. This also provides the answer to the interviewer's question of "how" the narrator came to work with Dixon. The tense is not as simple as we saw in (1) through (4), but we can see that tense-shiftings accompany a gradual attitudinal shifting. The tense shifts from "says," at the onset, through "saying" and "say," in the searching mode, to the past tense "said," the fourth remark, leading into the conclusion. Here Dixon's use of "you know" at the end indicates that following the series of information-searching remarks, he has established a mutual alignment with the narrator. He is seeking confirmation that they share the knowledge that there are few women singing the blues, which leads to the conclusion that he wants the narrator to sing the blues.

4.1.4. Summary of contrasts

So far, I have discussed how a narrator uses the present and past tenses in accordance with informational and attitudinal contrasts, such as question versus answer, offer versus acceptance, exclamation versus determination, and so on. But the significant common factor is the attitudinal contrast between the searching attitude and the clear, positive, and decisive attitude. This attitudinal contrast is reflected in the tense-contrast between the timeless present and the past. The tense-contrast appears in the reporting verb forms such as "says," "say," "saying," and "ø" versus "said." From the factors that we saw in this section, and from the way they appeared in discourse, I have abstracted the following summary of tense forms and their associated features:

said
1. result, decision, conclusion, determination, acceptance, answer
2. clear and positive attitude
3. claim, explanation, reproach, strong negation

says
1. search, search for help, new move, supposition, offer, question
2. future perspective, hope
3. addition

say, saying
1. succeeding utterance

[ø]
    1. no idea, search

So far, my tentative conclusion is that the past-tense dialogue-introducer ("X said") is used with a resultative or decisive attitude. It also reflects a clear and positive attitude. On the other hand, the present-tense dialogue-introducer ("X says") is used with a searching attitude. It also precedes additional remarks. In addition, "say" and "saying" are used with succeeding utterances, and zero-quotation (ø) is used also for no idea and for search. Dialogue-introducers take contrasting tense forms in accordance with the informational and attitudinal contrasts or shifts as follows:

Table 1

Past tense	decision; conclusion; clear and positive attitude
Present tense	search; new move; supposition; future perspective; addition

Some examples conform to CRM in that tense-contrast depends on the distinctions between the third persons and the first persons. In other examples, tense-contrast appears in a single speaker's speech in accordance with informational and attitudinal contrasts. In some cases, tenses are chosen independently of the psychological involvement that is a key factor for CRM. Tense-switching in such cases may function as an informational or attitudinal contrasting device.

4.2. CONFLICT VS. CONFLICT-AVOIDANCE

4.2.1. *Said* vs. *said* shows conflict; *says* shows watching the situation

Stories involving conflict present one of the situations that often involve attitudinal shifts and contrasts among participants. In narrating conflict-based stories, reporting speakers show subjective views and evaluations of conflicting speech events, especially when they are participants in the conflicts. Since narratives of conflict stories often contain tense-switching, I shall describe how tense behaves contrastively in such situations.

Conflict occurs when two people disagree about an issue and choose to support opposing sides. In most cases, both have concluded that, for the moment, their stances cannot coexist simultaneously with one another (Stein and Miller 1990; 1993a, b; Stein et al. 1997). In argument, both arguers believe that their stance is more legitimate and more viable than that of their opponent. The most frequent reasons for anger are unexpected violations of moral or social standards, and attempts by an angry person to seek revenge or to guarantee that these violations never occur again (Stein et al. 1994). For instance, the following excerpt narrates how a woman and her husband started an argument:

(6) I was at home .hh and um (0.4) and then we had an ar:gument didn't we (.) Jeff *said* what do you think (0.2) what hour do you think this is and (.) you shouldn't be home this late and (.) and I *said* >at least I had the decency to phone yuh I coulda lied< (Edwards 1997: 145)[4]

The narrator has come home late at night, for which her husband Jeff reprimands her. Jeff is angry because his wife broke a moral standard, which is expressed by "you shouldn't be home this late." If the wife had apologized or guaranteed that the violation would never occur again at this point, there would be no argument. But she answers in defense of her behavior. She believes that the fact that she phoned him justifies her coming home late. Both wife and husband believe that their stance is legitimate, which causes a conflict. Here, utterances in conflict are both introduced in the past tense:

(6)' Jeff *said*   {blame, anger}
      I *said*:   {defense, defiance}

I thus hypothesize, for now, that conflicting remarks are reported both in the past tense.

Stories of conflict often include more subtle balances of power and hostile negotiations that may develop into aggression and physical threats. Consider the following excerpt, a detailed conflict story. It contains zero-quotation (ø) and "say" in addition to overall use of "said" (underlines are added to draw attention to the features discussed in relation to tense forms):

(7) Three weeks ago I had a fight with this other dude outside. He got mad 'cause I wouldn't give him a cigarette. Ain't that a bitch? (Listener: Oh yeah?) He walked over to me. [ø] "Can I have a cigarette?" He was a little taller than me, but not that much. I *said*, "I ain't got <u>no more</u>, man," 'cause, you know, all I had was one left. An' I ain't gon' give up my last cigarette unless I got some more. So I *said*, "I don't have <u>no more</u>, man." So he, you know, dug on the pack, 'cause the pack was in my pocket. She he *said*, "Eh man, I can't get a cigarette, man? <u>I mean—I mean</u> we supposed to be <u>brothers an' shit</u>." So I *say*, "<u>Yeah, well, you know, man, all I got is one</u>,

you dig it? An' I won't give up my las' one to nobody." So you know, the dude, he looks at me, an' he—I 'on' know—he jus' thought he gon' rough that motherfucker up. He *said*, "I can't get a cigarette." I *said*, "That's what I said, my man." You know, so he *said*, "What you supposed to be, bad an' shit? What, you think you bad an' shit?" So I *said*, "Look here, my man, I don't think I'm bad, you understand? But I mean, you know, if I had it, you could git it, I like to see you with it, you dig it? But the sad part about it, you got to do without it. That's all, my man." So the dude, he on' to pushin' me, man. (Listener: Oh he pushed you?) . . .

(Myhill 1992: 62-65)

The story is about the narrator's conflict with a man who wanted to get a cigarette from him, and the narrator's rejection of the request. The narrator conveys how the man angered him. After this excerpt, the story continues until the narrator beats him. Let me closely examine how dialogue-introducer tense shifts along with the story's development. The narrative begins in the past tense. The first remark a man utters to the narrator is a request for a cigarette ("Can I have a cigarette?"). It is in zero-quotation form without any dialogue-introducer. It is explainable in terms of search and request, as we have already seen in the previous section. From here the conflict starts. The narrator is slightly hostile at this point, observed in his description of the man as a rival: "He was a little taller than me, but not that much." The narrator responds, rejecting the request. From here to the end, the narrator consistently uses the past tense except for once.

What causes the narrator to switch to the present tense once in his constant use of the past tense? I assume that the answer lies in the attitudinal contrast. The narrator rejects the man's request, saying, "I ain't got no more, man," and repeats, "I don't have no more, man." The man responds, confirming his rejection, "Eh man, I can't get a cigarette, man?" Here the man adds a remark which is considered to be a request for concession, "I mean we supposed to be brothers an' shit." To this request for concession and alignment, the narrator responds, "Yeah, well, you know, man, all I got is one, you dig it? An' I won't give up my las' one to nobody." This is the one that is introduced with the present tense ("I say"). In the two consecutive rejections of the request, the narrator uses the past tense ("I said"), while here the narrator's attitude is slightly different, giving an excuse for not offering a cigarette. The narrator's simple and strong attitude appears in the rejection words "no more" in the first two responses. On the other hand, in giving an excuse, the narrator steps back.

First, the narrator prefaces the rejection with "yeah," "well," and "you know." "Yeah" shows his acknowledgement of the previous request for alignment (Schiffrin 1987: 89). "Well" implies his not matching the man's expectation. "You know" indicates his attempt to draw the man's attention to his having only one cigarette left. He claims that his possession of only one cigarette is a shared knowledge which leads to a reasonable rejection of the request. These turn initiators used in a series not only soften his attitudes but also delay the rejection, which is a main portion of the answer.

Second, the narrator starts by giving an excuse followed by an explanation, rather than simply rejecting the request. He even admits that he has one cigarette left, compared to his previous claim that he had no cigarette, which he had made as a reason for rejecting the man's request. Third, he tags a question "you dig it?" With the prefacing "you know," it embodies his attempt to confirm the man's understanding of his explanation. These show the narrator's temporarily softened attitude and roundabout way of rejection, compared to the two previous simple rejections.

Fourth, we see a linguistic clue of the motivation for the narrator's softening attitude. Immediately before the narrator's response led by "So I say," the man softens his attitude to request for concession, saying, "we supposed to be brothers an' shit." The man's softening attitude is also reflected in his repeated use of "I mean" which signals a modification of the intentions of a prior utterance (Schiffrin 1987: 302). Since the man modified his attitude from confirming rejection to requesting concession, the narrator steps back and prefaces his rejection with turn initiators, and is also motivated to give an excuse. From the next remark by the man, from which the conflict resumes, the past tense is used constantly. Note that the last remark by the narrator also includes an explanation, but it is not introduced with "I say," which seems to contradict my claim that the narrator's previous use of the present tense accompanies an excuse or explanation. In this case, the man's preceding remark is too aggressive, containing repeated challenges with "bad an' shit?" In contrast to the narrator's stepping back at the man's "brothers an' shit," the repeated uses of "bad an' shit?" made the narrator hold a firm attitude. So the narrator's last remark starts as a rebuttal and persuasion, which are reflected in the past-tense dialogue-introducer. Only from the remark "But I mean, you know, if I had it, you could git it . . . ," he starts giving an explanation. But here already the two parties are in the mood for a physical fight, and the man starts pushing the narrator. The whole dialogues are featured in the following:

(7)' He [ø]: {request}
I *said*: {rejection}
I *said*: {rejection}
he *said*: {confirmation of rejection, request for concession}
I *say*: {TI, excuse, explanation}
He *said*: {confirmation of rejection}

I *said*:   {affirmation of rejection}
he *said*: {confirmation of hostility, reproach}
I *said*:   {rebuttal, persuasion, explanation, excuse}

I assume that in narrating a conflict story, a narrator uses the past tense ("said"), while the present tense is used when there is any softening or stepping back in the conflict. The tense forms show such a delicate balance of power in the conflict episode.

The same is true in the following narrative of a conflict story, which was told by actor Robert Lake on the Tonight Show on television:

(8) And I'm standing in line for like two and a half hours to get gas, and I get up there—just as I get to the pups, the guy *says*, "You only gettin' two dollars worth of gas." So I get <u>a little tense</u> in the first place because it cost me three dollars worth of gas just to get up to the gas pumps. (laughs) Now this big dummy with his suit and his tie on, pulls his little car up out there and then gets out with his gas can and just as my car gets there the gas can gets down and this guy's gonna get gas in front of me. And I *said*, "Mister, you're not gonna get any gas in front of me." And he *said*, "Get out of my way kid, or I'm gonna hit you." That's what he *said* to me. So I didn't bother explaining anything to him. I picked the gas can up and I threw it man, like a hand grenade. (laughter from the audience) The people behind me in the line—then they were all on my side.
(Listener: Well, I would think so.)
<u>All of a sudden</u> there was a reputation to defend, 'cause a old lady *says*, "There, that a boy, kid, hit him!" And I *says*, "Pal, you can hit me, but if I fall, I promise you I'm gonna fall on you." So he went and he got his gas can and he went down the road.   (Wolfson 1982: 38-39)

(8)' the guy *says*:   {false charge}
   I *said*:   {attempt to block, warning}
   he *said*:   {threat}
   That's what he *said* to me: {emphasis}
   a old lady *says*: {interruption, encouragement}
   I *says*:   {challenge, warning, precaution}

At the beginning of the story, a man makes a false charge against the narrator, from which the narrator senses a slight tension. After that, they fall into conflict. The man's false charge against the narrator, which is a cue for the following conflict, is introduced in the present tense ("says"). The conflicting part is introduced in the past tense ("said"). This beginning of the conflict is similar to the one in (7). In both (7) and (8), at the first challenging point, the narrator has sensed a slight tension and hostility, but is not sure of it. But for most of the interaction, there is an argument with pushing power from both sides. In (8), after "All of a sudden," there is an interruption by an old lady who has been observing the conflict. After that, the narrator reports his own remark to the man: "Pal, you can hit me, but if I fall, I promise you I'm gonna fall on you." These are both reported with "says." The old lady's encouragement to the man is not directly involved in the power balance between the two, but appears to have caused tension to escalate the conflict. At the old lady's encouragement to the man to hit the narrator, the narrator assumes a posture which leads to the narrator's next remark, as a precaution to the man. Here the conflict is suspended for the next move, and finally the man goes away. The use of the past tense is limited to the report of substantial conflicting dialogues between the man and the narrator, but when there is a suspension of the conflict, the present tense is used. From what we have seen so far, the basic pattern in the conflict story is summarized as follows:

>   *said* vs. *said*   :   conflict
>   *say(s)*   :   watch the situation, suspension

4.2.2. *Said* shows challenge; *says* shows step-back

While the above cases were obvious conflict stories, now consider some different situational cases of power balancing and stepping back from conflict, to further examine the uses of dialogue-introducer tenses. The following excerpt is a story about a fall:

> (9) Well, I walked over the boards, but I didn't fall over them. Then when I got down and started to walk on the path, I don't know, I must have missed my footing somehow—nobody seems to know what happened, all I know was, I was down, right? So he *said* to me, "Were you—did you have something to drink?" I *says*, "I don't drink at quarter to twelve in the morning. It's too early." And you know, what provoked me is, those people haven't even inquired about me. Now I think that's dreadful.   (Wolfson 1982: 65)

In 4.1., I described how reporting dialogues that are in question-answer pairs often accompany contrasting tense forms of present and past. Here in (9), at a glance, the dialogue between the man and the narrator seems to follow the pattern of onset-coda, with the man searching for some answer and the narrator giving the answer. Following the logic in 4.1., dialogue-introducer tenses in this narrative should have such forms as in "So he says to me" and "I said." That would match CRM, too. However, this is not the case. The dialogue-introducers which appear in this narrative are "So he said to me" and "I says." Here I claim that the situational context is different from the other onset-coda cases. The attitudinal context this narrator intends to convey is different from that conveyed in the mere searching-resultative interactions. The man is not simply asking with mere curiosity or without any idea. He is cautious of the stranger lying down on the street. He is suspicious, supposing that the stranger is drunk and may cause some danger to him. In addition, he has a blaming attitude. The narrator, sensing the man's suspicious attitude, attempts to dodge his question, giving an excuse-like response, to soften the tension between them. The attitudinal features for the dialogues are the following:

(9)' he *said*: {suspicion, anger}
    I *says*: {dodge, excuse}

This attitudinal contrast is different from that in the onset-coda situation. It is more similar to the conflict story, in which aggression is expressed with the past-tense dialogue-introducer, while a softer attitude with conciliation is expressed with the present-tense dialogue-introducer. The narrator's dialogue is not uttered simply to give an answer to the question, but with a clearly intended function of softening the atmosphere and as a 'perlocutionary act' (Austin 1962).[5] The tense-contrast between "he said" and "I says" in this narrative effectively conveys the attitudinal contrast between the two speakers.

The following case contains a similar attitudinal contrast:

(10) So he *says*, "All right, put your right hand up." So I *said*, "What the hell, right hand, left hand," I *says*, "I don't know what the hell to do with any of them—either hand."   (Ibid.: 51)

This excerpt contains a peculiar switch from "I said" to "I says" between the same first-person speeches. Such examples have been confusing for the researchers who have studied tense-switching. This is indeed one of the examples that led Wolfson to conclude that dialogue-introducer tense-switching is an anomaly. It is even a problematic case for CRM, too. It is hard to assume "I says" as a result of the third-person construal for the first-person ego, after such a quick switch from "I said." I prefer to view this case as a manifestation of the attitudinal shift of the first person that the narrator intended to convey. The remark by the "he" is an onset, watching the narrator's reaction, used even before a conflict occurs. The first remark by the narrator, "What the hell, right hand, left hand," is a challenging attitude, that shows that the narrator is not intimidated. The narrator refuses to raise a hand, even mocking the man. But after the remark, he steps back a while to give an excuse, which is taken as a way to dodge the man's hostility.[6] The attitudinal contrast is summarized as follows, with the dialogue-introducer tense-switching back and forth between the present and the past tense:

(10)' he *says*:   {order, threat}
     I *said*:   {rejection, challenge}
     I *says*:   {dodge, addition, excuse}

My observation suggests the following pattern to explain the tense-contrast:

said vs. *says*   :   challenge vs. step back, excuse

The narrator uses the past-tense dialogue-introducer ("X said") for the challenging attitude which precipitates a conflict. In contrast, the narrator uses the present-tense dialogue-introducer ("X says") for the conciliatory attitude which reduces or avoids a conflict. The attitudinal contrast of pushing toward and stepping back from a conflict emerges in each individual narrative. Contrast between tenses functions as an indicator of the speaker's sense of the power imbalance.

The next excerpt demonstrates a power balance and its temporary breakthrough:

(11) .. a=nd .. he just .. *said* "well, that theory was .. debunked." ... I *said* "Oh? by whom." ... He *said* "well by .. Peterson." ... I *said* ... "who's Peterson." .. He *says* "you don't know Peterson? ... Oh my goodness. .. Why he's one of our great ... local .. geologists." ... I *said* "well, .. uh that's nice, but why would he be the one to debunk this."   (Chafe 1994: 218)[7]

The narrator, a linguist, is reporting her telephone conversation with a man who had called her regarding the etymology of a place name. The linguist thought that he did not know anything about place names, or about the Indian language that was the source of the name. On the other hand, the caller insisted that the origin of the name had been "debunked" by a geologist, and the linguist thought that a geologist would not know anything about etymologies. In this excerpt, the narrator keeps introducing utterances both by herself and by the caller with "said," except for one utterance by the caller. We see that both parties involved in this conversation are experiencing an emotional conflict. Neither of them makes a concession. First, the caller denies the theory that the narrator has mentioned, by saying, "well, that theory was .. debunked." The narrator asks him to be clearer on the information that he used to deny the claim, by asking, "Oh? by whom." The caller gives a response, "well by ..

Peterson." The narrator still keeps asking for more clarification of who Peterson is. In response to this question, for the first time the caller takes a longer turn. His response is not only to answer who Peterson is, but also to claim that the narrator does not know Peterson, whom he claims to be one of their great local geologists. This claim is rather personal, deviant from debating on the theory or the theorist. The caller emphasizes the narrator's lack of knowledge. Against this claim about the narrator's ignorance, however, the narrator stays calm, and reverts to her point, requesting for a clarification of why Peterson is the one to debunk the theory. She points out the irrelevance of her lack of knowledge of Peterson in this debate. The narrator certainly does not give in. What we sense out of this short excerpt is that neither of the parties compromises. One is insisting that the theory has been debunked, while the other is not persuaded but keeps asking questions to object to his explanation. For the caller, the question by the narrator, "who's Peterson," is an opportunity to gain the upper hand, to lead to his superiority. Having found a chance to break through the conflicting power balance, he bursts into a personal remark, with heightened emotionality. These exchanges are featured as in the following:

(11)' he *said*: {claim, negation of the other's claim, challenge}
I *said*: {clarification Q}
He *said*: {A}
I *said*: {clarification Q}
He *says*: {A (Q), exclamation, claim, emotional burst, superiority}
I *said*: {acceptance, clarification Q, calm}

This fits well into the framework in which I have been discussing the power balance so far. When the conflicting power balance is kept more parallel by both parties challenging each other, the dialogue-introducer stays in the past tense ("said"). However, when the balance is broken, even temporarily, the tense switches to the present ("says"). Here we see the emotional burst of the speaker's gaining the upper hand. The narrator returns to the past tense ("said") for her next remark, which is uttered calmly, conveying the message that she is not giving in yet. The narrator's tense manipulation reflects a breakthrough in the subtle power balance. Here, I assume the following tense patterns:

said vs. *said* : challenge, conflict, balance of power
says : step forward

Notice that the characterization of "says" is rather different from what I discussed up to example (10) in which "says" introduced an attitude of conciliation in contrast to the challenging attitude of "said." I have characterized the use of "says" in (11) as stepping forward rather than escaping from the conflict. What is common to these two seemingly opposing attitudes is that the conflict annoys the speakers who attempt either to step forward or step backward from the conflict. The one in (11) who is stepping forward and finding a way to gain the upper hand is actually attempting to find a key to escape from the power impasse to superiority. Therefore, the pattern for conflict and conflict-avoidance reflected in tense choice is revised as follows:

> *said* vs. *said* : challenge, conflict, balance of power
> *says* : avoidance, softening, or escape from conflict

Another significant point in excerpt (11) is the way the one speaker breaks through the conflict. During the conflict, the issue was academic. The two talked about a theory, and the narrator who was asking questions stayed calm and rational. In contrast, the one who found a clue to break through the conflict shifted to a personal remark, with an emotional aspect. From this point, I tentatively suggest the following:

> *said* vs. *says* : professional vs. personal utterance, emotional aspect

The next episode contains a similar occurrence of a present-tense dialogue-introducer for a comparatively personal utterance:

> (12) So I uh—he *said*, "You go over and see X, tell him I sent you—tell him who you are, he'll give you a job here," he *says*, "I can't hire or fire, all I can do is run the place." So I *said*, "All right, where's he at?"
> (Wolfson 1982: 51)

About this episode, it is reasonable to suppose the following. By tense-switching, the narrator communicates that the secretary showed a rather businesslike attitude when uttering the first remark, and then showed a softer attitude with his second remark. The first remark led by "he said" simply directs the narrator to his boss. The second remark is an excuse why all he can do is to send the narrator who has come to find a job, to somebody else. He is showing his powerless status in the office. His implicit meaning is to apologize for not being able to do more for the narrator. It is more personal than his initial attitude of simply conducting his business. We see the following features in the exchanges, which lead to the contrasting pattern of "said" and "says":

> (12)' he *said*: {secretarial instruction}
> he *says*: {excuse, addition} (confession of lack of authority)
> I *said*: {acceptance, Q}

said vs. *says* : business like vs. personal utterance (step back, excuse)

Since the narrative continues further and this very part is not really the climax of the episode, the narrator does not take time to explain the shift of the secretary's attitude. But he consciously or unconsciously shows the subtle shift of the speaker's attitude through his dialogue-introducers.

4.2.3. *Said* shows never-intimidated attitude; *says* shows step-back

So far, we have seen the attitudinal contrast between escalating and retreating from the conflict. Now I shall consider some other cases, which Johnstone explains with the relative status hypothesis. I will examine whether they fit the account of the attitudinal contrasting use of dialogue-introducer tenses. In the following short excerpt, the narrator recounts the time when she was stopped by a police officer:

(13) and he *goes*, "you been drinking?" and I *said*, "WELL . . . yeahh . . . I had a few beers this afternoon."   (Johnstone 1987: 39)

The contrasting use of "goes" and "said" here is easily considered as a pair of onset versus coda, with the attitude of searching for an answer versus giving an answer. But is there any other subtle implication in this tense-switching, in terms of power balancing? Recall that example (9) contained a similar dialogue asking about drinking. Let us look at the relevant excerpt from the dialogue from (9):

(14) So he *said* to me, "Were you—did you have something to drink?" I *says*, "I don't drink at quarter to twelve in the morning. It's too early."
              (from 9)

In (14), the question is introduced with "said," while the narrator's response is led by "says." In (13), by contrast, the question is introduced with the present-tense verb "goes," while the narrator's answer is led by "said." While similar pairs of question and answer are reported in two different narratives as in these cases, I suggest that the narrators' conceptualizations of the two situational contexts are not the same. The narrator may reflect attitudinal information in the way she/he introduces dialogues. Before attempting to figure out the contrast of the dialogue-introducers in (13) and (14), let me cite another longer example, which contains more contextual information. The following is the narrative told by a woman about the time when she was stopped by a police officer:

(15) and I *said* "what's the problem" and he *says* "well misses um . . . I saw back down there by the high school I think you were going a little FAST there it's a thirty-mile-an-hour zone you know" and I *says* "yeah I know" I *said* "ah I know" . . . and he *says* ". . . oh . . ." he *goes* "well . . . I just want to let you know you're doing a good job"   (Johnstone 1987: 41)

The police officer claims that the woman committed a traffic violation by speeding. But his way of speaking to her shows that his attitude is not strong and authoritative. Or at least, this is how the narrator conveys his attitude. In his first claim, he stumbles, using "well" and "um . . ." He makes his claim more indirect by "I think" and "you know," and milder by "a little FAST." On the contrary, the response by the woman, the narrator of this narrative, is reported in repetition: "I says 'yeah I know' I said 'ah I know.'" This may be the repetition in the actual utterance,[8] but it is more likely that the narrator simply repaired herself at the time of the report.[9] In any case, the fact that the woman answered that she knew the speed limit of the street justifies her innocence, and the police officer steps back, saying ". . . oh . . ." As a discourse marker of information management tasks (Schiffrin 1987), "oh" displays receipt of an unanticipated answer, marking a reorientation toward a proposition whose completion had been differently anticipated. The police officer anticipated that the woman would not know the speed limit of the street, but finds out that she knew it. He then starts giving an excuse pretending that he never even thought of charging her with a traffic violation ("he goes 'well . . . I just want to let you know you're doing a good job'"). He is even flattering. The present tense dialogue-introducers for the police officer's remark reflect the narrator's evaluation of his ability and attitude as not particularly authoritative or strong. In contrast, the woman's first utterance, "what's the problem," which is introduced with "I said" signifies annoyance. The narrator's repair from "yeah I know" to "ah I know" suggests that she thinks that "I says 'yeah I know'" is not enough to express her exact words and attitude. Along with the correction of the dialogue itself, the narrator corrects the dialogue-introducer tense. The corrected remark "I said 'ah I know'" communicates her firmer confidence towards the police officer, which immediately made him step back. Her correction reflects the attitudinal correlation between the dialogue and the dialogue-introducer tense. The correlation is clear when we see the dialogue features in the following format:

(15)' I *said*:   {Q, annoyance}
   he *says*:   {mild charge of a traffic violation}
   I *says*:   {light A}
   I *said*:   {firm A, stiffening attitude}
   he *says*:   {step back}
   he *goes*:   {excuse, flattering}

says, goes vs. *said* : step back vs. never-intimidated attitude

The present tenses of dialogue-introducers reflect the attitude to step back from insistence, while the past tense conveys the never-intimidated attitude.

Now let us review example (13). In addition to the contrast of onset-coda, which is easily related to the present-past tense-contrast of dialogue-introducers, we can see that the police officer's attitude is not authoritatively strong, and the narrator responds with the firmer, never-intimidated attitude. Indeed, Johnstone (1987) states that the point of people telling their interactions with authority figures is to show that they are not intimidated by the authority. Thus, we may assume that excerpt (13) contains the following features:

(13)' he *goes*: {police checkup, simple Q}
　　 I *said*: {TI, A, acknowledgment, "So what?"}

Against the police officer's question whether the narrator had been drinking, she admits it, as if saying, "So what?" This unintimidated attitude is also related to the narrator's utterance "WELL" which is stronger than a simple response marker. It emphasizes that the police officer's presupposition is invalid (Owen 1983), in that the yes-no question format that he offers is irrelevant. She implies that she only had a few beers in the afternoon, but that she has not been drinking recently. It also indicates that she disagrees with the police officer, meaning "yes but . . ." (Pomerantz 1984). The narrator's attitude with this response is, "Yes, I only had a few beers this afternoon, but I haven't been drinking much. So what is wrong with it?" In this very short excerpt, it is hard to know more about the true meaning of tense-contrast. It is partly attributable to simple question and answer as onset and coda, and it is in accordance with the CRM's personal distinction of the first and third persons. But we can also agree that the narrator's intention may be to spotlight her never-intimidated attitude when facing the authority's professional checkups, as was the case in (15). Such a contrast is not intended in (14), on the other hand.

The following example contains a similar attitudinal contrast:

(16) and then I *said* "what's the problem here?" he *says* "well ma'am . . . ah . . . you didn't stop for that stop sign back there" I *said* "WHAT . . ." I mean I was mad I *said* "WHAT" and he *says* . . . he *says* "it's the In-" he just starts off rattling "it's the Indi- Indiana State Law you must come to a complete stop . . . before the stop sign da da da da" I *said* "I did" I *said* "there's a crosswalk there and the thing's before that" I *said* "where were you sitting anyway" [laughs] he *says* "I was right in that parking lot by the church" and

that parking lot's right back here [indicating on table] you can't even see the stop sign I *said* "I'm sorry" I *said* "you didn't see me" he *said* "it's the Indiana State Law da da da da da" (Johnstone 1987: 34)

Tense-switching in this narrative is analogous to what we have seen above. The police officer makes a mild charge of a traffic violation, against which the narrator counterargues very strongly. The police officer's speech contains a turn initiator "well" and stumbling expressions "... ah ... ," "Indi- Indiana State Law," "... before." The narrator's words show annoyance and anger by a strong remark "WHAT" with an added explanation "I mean I was mad." She claims her innocence, gives an explanation, and even advances a retorting question: "where were you sitting anyway." The attitudinal contrast between the two corresponds to the tense-alternation in this narrative, except for the last remark by the police officer. The last remark by the narrator, which is in the form of an apology ("I'm sorry"), is actually a sarcastic expression, with an air of superiority. She finds a way of gaining the upper hand, by claiming that the police officer had not seen her ("you didn't see me"). Notice that the officer's last remark is introduced with the past-tense dialogue introducer "he said," in contrast to the narrator's constant use of "he says." This reflects that his last remark is a repetition of the former explanation, which indicates his insistence upon his claim. His attitude shifts from mild to obstinate after his dishonest claim is pointed out to him. This is in contrast to the last remark of the police officer in example (15). In (15), when the police officer found out that his claim about the narrator's traffic violation was improper, he backed off, and his next remark was introduced as "he says '... oh ... .' he goes 'well I just want to let you know you're doing a good job.'" In (16) here, the police officer is far from retreating, and keeps insisting. This is reflected in the narrator's sudden switch from "he says" to "he said" at this point. The dialogue features and the dialogue-introducers correlate in the following ways:

(16)' I *said*:   {Q, annoyance}
he *says*:   {mild charge of a traffic violation}
I *said*:   {surprise, anger}
I *said*:   {surprise, anger}
he *says*:   {explanation, formulaic rattling}
I *said*:   {claim of innocence}
I *said*:   {explanation}
I *said*:   {retorting Q}
he *says*:   {A, explanation}
I *said*:   {apology with sarcasm}
I *said*:   {secure innocence, blame}
he *said*:   {repetition of formulaic rattling, insistence}

The narrators in both (15) and (16) illustrate their stronger attitudes than the police officers'. They start reporting the police officers' claims in similarly mild ways: "he says 'well misses um . . .'" and "he says 'well ma'am . . . ah . . .'" In both cases, the police officers signal by "well" that their following remarks are in some way dispreferred (Pomerantz 1984), and delay their claims. Their claims are described as mild ones in both cases. The narrators' description of the police officers in these ways confirms Johnstone's (1987) argument about the purpose of the narrators' telling the stories. The narrators try to convey their never-intimidated attitudes toward authorities. It is effective to contrast the police officers' attitudes with the narrators'. To demonstrate CRM, I raised the same example (16) and argued that the narrator's different construals for the first and the third persons motivated the overall contrast of "he says" versus "I said," and that the narrator's decrease of psychological involvement motivated the last "he said." The narrator's emotional heightening decreases because she was already winning the argument, while she views the police officer's attitude as still insisting on his claim in vain. The narrator's switch to the past-tense dialogue-introducer in the end accurately reflects her emotional state, and her interpretation of the police officer's attitudinal shift. The explanation by CRM and the attitudinal contrast account that I am giving here do not contradict each other, but in combination they lead to a verbal realization in the form in which it actually appears.

So far we have seen stories in which people described their interactions with police officers. Let us look at some other situations. The following is an excerpt of a narrator telling about her/his dialogue with a judge in a court:

(17) she *says* ". . . okay . . . I I see you plead guilty to this . . . to this charge you know is there anything you'd like to say on the record um . . . before I give you your uh . . . your fine or whatever?" I *said* "well I just . . . no I just want to get it over with I think this is just ridiculous"   (Ibid.: 39–40)

The court question by the judge sounds mild. The time lag indicator ". . . okay . . . ," and the stumbling expressions "I I see you plead guilty to this . . . to this charge," "um . . . ," "your uh . . . your fine or whatever?" mark the judge's utterances as not firmly motivated. The narrator's answer shows her/his feeling of annoyance and feeling of absurdity about the case. The contrasting attitude of the two fits with the tense-alternation in this narrative as explicated in the following:

(17)' she *says*: {mild court Q}
     I *said*: {A, feeling of absurdity}

Here is an important contradiction. With respect to (11) and (12), I discussed the contrast between professional and personal utterances. We saw that more businesslike utterances are introduced with "said" while the shift to more personal utterances is indicated by the tense-shift to the present. However, the professional utterances that we see here such as police checkups and court questions are introduced with "says." For this contradiction, I argue that what the tense-contrast reflects is not fixed situational features, but the narrator's subjective interpretation of the attitude of the reported speakers, and the narrator's egocentric view of the human relationships. In such cases as (11) and (12), the narrators attempt to communicate the shift in attitude of each speaker over the course of the interactions. The narrators focus on the gap between the professional attitudes and the personal phases. On the other hand, in (15), (16), and (17), which Johnstone calls authority stories, what the narrators emphasize with tense-contrast is their stronger, never-intimidated attitudes toward the authorities.

I shall confirm this type of contrast in the following excerpt in which the narrator reports his dialogue with his boss:

(18) and this jeep wheels up and it's this real hard-ass Lieutenant Mead and he hops out and he *says* "MALONE WHERE IN THE FUCK HAVE YOU BEEN?" [performing a tough voice] I *said* "Mead" a lieutenant you know I *said* "MEAD WHERE IN THE FUCK HAVE YOU BEEN?" [performing the same tough voice]
(Ibid.: 41)

(18)' he *says*:   {Q}
     I *said*:   {Q, sarcasm, blame}

The point in this narrative is the narrator's blame of his boss, with a strong attitude. By exact repetition of the boss's utterance, the narrator expresses his sarcasm. By using the same tough voice as the boss's, he expresses his unflinching attitude against his boss, suggesting that it is not he but the boss who is to be blamed. Actually the boss's first utterance is also uttered in a tough voice and therefore is reasonably reported in the past-tense ("he said"). But since the narrator's egocentric view of the situation and his point in reporting the dialogue is to emphasize his own strong attitude, he ends up using the tenses to contrast the two parties. It also conforms to the cognitive operation shown by CRM.

4.2.4. Summary of contrasts

In this section, I mainly dealt with conflict stories. I started with stories that exhibit high degrees of disagreement and aggression, and expanded my analysis to stories with more subtle emotional conflict. As I have suggested, Johnstone's (1987) 'authority stories' are indeed conflict stories. Attitudinal contrasts in conflict are the essential factors that appear as tense-contrasts in authority stories. Johnstone claimed that tense-switching is used to contrast authority versus nonauthority, but it is hard to apply her hypothesis to other situational contexts in which there is hardly any distinction of statuses. In that sense, the much broader category of conflict stories includes authority stories. Conflict stories often include a power differential and a status hierarchy between the two participants, just as authority stories do. Narrators of conflict stories contrast the power balances of the two participants, and use tense forms for such balances. The explanation that I have given for conflict stories easily applies to cases other than the authority stories.

One of the goals of telling conflict stories is self-justification (Georgakopoulou 1997). Narrators reassert or reaffirm their own positions, and justify their behaviors and arguments in contrast to those of other parties. By justifying their own behaviors, they attempt to create solidarity with their audience (Sakita 1999). For such purposes, narrators need to convey subtle power balances, feelings including anger and fear, and contrasting reactions between their opponents and themselves. As I have shown, tense-contrast conveys these essentials of conflict stories. Another significant aim of conflict stories is self-promotion (Georgakopoulou 1997). Reasonably, as I also have shown in examples above, conflict stories are frequently narratives of self-involving interactions. Narrators spotlight themselves, and create sympathetic alignments with the audience, gaining a widened base of support for their views.

The following lists categorize the relationships between the attitudinal and informational factors and tense forms as we have analyzed them in this section, according to how they appear in discourse:

said:
1. blame, anger, challenge, confirmation of rejection and hostility, request for concession, reproach, warning, threat, suspicion, claim, retorting question
2. defense, defiance, rebuttal, excuse, explanation, persuasion, claim of innocence, sarcasm, rejection, affirmation of rejection, acknowledgment, "So what?," feeling of absurdity, firm answer, insistence, stiffening attitude
3. secretarial instruction, professional
4. emphasis
5. surprise
6. calm, annoyance

says, goes
1. false charge, warning, precaution, order, threat, encouragement

106   *Reporting Discourse, Tense, and Cognition*

    2. dodge, excuse, confession, step back, explanation, flattering
    3. checkup, question, mild claim
    4. light answer
    5. exclamation, emotional burst
    6. addition

[ø]
    1. request

To summarize, the tense reflects the following attitudinal and informational contrasts:

Table 2

Past tense	conflict; challenge; never-intimidated attitude
Present tense	watching the situation; suspension; step back; excuse; emotional highlight; personal

Most interestingly, dialogue-introducer tenses are used to demarcate contrasts in power positions in situations as the following:

    said vs. *said*   : challenge, conflict, balance of power
    says   : escape from power conflict

The past-tense dialogue-introducer ("X said") in tandem reflects both parties' advances, with the balance of power in conflict. On the other hand, the present-tense dialogue-introducer ("X says") used in such power balances reflects withdrawal from the conflict. Attitudinal contrasts, indeed, appear in broader contexts than simple conflict stories, as we shall see in the next section.

4.3. WEAK VS. STRONG ATTITUDE

4.3.1. Degrees of assuredness in *I don't know*

In 4.1., we saw that tense contrasts attitudinal differences of reported speakers. The dialogue-introducer tense of the present and the past contrasted the searching mode with the resultative, decisive, clear, and positive mode. In 4.2., we further saw that the present-tense dialogue-introducer is used when the speaker holds a weaker attitude, is watching the situation, and steps back. The past tense is used for a conflict and for an unintimidated attitude. Now I can widen my focus and discuss more general cases, to see if a more general explanation can be given to the tense-contrast in discussion.

First, let us consider the following excerpt which contains reports of three persons' dialogues:

(19) One time my mom and my dad had went somewhere[.] And she left me and my brother and my little sister at home. And my brother he had got mad at me 'cause I was on the phone. And so he threw a pillow and I ducked and he hit the table and my mom's crystal was on it and he broke it. And I got in trouble for it and he didn't. I couldn't get back on the phone for like about three weeks. I was so mad. Then when he had broke it, I was trying to clean it up, and, you know, stick it back together. But some of it was just broken [into] too many pieces. I couldn't put it back together. Then she came home. It [She] *was like*, "Uh, uh, who broke this?" I'*m like*, "I don't know." (Laughs.) Then so my brother, he *said*, "She was on the phone and then she came in here and hit me and then I threw the pillow." And so she *said*, "Well, it's really your fault because you ain't supposed to be on the phone." (Rickford and Rafal 1996: 236)

The narrator uses the past tense all through this narrative except for the part "I'm like, 'I don't know.'" Facing her mother's anger, the narrator is in an awkward situation here. She is intimidated and fears that she will be scolded. It is reflected in her pretending not to know who broke the crystal. Her weak position is reflected in the use of the present tense. In contrast, the past-tense dialogue-introducer "It [She] was like" reflects the mother's burst of anger, which is a strong attitude. Her brother's remark is also introduced with the past-tense dialogue-introducer "he said," reflecting that he has a stronger attitude of telling on his sister, with a claim that he is innocent. The mother's final angry sentence is introduced in the past tense again. The tense-contrast displays the following features:

(19)' It [She] *was like*: {anger, emotional burst}
I'*m like*: {A, intimidated, pretension of not knowing, fear}
he *said*: {claim, explanation, telling on}
she *said*: {sentence, anger, reason}

The present tense is used for a weak attitude, watching the situation, while the past tense is used for a firm attitude. Here the contrast indeed reflects the weak versus strong positioning of each speaker.

108 *Reporting Discourse, Tense, and Cognition*

Observe some examples that involve the same utterance "I don't know" in different situations. Just as (19) did, the following excerpts (20) and (21) contain daughters' responses "I don't know" to their mothers' questions:

(20) B: Mm, tch! I wz gonnuh call you. -last week someti(h)me hhhhh!
     A: Yeh my mother a:sked mih I *siz* I don'know I haven't hea:rd from her. I didn' know what day:s you had. hhh   (TG: 15)

(21) K: Uh hu:h, so you're er- she said is he coming
     B: hhh hhh
     K: for vacation or for um (0.4) tsk! hhh work. An I said I:: do::n kno::w.
     B: KrisTI:na:!
     K: I said [both!
     B: [You're a lot of ba:ckup aren't you for me!
     K: I know, I said-no I said both. It's both! (0.4) Both. See? I defended you. hhh So:,   (AL: 4)

I discussed the way that the remark "I'm like, 'I don't know'" in (19) reflected the narrator's weak position and attitude. In (20), the daughter's response is reported as "I siz, 'I don't know . . .'" Its tense is the same as the one in (19). In (21), the daughter's response is reported as "I said, 'I:: do::n kno::w.'" Its tense is opposite to the other two cases. In (20), the second speaker A, when asked by her mother if the first speaker B is coming to visit them, responds that she does not know. In her report, after telling B of her response to her mother, she tells B that she did not know of it, saying, "I didn' know what day:s you had." On the other hand, in (21), K responds that she does not know whether B is coming for vacation or for work, when asked by her mother. By K's stretching out her response ("I:: do::n kno::w") and by B's uttering an exclamation ("KrisTI:na:!"), we see that the utterance "I:: do::n kno::w" has a great meaning for them. It is not a mere response showing no idea, but is an intentional control thinking of the effect of the words. It is an utterance in defense of B, and the speaker K is actually showing off the response, proud of it. Comparing the three cases of "I don't know," we come up with the following differences in speakers' attitudes:

I'*m like* "I don't know." : {pretension of not knowing}
I *says* "I don't know."   : {no idea}
I *said* "I don't know."   : {intentional control}

The present tense is used either without having any idea, or pretending not to know in an awkward, weak position. In such cases, the speakers do not feel enough certainty to express assured, strong attitudes. By contrast the past tense is used with more assured attitudes. Note that the tense reflects the attitudinal contrast that the narrator puts into the speech at the time of the narration, which may not reflect the actual attitudinal contrast of the original utterances of the speaker. As I mentioned above, the tense reflects the narrator's egocentric view of the world.

4.3.2. Degrees of firmness in negation and affirmation

A similar attitudinal contrast is seen in the following excerpt, in tense variation in report of negation. A woman is reporting a prior interaction with her daughter as an illustration of why she should date boys only of her own religion:

(22) //One// was a, his father was a friend of my husband's. And when I heard she was goin' out with him, I *said*, "You're goin' out with him," I *said*, "You're goin' out with a Gentile boy?" She *says*, "Well Daddy knows his father." I *said*, "I don't care." So she introduced him, and they went out, and she came home early, and I *said*, "Well, y' goin' out with him again?" She *says*, "Nope." I *said*, "Did he get fresh?" She *said*, "No!" She *says*, "But he's different!" She *says*, "I'm not used t' Gentile boys!" That cured her! She'd never go out with one again.
(Schiffrin 1990: 250-51; Georgakopoulou and Goutsos 1997: 133)

The tense-switching seems to follow the contrast preset by CRM throughout the narrative. The past tense is used for the first person, while both the present and the past tense are used for the third-person speaker. But are the switches between the present and the past tense used for the third person's remarks conditioned by degrees of the narrator's psychological involvement? Is the narrator more psychologically involved at the point "She says, 'Nope'" than at "She said, 'No!'" leading her to revert from "She says" to "She said"? It is hard to assume this explanation is correct, since in response to the narrator's question "I said, 'Well, y' goin' out with him again?'" the daughter's response is light in "She says, 'Nope,'" and emphasized in "She said, 'No!'" The psychic involvement is not decreasing in this context. I rather believe that in this case the tense-contrast reflects the shift of the speaker's assuredness, which the narrator intends to convey at this quote. When the narrator's daughter comes home from dating, the narrator asks if she is going out with him again, to which the daughter gives a light negation "Nope." The narrator further asks another question, "Did he get fresh?" The daughter is apparently annoyed by the mother's noisy interference, and even feels insulted and answers with a firm negation "No!" The following remarks are the explanation and excuse for why she is not going out with him again. The following summarizes the features and the tense-contrast in the narrative:

(22)' I *said*:   {blame}
    I *said*:   {repeated blame}
    she *says*:   {excuse}
    I *said*:   {rejection of excuse}
    I *said*:   {blame}
    She *says*:   {light negation}
    I *said*:   {Q, sarcasm}
    She *said*:   {firm negation}
    She *says*:   {excuse, claim}
    She *says*:   {excuse, claim}

The tense-contrast for introducing negation conforms to the tense-contrast for the report of affirmation which was seen in (15):

She *says*, "Nope."   vs. She *said*, "No!"   : light vs. firm negation
I *says*, "yeah I know." vs. I *said*, "ah I know.": light vs. firm affirmation

4.3.3. Degrees of upset in exclamation

Another feature common to tense-contrasts reflecting attitudinal contrasts is exclamatory remarks.[10] In the following excerpt, V and M, who are female housemates occupying different bedrooms in the house, tell about an amusing event involving themselves:

(23) V: So I stood on my bed
    M: She pounded on the ceiling,
    V: and I pounded on the ceiling,
    M: she was pounding . . .
    V: and I hear Marge and I hear Marge dash out of her room, come downstairs and open the door, and I *was like* ["No Marge . . ."
    M: [She *said* "Marge, it's me." I'*m like*, "What is . . ."
    V: I was pounding on my ceiling.
    M: Bizarre!   (Tannen 1989: 57-58)

This is a 'cooperative reporting' by two speakers (Sakita 1995; see also chapter 7). In lines 5-6, V narrates that Marge dashed downstairs being surprised at V's pounding, and that she attempted to appease Marge, saying, "No Marge . . ." At this point, Marge takes over the utterance and finishes it by "She said, 'Marge, it's me.'" She then reports her reaction to it by saying, "I'm like, 'What is . . .'" The tense-switching in this exchange is the following:

(23)' I *was like*: {negation, appeasement}
She *said*: {appeasement}
I'*m like*: {upset, lost}

The past-tense dialogue-introducers "I was like" and "She said" introduce negation in appeasement or in persuasion. In contrast, Marge's psychological state at "What is . . ." that is introduced with "I'm like" is the feeling of being surprised, lost, and upset. She has not grasped the situation and is asking, "What is going on?" or "What is this all about?" The remark "What is . . ." includes the mixed feelings of exclamation and attempt to grasp the situation. Recall the exclamation in (16). In the passage, "I said, 'WHAT . . .' I mean I was mad I said, 'WHAT,'" there were two exclamations that were emphatic and were reported with "I said." The attitudes attached to the remark are anger and annoyance. In contrast, the speaker in (23) has not even started to acquire any certain reactive feeling, since she has not grasped the situation yet. She is simply lost and upset here. The following contrast is suggested here:

said, was like vs. *am like*   :   firm vs. upset, lost, surprise

The following excerpt also contains exclamations. The narrator is telling of his experience going to the Japanese public bath when he visited Japan:

(24) Anyway, what was I say- Oh we were at the Japanese bath and um they didn't tell us, first of all, that we were going into the bath, so we were standing in the room, and they *said* "Okay, take your clothes off." We'*re like* "What?!" and um
[Listener: It's prison]
they gave us these kimono and we put the kimono on, they brought us to this other room, and they *said*, "Okay, take the kimono off." And we'*re like* "What are you talking about?" So then the the teacher left.
(Tannen 1989: 141)

At the abrupt request to undress, the narrator was just puzzled and shocked, uttering, "What?!" At another request to take the kimono off, the narrator was more puzzled and uttered, "What are you talking about?" The narrator was surprised, lost, and upset at the unfamiliar custom, unable to grasp the situation. To narrate such a progression, the narrator uses the dialogue-introducer tense-switching in the following way:

(24)' they *said*: {order}
We'*re like*: {upset, surprise}
they *said*: {order}
we'*re like*: {upset, lost}

The orders are introduced with the past tense, while the exclamations associated with feeling lost, surprised, and upset are introduced with the present tense. By considering this contrasting effect of tense, we can give a more reasonable account for the tense-shift in the following example that Johnstone (1987) explained with the relative status hypothesis:

(25) she called back on Sunday night she *said* "uh . . . car won't start" [laughs] I *says* "what do you mean the car won't start?" (Johnstone 1987: 40)

Johnstone explained the tense-switching in this exchange by the relative status hypothesis in that the narrator is an automobile expert and so is introduced with the present tense, in response to his wife's claim about automobile malfunction. I would argue, instead, that the present tense used for introducing the remark "what do you mean the car won't start?" reflects the narrator's surprise and lost psychology. He has not been able to grasp the situation. His wife's claim, "uh . . . car won't start," is a cause for his puzzlement. The tense-contrast accompanies the following features:

(25)' she *said*: {claim}
I *says*: {surprise, lost}

Compare the cases so far with the following case, in which tense-switching occurs in the last two lines:

(26) So meantime, I'm tying up the sail and getting everything secure and all and . . .
(Narrator's wife: And the boat is gone for fifteen minutes and Kenny comes back and as he's coming back he stands up in the boat and he waves his hand this way (motion)—You know what this (motion) is? That's the signal for distress. We thought he was kidding!)
(general laughter)
And he says, "Quick! Quick! Towels!" I said, "What do you mean, towels?"—"Nana fell in!" I says, "Kenny, let me . . ." (Wolfson 1982: 47)

Tense and Attitudinal Contrast   113

This is confusing, since the narrator's remark, "What do you mean, towels?" is introduced with "I said," which seems to contradict what we have been discussing so far. But considering the situational context, we can still account for this case in the framework that we have set. The remark by Kenny, "Quick! Quick! Towels!" cues the narrator's response, "What do you mean, towels?" The narrator is puzzled, and has not grasped the situation, but he is still not surprised or upset by what Kenny said. In (23), Marge was already upset when she said, "What is . . ." In (24), the narrator was surprised and upset by the concrete orders to disrobe. In (25), the narrator was already facing the concrete claim about the car malfunction. However, here in (26), at the remark, "What do you mean, towels?" the narrator is simply lost, but not upset yet. Only after the Kenny's next remark, "Nana fell in!" the narrator finds out that his mother has fallen into the pond. For the first time he becomes upset here, and utters the next remark, "Kenny, let me . . ." Here the narrator's upset emotion is reflected in the use of "I says." Therefore, the following correlation between the tense-switching and the narrative features is observed:

(26)' he *says*:   {upset, request}
   I *said*:   {<u>lost but calm</u>}
   he [ø]:   {upset, claim}
   I *says*:   {<u>upset</u>, offer}

The degree and nature of upset feelings, which the narrators attempted to show in reporting the exclamatory remarks, are manifested in the tense variations of dialogue-introducers. They are summarized as follows:

   I'*m like, "What . . ."*   : {surprise, upset, lost}
   We'*re like, "What . . ."*   : {surprise, upset, lost}
   I *said, "What"*   : {surprise, anger}
   I *says, "What* do you mean the car won't start?" : {surprise, lost}
   I *said, "What* do you mean, towels?"   : {lost but calm}

When the speaker is upset and lost, the present tense is used. When the speaker has a firm or a calm attitude, the past tense is used.

4.3.4. Summary of contrasts

Let me summarize the attitudinal and informational factors with tense forms that I have shown in this section:

114 *Reporting Discourse, Tense, and Cognition*

said
1. blame, rejection of excuse, sarcasm, firm negation
2. claim, order, explanation, sentence, reason, telling on, appeasement
3. anger, emotional burst
4. intentional control, calm

says
1. intimidated, pretension of not knowing, excuse
2. request, offer, plain greeting, light negation
3. lost, upset
4. no idea

[ø]
1. upset

In this section, I have shown cases in which the same speech acts are reported with different dialogue-introducer tenses. They reflected the narrator's interpretation of the speaker's different psyches and attitudes that accompanied the utterances. We examined the following speech acts here:

1) variation of "I don't know"
2) variation of negation
3) variation of "what"

When people say, "I don't know," they may be simply unsure of the information requested, or they may intentionally calculate some effect of the words on the listener. The dialogue-introducer tenses reflect the speaker's psychology and the attitudes that the narrator sensed in the situations and wants to put into the output. The narrators use the present tense for the speaker's uncertain and unassured attitude in a weaker position, while they use the past tense for the more assured, firm attitude of the speaker in a stronger position.

The ways people utter negation and affirmation also sensitively reflect their different positioning and attitudes. People may lightly negate something, or firmly negate something. In the latter case, people may feel anger, blame, annoyance, irritation, or they may simply be trying to negate the least possibility of the issue in question. In repeated negation, people's attitudes may become stronger. The same applies to the people uttering affirmations. The narrator utilizes the dialogue-introducer tenses in order to contrast the weaknesses and strengths of the reported speakers' assuredness in uttering the dialogues.

Exclamatory remarks starting with "What . . ." and short exclamatory remarks consisting only of "What" usually express the emotion of being surprised or lost. The speakers have not grasped the situations. I have shown that they involve varying psychological situations. A speaker may be upset about something because she/he is not sure what is happening. Or a speaker may be irritated and angry, but not in the emotional phase of upset. The contrasting use of dialogue-introducer tense forms reflects such emotional situations related to upset. When people are upset, their emotion is reflected in the present tense. In contrast, when people are not upset but their psychological situations include anger or firmness, and the narrator chooses to highlight the firmness of attitude, then the past tense is used. If the remark accompanies neither the strong nor unassured emotion, they are simply reported following the CRM patterns. Or if there is a contrast or shift in upset, the present and the past are used for it in combination.

Accordingly, tense reflects the following attitudinal and informational contrasts:

Table 3

Past tense	strong positioning; firmness; assuredness
Present tense	weak positioning; non-assuredness; upset

In the same manner, I can analyze the tense-alternation in the following excerpt, which at a glance is hard to explain:

(27) Wait! Listen! So I look up and I see Kenny, who is a very good sailor, Marion, who swims well, and my Mom in the dingy. And they *say*, "All right, look, we'll meet you at shore." And Kenny *said*, "all right, I'll go back with it." So they . . . (Narrator's wife: Kenny, Kenny is the operator of the dingy [*sic*]!) (Wolfson 1982: 47)

The remarks introduced with "they say" and with "Kenny said" both contain similar speech acts of wrapping up the preceding conversations. It seems hard to tell what is motivating the tense differences in dialogue-introducers of these remarks. But now that we have discussed tense forms reflecting attitudinal contrast of the speakers, we can come up with the following attitudinal contrast related to the two similar remarks here:

(27)' they *say*: {wrapping up conversation, greeting} - (plain)
Kenny *said*:{wrapping up conversation, claim} - (as evidence for confidence)

Kenny, Marion, and the narrator's mother are in the dinghy. They are going out to sail, and greet the narrator with their first remark, "All right, look, we'll meet you at shore." The story actually ends up in disaster, with their mother dropping down into the water and almost drowning. Here the narrator emphasizes that they departed in good cheer, compared to the fear and danger that will soon arise. Such a disaster is the last thing likely to happen in this situation since Kenny is a very good sailor, and Marion is a very good swimmer. The narrator's wife interrupts here to emphasize that Kenny is the operator of the dinghy. To maximize the effect of the narration, the narrator establishes the fact that the characters departed with confidence. He adds Kenny's remark, "all right, I'll go back with it," in addition to his and other two people's general remark, "All right, look, we'll meet you at shore." The first remark is rather a plain greeting, but the second remark, by Kenny, is added to emphasize the fact that he declared that he would go back with the dinghy. This is presented as evidence of Kenny's confidence in his sailing ability and the group's safety. The narrator stressed this subtle attitudinal factor, and it is well reflected in the use of the past tense for Kenny's assured, firm attitude at strong positioning. But it is not correct to say that the first remark introduced with "they say" reflects an unassured, weak attitude. It is better to say that in order to stress Kenny's confident and assured attitude, the narrator utilized the tense-shift from the present to the past.

It is important to note that the dialogue-introducer tenses are most often used in combinations or pairs. In some cases, contrasting tense forms reflect an actual attitudinal contrast, such as assuredness versus insecurity, or strong versus weak positioning. But in other cases, the tense contrast is used to highlight the attitude that accompanies one of the remarks. For instance, to emphasize the assuredness in one remark, the tense may shift from the present into the past, whether or not the preceding utterances reflected insecurity. Or, to focus on a weak position in one remark, the previous and subsequent remarks may be introduced with past-tense dialogue-introducers. The description of the attitudinal contrast depends, in most of the cases, on the narrator's subjective view of the situation and her/his interpretation of the human relationships. It depends on the narrator's conscious or unconscious decisions, which she/he makes in real time over the course of the narration, in order to communicate most effectively to the audience what she/he thinks the point of the story is.[11]

4.4. CONCLUSION

In turning thoughts into words and passing it on to somebody else, a narrator makes a creative effort to conduct the process as effectively as possible. The narrator wants to convey mental imagery as close as possible to her/his own. This chapter discussed the ways dialogue-introducer tense is one of the conversational devices available to the narrator for this purpose. It reflects how the narrator interprets the nature of information in utterances, human relations, and the attitudes of the speakers.

First, we saw that the present tense and the past tense contrast the searching mode with the resultative mode. Next, the same contrast applies to attitudes of conflict avoidance versus conflict escalation. Third, the present tense and the past tense contrast weak versus strong attitudes, with the past tense reflecting degrees of certainty, assuredness, and firmness, while the present tense reflecting degrees of upset emotions. The following table summarizes the contrasts:

Present tense:
1) search; new move; supposition; future perspective; addition
2) watching the situation; suspension; step back; excuse; emotional highlight
3) weak positioning; non-assuredness; upset

Past tense:
1) decision; conclusion; clear and positive attitude
2) conflict; challenge; never-intimidated attitude
3) strong positioning; firmness; assuredness

Overall, the past tense introduces a stronger and more assured attitude than the present.

When there are such attitudinal contrasts, why do narrators not clearly verbalize them? Why do they use dialogue-introducer tenses to mark attitudinal contrasts indirectly? The attitudinal factors are most often background contexts accompanying the narrative story-lines. But they certainly are the significant factors that help narrators guide their audiences to understand the point of the story. By using tense forms, narrators can convey such background information without lexicalizing it. In an indirect style, narrators use more lexical reporting verbs to carry speakers' attitudinal factors, such as "he claimed," "I suspected," "she shouted," and so on. But in the direct reporting style, dialogue-introducers are more neutral place markers, without variational lexical meanings that carry speakers' attitudes. Therefore, tense form is a useful means of interweaving into stories those attitudinal factors that are not sufficiently expressed by the verb itself.[12]

The attitudinal contrast between the reported speakers depends on the narrator's subjective bias and egocentrism. The story is developed according to the narrator's mental imagery which is constructed upon her/his interpretation of the event, and her/his purpose in telling the story. Therefore, the tense realization in each story is, in a sense, individualistic and particular to each situation. It nonetheless follows certain patterns shared by narrators and their audiences, since one of the narrators' primary goals in telling a narrative is to convey their mental imagery to their audiences.

5

CONSCIOUSNESS FLOW, DISCOURSE ACTS, AND TENSE

5.0. OVERVIEW

When a storyteller has to sustain a long turn in conversation, one of the requirements and responsibilities of the storyteller's role is to present information in discourse as effectively as possible. A smooth flow of information in coherent discourse holds the listeners' attention. Spoken narratives, however, are often not as well organized as written narratives and tend to be full of incomplete sentences, repetition of phrases (Tannen 1989) or of stories (Dumas 1997), repairs (Moerman 1977; Schegloff et al. 1977; Schiffrin 1987), digressions, and so on. In fact, these very features of conversational narratives make them attractive and attendable. Spoken narratives are produced along the narrators' natural consciousness flow following the sequence of events, and going back and forth between the narrative, meta-narrative, and para-narrative levels (McNeill 1992) to relate the story to the audience. The narrator's consciousness is thus a key factor for oral narrative development.

Emmott (1997: 76) claims that one of the major aims of discourse study is "to recognize units of structure and meaning above the level of the sentence." In the past, linguists considered only sentences as having structure, and regarded texts simply as conglomerates of sentences. However, a text has its own hierarchical structure. Larger structural units do exist, as texts consist of series of groups of sentences or even smaller 'intonation units' (Chafe 1994), with each group functioning together as a unit and having its own internal structure.[1] Thus, Emmott (1997: 85) further claims that text has overt connectivity. Smaller units such as sentences and intonation units are organized so that they flow from each other and this connection is often signaled linguistically.[2] This chapter views dialogue-introducers as linguistic markers to signal this connectivity between discourse units, and views their tenses as devices to mark the flow of consciousness over a series of discourse units.

I will show that dialogue-introducer tense manipulation (e.g., "X says" vs. "X said") often reflects modulation of narrators' 'consciousness flow' (Chafe 1994) and 'discourse acts' (Sinclair and Coulthard 1975; Tsui 1994). I shall begin by clarifying in 5.1., the descriptive units of conversational interaction upon which I will base my analyses. I will discuss discourse organization units such as act, move, pair, and exchange. In 5.2., I will characterize the flow of consciousness. Then, in 5.3., I will address two things: how dialogue-introducer tense-shifts relate to structures of moves and exchanges within conversational organizations embedded in narratives, and how the narrators' consciousness flow shapes such reported conversational organizations. By using Consciousness Stream Models, I will illustrate the correlations among discourse organization, consciousness flow, and shifts in dialogue-introducers. Specifically, I will first examine exchanges such as adjacency pair and three-part exchange. I will next examine the development of a narrative line over a series of remarks. Then I will address the repetition of dialogue-introducers, in the cases of pre-posing and post-posing dialogue-introducers, and repetitions at restatements. The whole analysis covers different directional tense-shifts, and demonstrates the significant functions of such tense forms as "I says," "he say," "I saying," that have been hitherto considered 'ungrammatical' or 'mistakes.'[3]

The previous two chapters looked at dialogue-introducer tense as (1) the manifestation of cognitive operation in the recall process, and (2) an attitudinal contrasting device. This chapter examines discourse organization in detail, and investigates the use of dialogue-introducers that seem to behave irregularly according to other frameworks.

5.1. Discourse Organization Units

A speaker organizes remembered events into discrete chunks in memory (Chafe 1977a: 222; Bower and Cirilo 1985: 97). In order to analyze how a speaker narrates events, it is significant to know how she/he separates events and organizes them into a discourse. As a descriptive framework for analyzing spoken discourse, I will follow Sinclair and Coulthard (1975) and Tsui (1994) for their choices of descriptive units: act, move, and exchange.

The 'act' is a unit in discourse (Sinclair and Coulthard 1975), characterized according to its function in the discourse:

the acts are characterized in terms of how they are related to each other in the discourse rather than the kind of function they are independently used to perform. (Tsui 1994: 10)

Thus 'discourse acts' are different from 'speech acts' (Austin 1962; Searle 1969), in which an 'act' refers to the action that is performed in making an utterance. Tsui (1994: 9) claims that in speech act theory, utterances are taken in isolation and no consideration is given to the discourse context in which the utterance occurs. Rather, the kind of speech act being performed is determined by considerations like the meaning conveyed by the words, the structures of utterances, the psychological conditions of the speaker, and so forth.[4]

The 'utterance' or 'turn' simply means everything one speaker says before another speaker begins to speak (Sacks et al. 1974; Tsui 1994: 7). It is not the smallest unit. Goffman (1981b: 23) points out that the talk during an entire turn cannot be used for a unit of analysis:

> one of the main patterns for chaining rounds is the one in which whoever answers a question goes on from there to provide the next question in the series, thereby consolidating during one turn at talk two relevantly different doings.

The following excerpt from a classroom discourse shows that 'turn' is not the smallest unit:

(1) T: Can you tell me why do you eat all that food?
    P: To keep you strong.
    T: To keep you strong. Yes. To keep you strong. Why do you want to be strong? (Sinclair and Coulthard 1975: 21)

T is a teacher, while P is a pupil. There are three turns. In the last turn, the teacher is doing two things: a follow-up and an initiation. It means that there are two 'moves' in the last turn. The organization of (1) is the following:

(1)' T: [initiation]
     P: [response]
     T: [follow-up] + [initiation]

'Move' is the smallest unit of discourse. It is made up of one or more than one act (Sinclair and Coulthard 1975: 23). The following example is again from a classroom setting:

(2) T: What does the next one mean? You don't often see that one around here. Miri.
    P: Danger falling rocks.
    T: Danger falling rocks. (Ibid.: 67)

This exchange is made up of three moves: an initiation, a response, and a follow-up. The first move by the teacher is further made up of three acts: a question, a statement, and a nomination. When a 'move' consists of more than one act as in the first turn in (2), it has obligatory and optional acts. The main act is the 'head act' which carries the discourse function of the entire move. It is obligatory. The rest are auxiliary or subsidiary acts, and they are optional. They are 'pre-head act' (or starter) and 'post-head act.' The first move in (2) is made up of an obligatory head act with two post-head acts (Tsui 1994: 13). The organization of (2) is the following:

(2)' T: [initiation move: {head act (question)} + {post-head act (statement)} + {post-head act (nomination)}]
     P: [response move]
     T: [follow-up move]

Two other important notions to describe conversational organizations, 'pair' and 'sequence' have yet to be defined. A 'pair' is made up of two turns taken by two different speakers (Schegloff and Sacks 1973; Sacks et al. 1974), and a 'sequence' is made up of more than one turn (Schegloff 1972; Sinclair and Coulthard 1975; Tsui 1994: 7).

As a basic conversational organization, Schegloff and Sacks (1973) propose the 'adjacency pair':

> Given the recognizable production of a first pair part, on its first possible completion its speaker should stop and a next speaker should start and produce a second pair part from the pair type of which the first is recognizably a member. (p. 296)

Utterances are related to form pair types so that a particular first pair part sets up the expectation of a particular second pair part. For instance, adjacency pairs are request-compliance, question-answer, greeting-greeting, offer-acceptance/refusal, and so forth. Schiffrin (1987: 84) defines adjacency pairs as "sequentially constrained pairs in which the occurrence of a first-pair-part creates a slot for the occurrence of a second-pair-part (a conditional relevance)." In real time communication, in such pairs, the non-occurrence of that second-pair-part is heard as officially absent (Schegloff and Sacks 1973; Schiffrin 1987: 84). There are semantic and pragmatic constraints for such adjacency pairs in immediate interactions.[5]

Sinclair and Coulthard (1975) and Tsui (1994) propose that a 'three-part exchange,' rather than an 'adjacency pair,' is the basic conversational organization. They claim that a typical exchange has three elements of structure: an initiation, a response, and a follow-up, as we already saw in (1) and (2). Tsui (1994: 29) raises the following example:

(3) B: Where where is he staying?
    A: He's staying at the ah the Chung Chi Guest House.
    B: Oh I see.

Goffman (1981b) also claims that three-part interchanges are typical in 'ritual interchanges' (Goffman 1967c). The general function of the follow-up move is to acknowledge the outcome of the interaction (Tsui 1994: 41). More precisely, it is evaluative (Berry 1981; Burton 1981; Coulthard and Brazil 1981), and shows acceptance of a preceding interaction (J. Davidson 1984). It further indicates the change of one's state of knowledge (Heritage 1984; Berry 1987; Schiffrin 1987), showing appreciation for the response (Goffman 1971; 1976), and thus saves face (Goffman 1971).

The concepts of act, move, turn, pair, and exchange will be important units in the following analysis of narrative dialogue organization with tense shifts.

5.2. CONSCIOUSNESS FLOW IN DISCOURSE

Language is a constantly changing process, and the constantly changing nature of language is the result of the restless movement of consciousness (James 1890; Chafe 1994; 1997). The metaphor of a 'stream' of speech captures the fluid quality of language. Chafe (1994) characterizes the overall nature of consciousness as "it involves the activation of small portions of the experiencer's self-centered model of the surrounding world" (p. 39). He presents the following as its constant properties (Chafe 1996: 38):[6]

(a) Consciousness has both a focus and a periphery.
(b) Consciousness is dynamic, with its restless movement from one focus to the next.
(c) Consciousness has a point of view.
(d) Consciousness has an orientation in space, time, society, and ongoing activity.

Chafe (1994) describes language and consciousness following the concept of the 'stream of consciousness' by the psychologist and philosopher William James (1890).

James claims that the stream of consciousness or the stream of thought is a continuous, unbroken stream. Relating the stream of consciousness to language, he claims that "large tracts of human speech are nothing but signs of direction in thought" (James 1890: 248-49). At the same time, the stream of consciousness has different pace of its parts, which Chafe compares to a bird's life that is composed of an alternation of flights and perchings: "The rhythm of language expresses this, where every thought is expressed in a sentence, and every sentence closed by a period" (James 1890, 1: 243). This is indeed very basic at every level of linguistic organization from sound, word, sentence, to discourse. Each sound has onset and coda. Each word has strong and weak accent. Each sentence has rising and falling intonation. Each discourse is divided and organized into certain length of sentences expressed generally by stops in spoken forms and by periods in written forms.

In narratives, consciousness dynamically flows and rests moving from one focus to the next, according to the interest of a narrator who is a conscious organism situated in a background orientation. Narrating interactional speeches between multiple participants or even in a single speaker's continuous speech, a speaker's consciousness flows like a stream and rests at islands on its way. In the following sections, I will examine how a narrator's consciousness shapes the organization and presentation of narratives. I will discuss how it relates to tense manipulations of narrative dialogue-introducers.

5.3. CONSCIOUSNESS FLOW IN NARRATIVE DIALOGUES

When a person tells a story, the person presents each separate sub-section of the story sequentially. Of course, she/he may have set a certain story plan with a certain motivation for telling a story.[7] She/he has some preset schema for the story. But what the narrator is actually doing at the time of storytelling or narrating the past events is to activate each small information chunk at a time and proceed on a flow from one focus to the next.[8]

For a discourse to be coherent, it must be organized around a topic. It may also have subtopics and extended supertopics. As Chafe (1997: 42) points out:

> In a typical situation that arises during a conversation, someone will open a basic-level topic, too big to be in active consciousness all at once, and successive foci will then navigate within it until its content has been judged to have been adequately covered. There are likely to be subtopics and sub-subtopics that emerge during this process, but any such hierarchical structure may be subject to modification as the development of the basic-level

topic proceeds, sometimes because of changes in plan by the person who introduced the topic, sometimes because other participants in the conversation may change its course in unanticipated ways.

Chafe (1994; 1997) suggests two different trajectories of topic development that keep language moving. One is an interplay between two interlocutors. The other is a self-sustaining monologic schema, of which narratives are a typical example. An initial setting establishes a background for a complicating action, which in turn leads on to a climax, after which a coda wraps up the topic as a whole.

Dialogues contained in narratives also have two schema types. One is a monologic schema, in which case a narrator may narrate her/his own speech or some other person's speech. In the other, a narrator narrates an interplay between two interlocutors. Let me illustrate one instance of topic developments in a narrative schema, in a very simplified way:[9]

Figure 1: Instance of Topic Development Schema of Narrative

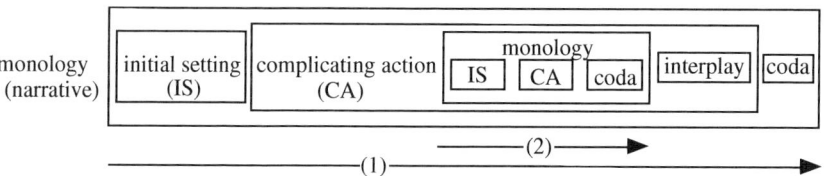

In this schema, a narrator's consciousness flows like a stream. At the level of whole narrative topic development, the consciousness starts flowing at the initial stage, and it flows on to a climax in complicating actions, then it rests at the coda. The consciousness flow is indicated by the rightward arrow (1). At the level of smaller units, consciousness also flows and rests at the initial stage and the coda. In this instance, in the monology embedded in the complicating actions, there is a flow and rest, as indicated by the arrow (2). At each level of hierarchical structure of narrative, there are both a flow and a rest of consciousness. The narrative development, matching the narrator's consciousness flow, guides a hearer's consciousness flow, fulfilling the hearer's expectation and curiosity.

Proceeding according to a narrative schema, a narrator activates each separate sub-part of the story one at a time. In the following section, I will show that the use of dialogue-introducers is motivated by such activation in a flow. I will also show that in narrative-embedded dialogues, consciousness flows and rests in relation to the move structure and also in relation to the sequence of discourse acts, and that such consciousness-flow-modulations are closely related to tense-shift in conversational storytelling.

5.3.1. Consciousness flow in exchanges

5.3.1.1. Adjacency pair

In an immediate communication, when one employs the first part of adjacency pairs such as question, invitation, offer, or greeting, the addressed person is expected to give the second part of the pair, such as answer, acceptance, agreement, or greeting. Similarly, in reporting a past event, when we start reporting the first part of an adjacency pair, we are naturally expected to continue by reporting the second part:

(4) A: X said, "How are you?" → Y said, "Good, thanks."
 A: X said, "Are you all right?"→ Y said, "Oh sure, no problem."
 A: X said, "Would you like some coffee?" → Y said, "No, thanks."
 A: X said, "What's up?" → Y said, "I just feel kind of bad."

Of course, in many cases in narrative-embedded dialogues, it is up to the narrator whether to complete reporting the pair or not, depending on what the narrative's point is and how she/he organizes the narrative. Still, there are cases in which dialogues are reported following the expectation in adjacency pairs, in which where there is an onset, a coda follows. A narrator's attention and consciousness flow according to such an expectation, and accordingly she/he chooses sub-sections of events and organizes them.[10] It is coherent and consistent in a certain span of discourse. Following the speaker's own consciousness flow, the information flows, and the listener's consciousness flows. Such discourse organization according to expectation matches the conversational maxims and the cooperative principle enunciated by Grice (1975):

> Cooperative Principle: Make your conversational contribution such as is required, at the stage at which it occurs, by the accepted purpose or direction of the talk exchange in which you are engaged. (p. 307)

The narrator needs to give required or expected information, which is the coda of the adjacency pair. In the case of the discourse flow in narratives, however, the speaker is not deliberately cooperating with expectation. Rather, what is at work in constructing narratives, I claim, is consciousness. A narrator's consciousness shapes a narrative organization, over which it flows naturally, and which presumably meets the narrator's and listener's expectation and information structure. Thus, when it is natural to complete adjacency pairs, a narrator gives both the onset and coda, while when the narrator's consciousness is not focusing on the fulfillment of adjacency pairs, the narrator simply does not complete them.[11]

In any event, one of the simplest patterns of the consciousness flow is the adjacency pair of onset and coda, which is closely related to the relationship between discourse topics and comments.[12] When a speaker introduces a topic in discourse, there is a move to comment on it, and that is what the audience expects, too. The following excerpt contains two adjacency pairs of statement and agreement. A female singer is telling how she came to work in a musical. She mentions that it was her sister who started planning their work in the musical:

(5)   . . . And she *says*, "You know, one of these days I'm going to write your life story." I *said*, "Well, great. Go ahead." And sure enough, down through the years, she came to Vegas, where I live now, and she *says*, "I got the idea. And I'm going to write it about your life story, and that way we can work together and you don't have to be away from home so much. You can be with us." I *said*, "Well, go ahead." . . .   (EJ 1995. 8: 16)

The first utterance is an initiation, which contains a statement of future perspective and an offer. It directs the narrator's consciousness to a response, which is a clear agreement ("Well, great. Go ahead."). Since the first remark is not a speaker's declaration of her own future but her offer to her sister, it is reasonable that her sister gives some kind of reaction to the offer. Then another similar adjacency pair is reported again. The move structures and dialogue-introducers in this case are as follows:

(5)'   X *says* [initiation] → Y *said* [response]
       X *says* [initiation] → Y *said* [response]

For reporting an initiation move, the present tense ("she says") is used, while the past tense ("I said") is used for reporting a response move. At the initiation move, the consciousness starts flowing, till it reaches the response where it rests. The speaker's consciousness 'flies and perches' in a rhythmic cycle in this excerpt. The listener's curiosity is aroused and satisfied cyclically, too. In other words, consciousness flows in search and rests in satisfaction. The flow and rest of consciousness can thus be modeled as follows:

128   *Reporting Discourse, Tense, and Cognition*

(5)" Consciousness Stream Model (CSM)

MV	[Initiation]	[Response]	[Initiation]	[Response]
DA	{Offer}	{Agreement}	{Offer}	{Agreement}
CF	start ──────▶ rest	start ──────▶ rest
DI	*says*	*said*	*says*	*said*
S	SHE	I	SHE	I

──────────────────── Discourse flow ────────────────────▶

(MV = Move)
(DA = Discourse Act)
(CF = Consciousness Flow)
(DI = Dialogue-Introducer [Verb])
(S = [Reported] Speaker)

An arrow outside the box indicates a consciousness flow at the level of the whole discourse. Inside the box, the rightward arrows show areas where consciousness flows, while vertical lines show points where consciousness rests.[13] At the introduction of the first utterance, which is an offer, the consciousness starts flowing. At the response, which is an agreement, the consciousness rests. At the second offer, the consciousness starts flowing again, until it reaches an agreement which is the resting point. Note that this model shows only the relationship of the dialogues to consciousness. As I discussed already, narratives have many layers of information interwoven at different levels. This example (5) is an excerpt from a larger narrative, where the narrator sets up background contexts and other events. Even between the first and the second adjacency pairs, there is a non-dialogic narration of the sister's actions. Following the dialogues the narrator talks about her and her sister's next moves. The consciousness continues to flow all through the narrative. In fact, the whole narrative is a response to an interview question. So on a broader scale, even before the narrator starts narrating, her consciousness had started flowing. At every part of the narrative, each cluster of events participates in directing, accelerating, and stopping the flow. The above model illustrates in a simplified fashion how dialogues relate to the stream of consciousness on a much smaller level. The reason I focus specifically on dialogues is to illustrate how narrators choose to report particular pieces of speech, arrange them, and choose dialogue-introducer forms and tenses. I will restrict my discussion mainly to dialogue-introducer tenses, which are the central concern of this chapter: why and how the tense switches and shifts along with the procession of discourse.

The next excerpt contains similar cyclic occurrences of adjacency pairs, but the move structure is more complicated:

(6) there wz anothuh girl walking around she *says* hhh uh-dihyou know where the science building is 'n I *said-* well I *said-* yihknow, the guard jus' told me thet this wz the bui:lding. So she *seh-* hh are you goin here fer 'n-hh fer en in:dian class by any chance 'n I *said* yes hh So I *said* c'mon we'll fi:nd it tuhgethuh (TG: 17-18)

The move structure in this excerpt is the following:

(6)' (a) X *says* [initiation] → [response Y *said* {pre-head act} + Y *said* {head act}]
X *say* [initiation] → Y *said* [response] + Y *said* [initiation (finality)]

It shows that a dialogue-introducer marks each move and act. The first pair contains a girl's initiation move and the narrator's response. The response move is made up of a pre-head act, which serves as the attitudinal marker (Schiffrin 1987; see also chapter 4), and a head act. The dialogue-introducing verb "says" is used for the initiation move and "said" for the response move. "Said" is repeated for each act in the response move. The second pair starts again with the girl's initiation move, which is introduced with "say." In (5), the first and the second moves were both introduced with "says," while here in (6), "say" is used in the second move. Narrators often use "say" to mark utterances in the midst of the flow. It indicates that in (6) the first and second pairs were produced repeatedly without interruption, thus the initiation of the second pair is not only the start of the flow of the pair but also is already in the flow at the whole dialogue level. (I will discuss the use of "say" in detail later.) The final turn is made up of two moves: a response move and the initiation of a new move. "Said" introduces the response. Although the last move is a new move which may be introduced with "says" or "say" according to our discussion so far, it is the end of this sequence of exchanges that the narrator reports in this narrative. In the original discourse a response for this initiation such as "All right" may have been produced, but it is not included in this narrative. The inclusion of any succeeding interactions such as "All right" could have changed the dialogue-introducers extracted in (6)'(a) to the ones indicated in the following:

(6)' (b) X *says* [initiation] → [response Y *said* {pre-head act} + Y *said* {head act}]
X *say* [initiation] → Y *said* [response] + <u>Y *say(s)* [initiation]</u> → <u>X *said* [response]</u>

In (6), the last move is an initiation but is indeed the end of the sequence of exchanges. The last "said" reflects two facts: it introduces the second part of the adja-

130   *Reporting Discourse, Tense, and Cognition*

cency pair; and there are no more dialogues reported. The consciousness flow in this excerpt is modeled as follows:

(6)" CSM

MV	[Initiation]	[Response]		[Initiation]	[[Response]	[Initiation]]
DA	{Q}	{A}	{A}	{Q}	{A}	{invitation}
CF	start ──▶	rest		start ──▶	rest	start ──▶
DI	*says*	*said*	*said*	*say*	*said*	*said*
S	SHE	I	I	SHE	I	I

──────────────── Discourse flow ────────────────▶

(Q=question; A=answer)

There are different levels of the consciousness flow. At the level of whole discourse topic development, the consciousness keeps flowing, as indicated by the long arrow outside the box. At the level of reporting dialogue exchanges, the consciousness keeps flowing as indicated by the long arrow within the box. At the level of each individual move, the consciousness flows and rests sequentially. The vertical line at the right end shows the termination of the flow of consciousness, while there are more frequent temporary pauses in the flow of consciousness, indicated by dotted vertical lines.

In the next excerpt, the flow modulation includes nonverbal behaviors. It also shows that the flow is marked by other linguistic forms as well as by tense-alternation:

(7)   . . . he comes running down the aisle, screaming at the airline hostess, "Does this plane go to Madrid?" and she finally *said*, "Yes," so she *says*, "Sit down," you know, so he finally went in the back and sat down.

(Wolfson 1982: 51)

The utterances in this excerpt are actually contained in one simple dialogue:

Man   : Does this plane go to Madrid?
Airline hostess : Yes, sit down.

But the way the narrator presents this dialogue reflects a more complicated move structure in the exchange and the consciousness flow. First, the narrator separates the airline hostess's turn "Yes, sit down" into two moves, i.e., a response ("Yes") and an initiation ("sit down"), prefacing each move with a dialogue-introducer. Second, for each dialogue-introducer, the narrator uses different tenses: the past tense ("said") for a response move, the present tense ("says") for the initiation of a new move, which is an invitation. Third, although there is no explicit verbal reaction to the airline hostess's invitation, the narrator completes it by telling of the man's nonverbal reaction. This reaction is reported with the past-tense verb "went." Fourth, for each response move, the narrator uses the adverb "finally" to indicate a move boundary. The move structure in this excerpt is the following:

(7)' X *screaming* [initiation] → Y (*finally*) *said* [response]
+ Y *says* [initiation] → X (*finally*) *went* [response]

The consciousness flow is modeled as follows:

(7)" CSM

MV	[Initiation]	[[Response]	[Initiation]]	[Response]
DA	{Q}	{A}	{Invitation}	{Action}
CF	start ──────▶	rest	start ──────▶	rest
DI	screaming	finally said	says	finally went
S	HE	SHE	SHE	HE

──────────────── Discourse flow ────────────────▶

We can observe that the use of dialogue-introducers and their tenses correlates with the discourse structure and the consciousness flow. The dialogue-introducers are used at the boundaries of moves. The present-tense dialogue-introducer appears when the consciousness flows, whereas the past tense conveys a sense of finality, which is also marked with the use of the adverb "finally." Interestingly, the past-tense dialogue-introducer is used at the boundary of moves even in the same turn, and this type of move boundary concurs with the pause in the consciousness flow within the turn.

From what we have observed in natural narratives so far, we can assume that when people report exchanges orally, they do not simply introduce each turn with a past-tense dialogue-introducer as in (4). Instead they use dialogue-introducers and tense variations in more flexible ways. For instance, when people report an exchange such as (8), what they produce in natural discourse is not always like (8)'(a). They may very likely produce a narrative discourse like (8)'(b) that shows the consciousness flow along with the discourse unit boundaries.

(8) X: How are you doing?
     Y: Good. Would you like some coffee?
     X: Oh, yeah.

(8)' (a) X *said*, "How are you doing?" Y *said*, "Good. Would you like some coffee?" X *said*, "Oh, yeah."
     (b) X *says*, "How are you doing?" and Y *said*, "Good." So Y *say*, "Would you like some coffee?" so finally X *said*, "Oh, yeah."

5.3.1.2. Three-part exchange

As Sinclair and Coulthard (1975) and Tsui (1994) propose, a 'three-part exchange' is the basic conversational organization; and thus, it is frequently reported in narratives. In the following narrative excerpt, the italicized part is the three-part exchange (with verbs underlined):

(9) *Anyway, we <u>went</u> to the Smiths' house after dinner and Mr. Smith very nicely <u>says</u>, "Would you like some brandy?" So I <u>said</u>, "Yes, I will have some brandy." So he <u>says</u>, "We have some very nice brandy." He <u>adds</u> that.* Then he goes to this cupboard and he opens it up and he said, "Too bad, you can't have any brandy 'cause I can't find any brandy snifters." . . . So he says, "Well, if that's the case," he said, "I will find you some other glasses."
(Wolfson 1982: 51)

The italicized part contains an initiation, a response, and a follow-up. It has the following move structure:

(9)' Y *went* <setting up a background>
     → X *says* [initiation] → Y *said* [response] → X *says* [follow-up]

The follow-up move is an additional remark, as indicated by the post-posed comment "He adds that." It acknowledges (Tsui 1994) and appreciates (Goffman 1971) the response. The narrator's point in including the follow-up move in this context is to stress Mr. Smith's confidence in the brandy and his delight to serve it, in contrast to the anticipated problem of his not being able to find brandy snifters.

In terms of the consciousness flow in (9), consciousness starts flowing at the initiation move and rests at the response, as in the adjacency pair. Since the follow-up is simply an additional move that acknowledges and accepts the outcome of the preceding interaction, the consciousness is still resting or floating at this point. It does not yet proceed to the next move. The consciousness flows according to the following model:

(9)" CSM

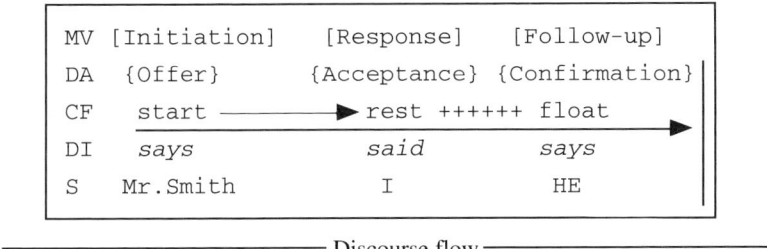

It shows two ways of dialogue-introducer tense-shifting. The dialogue-introducer tense shifts from "says" to "said" when the consciousness flows and pauses, while it shifts from "said" to "says" when there is an additional follow-up move.

5.3.2. Consciousness flow over a series of remarks

5.3.2.1. In a single speaker's speech

The rest of the italicized part of (9) is neither an adjacency pair nor a three-part exchange, but a continuous report of a single speaker's speech. Its dialogue-introducers still show tense variations. Below, I repeat (9) but now have italicized the part of a single speaker's speech:

(10) Anyway, we went to the Smiths' house after dinner and Mr. Smith very nicely says, "Would you like some brandy?" So I said, "Yes, I will have some brandy." So he says, "We have some very nice brandy." He adds that. *Then he goes to this cupboard and he opens it up and he said, "Too bad, you can't have any brandy 'cause I can't find any brandy snifters." . . . So he says, "Well, if that's the case," he said, "I will find you some other glasses."*

(=9)

Although the italicized part is a report of a single speaker's speech, it has a similar structure to that which we saw in adjacency pairs and in three-part exchanges. When we interpret the meaning of 'move,' more broadly, we can say that a single person's series of remarks in the italicized part in (10) consists of combinations of an initiation and a resultative move. The first move, which is nonverbal, is Mr. Smith's search for brandy snifters. It is an initiation. It results in his remark that he failed to find them. His next remark, "Well, if that's the case, I will find you some other glasses," is reported in two separate parts, introduced with separate dialogue-introducers. The conditional clause, "Well, if that's the case," is an initiation move, with which he starts searching for alternatives. It results in his stating a conclusion: "I will find you some other glasses." The move structure is thus seen as follows:

(10)' X *goes* + *opens* [initiation] → X *said* [result]
+ X *says* [initiation (conditional)] → X *said* [result (conclusion)]

The tense shifts from the present to the past cyclically, in conjunction with the shift from the initiation moves to the resultative moves. The consciousness flows along with the shifts as in the following model:

(10)" CSM

MV	[Initiation]	[Result]	[[Initiation]	[Result]]
DA	{Action, Search}	{Statement}	{Search}	{Conclusion}
CF	start ──────────▶	rest	start ──────────▶	rest
DI	goes+opens	said	says	said
S	HE	HE	HE	HE

──────────────── Discourse flow ────────────────▶

The narrator manipulates the move structure even at the clausal level, and the consciousness flows along with the structure.

The following example includes an instance of similar introductions of the separate parts of speaker's turn:

(11) And she *says*, "We have lots of room," she *said*, "even for-" Gary has a big dog, she *said*, "even for the dog!" So, it's really nice eh: y'know t'renew friendship.   (Schiffrin 1987: 206)

"We have lots of room," is the start of a remark, as yet unfinished. The narrator continues the report with "even for-," to finish the sentence. Here the narrator intends to report the reported speaker's humorous utterance that her house is big enough and has room even for a big dog. But the narrator is interrupted by a thought that the listener does not know that Gary, the reported speaker, has a dog. So she mentions the dog ("Gary has a big dog"). Then she ends the remark by "even for the dog!" In this case, it may be better to say that the turn is made up of one move, which consists of a head act and a post-head act:

(11)' [X *says* {head act} → X *said* {post-head act}]

The first act initiates the speech, and the post-head act concludes or wraps up the turn. Even though they are not separate moves, they convey a consciousness flow similar to the one in the initiation-result move structure. Separate dialogue-introducers are used to distinguish between the different sorts of acts. Tense shifts along with the shifts in the discourse acts.

In reporting a single speaker's speech, a narrator often separates the speech into several acts, and introduces each part with a dialogue-introducer. A narrator also uses different dialogue-introducer tenses according to the nature of the acts and the consciousness flow. Let us examine more cases of discourse acts and dialogue-introducer tense manipulations. Contrast the following two excerpts from narratives with similar formats. In (12), the narrator's mother issues a directive to her son (the narrator's brother) who was going out with a non-Jewish girl:

(12) And my mother *says*, "Now Jerry," And this is the God's honest truth. I'm not gonna hold no punches, y'don't want me to, do y'babe? She *said*, "I don' want y't'marry that- and I want y't'break it off right now."
(Ibid.: 243)

In (13), the narrator reports an argument between her husband and herself. She has been complaining that her daughter-in-law does not call her "Mom." She states that it is imperative to start using this form of address in the beginning of their relationship, and offers three examples to support her point. The following excerpt presents the third example that reports a disagreement with her husband about this issue:

(13) Now I remember when I first got married, and I was in that situation. And eh the first- like the first . . . few times, I wouldn't say anything. And my husband *said* to me, "Now look, it isn't hard. Just say 'Mom.'" He *says*, "And I want y't'do it." (Ibid.)

The reported dialogues in (12) and (13) have similar situational contexts and verbal forms: each narrative consists of two consecutive reporting discourses; a family member makes a personal directive. In relation to these two interpersonal arguments, Schiffrin (1987: 243) claims that "Now" in (12)'s "Now Jerry" and "Now" in (13)'s "Now look" both indicate the recipients' prior resistance to the directives. The directives in both (12) and (13) are issued as insistence and persuasion. However, there is a significant difference between the two excerpts. Their dialogue-introducer tense-shifts are in opposite directions. In (12), the tense shifts from the present in "my mother says" into the past in "She said." In (13), the tense shifts from the past in "my husband said to me" into the present in "He says." I assume that this is due to the different act structures in the dialogues in two excerpts. Let me compare the dialogues in the two:

from (12): my mother *says*, "Now Jerry," . . .
She *said*, "I don' want y't'marry that- and I want y't'break it off right now."
from (13): my husband *said* to me, "Now look, it isn't hard. Just say 'Mom.'"
He *says*, "And I want y't'do it."

They both have one initiation move, which starts with an act of summons followed by a directive. But the act structures are different:

(12)' [X *says* {pre-head act (summons)} → X *said* {head act (directive)}]

(13)' [Y *said* {pre-head act (summons)} {head act (directive)} → Y *says* {post-head act (confirmation)}]

In (12), the first reported segment is composed only of a summons, which is a pre-head act, and the second segment contains a directive, which is a head act. In contrast, in (13), the first segment has both a summons and a directive, a pre-head act and a head act. The second segment is a post-head act, confirming the directive. Thus, these two narratives have different information presentation formats. In (12), the first remark of a summons introduced with "my mother says" initiates the consciousness flow, which is on hold while the narrator gives some meta-narrative messages. Then the floating consciousness flows and reaches the resting point at the second remark, which is the directive. The consciousness flow from a pre-head act to a head act in this case parallels the flow along the move structure from an initiation to a response. This flow is modeled in CSM (12)". The dialogue-introducer tense shifts from the present ("says") to the past ("said") along with the consciousness flow. On the other hand, in (13), the first reported segment contains both summons and directive, which are the pre-head act and the head act. The consciousness already flows and rests in this one segment, and the interactive expectation is fulfilled at this point. The second segment is simply a confirmation which does not indicate a new move for the consciousness. The consciousness simply floats here. Such a floating consciousness at a post-head act parallels the floating consciousness at the follow-up move in (9). Recall the consciousness flow in the three-part exchange seen in (9). When the

Consciousness Flow, Discourse Acts, and Tense 137

(12)" CSM

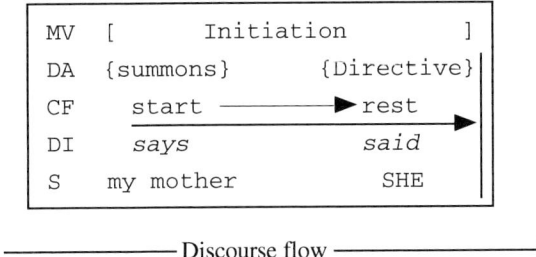

———————— Discourse flow ————————▶

consciousness proceeded from a response to a follow-up move, the consciousness was still resting, or floating at the point. Similarly, in (13), at the post-head act which is an additional act and does not start any new move, the consciousness is floating. Thus, the consciousness flow in (13) is modeled as follows:

(13)" CSM

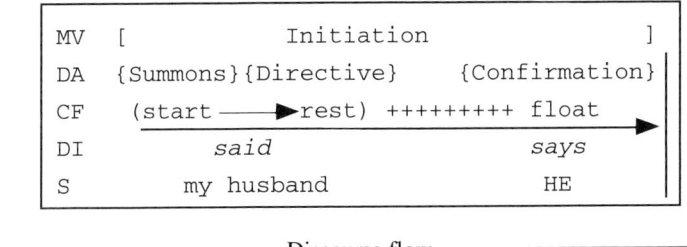

———————— Discourse flow ————————▶

The whole turn is one initiation move, which is made up of three acts. The consciousness flow starts at the pre-head act and rests at the head act. It floats at the post-head act. Since the narrator includes both the pre-head act and the head act in one quote, she first uses the past-tense dialogue-introducer ("my husband said to me") which indicates the resting of the flow of consciousness. For the additional remark where the consciousness floats, she uses the present tense ("He says").

By comparing Consciousness Stream Models (12)" and (13)", it is clear that the different consciousness flows are correlated with the opposite directions of dialogue-introducer tense-shift in these examples. In (12), in which the consciousness flows and rests, the present-tense verb "says" initiates the flow, which rests at the past-tense verb "said." In contrast, in (13), the past-tense verb "said" has already introduced period-like information, which does not introduce a new move. The second remark is a confirmation of the first remark, which is introduced with the present-tense verb "says."

So far, we have seen that the discourse act structure plays a significant role in a narrator's consciousness flow in reporting a single speaker's speech, just as the move structure does in reporting adjacency pairs or three-part exchanges. The narrator manipulates dialogue-introducers and their tenses along with the structural features. It is significant to note that when we examine act structures or move structures, we need to carefully consider the contextual information, i.e., how a certain utterance fits into the reporting frame in the narrative, and what the act or move actually does in the context. Consider the following excerpt, a conversation between the former U.S. President Jimmy Carter and Robert Fulghum, the best-selling author. Fulghum starts talking about Carter's private life:

(14) F: We watch your public life a lot, but I'd like to ask you some things about the life we don't see as much, things that are a little more private. We know a lot about your family, in a sense. I remember when you were first elected, and it seemed like it was a cast of unbelievable characters, and I thought people were making this up. I couldn't believe you had . . .

C: Let me tell you, one day the reporters came to Plains and *asked* Billy, "Billy, don't you think you're kind of a peculiar character?" He *says*, "Well, I've got a mother 70 years old in the Peace Corps, I've got a sister in her late 50s that's a leather biker—she rides a Harley-Davidson all the time. I've got a sister, another sister that's a Holy Roller preacher, I've got a brother that thinks he's going to be president." [long laughter] He *said*, "Why do you think I'm peculiar?" [long laughter]

(EJ 1997. 11: 3)

When Fulghum starts talking about Carter's family, Carter takes over the turn and elaborates it by reporting a particular interaction between the reporters and his brother Billy, by quoting their remarks. At a glance, the move structure in the interaction seems to be the following:

(14)' (a)   X *asked* [initiation]→ Y *says* [response] + Y *said* [initiation]

The reporters initiate the conversation by asking Billy a question, and Billy responds to it. After the response, he asks a question that starts a new initiation move. Such a move structure seems like it should be illustrated as in the following model, in which consciousness flows along with the structural features:

(14)"(a) CSM

MV	[Initiation]	[[Response]	[Initiation]]
DA	{Q}	{A}	{Q}
CF	start ────────▶	rest	start ────────▶
DI	*asked*	*says*	*said*
S	the reporters	HE	HE

──────────────── Discourse flow ────────────────▶

However, such featuring of the move structure and the consciousness flow runs counter to the tense-shift. I have already shown that the present-tense dialogue-introducer marks the flow, while the past-tense introducer marks a pause in the flow. I have claimed that dialogue-introducers and their tenses reflect the narrator's natural flow of consciousness along with the move or act structure in the report. But in the analysis of (14)'(a), the tense-shift is totally opposite to my prediction and appears to contradict my claim.

Let me reanalyze the move structure of Carter's report in (14), carefully taking the context into consideration. Fulghum starts talking about Carter's family, and when he is about to raise each family member by "I couldn't believe you had . . . ," Carter takes over the turn. Instead of simply listing family members, he tells about a particular occasion when his brother Billy was asked about his peculiar character and talked about his family. Carter chooses to provide the initiation move by the reporters as background information before getting into the main issue of how peculiar his family members are. To fully provide a background for the setting, he starts giving the context by saying, "one day the reporters came to Plains and asked Billy, 'Billy, don't you think you're kind of a peculiar character?'" Here he clarifies *when* ("one day") *where* ("Plains") *who* ("the reporters") did *what* ("asked") to *whom* ("Billy"). The mention of the reporters' question functions as background information, which is often reported with past-tense verbs. Recall (9) in which the background information ("we went to the Smiths' house after dinner") was reported with the past tense while "Then he goes to this cupboard and he opens it up" was reported with the present tense. Although both were nonverbal behaviors, the former functioned in the narrative as background information, while the latter was part of a consciousness flow in the main interactive issue. Here, in (14), the report of the reporters' remark initiates the interaction that signals the consciousness flow. But it is not a substantial part of what Fulghum and Carter are talking about in this narrative. Second, Billy's answer is reported in two parts. In proposing (14)'(a), I assumed that

140 *Reporting Discourse, Tense, and Cognition*

Billy's answer consisted of a response move and an initiation move. At first glance, this seems true. But the part "Why do you think I'm peculiar?" is in fact a rhetorical question which means, "That's why I don't think I'm peculiar." It wraps up his explanation on his family and concludes his answer to the question, "Billy, don't you think you're kind of a peculiar character?" rather than starting a new move. Thus, the two segmented reports are not separate moves but form one response move: the first part is a pre-head act; the second part is a head act that wraps up the response. In the first part, Billy raises peculiar characters of his family members and in the second part he concludes that in contrast he is not peculiar at all. His whole response is rhetorical, since he does not give a direct answer to the reporters' question but first raises his family members' peculiar characters and then questions whether he is peculiar in such a circumstance. From these points, I revise the analysis of the move structure in this narrative as follows:

(14)' (b) X asked [initiation] <setting up a background>
[response Y *says* {pre-head act} → Y *said* {head act (rhetorical question, resultative)}]

From a pre-head act to a head act, dialogue-introducer tense shifts from the present to the past. The consciousness flows accordingly, from the start of the response to the resultative claim. The consciousness flow in (14) is thus modeled as follows:

(14)"(b) CSM

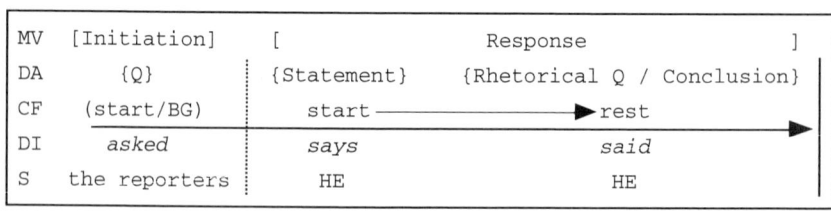

The initiation move is a background (BG). In a sense it starts the flow on the higher level of Carter's whole narrative, which is indicated by the longer arrow in the box. At the dialogue level, which is the main focus of the present analysis, the consciousness flow starts at the pre-head act, and rests at the head act which is the concluding remark. There are other points to support the theory that the initiation move functions as background information. First, it is clearly not a direct quote. As indicated by the dialogue-introducing part, "the reporters came to Plains and asked Billy," the subject of the report is plural ("the reporters"), and it is unlikely that all the reporters uttered the same question simultaneously. It is a choral dialogue which is a representation of what many people said (Tannen 1989) or a summarized report, rather than a direct quote of the utterance. Here the significance lies not in quoting the reporters' utterance, but in setting up the background for his brother's subsequent dialogues. Second, Carter introduces the reporters' utterance with "asked" which is a full lexical verb, rather than with a dialogue-introducing place-marker "say" as in other places.[14] Since the point in including the reporters' remark is to set up a clear contextual background, Carter uses a lexical verb that indicates the exact nature of the verbal event (Johnstone 1987: 42) rather than using "say." Therefore, the initiation move indeed functions to provide background information, so it is reported with a past-tense lexical verb. In the response move, along with the act structure of dialogues, consciousness flows and rests, so the dialogue-introducer tense shifts.

Note also that the pre-head act in (14) is not interrupted by dialogue-introducers, even though it is very long. It confirms that dialogue-introducers signal act boundaries as well as move boundaries. In the following, I will show that dialogue-introducers and their tense-shifts follow the development of story-lines.

5.3.2.2. Over a series of remarks

Flow of consciousness follows the development of a narrative line over a series of remarks. Dialogue-introducers mark the development, and their tenses shift when consciousness proceeds in conversational information from onset and flow to coda. The following excerpt from an interview of a female singer, Koko Taylor, involves tense-shift over a series of remarks. She tells how she met Willie Dixon and started recording:

(15) So, Willie Dixon heard me sitting in with them and after I was finished, he came over and *says*, he *says*, "My God, I never heard a woman sing the blues before like you sing the blues." He *saying*, "that's what the world needs today, a woman to sing the blues." He *say*, "We got plenty of mens out here singing." He *said*, "But we don't have no women, you know." He *said*, "That's why we need a woman to sing like you sing and to sing the blues." (EJ 1992. 3: 111-12)

Although the narrator does not report her reaction to Dixon's remarks, it is reasonable to assume that Taylor gave some kind of response in the original interaction. So this series of remarks by Dixon is a very long initiation move in the framework of an exchange format. The narrator has segmented it into some quotes, and introduces each segment with a dialogue-introducer. The discourse acts in this initiation move are 'informatives,'[15] which Tsui (1994: 135) characterizes as utterances that provide information, report events or states of affairs, recount personal experience, and express beliefs, evaluative judgments, feelings, and thoughts.[16] So, more specifically, what Dixon does in this initiation move is to assert his evaluative judgment of Taylor's song. It is positively directed to Taylor, so it is a compliment. Note, however, that it seems irrelevant to divide it into head act, pre-head act, or post-head act, since the utterances develop his idea in a series. In a sense, each part performs an obligatory step in the development of the coherent idea structure of the move. It is more significant to note the way the narrator segments his remarks as his assessment develops and constitutes a compliment.[17] The first quote, "My God, I never heard a woman sing the blues before like you sing the blues," reports his experience about gender and the blues, as a reaction to Taylor's song. It relates to the second part, "that's what the world needs today, a woman to sing the blues," with which Dixon assesses the world's needs, expressing his ideal concerning gender and the blues. Then the next two remarks further assess the world in terms of gender and the blues. The first part reports the present state ("We got plenty of mens out here singing"), and the second part points to the present problem ("But we don't have no women, you know"). The first and the second parts are Dixon's subjective assessments beginning with his exclamation. The next two parts are more objective assessments. The last quote, "That's why we need a woman to sing like you sing and to sing the blues," concludes his assessment, and presents his resolution for the present problem, namely, that Taylor, being a woman, should sing the blues. The move develops in a coherent series, in the following way:

(15)' [initiation {X *says* (experience) → X *saying* (ideal)} → {X *say* (factual) → X *said* (problem)} → {X *said* (resolution/conclusion)}]

The consciousness structure of this whole starts at the first remark, and flows over a series of remarks, to reach a conclusion where it finally rests. The narrator starts reporting with "he says," marks the development of the idea with "he saying" and "he say" where Dixon adds up information, and shifts to "he said" towards the end. But why exactly does the tense shift from "says" to "saying," and from "say," "said," to "said"? Upon a closer analysis, I would claim that the complicated tense-shift accompanies the consciousness flow in the act structure of the move. CSM (15)" illustrates the precise consciousness flows in this narrative. The narrator's consciousness is aroused at the opening exclamation "My God," where it naturally starts flowing. The present-tense dialogue-introducer "he says" is used here. The consciousness flows into the succeeding part where he mentions his ideal. Dixon's subjective assessment is complete here, but the consciousness does not rest but flows into the further remarks, as he continues the objective assessment. Such successive flow is expressed with "he saying," which bridges the flow between the closely related subjective and

(15)" CSM

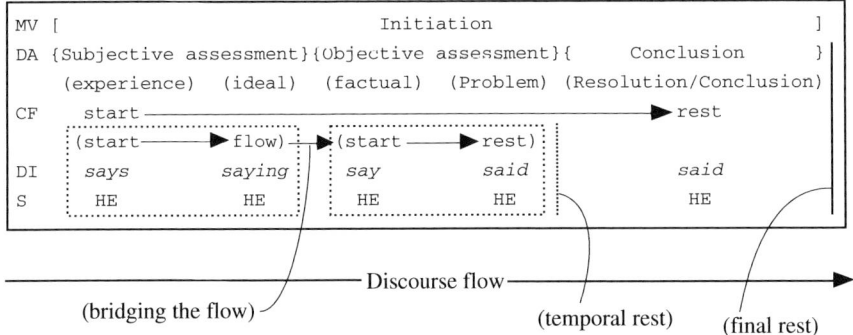

objective assessments. At the start of the objective assessment, the consciousness flow is marked with "he say." It receives the preceding flow and signals the further flow. Recall (6), in which the narrator used "she say" to mark an utterance in the midst of the flow, when reporting the speaker's continuous remark, as related to the preceding ones. The move structure in (6) was the following:

(6)' (a) X *says* [initiation] → [response Y *said* {pre-head act} + Y *said* {head act}]
X *say* [initiation] → Y *said* [response] + Y *said* [initiation (finality)]

"Says" marks the start of a flow at the level of the whole exchange, while "say" marks a successive flow when there is already a flow. Similarly, in (15) here, "he say" marks the start of the objective assessment, but the consciousness flow here is a successive one since the flow is carried over from the closely related preceding remarks with "he saying." The flow of consciousness temporarily rests at the end of the assessments with "he said." The whole flow finally rests at the conclusion which is introduced with "he said." Note also that Dixon's remark led by the progressive "he saying" indicates his forthcoming conclusion, which means that it is an evaluative point. According to Labov (1972b: 374), because the progressive indicates an event which is continuous and more extended in time, it momentarily breaks the sequence of action thereby calling attention to that part of the narrative and indicating to the listener that it has some connection with the evaluative point. Thus, the consciousness flow, begun with "he says," reaches a point, at "he saying" where the narrator indicates her/his connection to the story's purpose. At the same time the narrator shows that the discourse is continuous so the consciousness flows to the next related focus, Dixon's objective assessments of the world of gender and the blues.

144 *Reporting Discourse, Tense, and Cognition*

Let us examine other cases that contain the consciousness flow over a series of remarks. In the following, the continuous flow starts with "says," is carried along with "says," and reaches a conclusion with "said." Here, a man reports his negotiation exchange with a real estate dealer when he went to see a house:

(16) when I went to see it, the guy *says* to me, *says*, "We got a bid for thirty-three—thirty-four," *says*, "If you bid thirty-five," he *says*, "You'll get it." I *said*, "Okay, let me think it over." (Wolfson 1982: 25-26)

This is made up of two moves. The man makes an initiation move, and the narrator gives a response. The move structure is the following:

(16)' [initiation X *says to* Y, *says* {pre-head act} → {head act *says* (conditional) → X *says* (statement)}] → Y *said* [response]

In this case, the narrator presents an exchange as a series developing into his conclusion to start thinking about the price he would pay to buy a house. Indeed, this excerpt is the beginning of a long narrative on his negotiation with a dealer and finally getting the house with a very good deal. He marks the start of the consciousness flow with "the guy says to me" and the continuous flow with "says," and the rest at the response move with "said." The consciousness flow is diagramed as follows:

(16)" CSM

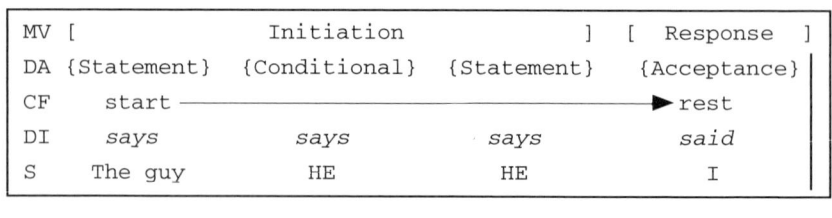

Let us see another case which is also made up of two moves: initiation and response. The excerpt is a part of a story told by a man about his reaction to his brother's refusal to carry him in the snow. The final event after the response is that he punches his brother in the nose.

(17) I *said*, "When we get home, Joe," I *says*, "You'll carry me in the house!" I *say*, "I ain't got no shoe:s, or no stockin's on." He *said*, "Carry yourself in the house! I ain't carryin' y'in!" So I went BOOM! (Schiffrin 1987: 203)

The narrator starts reporting the initiation move in the past tense ("I said"), which is contrary to what I have shown in reporting the beginning of a series of remarks. This is because the initiation move, "When we get home, Joe," functions to set up the background for the succeeding directive. Wolfson (1979; 1982) claims that there is a strong constraint on the use of the historical present tense in *when*-clauses. She explains that the verb in the *when*-clause is in the past tense because "when" locates the action in time, like the background information normally given as an introduction before the beginning of an actual narrative.[18] Since the *when*-clause in this excerpt (17) sets up the background, it is introduced with "I said," regardless of the fact that it is introducing the initiation move. I showed in (9)' and (14)'(b) that the part that sets up a background is reported in the past tense whether it is a nonverbal or a verbal action:

(9)' Y *went* <setting up a background>
→ X *says* [initiation] → Y *said* [response] → X *says* [follow-up]

(14)'(b) X *asked* [initiation] <setting up a background>
[response Y *says* {pre-head act} → Y *said* {head act (rhetorical question, resultative)}]

In (17), after setting up the background, the narrator marks the start of the consciousness flow with "says," and the succeeding remark with "say," and the response with "said." The move structure is as follows:

(17)' [initiation {head act X *said* <temporal-setting-up> → X *says* (statement)}
→ X *say* {post-head act}] → Y *said* [response]

Consciousness flows along this structure as modeled in CSM (17)".

Let me examine a more complicated case, in which, for a strategic reason, a narrator basically does not mark the consciousness flow but still marks the flow when it is crucial to indicate it in a series of remarks. (18) is an excerpt from a conversation between two men, Peter and Bill. They are talking about a woman named Jane. Peter criticizes her.

146 *Reporting Discourse, Tense, and Cognition*

(17)" CSM

MV	[	Initiation		]	[Response]
DA	{Temporal}	{Statement}	{Statement}		{Rejection}
CF	(start/BG)	start		⟶	rest
DI	said	says	say		said
S	I	I	I		HE

⟵——————————— Discourse flow ———————————⟶

(18) P: My- .. my feeling is, .. as I told them, I *said*, (H) if it's that issue, .. I *says*, .. you know, ... I *said* let's just get real here. .. I [*said*],
 B: [Yeah].
 P: we all know Bill, ... (H) I *said*, we all know Jane, I *said*, and I don't know anybody on this board who does not tiptoe around Jane. ... [Period].
 B: [Y e a h].
  .. [Unhunh].
 P: [(H)] I *says*, I don't know anybody who would even go as far as to say .. anything of that nature, .. I *said*, (H) = a=nd, .. there- —it was very clear . . .   [Personal names are changed] (CSAE)[19]

Peter is reporting his own series of remarks about Jane that he previously uttered in talking with other people. The remarks are segmented into many smaller chunks prefaced with dialogue-introducers. Most of the dialogue-introducers are in the past tense ("I said"), although two of them are in the present tense ("I says"). The following is the move structure that I assume for this series of remarks:

(18)' [X *said* {pre-head act (conditional) X *says* → X *said* (statement)}
 {head act X *said* (A) X *said* (B) X *said* (C)
 + X *says* (D) X *said* (statement)}]

In the whole move, Peter talks about his feelings about Jane. I assume the dialogues are basically reported in the past tense in order to reflect the fact that Peter is criticizing Jane and insisting on his point (see chapter 4). But, he uses the present-tense dialogue-introducers when he chooses to mark the flow of consciousness. The first remark, "If it's that issue, let's just get real here," is the pre-head act, and the rest is the head act. I will discuss the first remark with the first use of "I says" later in 5.3.3.2. Here let me discuss the head act in which a series of remarks is reported with the past tense, while only once the present tense "I says" is used. Let me excerpt the reported dialogue part in this head act in the following:

(18)'(a) We all know Bill, we all know Jane, and I don't know anybody on this board who does not tiptoe around Jane. Period. I don't know anybody who would even go as far as to say anything of that nature, and, there it was very clear . . .

It has a parallel arrangement structure in the following form:

(18)'(b) (A), (B), and (C). <u>Period.</u> + (D), (statement)

The speaker starts with parallel presentation of A, B, and C. The speaker ends the row by saying, "Period." After that, he adds another piece of information D that reenforces the preceding C. After that he starts another statement. To report such a long series of utterances, the narrator segments it according to the parallel arrangement structure by using dialogue-introducers as follows:

(18)'(c) {head act X *said* (A) X *said* (B) X *said* (and C <u>Period</u>) + X *says* (D) X *said* (statement)}

(18)'(d) {I *said* (We all know Bill) I *said* (we all know Jane) I *said* (and I don't know anybody on this board who does not tiptoe around Jane. <u>Period</u>) + I *says* (I don't know anybody who would even go as far as to say anything of that nature) I *said* (and, there it was very clear . . .)}

This shows that the present-tense dialogue-introducer "I says" marks the addition of one more piece of information to the parallel structure. Since the speaker has already marked the completion of the information flow by saying, "Period," it is important for the narrator to mark the still-ongoing information flow. In this way, even though the narrator uses the past tense through a whole series of remarks for a strategic reason, such as showing a strong attitude, he still marks the flow with the present tense when it is necessary to indicate the continuity of the flow of consciousness.

Finally, let me show that the cyclical flows of consciousness in reporting a single speaker's series of remarks observed in (15) operate also in reporting two people's exchanges. In the following excerpt, a man is telling his friend that he met a man at an auto-show, who was selling a very good car because he was afraid that his ex-wife would get to it and harm it:

(19) En he wz tel//lin' us, we were kind'v admiring th'//car en 'e *siz* yah, I gotta get rid'v it though. I *said* why dihyou have tih get rid'v it. 'n 'e *sid* well I'm afraid my wife will get it. er: my ex wife. (1.0) Uh::, (0.4) (Tehyuh) [ø] whatwuddiyuh mean yer afraid (yer wife'll) get it well she's afrai-he's afraid ss::

148   *Reporting Discourse, Tense, and Cognition*

>   she'll get it PLANE 'n do sumpn to it. [ø] like what the hell could she do:. HHHH He *seh* we::ll I drove it down t'this car show, (0.8) uh someplace in Ohio. An' uh, he got down (innit) en th'engine heated up'n ble:w. on the ways ba:ck. (0.4) Took it up tore d'damn thing apart'n found a ra:g stuffed in th'radiator hose. (1.2) *Said* I'm afraid m'wife will get to it again I gotta sell it. (0.3) hhh(h)h [ø] Je//(h)sus Chri:st yer kiddin' me.   (AD: 27)

The narrator's uses of dialogue-introducers in this report seem totally unsystematic, at first glance. The narrator starts with "he says" followed by "I said" and "he said." Then he uses a zero-introducer (ø), but soon shifts to summary style, which is one of the variations on indirect reporting style (Sakita 1995; see also chapter 7). He shifts back to direct reporting style with a zero-introducer (ø) again, and then uses "he say" but again shifts to summary style. He shifts back to direct reporting style with "said," but ends with a zero-introducer (ø). The narrator not only shifts tense forms between "says," "said," "say," and zero-introducers, but also shifts reporting styles. His narrative has a very complex reporting structure. However, there is still a synthetic coherence in such an apparently chaotic discourse, and the consciousness flow and tense forms are well modulated within it.

The arrangement of the dialogues in (19)' clarifies the discourse organization (lines are numbered for convenience; timed pauses are erased; reporting verbs are underlined). Line 1 is the background information that the man was telling the nar-

(19)'

1	(BG) En he wz tel///lin us, we were kind'v admiring th'//car
2	en 'e siz yah, *I gotta get rid of it though.*
3	(N) said why dihyou have tih get rid'v it. (1)
4	'n 'e sid well *I'm afraid my wife will get it.* er: my ex wife. Uh::, (Tehyuh)
5	(N) ø what- wuddiyuh mean yer afraid (yer wife'll) get it
6	well she's afrai-he's afraid ss:: she'll get it PLANE 'n do sumpn to it.
7	(N) ø like what the hell could she do:. HHHH (Summary style)
8	He seh we::ll I drove it down t'this car show, uh someplace in Ohio.
9	An' uh, he got down (innit) en th'engine heated up'n ble:w. on the ways ba:ck. (2)
10	Took it up tore d'damn thing apart'n found a ra:g stuffed in th'radiator hose.
11	Said *I'm afraid m'wife will get to it again I gotta sell it.* hhh(h)h
12	(N) ø Je//(h)sus Chri:st yer kiddin me.

rator about the car, and that they were admiring the car. Therefore it is presented in the past tense. I have written the reports of the man's remarks along the left end, and indented the reports of the narrator's own remarks and marked them with (N). Notice that the zero-introducers in this narrative are all used for introducing the narrator's remarks, and not the other man's remarks. The narrator's first remark in line 3 starts with "I said," but the rest are all introduced with zero-introducers. The narrator's remarks are all reactions to the man's remarks, and they introduce or cue the man's remarks, since the man's remarks are the central issue in this narrative. The narrator first contextualizes himself as a reactant by using "I said" in line 3, and places himself in the background for the rest of the remarks. So, after this point, he no longer uses dialogue-introducers to introduce his own remarks.[20]

The main issue in this narrative is the man's remarks, and the point of this narrative is given in his remarks, indicated in italics: *the man has to sell the car for he is afraid that his ex-wife will get to it*. The narrator is very much surprised at the fact that he has to sell such a nice car, and at the reason for it, which is the reason for his telling this story to his friend. So his consciousness focuses on them. In presenting the man's remarks, the narrator's consciousness flows over the man's remarks. I illustrated the consciousness flows in (19)' by two arrows at the right side. First, the consciousness flow starts at line 2, which flows over to line 4 where it rests. The narrator's consciousness focuses on the fact that the man has to sell the car (line 2), and it is triggered to flow over to the reason (line 4) by his curiosity indicated in line 3. The tenses of dialogue-introducers mark this flow of consciousness. At this point, the tense shifts from "says" to "said," when he inserts the explanation of why the man is afraid of his ex-wife's getting to the car. He summarizes the man's answer in line 6 instead of quoting him. The second flow starts at line 8, which flows over to line 11 where it rests. At line 8, the narrator starts reporting what he's afraid his wife will do to the car.

Once the flow starts, he switches to summary style in lines 9 and 10. This may be because the man's answer was quite lengthy, narrating an episode (Sakita 1996a; see also chapter 7).[21] The man's remarks reach a conclusion in line 11, where he repeats his point that he's afraid his wife will gets to his car again, so that he definitely has to sell it. This second flow is also marked with dialogue-introducers' tense-shifts. This time, the tense shifts from "say" to "said." Recall that the second cyclic flow in the midst of a flow in (6) and (15) started with "say" rather than with "says." What is happening here in (19) is exactly the same. There are two cyclic consciousness flows in this episode over evaluative points. Tense-shifts clearly mark the cyclical consciousness flows. The first cycle accompanies the shift from "says" to "said," and the second one accompanies the shift from "say" to "said."

150 *Reporting Discourse, Tense, and Cognition*

In this section, I have shown that consciousness flows along with the development of a narrative line over a series of remarks. A narrator marks the development with dialogue-introducers' tense-shifts along with her/his consciousness flow. Generally "says" marks the start of the flow, while "said" marks the pause or conclusion. In the midst of the flow, "saying" and "say" show continuity. "Said," and other past-tense general verbs, also indicate remarks which set up contextual backgrounds. With example (18), I showed that even when a narrator does not mark the consciousness flow for strategic reasons, she/he may still mark the flow in order to relate it to a series of remarks. We saw that the consciousness flow focuses on evaluative points and is marked with tense-shifts even in complicated narratives. In the following, we shall further examine the previously baffling issue of the repetition of dialogue-introducers. The present framework accounts for them reasonably well.

5.3.3. Consciousness flow in repetition of dialogue-introducers

5.3.3.1. Pre-posing double dialogue-introducers

In example (17), I showed how the past-tense dialogue-introducer ("X said") marks the setting up of a background for the consciousness flow. The same thing happens in the following case, in which the dialogue-introducer is used repeatedly. In the second line, there are two dialogue-introducers for Lottie's report of Claude's remark (the corresponding part is underlined):

(20) Lottie: An' I didn' wanna say-eh: A:deline said she a'ways wanted uh see it so .hnhh I never said anything but- uh: <u>Claude *said* today he *says*</u> <u>wasn' that the dirtiest place?</u>=
Emma: =[Y e : s]
Lottie: =['n I s]ai:d you know? (.) I: felt the same thing but I didn't wanna say anything to you but I jus' fe [:lt=]
Emma: [Ya:]h
Lottie: =dirty when I walked on the ca:rpet. (Edwards 1997: 147)

Lottie first introduces Adeline using indirect reporting style, which is often used to set up the background. After that, Lottie introduces Claude with a remark, "Claude said today he says." The repetition of the dialogue-introducer seems redundant, but the first phrase "Claude said today" functions not as a dialogue-introducer, but rather to set up a background. It informs *who* ("Claude") did *what* ("said") and *when* ("today"), while the second part "he says" simply introduces the succeeding dialogue and initiates a flow. Thus the move structure in this adjacency pair is seen as follows:

(20)' X *said* <setting up a background> X *says* [initiation] → Y *said* [response]

The repetition of pre-posed dialogue-introducers in such a case first sets up background information, then proceeds onto a succeeding flow. The same is true for the repetition of introducers in forms such as "X said to Y, says, '...'"

5.3.3.2. Post-posing dialogue-introducers

A narrator usually pre-poses a dialogue-introducer to introduce a dialogue, but sometimes post-poses another one immediately following the dialogue, accompanying a tense-shift. Such a tense-shift guides a quick change of the consciousness flow. The pre-posed one marks the consciousness flow, while the post-posed one marks the change of the flow. In the following excerpt, in reporting the narrator's remark "Hey Joe," two dialogue-introducers are used, one pre-posed and the other one post-posed, but they have different tense forms:

(21) We went to clean the drain in the sn- in the snowstorm. This was right after the war. So, w- we- it was- my feet were wet. We were riding in the truck. In a car. I <u>say, "Hey Joe." I said-</u> I took my stockin's off, and my shoes. So we get t'29th and Green, we live on 41st and Green, so we g- get t'29th and Green. (Schiffrin 1987: 192)

The narrator first contextualizes the background in lines 1-2, then starts reporting his own initiation move, with a remark "Hey Joe." This remark is a summons. As I showed in relation to (12) and (13), a summons is usually a pre-head act before a head act. Thus in reporting dialogues that contain a summons, a narrator's consciousness starts flowing at a pre-head act, and flows over to a head act, where it may rest. Recall a dialogue from excerpt (12):

from (12):
my mother *says*, "Now Jerry,"...
She *said*, "I don' want y't'marry that- and I want y't'break it off right now."

(12)' [X *says* {pre-head act (summons)} → X *said* {head act (directive)}]

Along with the consciousness flow, the narrator starts reporting the pre-head act with "says" while he marks the consciousness pause at the head act with "said." Likewise, in (21) here, the narrator starts narrating the pre-head act "Hey Joe" with the present-tense dialogue-introducer "I say." Naturally, the consciousness starts flowing at this pre-head act. But the narrator stops reporting succeeding remarks. Instead, he describes his action of taking off his stockings and shoes. The consciousness flowing over a dialogue is interrupted here by a shift to a nonverbal action and situational features. Indeed, it is not unnatural for consciousness to move this way. As I discussed in 5.2., one of the characteristics of consciousness is that it is dynamic, with its restless movement from one focus to the next. What is happening in this case is the natural movement of the consciousness from recalling a dialogue to recalling other actions related to the event. The significant point in this case then is that the narrator marks the movement of consciousness with dialogue-introducers. The move structure in the dialogue is as follows:

(21)' [X *say* {pre-head act (summons)} X *said*]

There is no head act in the move. The narrator first marks the start of the flow with the present-tense dialogue-introducer. Then he marks the stop of the flow immediately after the pre-head act with the past-tense dialogue-introducer. The post-posed "I said" functions as a terminator in this case. The consciousness flow in this structure is thus illustrated as follows:

(21)" CSM

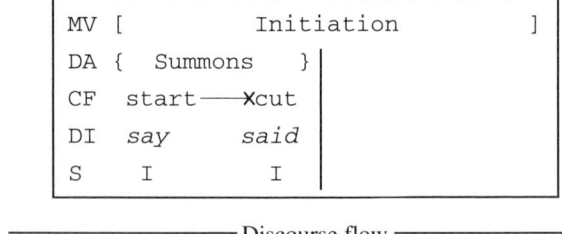

The act of summons is started with "I say" and the consciousness starts to flow, but is terminated immediately with "I said." The lack of a head act is also at odds with the listener's expectations of the narrator's relation to him, when his consciousness is directed toward the succeeding head act, cued by the pre-head act with the present-tense dialogue-introducers. Thus, the post-posed terminator functions, in a sense, to guide the listener's consciousness by reorienting his expectation and indicating the movement of the narrator's consciousness.

The following excerpt includes a similar report of a summons only. It also accompanies the repetition of dialogue-introducers with a tense-shift:

Consciousness Flow, Discourse Acts, and Tense 153

(22) And Mrs. Katz freaked out today because I had t' give her a reinstatement card and YOU know Mrs. Katz. She- I had- I had t' get her t' sign the card, and she looked at it, and she *goes* . . . "Sandy! Sandy!" hhhh, she *was sayin'*- an' Sherry an' Karen an' Lynn in the front row, they're all sittin' up there hysterically laughing, 'cause this is like a very novel thing, for me t' get suspended. (Schiffrin 1981: 49)

The report of Mrs. Katz's call for Sandy is prefaced with the dialogue-introducer "she goes." But the narrator does not report any succeeding remarks by Mrs. Katz. It may be that the fact that the narrator was suspended because of Mrs. Katz' caprice is more important to her/him than any further words she subsequently uttered. The narrator instead reports the three women's laughter over her/his suspension, which supports this point. Mrs. Katz' remark is reported with the following move structure:

(22)' [X *goes* {pre-head act (summons)} X *was sayin'*]

Along with this structure, the consciousness flows as follows:

(22)" CSM

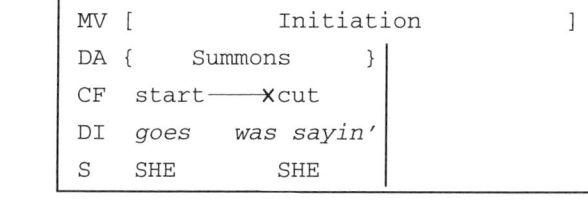

MV [	Initiation]
DA {	Summons }
CF	start ─────×cut
DI	goes was sayin'
S	SHE SHE

────────── Discourse flow ──────────▶

The move structure and the consciousness flow in (22) are similar to those in (21). But in (22), the post-posed dialogue-introducer tense is not the simple past but the past progressive. While the narrator stops the consciousness flow by post-posing "she was sayin'," its progressive aspect suggests that Mrs. Katz' action of speech is not period-like but is more continuous. Because the progressive is a 'correlative' and it highlights and evaluates an event by aligning it with another event which occurred at the same time (Labov 1972b: 387), post-posing the progressive phrase "she was sayin'" reflects the fact that Mrs. Katz may be further interacting with Sandy, while three women were laughing at her/him. I can assume this by the fact that she/he was suspended. The narrator's consciousness here moves to the three women laughing at her/him.

Let us examine another case of post-posing dialogue-introducers. When the pre-posed dialogue-introducer tense does not match the discourse act of a local clause, a narrator may post-pose another dialogue-introducer with the relevant tense form to mark the consciousness flow. The following is the opening remark from excerpt (18). Peter starts reporting his own remarks about a woman named Jane:

(23) P: My- .. my feeling is, .. as I told them, <u>I *said*, (H) if it's that issue</u>, .. I <u>*says*</u>, .. you know, ... I *said* let's just get real here. ..   (from 18)

The remark, "If it's that issue, let's just get real here," is a pre-head act that prefaces a head act that follows. It seems enough to use one dialogue-introducer for the whole pre-head act, but the narrator uses three. Why? Let me examine it in detail. The whole pre-head act starts with the past-tense dialogue-introducer "I said," reflecting Peter's strong critical attitude (see chapter 4) which remains consistent in the succeeding head act as already discussed in relation to (18). The pre-head act is reported in two segments: "If it's that issue" and "let's just get real here." Note that the first segment is a conditional clause. I showed in examining (10) and (16) that conditional clauses are often prefaced with "says," since they are in search of some concluding ideas or are preparing conditions for certain ideas that are given in main clauses:

from (10): . . . So he *says*, "Well, if that's the case," he *said*, "I will find you some other glasses."
from (16): . . . *says*, "If you bid thirty-five," he *says*, "You'll get it." I *said*, "Okay, let me think it over."

In (23), since the narrator had already prefaced the whole pre-head act with the past-tense dialogue-introducer "I said" to reflect the attitudinal factor at the whole sentential level (or dialogue level), he post-posed the present-tense dialogue-introducer "I says" to mark the continuous flow of the consciousness over to the succeeding main clause. Then another dialogue-introducer "I said" prefaces the conclusive nature of the main clause. Thus the act has the following structure:

(23)' X *said* {pre-head act (conditional) X *says* → X *said* (statement)}

In this way, when the pre-posed dialogue-introducer tense does not fit in the consciousness flow at the local clause level, a narrator may post-pose another dialogue-introducer to mark the flow more clearly.

In this section, I have shown that dialogue-introducers are not only pre-posed but also post-posed to mark the flow of consciousness. Post-posed introducers with tense-shifts mark a change in the flow, against an already aroused expectation. I discussed the ways that, even in a mostly past-tense narrative, a narrator still marks the consciousness flow with a present-tense dialogue-introducer to clearly follow the flow.

5.3.3.3. At restatements

There is another significant tense-shift of dialogue-introducers in narratives. It occurs when a narrator restates a quote after inserting some information, or when she/he corrects a quote. For instance, consider the following excerpt. It is a story about the speaker's fear when she discovers that the man in her bedroom is not her husband:

(24) So I felt him lean over the bed. And I- I start laughin'. <u>I *says*, "Oh you s-" excuse the expression I *said*, "Oh you son of a bitch,"</u> right, And he came, he kissed me. When he kissed me I felt his beard. And I'm pushin' I'*m saying*, "Ooh, my God! It isn't you!" And I'm pushin' with all my might, right? I'*m saying*, "Oh my God! Who is he?" y'know. And I PUSH. And I'm- uh-uh I try to scream and I was too scared.   (Schiffrin 1981: 59)

The narrator starts reporting her verbal reaction to the man, saying, "And I- I start laughin'. I says, 'Oh you s-.'" At this point, she feels uneasy using the slang expression, "son of a bitch." She interrupts her report to include a para-narrative message to the listener, apologizing for using the expression. She then re-states her utterance. Interestingly, the narrator first uses the present-tense dialogue-introducer, and switches to the past-tense one in restatement in the following way:

(24)' [X *says* (A) <insertion> X *said* (A')]

I assume that consciousness flows in this structure as illustrated in CSM (24)". The consciousness starts flowing, which is marked by "I says." At the interruption, it is suspended. The restatement is made with a sense of confirming the remark, which is indicated by the mention of "right" after the restatement. This is presented as a period-like information with certainty. The consciousness rests at this point. In chapter 4, I discussed the correlation between tense and the reported speaker's attitude. Here it applies to the narrator's attitude of certainty toward reported information.

(24)" CSM

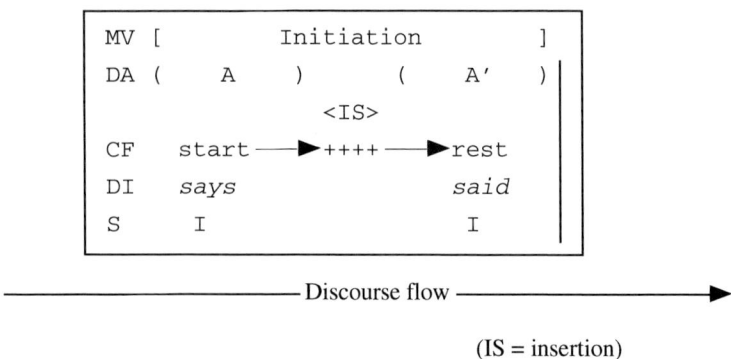

(IS = insertion)

5.4. CONCLUSION

In this chapter, I have explored how a narrator's consciousness flows in reporting discourse along with discourse structures, and how it manifests itself in the use of dialogue-introducers and their tense manipulations. I explicated systematic occurrences of the past- and the present-tense dialogue-introducers, and showed that the dialogue-introducers' occurrences and their tense-shift mark how a narrator's consciousness flows along with dialogue structures. Previous studies on tense have neglected tense usage such as "I says," "he say," "I saying," and "he saying." I have shown that all these forms perform significant work toward making a narrative a coherent whole with a natural consciousness flow.

In narratives, consciousness dynamically flows and rests moving from one focus to the next. I demonstrated that in narrating interactional speeches between multiple participants or even in a single speaker's continuous speech, a speaker's consciousness flows like a stream and rests at islands on its way. At each level of the hierarchical structure within a narrative, there appear both a flow and a rest of consciousness. Along with the narrator's consciousness flow, the narrative development guides a hearer's consciousness flow, fulfilling the hearer's expectation and curiosity. In narrative-embedded dialogues, consciousness flows and rests in relation to the structures of move and of discourse act, and this consciousness-flow-modulation manifests itself in tense-shifts.

I started with discussions of the consciousness flow in exchanges. In adjacency pairs, consciousness starts flowing at an initiation move and rests at a response. To report an initiation move, the present-tense dialogue-introducer "X says" is used, while "X said" is used to report a response move. In a three-part exchange, consciousness stays resting or floating at a follow-up move. The dialogue-introducer shifts from "X says" to "X said" when consciousness flows and rests, while it shifts from "X said" to "X says" when there is an additional follow-up move. I showed that the flow-modulation may also include nonverbal behaviors, and the flow may be marked by other linguistic forms as well as by tense-alternation.

I then proceeded to examine the consciousness flow over a series of remarks. First, in reporting a single speaker's speech, a narrator often separates the speech into separate acts, and introduces each part with a dialogue-introducer. The dialogue-introducer tense varies according to the nature of the acts and the consciousness flow. I showed cases in which different forms of the consciousness flow are correlated with opposite directional tense-shifts of dialogue-introducers. Second, I showed that consciousness flows along with the development of a narrative line over a series of remarks. Dialogue-introducers mark this development, and their tenses shift when consciousness proceeds over conversational information, from onset and flow to coda. Generally, "X says" marks the start of the flow, while "X said" marks the end or, a pause. In the midst of the flow, "X saying" and "X say" show continuity. More specifically, "X say" marks the beginning of a subsequent flow without a break in the flow, whereas "X saying" signals that the consciousness flow is moving on to the next related focus. I showed systematic behaviors of dialogue-introducer tenses in some complicated cases. In some, narrators do not mark the consciousness flow for a strategic reason, but still mark the flow when it is helpful to indicate it in a series of remarks. In others, narrators not only shift tense forms between "says," "said," "say," and zero-introducers, but also shift reporting styles. I demonstrated that in an apparently chaotic discourse, there is still a synthetic coherence, and the consciousness flow and tense forms are well modulated in it. In addition, I showed that the past tense ("said") denotes remarks used to set up contextual backgrounds.

I further examined the consciousness flow in the repetition of dialogue-introducers, in which tense-shifts have been considered irregularly behaving. First, narrators often pre-pose double dialogue-introducers. I discussed that the first dialogue-introducer sets up some background information, then the second one introduces a subsequent flow. Second, narrators also often post-pose dialogue-introducers immediately following dialogues, accompanying tense-shift. I showed that such a tense-shift guides a quick change in the consciousness flow. The pre-posed one initiates the consciousness flow, while the post-posed one shows the change. There are also cases in which the pre-posed dialogue-introducer tense does not match the discourse act of a local clause, and then a narrator post-poses another dialogue-introducer with the relevant tense form to mark the consciousness flow. Third, I examined uses of dialogue-introducers at restatements. While a consciousness flow is marked with "says," its suspension upon interruption is marked with "said."

My discussion in this chapter agrees with Fleischman's (1990: 207) claim that "oral narratives of any length do not unfold in a single seamless continuum, but segment themselves naturally into chunks." Indeed, dialogue-introducers reflect exactly how speakers package information into units of 'blocks' (Grimes 1975) naturally reflecting the flow of consciousness over the course of discourse. In my general discussion, I showed dialogue-introducers as devices to signal "varying degrees of continuity or discontinuity between narrative segments" (Georgakopoulou 1997: 89) along which consciousness flows and rests. In this regard, dialogue-introducers behave as connectives, linking one chunk of information with another, providing what previous discourse studies (e.g., Grimes 1975; Chafe 1980; Longacre 1985; Johnstone 1990) have labeled "the main anchor points for uncovering the web of a story's organizational relations" (Georgakopoulou 1997). While the previous chapters explored dialogue-introducer tenses as manifestations of cognitive recall, and attitudinal contrasting devices, this chapter examined special cases of tense-alternation as a function of the flow of consciousness through a dialogue. With regard to chapters 3 through 5 in general, I will discuss how to integrate these different forces influencing the choice of tense in chapter 8.

6

TENSE IN INDIRECT
REPORTING DISCOURSE

6.0. OVERVIEW

Reporting discourse is characterized by two different contexts in an interaction within a single unifying syntactic structure (Voloshinov [1929]1986). Therefore, one sentence carries two tenses, one in the reporting clause and the other in the reported clause. In chapters 2 through 5, I explored tense-alternation phenomena in reporting clauses, focusing mostly on direct reporting discourse. This chapter will focus on the ways tense in reported clauses is determined in indirect reporting discourse. I will show that tense-alternations may still occur in indirect reporting discourse, as natural discourse phenomena. Taking a flexible view of tense in indirect reporting discourse, I will introduce a new perspective on the issue.

Traditional grammar has analyzed tense in English reporting discourse based on a theoretical dichotomy of direct and indirect styles (e.g., Jespersen 1931; 1964; Quirk, et al. 1985). Celce-Murcia and Larsen-Freeman (1983: 459) show the following examples:

(1) (a) Allen said, "I will buy this car tomorrow."
    (b) Allen said that he would buy that car on the following day.

(1a) contains an example of direct discourse, retaining the verb and its tense from the reported speaker's discourse. (1b) as an example of indirect discourse, does not directly adopt the original discourse, and hence must follow some rules to determine the tense in its complement clause. The most widespread principle for such rules is the sequence of tenses (SoT) formalized by Comrie (1986). He considered the principles only within the scope of a single sentence, treating tense in reporting discourse as a purely syntactic phenomenon. His treatment of tense is too mechanical, because it does not cover the whole range of reporting behaviors in language performances.

Declerck (1990) has incorporated semantic and pragmatic information into the SoT rule, in an attempt to account for wider sets of examples. In this chapter, I will examine tense in reporting discourse within the scope of actual language performances. I will show that the standard treatments of the English grammar of tense in reporting discourse are unsatisfactory. I will essentially support Declerck's proposal, and will further introduce discourse perspectives in which tense in indirect reporting discourse is viewed as a discourse functional phenomenon. Speakers often report from their own perspectives to maintain discourse coherence rather than maintaining syntactic integrity.

I will discuss, first, how traditional English grammar has treated tense in reporting discourse by briefly introducing Comrie's formal rule. Second, I will show that the formal tense rule overlooks pragmatic information, which is important for successful communication. Third, I will outline Declerck's hypothesis which incorporates pragmatic and semantic information in the tense theory. Fourth, I will show that tense in indirect reporting discourse in naturally spoken English does not behave as rigidly as standard theories have assumed. From naturally occurring language data, I will raise examples in which the standard theories do not work. I will present discourse perspectives to supplement Declerck's theory. Finally, I will suggest that in spoken discourse, the reported clause is not subordinated to the reporting clause as has long been assumed. Tense in the complement clause is often determined not by its relation to the head clause, but rather by its direct relationship to the moment of speaking. I will show that in many cases in spoken English, tenses of reported verbs are naturally determined by the reporter's perspective. I will cite three pieces of evidence to support my view. First, speakers often avoid the past perfect tense in spoken English. Even when they use it, they use it as the absolute tense for a discourse functional necessity, rather than as a backshifted or relative tense. Second, indirect reporting discourse has tense-alternation phenomena, which have long been considered a feature in direct reporting discourse. Third, reporting clauses behave flexibly as dialogue markers. In these three cases, it is necessary to maintain the internal discourse coherence of the reporters' perspectives.

6.1. TREATMENTS OF TENSE IN GRAMMAR

Traditional English grammar (e.g., Quirk, et al. 1972; 1985; Leech and Svartvik 1975; Thomson and Martinet 1980) has presented tense in indirect reporting discourse with a very formal sequence of tenses (SoT) rule. Jespersen (1924: 290-99) made it popular, and its recent proponents are Comrie (1986) and Hornstein (1990). They treat it as a purely syntactic operation, which is applied mechanically without semantic motivation. The rule is summarized as follows:

> If the tense of the verb of reporting is non-past, then the tense of the original utterance is retained; if the tense of the verb of reporting is past, then the tense of the original utterance is backshifted into the past, except that if the content of the indirect speech has continuing applicability, the backshifting is optional. (Comrie 1986: 284)

To illustrate the operation of the second part of this rule, grammar books often present charts such as the following:

simple present	→	simple past
present continuous	→	past continuous
simple past	→	past perfect
present perfect	→	past perfect
past continuous	→	past perfect continuous
future	→	conditional future
perfect	→	conditional perfect
conditional	→	conditional perfect

The grammar books provide examples in pairs of direct and indirect discourse such as the following to demonstrate the above rule:

(2) (a) Eric said, "I am ill."
 (b) Eric said that he was ill.
(3) (a) Joy said, "I saw her the other day."
 (b) Joy said that she had seen her the other day.
(4) (a) David said, "I have not yet seen her."
 (b) David said that he had not seen her yet.

However, there are some cases for which the formal SoT rule cannot account. In the following examples, the formal SoT rule fails to predict accurate forms of indirect reporting discourse:

(5) (a) Shigeru regrets saying to Chia-Yi, "I feel lonely."
 (b)* Shigeru regrets telling Chia-Yi that he feels lonely.
 (c) Shigeru regrets telling Chia-Yi that he felt lonely.

(6) (a) Anne remembers thinking, "It is impossible."
    (b)* Anne remembers thinking it is impossible.
    (c) Anne remembers thinking it was impossible.

For the direct reporting discourse examples (5a) and (6a), the formal SoT rule predicts (5b) and (6b) as indirect versions. This is simply because there are no past-tense reporting verbs to trigger backshifting in the head clauses. But normal speakers use (5c) and (6c) for indirect discourse.

Declerck raised the following cases for which the formal SoT rule cannot make correct predictions:

(7) (a) This is John's wife.—Yes, I THOUGHT he was married.
    (b)* This is John's wife.—Yes, I THOUGHT he is married.

(8) (a) I knew you liked her.
    (b)* I knew you like her.   (Declerck 1991: 185)

The state in (7) that John is married and the state in (8) that "you" like "her" have continuing applicability. The formal SoT rule predicts (7a or b) and (8a or b) instead of (7a) and (8a). (Recall that if the content of the indirect discourse has continuing applicability, the backshifting is optional.) However, (7b) and (8b) are wrong predictions.

The above cases (5), (6), (7), and (8) show that if we mechanically apply the formal SoT rule, in some cases we will form unacceptable sentences. Indeed, such a mechanical way of viewing reporting discourse is what Voloshinov ([1929]1986: 128) pointed out as "a typical grammarian's error." He claimed that the "mechanical, purely grammatical mode of translating reported speech from one pattern into another, without the appropriate stylistic reshaping" is a highly objectionable way of manufacturing classroom exercises in grammar. As he emphasized, "This sort of implementation of the patterns of speech reporting has nothing even remotely to do with their real existence in a language."

6.2. PRAGMATIC VIEW

Comrie's formal SoT rule described tense in indirect reporting discourse by reference to the relationship between a subordinate clause and its main clause counterpart. Comrie attempted to predict direct reporting discourse is switched into indirect style, and how tense in the complement clause is realized in indirect discourse. He tested the mechanical operation of his rule in single sentences, and provided English grammar with a formal rule at the sentential level.[1]

However, it is doubtful whether this formal rule actually operates in real communication. Goodell (1987) showed some cases where the formal rules could fail to form utterances suitable to the situations. For instance, suppose that a mother has made the utterance (9). (10) is a case in which Mary reported it immediately after her mother's utterance. (11) is a case in which Mary reported it after a distinct period of time:

(9) Mother : Girls, I want you to clean up the kitchen.
(10) Debbie : What did Mom say? I couldn't hear her.
     Mary : She said she *wants* us to clean up the kitchen.
(11) Debbie : What did Mom say before she left yesterday? I couldn't hear her.
     Mary : She said she *wanted* us to clean up the kitchen.
                                                (Goodell 1987: 309)

The appropriate tense forms in the complement clauses are the present in (10) and the past in (11). If we mechanically apply the formal SoT rule, we cannot distinguish such context-sensitive differences. The example suggests that we need to know the semantic and pragmatic concerns to determine the tenses in some indirect reporting discourses. The formal theories have long set aside such cases as exceptions to their rules. We need to see if tense is used with certain discourse functions, or in some context-sensitive ways. In order to do that, we need to investigate reporting discourse in natural language situations and see how tense behaves in real communication.

6.3. DECLERCK'S HYPOTHESIS

Because of deficiencies in Comrie's SoT rule such as those briefly illustrated above, Declerck (1990) proposed the incorporation of pragmatic and semantic information into tense theory. He proposed a new hypothesis by combining the relative time hypothesis and the absolute deixis hypothesis.[2] I will call it 'the combination of relative and absolute tense (CoRA) hypothesis' in this chapter. According to this new hypothesis, tense in an indirect discourse complement clause is usually a relative tense, relative to tense in a head clause. The hypothesis also includes an absolute tense which can appear, subject to certain conditions. Table 1 summarizes his explanation of relative tense.

Table 1: Relative Tense

	Temporal relation between complement clause & head clause		
	simultaneity	anteriority	posteriority
head cl.: past	preterit	past perfect	conditional
head cl.: non-past	present	preterit, present perfect	future

(Sakita 1996b)

For instance, in (2a), the tense of the head clause is the past and the temporal relation between the head clause and the complement clause is simultaneity. Therefore, the reported verb is realized as preterit in (2b). In (3a) and (4a), the head clauses are both in the past, and the information in the complement clauses is anterior to the head clauses. So, the reported verbs are both in the past perfect in (3b) and (4b). Also, the following is a case in which the head clause is in the non-past:

(12) (a) My father will say, "I am baking cookies."
 (b) My father will say that he is baking cookies.

Here, the head clause is not in the past, and the content of the complement clause is simultaneous with the head clause. So the reported clause has the verb in the present.

In addition to the use of the relative tense as the unmarked choice, Declerck includes the absolute tense in his hypothesis, by allowing it in marked, restricted cases. In some restricted cases, tense in the reported clause may be directly related to the moment of speaking, having the speaker's deictic center as the reference point. Declerck raised the following example:

(13) John said that Bill was in London the day before.
(Declerck 1990: 519)

In this sentence, neither the formal SoT rule nor Declerck's relative tense explanation works. They both predict the reported verb in the complement clause to be "had been" instead of "was." Declerck solves this problem by saying that in such sentences the complement clause shifts the domain instead of incorporating its situation into the head clause domain.[3] That is, the situation is reported from the speaker's deictic center, not from the reportee's. He explains that the absolute tense is allowed only if the temporal order of the situations is clear from a temporal adverb, the context, or from the hearer's pragmatic knowledge of the world.[4] Since (13) contains the time adverbial phrase "the day before," it is clear that Bill's being in London is anterior to John's report of it.

In this way, Declerck introduced the possibility that the tense used in a complement clause in indirect speech may be either a relative tense or an absolute tense.[5] The complement clause situation can either (1) be incorporated into the domain referred to in the head clause and express a relation internal to the domain, or (2) shift the domain (i.e., create a new domain). The speaker's choice of relative or absolute tense forms is governed by the following principle:

> If both clauses refer to the same time-sphere, the use of relative tense in the complement clause is the unmarked choice. This means that, in such sentences, relative tense is always possible, whereas there are restrictions on the absolute tense form. For example, absolute tense is allowed only if the temporal order of the situations is clear from a temporal adverb, the context or from the hearer's pragmatic knowledge of the world.
> (Declerck 1990: 519)

Declerck raised two main reasons for using the absolute tense: (1) the tendency towards tense simplification; (2) the speaker's occasional desire to represent a past situation as still relevant at the speaker's deictic center (1991: 183).

6.4. TENSE IN DISCOURSE

6.4.1. Prevalence of speaker's viewpoint

I will now show that tense in indirect reporting discourse in spoken English does not behave as rigidly as standard theories have claimed. I agree with Declerck's CoRA's inclusion of semantic and pragmatic concerns in tense theory. He has shown examples in a variety of sentences. I will apply discourse perspectives to his hypothesis, and show that the absolute tense is common in spoken discourse. In spoken discourse, it is not only contextual clarity that calls for the absolute tense. Speakers often prefer the absolute tense to the relative tense to preserve the coherence of the discourse. In addition, the type of verb chosen introduces linguistic restrictions that affect the choice of tense. The following discussion will show uses of tense within a wider scope of discourse with contextual variations. Examples will include naturally occurring language data in such settings as casual talks, telephone conversations, elicited narratives in semi-formal settings, movies, news reports, etc.

166 *Reporting Discourse, Tense, and Cognition*

The first examples show verbs that obviously do not behave as Comrie's SoT and Declerck's relative tense rule in CoRA predict. The first two examples are from a telephone conversation between a woman (W) and a man (M). In (14), M is referring to their previous conversation about his class:[6]

(14) M: ahh I wrote one thing about .hh remember I told you the first couple days a cl:ass
W: un hum
M: *was* kind of ah .hh a weird game situation
W: uhyeah
M: ynah I sit down I sat done n en wrote that   (JR: 20)

In the reporting discourse which starts with "I told you," M used the past-tense verb "was" in the complement clause. Here the formal SoT and the relative tense rule both predict "had been," since the original discourse for this utterance is assumed to be:

(15) The first couple of days a class *was* kind of a weird game situation.

Here, contrary to what the formal SoT and the relative tense rule predict, the tense of the original discourse is retained in the indirect discourse. The next example is a similar case. M asks W if she has seen her mother:

(16) M: Have you seen her yet
W: Yeah we saw her tonite=
M: =What was the reaction (0.2)
W: Uhhum (0.3) good you know after I kn- I knock on the doo:r (0.8) Who's there Alice no she starts laughing wow y'know, heh (0.2) en y'know sorta like waited a while en then told her we *had* hitchhike cause she didn't know y'know an then   (JR: 22-23)

In answering M, W mentions that she told her mother about hitchhiking. Here, W uses the simple past form "had" rather than the past perfect form "had had," which the formal SoT and the relative tense rule predict from the original words that W spoke to her mother:

(17) We *had* a hitchhike.

Only the absolute tense explanation works for (14) and (16). The following example is from a news report:

(18) Tokyo Governor Yukio Aoshima announced that he *decided* to cancel the World City Expo which was scheduled for next year. The writer-turned governor made the decision although the Tokyo Metropolitan Assembly overwhelmingly adopted a resolution demanding the Expo proceed.
(CE 1995. 8: 92)[7]

In (18), since the verb "announced" is in the past tense in the head clause, and the assumed original discourse by Yukio Aoshima is (19), both the formal SoT and the relative tense rule predict the past perfect form "had decided" in the complement clause. However, the verb in the complement clause retains the past tense from the assumed original discourse:

(19) I *decided* to cancel the World City Expo which was scheduled for next year.

The following is a similar case:

(20) U.S. voters are going to the polls in the most important day so far in the presidential election season. Primary elections and party caucuses are under way in seven states and American Samoa. The southern state of Georgia is in the spotlight because the primary there is a crucial test between President Bush and Republican challenger Patrick Buchanan. Several voters in Athens, Georgia, however, told reporters today they *are* less than impressed with the choice of candidates. (VOA News 1992)

In the last sentence in (20), the verb in the complement clause retains the present-tense form "are" from the original discourse (21):

(21) We *are* less than impressed with the choice of candidates.

It does not follow either the formal SoT or the relative tense rule.

In these four cases, we observe the use of the absolute tense, i.e., the reporter's deictic center is the reference point. The tense in the complement clause is not back-shifted as the formal SoT predicts, nor is it determined relative to the tense in the head clause. The reporter chooses her/his tense according to the temporal relation of the event to her/his own standpoint. Declerck's hypothesis allows the absolute tense as a marked restricted case only when the temporal order is clear from the context. (14) exactly fits with this idea. What M is reporting is the repetition of his former conversation with W, thus the temporal order of M's reporting and the event in the complement clause is a shared knowledge between the speakers. In natural language use, speakers and hearers generally share some pragmatic knowledge or, at least, some common knowledge of the world. Or the speakers contextualize their stories beforehand. Therefore, it is natural that speakers use the absolute tense frequently in spoken English discourse.

In (16) and (18), the temporal order is supported by common linguistic information. That is, because of the characteristics of the reported verbs in (16) and (18), the temporal orders are clear between the reporting and reported clauses. It is clear that the verbs in the original discourses of (16) and (18) are not in the present tense, because the verbs "have" and "decide" generally do not appear in the present tense:

(22) (a)   We had a hitchhike.
 (b)(*) We have a hitchhike.
 (c)   We are having a hitchhike.

(23) (a)   I decided to cancel the World City Expo which was scheduled for next year.
 (b)(*) I decide to cancel the World City Expo which was scheduled for next year.
 (c)   I will decide to cancel the World City Expo which was scheduled for next year.

In these cases, "have" and "decide" are used as event verbs, and so they will not appear in the present tense unless the event occurs habitually, e.g., "I walk to school." According to Leech (1987), there are event verbs and state verbs that are used to refer to events or states. For instance:

> event verbs : *jump, nod, get, put, land, begin, find, hit, fall, go, become, take.*
> state verbs : *be, live, belong, last, like, stand, know, have, contain, seem, owe.*
> (Leech 1987: 9)

'Event' and 'state' are semantic rather than grammatical terms. "Decide" is an event verb. Although "have" is usually a state verb, when it appears in the *'have a* verb' construction (Dixon 1991: 346) with an emphasis on the activity, it is used as an event verb. With event verbs, the instantaneous use of the present tense, that signifies an event simultaneous with the present moment as in (22b) and (23b), is generally the marked or abnormal alternative to the progressive present tense, "because there are few circumstances in which it is reasonable to regard an action as begun and completed at the very moment of speech" (Leech 1987: 7).[8] So, Leech's findings suggest that event verbs are generally used in the past tense. When event verbs ("jumped"; "got") occur in indirect reporting discourse (24a), it is generally assumed that the direct discourse version resembles (24c) instead of (24b), except in contextually restricted cases.

(24) (a)   He said that he jumped and got hurt.
    (b)(*) He said, "I jump and get hurt."
    (c)   He said, "I jumped and got hurt."

There is no ambiguity in temporal relations between the content of the reporting clause and the content of the reported clause in (24a). Therefore, even without any contextual information to clarify the temporal order, there is no ambiguity in (16) and (18). Therefore, these sentences may keep the absolute tense.

The case (20), I assume, is explained as a matter of discourse coherence in a flow of speech, rather than as a matter of temporal clarity. The speaker consistently uses *be*-verbs in the present tense throughout his speech, except for the reporting verb "told," which is included to make clear that the last sentence is a subjective opinion. The verb "are" in the last sentence maintains the present tense in harmony with other present verbs in this discourse. Declerck may explain this case by saying that the past situation is still relevant at present (Declerck 1991). This interpretation is also supported by the temporal adverb "today."

Let me cite a few more examples which contain the absolute tense:

(25) The study showed that under normal circumstances, high quantities of allergen *were* needed to cause an asthma attack, but when other pollutants *were* also introduced, the amount of allergen needed *decreased* significantly.   (EJ 1995. 7: 21)

(26) Ann Stone, leader of Republicans For Choice, says 50,000 people have joined to seek pro-choice language in the platform. She complained that Republican convention planners *allotted* her only a few moments to discuss the question of abortion.   (ABC News 1992. 10)

(25) is from an interview on scientific research. (26) is from a news report. At first glance, if we do not examine the contents with their contexts, we may think that the formal SoT applies in these examples. Since the head and complement clauses are both in the past tense, the two tenses seem to be in sequence. For instance, in (26), "she complained" and "allotted" are both in the past. But the formal SoT works only if we assume Ann Stone's complaint to be (27). (The same is said of the relative tense rule.) But according to the context, it is natural to assume that her complaint was not (27) but (28):

(27)*Republican convention planners *allot* me only a few moments to discuss the question of abortion.
(28) Republican convention planners *allotted* me only a few moments to discuss the question of abortion.

(26) retains the past tense from its original discourse (28), since it is the past event also from the present speaker's viewpoint. That is why it is the absolute tense. In (26), the reporting verb "says" in the first sentence is in the present, and the reporting verb "complained" in the second sentence is in the past. This is a case of tense-alternation in which the tense in the head clause is not fixed, but rather freely switches between the present and the past (e.g., Wolfson 1979; 1982; Schiffrin 1981; Johnstone 1987; see also chapters 2-5).[9] If the reported verbs switch their tenses as freely as the reporting verbs, discourse coherence is broken. To maintain coherence, the speaker keeps her/his point of view.

The formal SoT and the relative tense rule are based on the assumption that the tense in the complement clause is determined in relation to its head clause. However, the above discourse examples show that this is not the case. The complement clause is uttered from the speaker's (reporter's) viewpoint. The head clause does not have as strong an influence on the complement clause as was supposed in previous theories. This is partly supported by the free indirect discourse in which the reporter does not use the reporting clause.[10] It is also supported by the tense-alternation shown in (26), where the tense in the head clause freely switches between the present and the past.

6.4.2. Avoidance of the past perfect tense

In spoken discourse, people try to avoid using the past perfect when it is not necessary (and even sometimes when it is). The examples shown above had the past tense where the formal SoT and the relative tense rule would predict the past perfect. Here is another example:

(29) V: But still it covers eighty percent.
C: Yeah
V: hh Anyways hh so the next day your Mom told me that she *talked* ta my Mom n that it *wz* a:ll confusing n that she *didn't*- my mother *sounded* real upset that she she *didn't* know what was going on about why they didn't change the knee. (VK)

This is a conversation between female friends. V says that C's mother told V that V's mother had been upset about V's father's operation. The formal SoT and the relative tense rule predict that all the reported verbs in this example would be in the past perfect. But the simple past tense is used throughout the report. The following is a similar case from a casual talk between two men:

(30) G: Well 'e took Jim, a good friend a' mine, he weighs about two hunnerd'n s:;
     B: rrrraaaaaah
     (0.5)
     B: hh AAW YAWWWW!
     G: two hunned's five pounds I think 'e weighs. Took im fer a ride on that'n Jim said thet he *wz* et least goin eighty miles'n hour. With the two of 'em on it.=   (AD: 36)

Here, G tells B of an episode in which one man took his friend Jim for a ride on a snowmobile. In his last remark, Jim's speech is reported with the past-tense verb "was" rather than with the past-perfect-tense verb. There are many such cases in which the past tense is used instead of the past perfect tense.

The phenomenon of avoiding the past perfect tense has been largely absent from the frameworks of SoT and CoRA. Previous studies describe the tense in reference to the relation between a subordinate clause and its main clause counterpart, rather than by the relation between indirect reporting discourse and the actual speech being reported (Huddleston 1984). Such a rigid mode of analysis leads to serious errors in discourse interpretation. Previous studies often present pairs of indirect and direct reporting discourse such as the following:

(31) (a) The guy in the visitor's chair responded that he *wasn't* feeling well either.   (Sakita 1996a)
    (b) The guy in the visitor's chair said, "I'*m not* feeling well either."

When they face the indirect reporting discourse (31a), SoT and CoRA are most likely to predict that its direct speech counterpart is (31b) with its verb in the complement clause having the present tense. However, this could be a mistaken interpretation of the utterance (31a). The sentence (31a) is indeed a report that was uttered in elicited narratives that I collected (Sakita 1996a; see also chapter 7). I asked 19 native speakers of English to describe a film that contained short conversations, and the outcomes contained various ways of reporting. (31a) is one of the typical ways of reporting the original utterance (32) in the film:

(32) I *wasn't* feeling well, but I got the muffin because I thought it would help my stomach.   [original discourse] (Ibid.)

172 *Reporting Discourse, Tense, and Cognition*

It is clear that, in reality, the speaker who produced (31a) has not chosen the tense in the complement clause based on its relation to the verb tense in the main clause. The speaker simply conveyed the fact that the man was not feeling well from her own viewpoint. The speaker's use of the simple past rather than the past perfect in (31a) does not mean that the situation in the complement clause (the man's not feeling well) is happening simultaneously with the man's utterance. Such an interpretation distorts the fact. The original speaker's point is that he was not feeling well, but that he feels better now because of the muffin. The speaker who produced (31a) simply used the past tense from her own viewpoint, and not the past perfect. Following SoT and CoRA, one would have reported the original utterance (32) by using the past perfect as in (33):

(33) The guy said that he *had not been* feeling well, but he *had gotten* the muffin because he *had thought* it would help his stomach.
[predicted direct discourse]

But many people actually reported (32) using the simple past tense as in the following ways:

(34) The guy in the visitor's chair responded that he *wasn't* feeling well either, but he *got* a muffin because he *thought* it would settle his stomach . . .
(35) The other guy, Kevin, said he *wasn't* really feeling well either, but he *got* a muffin because he *thought* it would make him feel better . . .
(36) Kevin said that he *didn't* feel well also, and ah once he *had* the muffin, he *was* feeling better . . .
(37) Kevin said that he *got* the muffin because he *thought* it would make him feel better . . .   (Sakita 1996a)

6.4.3. Discourse functional use of the past perfect tense

There still are some cases, however, in which the past perfect is used. In these cases, I argue that the past perfect is used not as a result of the formal SoT nor the relative tense rule. Rather, it is used as an absolute tense simply because of a discourse functional necessity.[11] Consider the following example. It is an extract from the elicited narratives mentioned above:

(38) The man on the right said that he *had not been* feeling well, but he *got* his muffin so he now *feels* better.   (Ibid.)

In this sentence it is odd to say that the past perfect form "had not been" is determined relative to the reporting verb "said," since we cannot explain the other verbs "got" and "feels" in this way. Rather, the reported clause is seen from the reporter's viewpoint and organized in a sequence of events. The tenses in the reported clause are realized as absolutes to clarify the causality of the three events: the man's not feeling well; his getting a muffin; his feeling better. The speaker used the past perfect and showed that the man's feeling unwell was a continuous state until he got a muffin. It may be argued that the latter half of this sentence is not a reporting discourse, thus the reporting verb "said" influences the tense only in the reported part, "he had not been feeling well." But we can see in (39) that the absence of the reporting phrase from (38) does not affect the coherence of this sentence:

(39) He *had not been* feeling well, but he *got* his muffin so he now *feels* better.

The whole reported clause in (38) keeps its coherence, independent of the reporting clause.

The following example shows how reporters attempt to maintain the causal relationship or order of reported events:

(40) The man on the right <u>talks</u> about, ah excuse me, the man on the left <u>mentions</u> that he *had ah contemplated* buying a muffin but he <u>said</u> he *didn't feel* well, and the man on the right <u>says</u> he also *did not feel* well but *decided* to buy the muffin anyways. (Ibid.)

The tenses of the reporting verbs (which are underlined) alternate between present and past in this example. Here, the tenses of the reported verbs are determined not in relation to the switching tenses of the reporting verbs. Rather, the reported discourse keeps its own coherence. The speaker reports the events involving the man on the left in chronological order: the man had considered buying a muffin, then he gave it up since he did not feel well. So the past perfect tense comes first and the past tense comes next.

The following example also shows the use of the past perfect tense as a reporter's attempt to clarify the order of reported events:

(41) Bill said that something to the effect of he *thought* of getting a muffin but *didn't* feel well, . . . and Kevin, Kevin said that ah earlier he *hadn't been* feeling well either, and they seemed a little bit more happy and I think I saw Kevin smiling at the very beginning, they were both seated at a desk, in about the same position except that Kevin was leaning over and eating, and

I believe that Bill said that the problem *was* with his stomach, an that's why he *didn't* want to have a muffin, because he *was* having some kind of stomach problem. (Ibid.)

Here, the formal SoT and the relative tense rule would conclude that the use of "hadn't been" in line 2 is determined relative to the past-tense verb in the head clause "Kevin said." But I argue that this past perfect is triggered by "earlier" immediately before "he hadn't been." This speaker keeps the absolute tense throughout his discourse. It is natural that he consistently uses the absolute tense, and only once does he use the past perfect in combination with "earlier" in order to clarify the temporal relation of the events within his speech.

Let us look at another example in which we can see the discourse functional use of the past perfect:

(42) U.S. Secretary of State Warren Christopher announced that Israel and Syria *had agreed* on a framework clearing the way for detailed negotiations on security agreements. Christopher said that top military officials from Israel and Syria *agreed* to meet in Washington by the end of June to resume their stalled peace talks mainly concerning conditions of Israeli withdrawal from the Golan Heights. Peace talks between the two countries had been frozen since last December. (CE 1995. 8: 89)

The formal SoT and the relative tense rules fit the first sentence, but they cannot explain the second sentence. If we consider that both the verbs "had agreed" and "agreed" are in the absolute tense, we can give a consistent explanation for the whole discourse. The two italicized verbs are in chronological order and in a causal relationship. Thus, it is common that the simple past tense is used in spoken discourse where the past perfect is expected by the formal SoT and the relative tense rules. The past perfect tense is rarely used unless there is a discourse functional necessity to report a sequence of events.

6.4.4. Reporting clause as dialogue marker

In examining (26) and (40), I pointed out that tense-alternation may occur in indirect reporting discourse. Previous theories assumed that the tense of the reporting verb is faithful to the event time, and that the tense in the complement clause is determined by its relation to the reporting verb tense. But in spoken discourse, the tense in the head clause may remain in the present or past, or more flexibly switch between the present and the past, regardless of the actual speech settings. It seems that reporting clauses in such cases neither indicate temporal settings nor provide reference points for reported clauses.

Narrators often keep whole discourse coherence rather than sentential coherence by relating reporting clauses and reported clauses. In such cases, a reporting clause simply functions as a marker to introduce dialogue. Consider the following narrative excerpt, where a woman tells the story of an emergency that she heard from her friend who fell on the floor and could not get out of her house. People lifted a little girl through the kitchen window to help the woman. After reporting detailed exchanges with direct reporting style, the narrator switches to indirect style:

(43) So that's what they did. So she goes through and <u>she says</u> she *landed* in the sink . . . well, naturally, it's like our kitchen. So she had taken her shoes off, right? She had heels on and she took them off when they hoisted her. She was on a little step ladder but then they still had to give her a little push, right? So she got in, <u>she said</u> she *sat* right in the sink. So she had to work her way out of that and she got in and here she opened up the front door and it took the four of them to get her up and she was screamin' when they got her up, she was in such pain. (Wolfson 1982: 94-95)

There are two indirect reporting parts in this excerpt (reporting clauses are underlined). In line 1, the narrator states the fact that the little girl entered the house and landed in the sink by saying, "So she goes through and she says she landed in the sink." Here she adds detailed explanations of how she went into the house (". . . well, naturally, it's like our kitchen. . . . they still had to give her a little push, right?"). In line 5, the narrator resumes describing the little girl's entering the house, saying, "So she got in, she said she sat right in the sink," and continues the story. Although these repeated reporting parts are about the single event of the little girl's landing in the sink, they have different tenses. In line 1, the reporting clause ("she says") is in the present tense,[12] while in line 5, the reporting clause ("she said") is in the past tense. We see that the tense variation of these reporting clauses has not affected the past-tense forms in the reported clauses. It indicates that the reporting clauses in these cases are not temporal reference points for the reported clauses. The reporting clauses are more like dialogue introducing markers, while the reported event of the girl's landing in the sink is in the discourse flow over the event line. Even if the reporting clauses were not present, the reported event would fit in the narrative line and would not confuse the listener:

(44) (a) So she goes through and she landed in the sink . . .
     (b) So she got in, she sat right in the sink.

176 *Reporting Discourse, Tense, and Cognition*

In these cases, the reported clauses belong to the main event line. The reporting clauses are markers that indicate the source of the reported information, and their tense variations may serve some discourse functions, just as dialogue-introducer tense-shifts in direct reporting discourse serve significant discourse functions as I have illustrated in chapters 4 and 5.[13]

The same is true in the post-posed reporting clauses. In the following excerpt which occurs before (43) in the same narrative, the reporting clause in line 2 is post-posed:

(45) So then after a while, she thought one of them'll have enough sense to come to the door, ring the bell, right? So she couldn't get up she said, she, it was a- —so she crawled to the door and then finally one of the women came and rang the bell and she said to 'em, "I'm on the floor, I fell and I can't get up." So Nancy said, "Well, open the door,"   (Ibid.)

In this case, the reporting clause "she said" could be pre-posed (46a) or could even be omitted (46b) without changing the tense in the reported clause:

(46) (a) So she said she couldn't get up, she, it was a- —so she crawled . . .
     (b) So she couldn't get up, she, it was a- —so she crawled . . .

Since the whole story that the narrator is telling is based on her friend's report, the inclusion of the reporting clause is not obligatory as an indication of its being reported by her friend.

When we look at the flexibility of these reporting clauses, we notice that they behave more like comment clauses which are characteristic of spoken English. "Comment clauses are either content disjuncts that express the speakers' comments on the content of the matrix clause, or style disjuncts that convey the speakers' views on the way they are speaking" (Quirk et al. 1985: 1112). Comment clauses are parenthetical disjuncts, and they may occur initially, finally, or medially, and generally have a separate tone unit. They are generally marked prosodically by increased speed and lowered volume. Some reporting clauses in spoken English, as we saw above, share these characteristics with comment clauses. From among six types of comment clauses that Quirk et al. distinguish,[14] I assume that reporting clauses are related to the type (i) comment clauses that are "like the matrix clause of a main clause." As in (47a), this type of comment clause generally contains a transitive verb or adjective which elsewhere requires a nominal *that*-clause as object (47b):

(47) (a) There were no other applicants, I believe, for that job.

(b) I believe that there were no other applicants for that job.
(Quirk et al. 1985: 1113)

In (47), the sentences (a) and (b) are not exact paraphrases, but have different meanings. The verb in the comment clause in (47a) may have only one of the meanings possible for the verb in the matrix clause. Especially, verbs like "believe" and "think" in comment clauses may have merely a hedging function.[15] Although the verbs in most of the comment clauses of this type (i) are in the simple present, Quirk et al. (ibid.: 1114) admit that, in some cases, clauses can be fairly freely constructed, permitting variations of subject, tense, and aspect, or additions of adjuncts, etc.:

(48) The Indian railways (my uncle was telling me some time ago) have always made a profit. (Ibid.: 1114)

Some reporting clauses in indirect reporting discourse function as comment clauses in this category. They are constructed like the matrix clause of a main clause, but are more freely constructed with variations of tense and aspect. What is significant is that the reporting clauses that have been definitively considered to be main clauses according to the previous frameworks may also function as comment clauses in spoken English. In such cases, they do not function to indicate temporal reference points for reported clauses in tense determination. The use of reporting clauses as comment clauses is often seen in narratives. It also appears in casual conversations:

(49) Yihknow she really eh—so she said you know, theh-ih- she's *had* experience. hh with handicap' people she said but hh ih-yihknow ih-theh- in the fie:ld. —thet they're i:n::.= (TG: 8-9)

Here reporting clauses are positioned before and after a reported clause, "she's had experience with handicap' people." The tense in the reported clause is not backshifted. Quirk et al. (ibid.: 1115) note that reporting clauses for direct reporting discourse are related to the semantic roles of type (i) comment clauses, and may be considered an additional semantic category within type (i):

(50) "It's time we went," I said. (Ibid.: 1115)

Reporting clauses in indirect reporting discourse, which I characterized as comment clauses function similarly to the dialogue-introducers in direct reporting discourse in (50). In both indirect reporting (49) and direct reporting (50), the speaker comments, by using the reporting clause, that the content of the matrix clause is not the present speaker's immediate utterance but is a report.

The use of reporting clauses as comment clauses in indirect reporting discourse seems to be related to the 'syntactic dependency' that Declerck and Tanaka (1996: 293) observe in discussing the factors that prevent the use of the present tense in reported clauses. They point out that the degree of syntactic dependency of the reported clause on the reporting verb is one of the factors that restrict the tense in reported clauses.[16] In the case of the basic comment clauses that Quirk et al. (1985) raise, they are surely syntactically independent of the main clauses since they are parenthetical disjuncts. Seen from this perspective, some reporting clauses serve as comment clauses. The reporting clauses are independent of reported clauses and may be easily omitted or moved to other positions.

However, the dependency between reporting clauses and reported clauses should be defined in a more flexible way than in terms of syntax, when we study spoken English discourse. If a speaker uses a reporting clause to comment on, add information to, or even contextualize the reported event, then the reporting clause behaves as a comment clause and does not necessarily function as a temporal reference point. It depends on how the reporter conceptualizes the relation between the information in the reporting clause with the information in the reported clause. In the following excerpt, the speaker P introduces a new topic in the form of a report. At the beginning, he provides an information source, Jack, in a reporting clause:

(51) P: Jack siz there wz a big fight down there las'night,
     C: Oh rilly?
          (0.5)
     P: with Sam en, what. Gene Callaha:n?]
     J: Gene Callahan.] Guy out of,=
     C: =Callaha:n yeah I know 'm.   (AD: 8)

The speaker's focus is on the reported event that there was a fight, and the hearer's response "Oh really?" is a reaction to the content of the reported event ("there was a big fight down there last night") and not to the report itself ("Jack says . . ."). Although the reporting clause provides the source information, the speaker does not relate the reported event as dependent on the source information. So it could be more directly presented as source information as follows:

(52) (a) According to Jack, there was a big fight down there last night,
     (b) You know what I heard from Jack? There was a big fight down there last night,

In (52a), the reporting clause from (51) behaves more like a comment clause, and in (52b), it even becomes a totally independent sentence. Again, in the following:

(53) he said he *was* standing there and he *was* just out dancing around on the edge of the dance floor and Don who looks real Butch but is this major Nillie Queen comes running up to him and goes: "now just nod your head—nod your head"—and Bob was standing over there watching with this horrified—Alan said he *had* this totally horrified look on his face—and eh—Don goes: "nod your head—nod your head" and so Alan's like: "oh okay"... (Yule and Mathis 1992: 208)

In both occurrences of indirect reporting discourse in this excerpt, the tenses in the reported clauses are not backshifted in their relations to the reporting verbs. The second occurrence is excerpted in (54a) below:

(54) (a) and Bob was standing over there watching with this horrified—Alan said he *had* this totally horrified look on his face.
(b) and Bob was standing over there watching with this horrified look.
(c) and Bob was standing over there watching with this horrified look, which Alan told me.

In (54a), the speaker describes how Bob looked when Don came up to Alan (the first "he" in [53]) and gave a strange order. Here, the speaker makes a repair. At first, the speaker is about to describe Bob as shown in (54b). But since the description "horrified look" is a subjective assessment, the speaker repairs himself and makes clear that the source of the subjectivity is Alan, to support his point. Such source information could also be post-posed as in (54c). There is no dependency or subordinate relationship between the source and the reported event. The event line has its own discourse flow with its own coherence. The source information is added as a comment to supplement the event line. In this way, the speaker's consciousness smoothly flows over the narrative line.

In spoken English, people do not always set temporal reference points in reporting clauses in either indirect or direct reporting discourse. Reporting clauses function more often as hedges, evidential markers, source markers, or personal deictic markers, rather than as reference points for temporal relationships with reported clauses. The reporting clauses commonly seen in news reports may also be considered as comment clauses. The following excerpt contains two indirect reporting sentences:

(55) The World Health Organization announced in a statement that the acute phase of the Ebola hemorrhagic fever epidemic in southwest Zaire *was* over. At least 164 people died after contracting the deadly virus. WHO said that although the disease *was* stabilized, it *anticipates* a number of new cases will

180 *Reporting Discourse, Tense, and Cognition*

be reported from people who are currently in the incubation period which lasts between two to 21 days. (CE 1995. 8: 90)

In both of the indirect reporting sentences in this report, none of the verbs in the reported clauses are backshifted. Reporting clauses in this type of news report function as evidential markers and as source markers, but do not set temporal reference points, since it is commonly assumed that news reports are based on past events. Even if we totally omit reporting clauses, there is often no confusion as to the information structure of the whole discourse, nor as to the temporal relationship between the events, as we can see in the following:

(56) The acute phase of the Ebola hemorrhagic fever epidemic in southwest Zaire *was* over. At least 164 people died after contracting the deadly virus. Although the disease *was* stabilized, a number of new cases will be reported from people who are currently in the incubation period which lasts between two to 21 days.

What the reporting clauses do in (55), then, is to indicate that the report is not based on the reporter's subjective opinion. They do not function to set temporal reference points. Therefore, news reports often have tense-alternation in reporting clauses without confusing the temporal relations between events, as in (26) and (57), or they may use the present tense in reporting clauses as in (58):

(57) The government says a law permitting soldiers to serve in foreign countries will take effect August 10th. Officials said the Japanese cabinet also decided to permit some troops and civilians serving in foreign countries to carry guns. But they will be able to use them only in self-defense. Troops will not be permitted to fight. Japan plans to send troops to Cambodia to join other United Nations forces to help secure the peace between the country's opposing groups. A law permitting Japanese soldiers to operate as U.N. peacekeepers was passed by parliament in June after a major debate.
(VOA News 1992. 8. 4)

(58) Japan says it will send another fact-finding team to Cambodia next week to prepare for Japan's first involvement in a United Nations peacekeeping force. The team will seek to learn how a Japanese peacekeeping group can help repair roads and bridges. Team members also want to learn more about the Cambodian peace agreement. (Ibid.: 8. 6)

In these two cases, the reporting clauses function as source markers, marking where the information came from, and as evidential markers to support the credibility of the information. They do not carry any temporal information.

In summary, in naturally spoken discourse, tense in reporting discourse is more flexible than previous studies have assumed. In this section, I discussed the flexible behavior of reporting clauses. Some may have tense-alternation, which shows that the tense forms of reporting verbs do not directly reflect their tenses. Some may even function as comment clauses. In such cases, reported events themselves are cohesively constructed in whole discourse, and reported verb tenses are determined according to how the present speakers view the reported events. This does not mean, however, that the reported verb tense has no relationship to the reporting verb tense. When speakers focus more on their reported events and construct discourse cohesively around them, the events are more likely to have their own coherence independently from reporting verbs. On the other hand, if the speakers believe that the temporal relationship between the time of reported speakers' speaking and the spoken events is significant, they may clarify the relations by what appears to be backshifting. In spoken discourse, however, there are many cases in which it is more important to keep the discourse coherence of the reported events themselves, and the reporting clauses simply function as speech introducing markers.

6.5. Conclusion

In naturally spoken English, tense in indirect reporting discourse does not behave as has been supposed in traditional grammar. Comrie's formal SoT rule and the relative tense rule of Declerck's CoRA are based on the assumption that the tense in the complement clause is determined by its relation to the head clause. But the absolute tense rule in Declerck's CoRA is common in spoken discourse. Tense is often determined by the reporter's here-and-now, relating directly to the moment of speaking. The prevalence of the absolute tense in spoken discourse is due in part to the fact that the temporal order of the events is often clear from the context. In natural language use, typically, speakers and hearers share some common knowledge of the world, or speakers contextualize their stories beforehand. In addition to Declerck's account of the absolute tense, linguistic restrictions and discourse coherence are keys to the use of absolute tense in spoken English.

Backshifting of tenses once seemed necessary to fulfill logical grammatical requirements aesthetically. But in natural discourse, speakers invest more effort to maintain discourse coherence that fits in the communicative framework at the expense of syntactic integrity. In addition, as Coulmas (1986: 15), one of the followers of SoT admits, shifting of tenses is "by no means logically necessary or implied by the presence of a tense system,"[17] although he viewed SoT as "natural" at least within the confines of a given grammatical system.

In spoken discourse, the relationship between the reporting clause and the reported clause is more flexible than has previously been considered. The previous theories viewed this relationship as a subordination of a complement (or subordinate) clause to a head (or main) clause. However, in spoken discourse, a reporting clause often appears as extra information which the reporter can choose to include or not. In spoken discourse, the main information is the content in the reported clause, and the reporting clause often behaves as if it were a comment clause. For discourse coherence, it is more natural to base tense determination consistently on the reporter's viewpoint rather than on extra information. Some reporting clauses behave flexibly as dialogue markers that function not as temporal reference points, but rather as hedges, evidential markers, source markers, and personal deictic markers. This study demonstrates the prevalence of the speaker's viewpoint by the fact that indirect reporting discourse exhibits tense-alternation. Reporting clauses that have tense-alternation cannot serve as temporal reference points, thus speakers are reporting from their own perspectives.

We further need to elucidate how tense in indirect reporting discourse behaves in actual language performance. The choice between relative and absolute tenses seems more a matter of different uses of reporting discourse for different genres, such as spoken and written discourse, or formal and informal language. In written discourse, temporal order and pragmatic knowledge of the reported events may not be shared as much as in spoken discourse. Therefore, writers more carefully monitor the choice, sequence and relationship of tenses. In spoken discourse, backshifting tenses may obstruct the flow of conversation. Speakers may ignore details of tense to maintain discourse flow and coherence. For successful conversations, the important thing is to maintain the discourse flow and coherence.

7

REPORTING DISCOURSE STYLE AND FUNCTION

7.0. OVERVIEW

In the previous chapters, I have focused on micro-level style choice or shift of reporting discourse: dialogue-introducers with their tense forms in direct reporting discourse, and reported verb tense in indirect reporting discourse. In this chapter, I aim to better understand macro-level style choices in reporting discourse: what determines reporting style itself. Traditional theories have distinguished two kinds of reporting discourse: direct reporting discourse and indirect reporting discourse. Numerous studies in linguistics, literature, and related fields have looked at differences between the two styles. Pragmatic studies started to explore what factors operate to determine reporting discourse style, looking at transactional and functional phases of reporting discourse. However, reporting style choices, when, why and how people choose one speech style over another, are still incompletely understood (Janssen and Wurff 1996). In fact, many factors are interwoven to determine reporting discourse style. In my view, those factors interact with each other in each communication context. Some factors override others depending on the situation, and certain situational orderings and patterns affect reporting style.

My goal in this chapter is to better understand the whole picture of reporting discourse and to clarify the interwoven factors affecting style choice. For that purpose, I first need to know if any structural factors are operating before interactive factors come into play. I need to clarify whether any such factors are not related to pragmatic functions. In discourse studies of language in communication, it is hard to know what is really interactive, goal-directed, and functional, and what is not. Indeed, what the speaker is doing is of a multifaceted nature. Using the combined approaches of discourse analysis and experimental analysis toward reporting discourse, I examine whether structural factors influence a speaker's style choice between direct and indirect styles. At the same time, I show that reporting styles vary along a continuum. Second, although previous pragmatic studies have revealed some functional factors at work for direct and indirect reporting style choice, it has not been clear yet how reporting discourse itself is patterned in discourse and how such patterns interact with styles and functions. After describing reporting discourse patterns and functions, I summarize the correlations between style and function.

In the following section, I first review some fundamental differences between direct and indirect styles, relating to different theoretical backgrounds. I also review the functional differences that the pragmatic studies have revealed. Then I present two studies that I conducted with different approaches to reporting style choice. The first study in 7.2. explores how sentence structures affect reporting style before such pragmatic factors come into play. In this section, I focus on the structural complexities and the length of the original discourse, and experimentally test how they correlate with reporting style. The second study in 7.3. explores interactional functions of reporting discourse in linguistic performance. Here, I explore how functions of reporting discourse correlate with discourse patterns and styles. I show reporting discourse as rule-governed, goal-directed and purposeful linguistic action, by discussing some of its main functions related to evidentiality, information grounding, and dramatization. To synthesize the two studies, in 7.4., I attempt to locate correlations of reporting styles and functions on a continuum.

7.1. GENERAL CHARACTERIZATIONS OF REPORTING DISCOURSE STYLE AND FUNCTION

7.1.1. Theoretical backgrounds

Reporting discourse has been traditionally viewed as a dichotomy. Quirk et al. (1985: 1021) show the following two kinds of reporting discourse:

(1) (a) David said to me after the meeting, "In my opinion, the arguments in favour of radical changes in the curriculum are not convincing."
 (b) David said to me after the meeting that in his opinion the arguments in favour of radical changes in the curriculum were not convincing.

Traditional theories view (1a) as direct reporting discourse, which purports to give the exact words of the original speaker, while viewing (1b) as indirect reporting discourse, which conveys in the words of a subsequent reporter what has been said or written by the original speaker or writer. There are many differences between direct and indirect reporting discourse. The two styles have surface observable differences such as pronominalization, verb tense, place and time deixis, word order, and the presence or absence of the complementizer "that" (Li 1986). They also differ in perspective (Coulmas 1986). In direct style, the reporter quotes the reportee's speech and reports it from the reportee's perspective. The reporter simply lends her/his voice to the reportee and plays the role of the reportee. By contrast, in indirect style, the reporter interprets the reportee's discourse and reports it with her/his own words. The reporter does not assume the reportee's perspective. Direct reporting discourse and indirect reporting discourse also have phonological differences in terms of pause and intonation pattern (Longacre 1976), and semantic differences (Partee 1973).

Often, traditional theories have supposed a syntactic derivational relationship (e.g., Jespersen 1964; Jackson 1990) between the two reporting styles. They assume transformational derivations of instances of indirect reporting discourse from direct discourse:

> You will note a number of changes (e.g., *won't* to *wouldn't*, *this* to *that*, *have* to *had*, *my* to *his*) that occur as a consequence of transforming direct speech into indirect speech. (Jackson 1990)

> It is always possible to reconstruct a direct speech utterance from its reported speech [indirect speech] counterpart or to deduce a reported utterance from a direct one. The adaptations required by the extralinguistic context concern deictic categories. (Cate 1996: 190)

A direct reporting discourse quotes the exact words of the original discourse, and an indirect reporting discourse is derived from the direct discourse.

Traditional theories are typically based on the assumption that direct reporting is a verbatim reproduction, representing the wording of the original speaker. The difference between direct and indirect discourse is thus often discussed as a question of how accurately the reporter reproduces the original discourse:

> in direct speech the reporter is committed to repeating the exact words of the original speaker (or an accurate translation thereof into another language), whereas in indirect speech all that need be communicated is the information contained in the original speaker's utterance.
> (Comrie 1986: 266)

> In direct speech, the utterance of a person (the reported speaker) is conveyed by the reporter in exactly the form in which it originally was said or written (or at least could have been said or written), or even will or can be said or written in the future .... In reported speech [indirect speech], the

utterance of the reported speaker is reported in a form adapted to the linguistic as well as the extralinguistic context . . .   (Cate 1996: 190)

Clark and Gerrig (1990) characterize the verbatim assumption of direct quotation as a strong wording theory, which is adopted in mention theory (e.g., Quine 1951; 1960; Church 1964), demonstrative theory (D. Davidson 1984), dramaturgical theory (Wierzbicka 1974), and others.[1] Prescriptive grammar and style manuals (e.g., Urdang 1991) especially for writing rigidly restrict the accuracy in verbatim quotations.[2] There is also a weak wording theory that characterizes direct quotation as merely an attempt to reproduce the wording of the original, while characterizing indirect quotation as a representation of only the content.

There are other researchers, however, who argue against such traditional views of reporting discourse, and treat reporting style in more flexible ways (e.g., Banfield 1982; Tannen 1989; Clark and Gerrig 1990; Mayes 1990; Sakita 1995; 1996a; Perridon 1996). First, they deny the view that a direct reporting discourse directly quotes the original discourse. Tannen (1986; 1989) points out that direct quotes cannot be exact repetitions of previous utterances, because of the limitations of memory. "Rather, even seemingly 'direct' quotation is really 'constructed dialogue,' that is, primarily the creation of the speaker rather than the party quoted" (Tannen 1989: 99). Mayes (1990) demonstrates that many direct quotes in informal spoken discourse are in fact invented. She places quotes on a continuum from those which could be authentic renditions to those which are entirely invented. Studies of memory (e.g., Wade and Clark 1993) support such a view, demonstrating that from a conversation or text presented only once, memory of exact words is limited to keywords and phrases after even a short delay. Such claims are quite reasonable, since the verbatim assumption cannot account for a number of uses of direct quotation, such as when there is no original wording to reproduce. Following Tannen, Perridon (1996: 165-66) recently claims that direct reporting discourse is as subjective as indirect reporting discourse, since the former is "a kind of acting on the part of the speaker, who casts himself in the role of a real or imagined person whose words or thought he wants to communicate to his audience." The speaker is really performing as an impromptu actor most of the time, even when it seems as if she/he is repeating the original discourse. In indirect style, the speaker's role as interpreter is simply more evident. Perridon claims:

> There is therefore no reason to subscribe to Coulmas' view (1986: 4) that "direct speech always has a *de dicto* interpretation." The expression *that fool*, for example, in *She said, "I don't want to see that fool again,"* is not necessarily a faithful rendering of what the 'original speaker' has actually said (the *de dicto* interpretation), but may as well reflect the opinion of the

reporting (or 'acting') speaker (*de re* interpretation). This becomes evident when the introductory phrase *She said* is expanded to *She said something like*, or changed into *She thought*. (p. 165)

Clark and Gerrig (1990) propose a theory of demonstration. They claim that direct quotation is a demonstration, which works by selective depictions of their referents from a particular vantage point, while indirect reporting discourse is a description.[3] Since quotation has characteristics of demonstration, there are three principles that speakers and hearers share:

(a) Decoupling Principle: Demonstrators intend their audience to recognize different aspects of their demonstrations.
(b) Partiality Principle: Demonstrators intend the depictive aspects to be the demonstration proper.
(c) Selectivity Principle: Demonstrators intend their demonstrations to depict only selective aspects of the referents.

Thus, in direct quotation, the speaker may depict some aspects of the original speaker's utterance, and they usually do not include its exact wording. The speaker depicts features such as sentences (or parts of sentences), emotional states, accents, voices, non-linguistic actions, and non-linguistic events.

Second, the linguists who argue against the traditional theory of reporting discourse claim that the two reporting styles are constructed independently of each other. Banfield (1973; 1982) points out that there are many syntactic constructions that cannot occur in subordinate clauses (indirect quotes) but only occur in main clauses (direct quotes). In many cases, it is hardly possible to assume a transformational relationship between the two styles. Since direct quotes have no stylistic restrictions, a speaker can use many constructions that would be ungrammatical in an indirect style, such as interrogatives, pre-posed adverbs and nominals, imperatives, truncated sentences, exclamations, vocatives, and so forth.[4] She claims that the direct and indirect constructions are independent of each other, and that speakers choose direct or indirect reporting style depending on how much affective information they want to convey. This depends on the context and the speech event.

Third, direct and indirect reporting styles are not discrete entities; the boundary between the two is fuzzy (Tannen 1989). Rather, they are situated on a continuum (Sakita 1992; Yule 1993). Sakita's quantitative analysis (1992) of direct and indirect discourse showed that some items which are generally considered characteristics of one of the two styles are not used exclusively for either one. For instance, although some proponents of prescriptive grammar (e.g., Jespersen 1931; Celce-Murcia and

188 *Reporting Discourse, Tense, and Cognition*

Larsen-Freeman 1983) claim that the complementizer "that" appears only in indirect, it may also be used for direct style. Chafe (1994) also raises a case in which the complementizer "that" is used with direct reporting discourse:

(2) She put that, I gave this car to Robert Ingalls for a gift.
(Chafe 1994: 217)

For more than a century, the 'fuzzy' view of the boundary between direct and indirect reporting styles has been quite common among scholars studying literary narratives. There are intermediate forms that exhibit features of both direct and indirect styles, and Tobler (1894) first defined such forms as "peculiar mingling[s] of direct and indirect discourse."[5] Other researchers as Kalepky (1899), Bally (1912), Lerch (1919), Lorck (1921), Jespersen (1924), Voloshinov ([1929]1986), and Chafe (1994) proposed their views on such intermediate forms, defining characterizations and introducing different terms for such forms.[6] Quirk et al. (1985) show the following examples that contain free direct and free indirect reporting discourse respectively:

(3) (a) I sat on the grass staring at the passers-by. Everybody seemed in a hurry. *Why can't I have something to rush to?*
[The reporting part is italicized]
(b) So that *was* their plan, *was* it? He well *knew* their tricks, and *would show* them a thing or two before he *was* finished. Thank goodness he *had* been alerted, and that there *were* still a few honest people in the world!   [The backshifted verbs are italicized]
(Quirk et al. 1985: 1032-33)

Quirk et al. (1985) also show indirect reporting style variations which are paraphrase or description styles. In such cases, the act of communication may even not be indicated at all. They raise (4b) as an alternative to indirect reporting discourse (4a):

(4) (a) David told me after the meeting that he remained opposed to any radical changes in the curriculum.
(b) I saw David after the meeting. It's a pity that he remains opposed to any radical changes in the curriculum.   (Ibid.: 1021)

7.1.2. Pragmatic studies

Recent pragmatic approaches considering the interactional and transactional functions of language (e.g., Brown and Yule 1983) raised the questions of when and why people choose one speech style over another. Based on their fundamentally different characteristics, direct and indirect reporting styles have different discourse functions or purposes in communication. Studies have shown that contextual and interactional factors crucially influence the choice of reporting styles.

Direct reporting discourse is used for vividness and for dramatic effect (Tannen 1988) based on its 'theatrical' nature (Wierzbicka 1974),[7] and to project authenticity (Macaulay 1987). Accordingly, it can be used to depict future or imaginary events (Sakita 1995). It is also often used to engage the listener, especially at climaxes and punch-lines, by 'showing' rather than 'describing' the climactic speech events (Sakita 1992; 1995; Yule 1993). It reflects the speaker's involvement in the story (Chafe 1982; Tannen 1982b; Li 1986). Since direct reporting discourse is usually felt to be more vivid than indirect reporting discourse, it is often used to create "interpersonal involvement among speaker or writer and audience" (Tannen 1986: 312).[8] Sakita (1997b; 2001a) accounted for cognitive backgrounds of direct and indirect style choice, in terms of the speaker's involvement with the narrative. Depending on the speaker's psychological involvement in the reported events, the speaker construes his recollection of events in different ways (see chapter 3).

In narratives, direct reporting discourse functions to internally evaluate the point of a story (Labov 1972a). Labov defines evaluation as anything that highlights or points to the main point. There are internal and external forms of evaluation.[9] Direct quotation is one type of internal evaluation with which the narrator 'shows' rather than 'tells' the audience what the point is. He claims that many stories contain the largest amount of direct quotation at the main point. Chafe (1994: 217) acknowledges that introducing evaluative information associated with an earlier speech event is the most common motivation for direct reporting discourse.

Direct reporting discourse is often presented as evidence. Mayes (1990) claims that this is because of the popular belief that direct quotes are exact, and therefore more factual or reliable than indirect quotes. Philips (1985) shows that in court, direct quotation is used for evidence pertaining to the elements of the charge, while indirect speech is used for background information. Haverkate (1996: 100) claims that direct reporting discourse functions as a type of evidentiality marker because of its characteristic ability to instill in the listener a presumption of the truth of reported events, by creating the illusion of the listener also being an eye-witness (Fónagy 1986). On the other hand, such assumed exactness of direct reporting discourse accompanies an effect of indirection in presentation. Quoted direct speech conveys information implicitly that might be more awkward to express explicitly. Direct reporting discourse reduces the reporter's responsibility (Goffman 1974; Kuhn 1989), and thus is used for taboo expressions and for self-praise (Macaulay

1987). Direct quotation also functions as mimicry (Macaulay 1987). A speaker can show knowledge of linguistic features such as social dialect, or draw attention to a form of speech.

Banfield (1973) argues that 'expressive elements' only occur in direct reporting discourse and convey something other than propositional content. With such expressive elements, a speaker can communicate affective aspects of meaning. As Haiman (1989) points out, the purpose of expressive language is to indicate internal information about the speaker's state. According to this characterization, direct reporting discourse often projects emotion (Sakita 1995). Similarly, direct reporting discourse also contains discourse markers as "oh" and "well" (Schiffrin 1987),[10] that have clear discourse functions which would not be contained in a paraphrase or in indirect reporting discourse. Sakita (1996c) shows that speakers reporting in direct style frequently use interjections that are not in the original speech, which supports the theory that reporters include affective elements in direct style.[11]

Direct reporting discourse is also often used for reporting interactive elements (Macaulay 1987). There are frequently adjacency pairs such as question and response in direct reporting discourse.

Direct reporting discourse is used when the verbatim language itself has some special relevance (Chafe 1994), for instance, to report some authoritative speech act such as an instruction, advice, demonstration, or explanation, in which the language that was actually used has some importance. There are also cases in which the specific wording has some legal or instructional significance.

On the other hand, indirect reporting discourse reports background facts or contexts, and is often used when the exact contents are uncertain (Li 1986). It is also used when clarifying information or correcting errors (Mayes 1990). Indirect reporting discourse is often used to report inner language and can express beliefs, opinions, or decisions (Chafe 1994), while direct reporting can not report a represented thought that is simultaneous with an attribution like "I think" or "I'm thinking."[12] Narrational summary speech, an indirect style version that condenses, summarizes or recasts characters' speech, is useful in reporting unimportant conversation, or for referring a second time to a conversation that has previously been presented more fully (Toolan 1988: 122).

Socio-cultural factors also operate as keys to the choice of reporting styles. For instance, some studies reported on age and sex (Sanchez 1987; Ferrara and Bell 1991; Sakita 1992; Ely 1993),[13] and others reported on occupation and genre (Thomas 1987; Tannen 1988; Kuhn 1989),[14] as specific socio-cultural situations that affect style choice of reporting discourse. Status differences also affect the choice of reporting styles (Macaulay 1987).

7.2. REPORTING STYLE AND STRUCTURE

7.2.0. Overview

Direct and indirect reporting discourse have different purposes in communication. Pragmatic studies have begun to reveal when and why people choose one speech style over another, focusing on contextual and socio-cultural factors. In this section, I will show that sentence structures also affect reporting styles, before those pragmatic factors come into play. I have experimentally tested the correlations between structural factors and choice of reporting style, focusing on the length and structural complexity of the original discourse, which had emerged as influential factors on reporting style choice in a preliminary analysis of English conversations.

The experiment was designed based on Voloshinov's ([1929]1986) point that reporting discourse is grounded in the interrelationship between the reportee's and the reporter's speech. I will test how the length and structural complexity of the original discourse are correlated with reporting styles. I will also test the hypothesis proposed in previous studies (e.g., Macaulay 1987; Mayes 1990) that direct style is far more frequently used than indirect style, based on a recategorization of indirect styles. I will discuss the results within the framework of speech act theory. I will argue that while structural factors are theoretically primitive factors for style choice, in real conversation, interactive factors tend to override them.

7.2.1. Preliminary study

I first observed twelve casual conversations in natural settings, and generated hypotheses about the influence of structure on reporting style choice. One concerns the length and complexity of reported clauses.

Short sentences often appear with direct reporting style:

(5) (a) Didn't he say I'll write you?
 (b) She goes, that's great.
 (c) but then she said, No, I'm only teasing.
 (d) I was frustrated like Oh that's ridiculous.

192 *Reporting Discourse, Tense, and Cognition*

    (e) well you know she didn't say, Yes your Dad will, but she said, when you see him and . . .
    (f) I can imagine your Dad saying, no no that's all right I won't be active.
    (g) I kept asking her you know, Are you sure . . .

On the other hand, long sentences such as the following employ indirect style:

(6) (a) so the doctor said that they would . . . if he didn't wanna keep being active and do sports and things, right now at his age and with the bad condition of his knee, they normally put in a plastic knee.
    (b) doctor knew what he was talking about, made my Dad feel comfortable, said that he's gonna have this same operation when he's in about twenty years cause he had bad knees from football in high school.
    (c) the next day your Mom told me that she talked to my Mom and that it was all confusing and that she didn't . . . my Mom sounded real upset that she didn't know what was going on about why they didn't change the knee.

These examples suggest that discourse length affects reporting style. However, see also the following:

(7) (a) she said, It's gonna be better. He's gonna walk better, he's gonna feel better, his knee's not gonna hurt, we've seen it over and over . . .
    (b) He goes, Ooo:: you are so smart, what were you, a cheer leader in a high school?

These are reported in direct style. By contrasting (6a)(6b)(6c) with (7a)(7b), we see that the former reporting discourses contain conjunctions, embedded sentences, subordinate interrogative clauses, adverbial clauses, and so forth. On the other hand, the latter contain clusters of short utterances combined by commas to show intonation breaks. So, it seems that the length of reported discourse does not in itself matter; rather the underlying relationship between length and structural complexity ultimately affects the choice of reporting style.

However, observational study has two inadequacies. First, although reporting styles seem to be affected by structural variations in the original discourse, it is hard for researchers to grasp the original discourse by observing surface language phenomena. The reporters often do not reproduce all the verbal and nonverbal features of the original discourse. It is inadequate to examine people's way of reporting without knowing what they are actually reporting. Voloshinov ([1929]1986) emphasizes that the true object of inquiry ought to be precisely the dynamic interrelationship of the two factors, the speech being reported (the reportee's speech) and the speech doing the reporting (the reporter's speech). Second, it is difficult for observers to control for the many interactional factors interwoven in natural conversations, enough to place a clear focus on the structural factors.

7.2.2. Experimental study

To further examine the hypothesis that reporting styles are affected by the structural variations of the original (reported) discourse, I designed an experiment. I showed native speakers of English a film which contained discourse of different lengths and complexities. I observed how people report the differently structured original discourse in different styles by comparing the reportees' and the reporters' speech.

The following hypothesis was tested:

> Long and structurally complicated discourse tends to be reported in indirect style, whereas short and simple discourse tends to be reported in direct style.

7.2.2.1. Method

The subjects were native speakers of English. They were enrolled in the University of Wisconsin-Madison, as undergraduate or graduate students. Their ages ranged from 18 to 32 years. There were 10 females (24.8 years old on average) and nine males (23.9 years old on average). I showed the subjects a film in a language laboratory. They saw a total of three scenes. After each scene, they were asked to describe the scene. The direction given was, "Please describe what you witnessed in the film." They were in individual booths, and recorded what they had seen or heard in the film, using microphones. So this was a non-interactive, monologic reporting discourse.

The film was specifically designed and filmed for this experiment, so as to focus on the discourses' length and structural complexity by controlling the variables:[15]

(a) Actors (reportees): two males.
(b) Context: the subjects had been told that Bill and Kevin were talking in their office.
(c) Topic of the conversation: casual talk about coffee.
(d) Sentence type: statement.

(e) Interactions in each scene: the actors were talking all through the film, but some parts of their voice had been erased. All that the subjects heard was one discourse per person per scene, except in scene 3, when each actor had an additional short remark at the end.

(f) Length and structure of the discourse (independent variable): in scene 1, each actor uttered a simple, short discourse; in scene 2, each actor had one semi-long discourse with simple conjunctions "but" and "because"; in scene 3, each had a long and complicated discourse which contained conjunctions, relative clauses, embedded sentences, adverbial clauses, subordinate interrogative clauses, *to*+infinitive verbs, and so forth. Additionally, in scene 3, each uttered a simple short discourse at the end.[16]

The following is the discourse that the subjects heard in the film:

SCENE 1
B: Oh, coffee is ready.   (4 words)
K: It's about time, I really wanna have my muffin.   (9 words)

SCENE 2
B: I was gonna get a muffin too, *but* I just don't feel that good.
                                                       (14 words)
K: I wasn't feeling well, *but* I got the muffin *because* I thought it would help my stomach.   (17 words)

SCENE 3
K: Usually I buy Colombian coffee. This time the coffee *that* I bought is *I think* it's called Hawaiian something or other. *I just decided* I would take a different kind of coffee.   (32 words)
B: Friend of mine from Brazil knew somebody *who* ran a coffee farm, *and* we have talked a lot about maybe um starting some type of a, of a business, *where* we will import in coffee, *because we know how much* I like to drink coffee. (I'm a big) coffee drinker, too. (Good) deal to make some money. Could be good idea.   (61 words)
K: Yeah, it's a good business, it's been going on for a while. (12 words)
B: See what happens.   (3 words)

7.2.2.2. Data analysis procedures

From the subjects' description of the film, the parts in which they reported Bill's and Kevin's speech were extracted and analyzed. First, they were classified into direct and indirect styles.[17] To distinguish the two styles, the general features raised in 7.1. were considered. In direct style, the speech is reported from the reportee's perspective. In indirect style, the reporter interprets the reportee's discourse and reports it in her/his own words. Syntactic differences, such as pronominal forms, verb forms (tense), demonstratives, and adverbials of time and place, were also considered. The audiotapes were examined along with the transcriptions, because intonation, stress, pause, as well as voice change could support the classification of the speech as direct or indirect. The same classification procedure was conducted again, three weeks later, in order to ensure the reliability of the classifications.

The frequency of usage of direct and indirect styles was counted. Indirect styles were separated into three subcategories: indirect style using a gerund or a noun phrase; indirect style using a sentence; and description style. The frequency of direct and indirect styles in each reported scene was further calculated into a percentage, and the distribution of the three scenes was compared with each other.

7.2.2.3. Results

The subjects employed direct and indirect styles in reporting the actors' speech according to the frequency distribution shown in Table 1.

In scene 1, Bill's speech, which consisted of four words, was reported twice in indirect style using a gerund (reported parts are italicized):[18]

(8) (a) They were talking about um *the coffee being ready*.
    (b) We heard about *the coffee being ready*.

It was reported three times in indirect style using a sentence. For example:

(9) (a) Bill said something to the effect of that *the coffee was ready*.
    (b) The gentleman on the left did say *coffee was ready*.

It was reported in direct style six times. For example:

(10) (a) The guy behind the desk says, *coffee is ready*.
     (b) The man without a beard said, *I hope my coffee is ready*.

Table 1: Frequency of Direct & Indirect Styles

SCENE 1

		4 words Bill	9 words Kevin
Indirect	(Gerund)	2	3(1*)
	(Sentence)	3	5(1*)
Direct		6	7

(N.B. The symbol * stands for the thing which did not actually happen.)

SCENE 2

		14 words Bill	17 words Kevin
Indirect	(Gerund)	1	0
	(Sentence)	12	15(1#)
	(Description)	6	3
Direct		2	4

(N.B. The symbol # stands for a subordinate interrogative clause.)

SCENE 3

		32 words Kevin	61 words Bill	12 words Kevin
Indirect	(Gerund)	6	5	0
	(Sentence)	13(5#)	17(7#)	3
	(Description)	2	5	2
Direct		1	0	3

Kevin's speech, which consisted of nine words, was reported three times in indirect style using a gerund, five times in indirect style using a sentence, and seven times in direct style. An example of each style follows:

(11) The man says something about *getting a muffin*.
(12) Gentleman on the right then said *he couldn't wait to have his muffin*.
(13) *Oh, good I want the coffee now to have with my muffin*, is what is, what Kevin says.

The case with the symbol * in the parenthesis did not actually happen, as shown here:

(14) They, the gentleman on the right talked about *wanting coffee* asking if *the coffee was ready*. The gentleman on the left did say *coffee was ready* . . .

This turn-taking did not happen in the film. In the real scene, only Bill (on the left) said, "Coffee is ready." However, this case is counted along with other factual reported events, because this was in the reporter's own memory, hence, it is psychologically real for her.

In scene 2, Bill's speech of fourteen words was reported once in indirect style using a gerund, twelve times in indirect style using a sentence, and six times in description style, which is also considered to be one of the subclasses of indirect style. On the other hand, his speech was reported twice in direct style. The following examples show each of these styles in order:

(15) Bill says something about *getting wanting to get a muffin* . . .
(16) The first, the one man who was on the left which was Bill was saying that *he wanted a muffin but he didn't get one, because he didn't feel well.*
(17) *Bill didn't wanna eat because he wasn't feeling very well.*
(18) The man without the beard said *I was thinking of having a muffin, too, but I'm not feeling so well.*

(17) is in description style, so there are no reporting verbs. The reporter seems to be describing the scene in his own words or as his own interpretation of the scene, although the reporter actually used Bill's perspective. This is considered to be a case of indirect style. Recall (4b), which Quirk et al. (1985: 1021) cite as an example of one of the variations of indirect reporting style:

(4) (b) I saw David after the meeting. It's a pity that *he remains opposed to any radical changes in the curriculum.*

After noting the possibility of this type of paraphrased indirect style, Quirk et al. (1985) exclude it from their definition of reporting. By simply looking at (4b), it is hard to know if it is a report of somebody's speech or is simply the speaker's immediate remark based on her/his observation of the situation. However, Table 1 shows that a significant portion of the instances of indirect reporting use this style.

Kevin's speech of seventeen words was reported fifteen times in indirect style using a sentence, three times using description style, and four times in direct style. Listed below is one example of each in order:

(19) Kevin said that *he got the muffin because he thought it would make him feel better*.
(20) *One of them ate the muffin because he felt it would help his stomach.*
(21) He said *well I wasn't feeling well either but I thought maybe this would help.*

The following is the case labeled with the symbol # in the parenthesis in scene 2 of Table 1. It is a subordinate interrogative sentence, which contains a clause starting with "what" or "how." It is considered to be one of the indirect styles using a sentence:

(22) Kevin responds with a comment about *how he thought a muffin*.

In scene 3, Kevin's speech of 32 words was reported six times in indirect style with a gerund, thirteen times in indirect style using a sentence (including five cases of subordinate interrogative sentences), twice in description style, and only once in direct style. I have taken two distinct cases, indirect style with a gerund and indirect style with a noun phrase, and grouped them together for the purpose of this classification. Here is an example of indirect style with a gerund:

(23) The man on the right talks about *usually buying Colombian* and . . .

Of the six cases counted as indirect style with a gerund some exemplify indirect style with a noun phrase, such as:

(24) Kevin was talking about *the different kinds of coffee that he had he'd er that kind Colombian that he liked that tried some Hawaiian kind.*

The following example of indirect style uses a sentence:

(25) Kevin said that *he usually drinks Colombian coffee, however, this time he tried something different* . . .

Here is an example of indirect style using a subordinate interrogative clause:

(26) He's talking about *how he usually drinks*, he talked about *how he usually drinks Colombian coffee*, . . .

In scene 3, it is rather difficult to judge whether the indirect style is description or some other variation of indirect style. In the following example, the italicized part could be considered a description without a reporting verb, but could also be interpreted as an object of the reporting phrase "talks about":

(27) The man on the right talks about usually buying Colombian and *this time he bought Hawaiian version, Hawaiian type of coffee.*

Similar cases, in which the reporter shifts to report by her/his own interpretation in the middle of a sentence, are frequently seen in the reports of scene 3, presumably because of the complexity and the length of the reported event. This ambiguity between typical indirect style and description style does not affect the frequency of counting direct and indirect styles though, because description style has been classified as one of the subcategories of indirect style. The only case in direct style was the following:

(28) The man with the beard said *usually, I drink Colombian coffee* or something,

In scene 3, Bill's speech of 61 words was reported five times in indirect style with a gerund, seventeen times in indirect style with a sentence (including seven times with subordinate interrogative clauses), and five times in description style. One example of each, including one with a subordinate interrogative clause, is shown below:

(29) The guy on the left, kind of rocking his chair, was talking about maybe *opening a business of um importing or exporting coffee, since he drinks so much coffee*, or something I guess.
(30) Bill said that *he had a friend who knew somebody who had a coffee business in Brazil, sort of a farm, and he had been thinking about maybe going into that business.*
(31) The guy behind the desk told a story about . . . *how they had discussed um starting up a coffee import business, importing coffees into the United States.*
(32) *The man on the left plans to start like a coffee business with some friend who ah owns the coffee plantation in Brazil.*

None of the subjects used direct style to report Bill's speech in scene 3.

Lastly, Kevin's additional twelve word remark was reported three times in indirect style with a sentence, twice in description style, and three times in direct style. Examples of each of these follow:

(33) Kevin said that *he thought that was a goo- you know it sounded like a good business.*
(34) And so *this other guy thought that would be a good idea.*
(35) And both agreed *yeah it was a good business.*

Table 2: Ratio of Direct & Indirect Styles Used in Reporting

(Original sentence types: simple short discourse)

SCENE 1

	4 words Bill	9 words Kevin	Total
Indirect	45.5%	53.3%	49.4%
Direct	54.5%	46.7%	50.6%

(Original sentence types: semi-long discourse with one or two conjunctions)

SCENE 2

	14 words Bill	17 words Kevin	Total
Indirect	90.5%	81.8%	86.15%
Direct	9.5%	18.2%	13.85%

(Original sentence types: long discourse with complicated structures)

SCENE 3

	32 words Kevin	61 words Bill	Total	12 words Kevin
Indirect	95.5%	100.0%	97.75%	62.5%
Direct	4.5%	0.0%	2.25%	37.5%

The results of Table 1 are converted into percentages in Table 2. Table 2 shows the correlation between the sentence type and the use of direct and indirect styles. To report short and simple discourses, 50.6% were in direct style. To report semi-long discourses with one or two conjunctions, 13.85% were in direct style. To report long and complicated discourses, only 2.25% were in direct style. Let us also look at Kevin's last additional remark in scene 3 ("Yeah, it's a good business, it's been going on for a while"). This was not included in calculating the total percentages for scene 3, because it is obviously a different type of sentence from the other two speeches in this scene, in terms of both the complexity of its structure and its length. It consists of twelve words and has no conjunctions. This remark should be situated between the sentence type in scene 1 (four and nine words) and the sentence type in scene 2 (fourteen and seventeen words). 62.5% of the reportings of this remark by Kevin were in indirect style and 37.5% were in direct style. And in fact the ratio of indirect to direct reportings is greater than that of scene 1 and less than that of scene 2, as seen in Table 3. The shift of reporting style from direct to indirect, follows the shift

Reporting Discourse Style and Function 201

Table 3: Shift of Reporting Styles (1)

	Direct style	Indirect style
Scene 1	50.60%	49.40%
Kevin's remark in Scene 3	37.50%	62.50%
Scene 2	13.85%	86.15%
Scene 3	2.25%	97.75%

Table 4: Shift of Reporting Styles (2)

style \ words	4	9	12	14	17	32	61
Indirect style	45.5%	53.3%	62.5%	90.5%	81.8%	95.5%	100.0%
Direct style	54.5%	46.7%	37.5%	9.5%	18.2%	4.5%	0.0%

Figure 1: Correlation of Reporting Styles with Length & Complexities

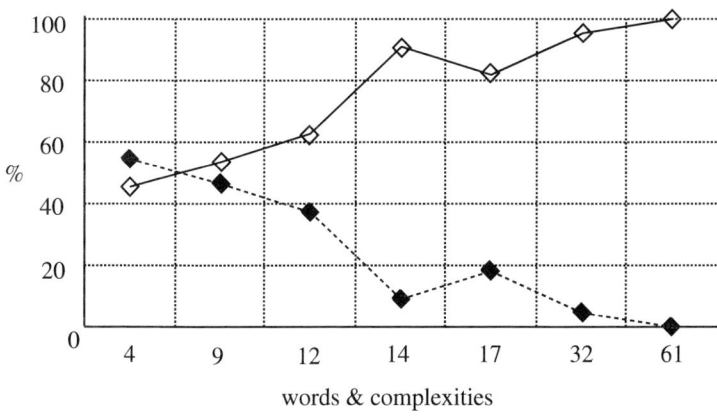

of the sentence type from short and simple to long and complicated. In Table 4, we can see the style shift for each utterance, which is graphed in Figure 1.

The results partially support the hypothesis. For reporting simple and short discourse, indirect style is used almost as frequently as direct style. For longer and more complicated discourse, indirect style is used more frequently. The longest discourse was reported exclusively in indirect style.

7.2.3. Backgrounds of structural influence on style choice

There are several possible explanations for the shift in reporting style in response to structural complexities. First, as wording theories suggest, it may be due to the limitations of memory. To report complex sentences, speakers shift to indirect style that is a representation of the content alone, rather than attempting to reproduce the wording of the original, which is almost impossible for such complex sentences. About length, Macaulay (1987: 14) points out that when the remark is short and the point depends on the form, "the listener has no reason to question its validity. With longer utterances, the validation may be less obvious." Ely (1993) states that people use direct reporting style more frequently when they remember the reported speech event clearly enough to reproduce it, such as in reporting an event that happened in the immediate past. Of course, such claims cannot rely on a speaker's exact memory of short and simple sentences, since memory of exact words is limited after even a short delay (Wade and Clark 1993). But in any case, even if it is not an exact quotation, if the speaker still thinks she/he remembers the forms of short sentences better than those of long sentences, the memory explanation may work.

Second, the influence of structural complexity on reporting style may be due to the communicative need to avoid ambiguity. Although I attempted to make the setting in the experiment neutral and monologic to exclude interactional factors, such a speech situation is still a valid example as one type of situation prompting spoken language. When structural factors such as length and complexity influence reporting style, it is not totally independent of communicative motivations. It may be explained in speech act theory (Grice 1975). As one of his maxims about conversation, Grice includes the maxim of manner: "Avoid ambiguity." I assume that following this maxim, speakers try not to exceed the limits of the listeners' ability to decode structurally complicated sentences. For instance, suppose a speaker utters a sentence (36a) which is written out without quotation marks. It is ambiguous in two ways, (36b) and (36c):

(36) (a) I said it's not my fault 'cause she made it.
(b) I said, "it's not my fault," 'cause she made it.
(c) I said, "it's not my fault 'cause she made it."

(36b) represents the interpretation that the adverbial clause with the conjunction "because" is the reporter's immediate utterance, conjoined to the reporter's utterance, "I said, 'it's not my fault.'" On the other hand, (36c) shows the adverbial clause as included in the reported speaker's utterance, conjoined to the reported discourse, "it's not my fault." Complex sentences with conjunctions may cause such ambiguities. To avoid the ambiguity that may result from such complex sentences, speakers may choose to use an indirect style, including description or summary style, and focus on the content.

Deictic relations also may cause ambiguity in direct discourse. Direct quotes have a deictic center, the same as in the original event (Mayes 1990). Since the deictic center of direct quote is the present time, it is easily confused with the narrator's present. For instance, in the utterance (37a), both personal deixis and temporal deixis are ambiguous. The utterance (37a) could mean either (37b) or (37c):

(37) (a) The doctor said you are OK, you are just a bit tired, but do you believe it?
(b) The doctor said, "You are OK, you are just a bit tired," but do you believe it?
(c) The doctor said, "You are OK, you are just a bit tired, but do you believe it?"

In indirect style, such deictic confusion is avoided, since all the deictic elements are centered around the narrator's immediate present. The meanings in (37b) and (37c) are expressed clearly in indirect style as follows:

(38) (a) The doctor said that I was OK, and that I was just a bit tired. But do you believe in it? (for 37b)
(b) The doctor said that I was OK but was just a bit tired. He then asked me if I believed in it. (for 37c)

However, in natural discourse, such ambiguities are often left to be solved by contextual cues. Interactional factors often override structural factors. For instance, a sentence with a long adverbial clause is reported in direct style when the speaker is highly involved in the reporting. In such cases, features such as pause and voice quality help overcome the ambiguities in the flow of conversation. In contrast, in the present experimental situation, there were no interactional or interpersonal factors to induce speakers to use direct style to report long complicated sentences.

When reporting long and structurally complicated sentences, indirect reporting style reduces ambiguities caused by the complexities. Indeed, in reporting very long sentences, speakers often shift from direct to indirect style in mid-sentence. In short and simple sentences, there is usually less ambiguity, so there is less motivation to use indirect style to avoid ambiguity. Accordingly, the speakers in the present experiment used direct and indirect style equally to report short and simple sentences, since interactional factors that could also influence style choice were excluded. But for reporting long and complicated sentences, they used indirect style more frequently.

7.2.4. Summary

The present study shows that reporting style correlates with length and structural complexity. Reporting style shifts to indirect style, concomitant with the shift of sentence type from short and simple to long and complicated. When the sentence was short and simple, people generally used the direct style slightly more frequently than the indirect style. The longer and the more complicated the sentence structure was, the more often it was reported in indirect style. In fact, a very long and complicated speech of 61 words was reported in indirect style by all subjects.

Although many discourse studies of conversations and interviews have reported that direct style is used far more frequently than indirect style (e.g., Macaulay 1987; Mayes 1990), the present study showed that this is not true. Direct style is not always favored over indirect style. Indirect style is used more frequently than direct style in reporting long and complicated sentences. Previous observational studies overlooked some forms of indirect style, such as indirect style with a gerund, indirect style with a noun phrase, and description style. In the present study, the inclusion of these styles made it possible to accurately judge the frequency of occurrences of indirect reporting discourse. This is because the present study sees reporting discourse as the interrelationship between the reportee's speech and the reporter's speech, and surveyed reporting discourse by comparison with its original discourse.

The present study indeed demonstrated that there are many varieties of ways of reporting a single original utterance, either in direct or in indirect styles. Although some studies (Bates, Masling, and Kintsch 1978; Hjelmquist 1984) claimed that people have a substantial memory for surface structure as well as for meaning, more recent studies on memory (e.g., Wade and Clark 1993) report that memory for exact words is limited after even a short delay. The present experiment confirmed that people do not report the exact original utterances in direct style but in a variety of ways, which supports Tannen's (1986; 1988) view that all quotation is constructed.

Monologic reporting in controlled settings gave evidence of structural influence on style choice. In natural conversations, many factors come into play simultaneously. I assume that structural factors such as sentence length and structural complexity are primitive factors for style choice, but interactional factors override them in conversations. A very long discourse may, in fact, be reported in direct style, seeking an effect such as vividness, or the avoidance of responsibility. We need to investigate further how the interactional and the socio-cultural factors interact with the structural factors in natural language processing.

7.3. REPORTING FUNCTION AND PATTERN

7.3.0. Overview

In the previous section, I examined structural factors that influence reporting style. In this section, I will look at interactional and functional aspects of human reporting behaviors. I will explore reporting discourse patterns with a discourse analytic approach, and at the same time, I will show how interactional functions of reporting discourse are correlated with reporting style and patterns.

Human reporting behaviors fall into some routine patterns or scripts that people in the same language community share. Of course, they are not scripts in a narrow sense as often discussed in script theory (Schank and Abelson 1977; Mandler 1984), which associates people's linguistic actions in particular kinds of social occasions, places, or settings with routine, recognizable patterns. Rather I am interested in a wider interpretation of 'script,' on the assumption that reporting discourse may have sequential patterns or rules associated with certain functions. Moreover, the 'rules' that I have in mind are not behavioral rules that people must follow in order to make sense. Rather, they are 'script schemas' that are "derived from concrete experience of events" (Nelson 1986: 6) and are abstractions of how reporting proceeds in interactions in order to achieve certain goals. This chapter explores one of the central questions of discourse analysis: "Are there principles underlying the order in which one utterance follows another?" (Schiffrin 1994: 41). Labov (1972a: 252) acknowledges that the "fundamental problem of discourse analysis is to show how one utterance follows another in a rational, rule-governed manner." There are attempts (e.g., Hundsnurscher 1980; Franke 1990) to identify systems of rules that determine well-formed sequences of speech acts and coherent dialogues. But rather than adopt their methodology of working out the rules without looking at actual dialogue performances,[19] I take a discourse analytic approach and examine the daily linguistic performances documented in transcriptions.

In this section, I will present observations of reporting discourse in English, focusing on its interactional functions. I will focus on some of its main functions related to 1) evidentiality; 2) foreground and background information; and 3) dramatization, to show reporting discourse as a discourse strategic device. The dialogue patterns are shown for some of the main functions. Certain tendencies of different reporting styles emerge as characteristics of each function, and the correlations between styles and functions are summarized on a continuum in 7.4.

7.3.1. Method

This study takes a qualitative approach to reporting discourse in American English. After preliminarily examining seventeen conversations situated in different settings, seven are chosen for more detailed analyses: a telephone conversation between two females; a telephone conversation between two males; a face-to-face conversation involving two females and one male; two dinner-table conversations involving groups of both genders; a female interviewed by a female; and a male interviewed by a male.[20] The first five represent casually spoken language among friends, in which the participants are less conscious of their discourse style and have fewer psychological constraints on their speech. The two interviews are semi-formal. The transcripts as well as the audiotapes were examined.

7.3.2. Reporting discourse functions

7.3.2.1 Evidentiality

Reporting discourse is a manifestation of evidentiality in English (Thurgood 1981; Li 1986). As defined by Chafe (1986), evidentiality is the linguistic means of indicating how the speaker obtained the information on which she/he bases an assertion.[21] Anderson (1986: 274) also identifies 'evidentials' as the linguistic devices to show the kind of justification for a factual claim which is available to the person making that claim. He raises the following as part of his generalizations:

(a) Evidentials are normally used in assertions (realis clauses), not in irrealis clauses, nor in presuppositions.[22]

(b) When the claimed fact is directly observable by both speaker and hearer, evidentials are rarely used (or have a special emphatic or surprisal sense).
(c) When the speaker (first person) was a knowing participant in some event (voluntary agent; conscious experiencer), the knowledge of that event is normally direct and evidentials are then often omitted.   (p. 277)

Reporting discourses share these characteristics when used as evidentials. Accordingly, in the following, I will demonstrate that speakers use reporting discourse to state their opinions, for example, to express disagreement, or to attempt to convince others. Speakers also use reporting discourse when they lack enough background information to answer questions. I will show that the use of reporting discourse as evidentials follows some common patterns.

7.3.2.1.1. Disagreement and persuasion

When people disagree with others or need to convince them of something, they often use reporting discourse as a form of evidence. Because evidentiality functions as an indication of the source and reliability of a speaker's knowledge, the speaker can strengthen her/his argument by quoting other people's speech. In the following conversational excerpt, N tells H about her pimples, and describes how badly it hurt when a doctor opened the pimples (reported clauses are italicized):

(39) N: It (js) hu:rt so bad Heidi I wz cry:::ing,=
H: =Yhher khhiddi[: n g.]
N: [nNo:]::. He really hurt me he goes *I'm sorry, hh wehhh .hh I khho th(h)at dznt make i(h)t a(h)n(h)y better* yihknow he wz jst (0.4) so, e-he didn't mean to be but he wz really hurting me.
(HG)

N starts talking about the doctor opening her pimples. She emphasizes the acuteness of her pain by first saying, "It hurt so bad." H seems to be surprised and cannot believe the seriousness, so she utters the remark, "You're kidding." Against this, N says, "No," and repeats, "He really hurt me." Then she quotes the doctor's remark, "I'm sorry, well I know that doesn't make it any better," and concludes by saying, "he was really hurting me," again. In (39), N uses reporting discourse as a means to convince H that the pain was really serious. This exchange is patterned around the proposition as follows:

N: proposition
H: disagreement or doubt
N: "No"; proposition; *speech reporting*; proposition

Here, the speaker uses the reporting discourse as evidence to support her proposition when facing disagreement from the other party.[23] Since the degree of pain is subjective, she supports her insistence on the reality of the pain by reporting that the doctor himself was aware of the pain and indeed apologized to her. Quoting the doctor validates, authenticates and emphasizes her proposition.

In the next example from the same conversation, similar exchanges occur: the speaker, H, is not convinced by what her friend, N, says, and N quotes the doctor in order to strengthen her remark. Here, N and H are discussing what is good and bad for pimples. N starts by saying that the doctor gave her some pills to take:

(40) N: So 'e gay me these pills tih ta:ke?=
     H: =What. Tetracykuhleen?
     N: No: cuz I usetuh take that an' it didn' he:lp so 'e gay me something e:lse.=
     H: =Hm:.
     N: He sai:d- yihknow, (0.2) *sometimes Tetracycline jus doesn' he:lp.*
     N: Also he sid that (0.3) t *what you ea:t, (0.2) end how you wash yer face has nothing tih do with it,*
     H: Yer kiddin[g.
     N: [nNo:,
     N: He says *'t's all inside you it's 'n emotional thing'*n, hhh [e : n,]
     H: [Yeah] buh whatchu ea:t if you eat greasy foo:d=
     N: =We:h he said *it's no:t the fact thet you've eaten the greasy food it's a fact thet you worry about it. En that makes you break ou:t.* (HG)

In line 2, H expresses her idea that Tetracycline, a kind of medicine, is good for pimples. Against this, N says, "No . . . it didn't help." Then she quotes the doctor, "sometimes Tetracycline just doesn't help," in order to support her remark. We can observe the pattern in which the speaker first faces an unexpected opinion ("Tetracycline?") which is different from her own, negates it ("No"), states the proposition ("it [Tetracycline] didn't help"), then quotes another person's speech (doctor's remark). In this way the speaker uses reporting discourse as a tool to support the proposition when disagreeing with others. It is patterned as follows:

     H: unexpected or different opinion
     N: "No"; proposition; *speech reporting*

In this case, the doctor's remark is provided as an authority for a statement. Du Bois (1986: 323) claims that the critical listener sifts through what is said, deciding what she/he will accept as reliable and what she/he will not. He lists four basic questions that the hearer may ask in order to gauge the reliability of the utterance:

(a) How does the speaker know?
(b) What are his interests, and how might interests distort assertions?
(c) Is he sincere, or is he lying?
(d) Is he fallible? (1986: 323)

These four questions—knowledge, interests, sincerity, and fallibility—stand at the core of the problem of reliability. Quotation attempts to shift the hearer's scrutiny of knowledge, interests, sincerity and fallibility to others who are more able to bear it. In the above case, by quoting the doctor, the speaker defers the responsibility to an authority who the speaker expects will withstand the scrutiny.

In lines 7-8 in (40), N tells H her belief that what one eats and how one washes one's face has nothing to do with pimples by quoting the doctor's remark. Against H's remark "You're kidding," N says, "No," and quotes the doctor's remark ("It's all inside you it's an emotional thing") to support what she said. But H is not convinced yet and still disagrees, saying, "Yeah but . . . if you eat greasy food . . ." N further quotes what the doctor said to convince H. Here, we can observe a similar pattern of exchange as above:

N: proposition
H: disagreement or doubt
N: "No"; *speech reporting*
H: disagreement
N: "Well"; *speech reporting*

Here is another example of this pattern:

(41) M: they wanted t'get my au:tograph.]
R: uh huh!]
S: Yer kidding.
R: Oh my go::sh=
M: =No, They said thet *they wanted my au:tograph*. (SN: 15)

Against M's remark that some girls wanted his autograph, R and S show surprise and doubt, then M says, "No," and indirectly quotes the girls' remark to convince his friends.

The basic pattern for evidential use of reporting discourse observed in (39), (40), and (41) is summarized as follows (parenthetical listings of the 'proposition' indicate that it may appear in any of these positions):

1: (proposition)
2: disagreement, doubt, or different opinion
3: negation (e.g., "No"); (proposition); *speech reporting*; (proposition)

In all the above cases, presenting reporting discourse attempts to change the hearer's belief, expectation, or state of mind. It conforms to what Du Bois (1986: 323) claims about the function of evidentials: "evidence is used to persuade, and persuasion is a perlocutionary act, involving a change in the state of mind of the hearer."

7.3.2.1.2. Response

Since reporting discourse incorporates the functions of evidentials, it is used as a discourse strategy to compensate for one's lack of information or even to state a proposition itself. This is observed when people are expected to answer questions but lack enough background information to answer them. In the next example, N asks H about a man, but H has not yet met him, so she answers by reporting the words of her friend:

(42) N: Well wt's (.) wt's he li: [ke.
    H: [hhhhhhhh a-ah: she says (.) *he* y'know, *th'las'-time she saw im which wz (.) three years ago he wz pretty good looki-*[*ng,*
    N: [Uh hu [:h,
    H: [t hhh
    H: A:nd u:m,
    H: you know she says *eez a veewy nice guy.eez a rea:l, (0.7) t good pers'n.*
                                                                                                                                                                                       (HG)

To answer N's question, "What is he like?" H cannot give her personal opinion because she has never met him. She tries to answer the question anyway by quoting a friend who has already met him ("she says he- you know, the last time she saw him which was three years ago he was pretty good looking"). This is a convenient discourse strategy to carry on the conversation. It also enables the speaker to answer questions while avoiding personal commitment or responsibility for the answer, since the speaker does not give her/his own personal opinion. In the following example, the speaker shifts the responsibility to an authority even though his personal opinion is requested:

(43) K: Just from your own personal point of view, what are the important issues?
N: Well, in the words of George Bush, *jobs, and jobs, jobs*, or maybe he said, *jobs, jobs and jobs*.
K: *And jobs*, right. (AE 1992. 6: 105)

Although the speaker, K, has confined his question to "Just from your own personal point of view," the speaker N refers to the words of an authority, George Bush. Based on the audiotape, K's follow-up confirms the exactness of N's quote, which suggests that Bush serves as an evidential with high reliability. Studies have shown that the use of reporting discourse as a means of avoiding personal responsibility is cross-linguistically observed (e.g., Kuhn 1989; Besnier 1993).

7.3.2.2. Foreground and background information

Yamanashi (1995) discusses the ways style choice in natural language reflects the speaker's perspectives, contrasting foreground and background information in five aspects: new and old information; conclusion and premise; existing object and background place/space; moving object and scene; coded part and omitted part. Hopper and Thompson (1980: 280) had formulated:

> In any speaking situation, some parts of what is said are more relevant than others. That part of a discourse which does not immediately and crucially contribute to the speaker's goal, but which merely assists, amplifies, or comments on it, is referred to as BACKGROUND. By contrast, the material which supplies the main points of the discourse is known as FOREGROUND.

Although Thompson (1987) later questions the foreground/background distinction in terms of 'importance' in narratives,[24] in general, one of the cognitive foundations of the foreground/background distinction of information is the contrast of salient versus contextual information. In the following sections, I will demonstrate that reporting discourse can either 'show' salient information or 'describe' contextual information, depending on its style. Typically, direct quotation functions to highlight climaxes within the foreground of a series of speech events in contrast to background

212 *Reporting Discourse, Tense, and Cognition*

contexts, while indirect style is used to report background information.

7.3.2.2.1. Showing climaxes or punch-lines

Speakers often use reporting discourse to 'show' instead of to 'describe' a climax or punch-line in a series of narrated events. Let us consider the first example:

(44) H: ='n then, hhm (0.2) tch en the:(w)- the mother's hh sister is a real bigot.
    N: [i - Y a : h,   ]
    H: [Yihknow en sh]e hates anyone who isn' a Catholic.=
    H: =hhh a:nd this boy is Jewish. hh An' tshe- this girl's fixed up onna da- a bline da:te. An' the(g)- en turns out t'be this gu:y.=
    N: =[Uh hu[:h,
    H: =[hhhh [An' they goes *oh I hear yer of the Jewish faith* yihknow so 'ere's a whole thing in that, hhhhhh=   (HG)

H relates the plot of a movie. Before this paragraph, she has described the boy in the excerpt as very handsome, rich, and nice. H wants to explain why the girl was not successful with him and the result was sad. The context from the first to the fourth line makes clear that the mother's sister hates anyone who is not a Catholic. In the fifth line, she says that the boy is Jewish. In this circumstance, the boy and the girl were fixed on a blind date. By this point, anyone would naturally expect the mother and her sister not to like the boy and predict that the girl and the boy cannot get together. There is little need to describe what happens next. Rather, the hearer is curious to know how the next episode happened rather than simply what it was. For this purpose, 'to show' the climax is more effective than simply to summarize or describe it. H uses a direct quotation from the movie to achieve this effect.

In contrast to this example, let me show an example in a similar context which does not have the same function. H describes a movie using reporting discourse:

(45) H: It's jist like the psychological backgroun' behind all these different people in this: f[am'ly.]=
    N: [Mm hm:]=
    H: = hh Li:ke, the husbin:d (.) i:s, (.) He's- yihknow(t)- (.) he's lahst iz job becuz they said *'e wz too o:ld* yihknow en eez tryina make a l:living en, hh en 'e can't s'pport iz fam'ly, hh en the wi:fe hh therefore can't give hi:m: any sex becu:z she figures he's no:t yihknow (.) being responsible enough en she's s:so worried about the chi:ldren,=   (HG)

Although here, as in example (44), H describes a movie using reporting discourse, the point at which the reporting discourse is used in the fifth line is neither the climax nor the punch-line. We can even expect that a climax will come later. So the reporting discourse is used to set the scene for the coming climax. This seems to contradict the analysis of (44) in that reporting discourse is used for background information as well as for presenting the climax. An important difference between (44) and (45) lies in their respective reporting styles. The one used in (45) is indirect style, while the one in (44) is direct. In comparing these two examples, I assert that when reporting discourse is used to 'show' the climax in a series of events, direct rather than indirect style is used for this function. This is in agreement with what Yule (1993) points out. According to Yule, direct speech style is used to report how something was said, and indirect style is often used to report what was said. Although Yule's argument is mainly focused on the direct reportings which occur with no introductory verbs (i.e., zero-quotation), example (44) shows "go" as another matrix verb for this function. Direct style has a demonstrational effect, pushing climactic lines to the fore, while indirect style describes background information.[25]

7.3.2.2.2. Exemplification and demonstration of emotion

The function of direct presentation as illustrated above often appears in an emotional situation, when a reported speech is emotionally charged. In order to exemplify someone's emotion, reporting discourse is used to show it rather than to simply state it. Such exemplification often follows a stylistic pattern in that the speaker first identifies an emotion and then demonstrates what the speaker felt. In the next example, V's father had surgery, and C's mother told V that the surgery was unnecessary:

(46) V: There was no confusion. An I was calm with it n then- when- when yer Mom said that I was frustrated like *oh that's ridiculous*. But then when I talked to my Mom an she wz all hysterical, then I started getting hys-[t e r i]cal.
C: [Yeah.]
V: Like *oh my Go:d all this for nothing, my D[a d] was Okay:*,
C: [Yeah]
K: O:h(h)
V: *he could ski, he could wa:lk, why's he going though this pai:n*=
(VK)

In line 2, V says, "I was frustrated," then she shows what she actually thought by saying, "like oh that's ridiculous." Again in lines 3-6, V says, "I started getting hysterical," and then she shows what actually was in her mind by saying, "Like oh my God all this for nothing, my Dad was Okay." In both cases, V modulates her voice and demonstrates her emotion vividly. These reported events might have been actually uttered to "your Mom" and "my Mom," or might be what she was saying to herself out loud or simply in her mind. Both of the above cases are introduced by "like" and in direct style, in the following pattern:

emotion; "like"; *direct style*

Let me cite a similar example, with a different introductory phrase. This example springs from the same context as above. Here, K is talking about V's emotional episode:

(47) K: An uh she got off the pho:ne an she was incredibly upset?
C: [Mm hm]
K: [She wz goin'] *God do you think they're performing unnecessary surgery on my Dad* or some'm like that? (VK)

In the first line, K describes V's emotion, saying, "she was incredibly upset," and shows how upset she really was by saying, "She was goin' God do you think they're performing unnecessary surgery on my Dad." A basic pattern for (46) and (47) is summarized as follows:

emotion; introducer; *direct style*

Reports serve to describe emotion vividly in this pattern. In all cases the reporters change their voice. Although it is possible to convey the propositional emotion by simply stating it, the reporter demonstrates it in order to make it sound vivid. These patterns also have the effect of arousing the listeners' interest about how and to what degree the reported speaker was frustrated or hysterical, by first simply mentioning the emotion. Thus the speaker first builds a foundation in the hearer's mind, and then shows the emotional content as the foreground. To accomplish this, direct style is used. The dialogue-introducers "(be) like," "go" are preferred for this function. When we consider that emotions are often mixed, and it may be hard to isolate and report only one feeling from the mixture, the dialogue-introducer "(be) like" elucidates the feeling adequately. It is used as "for example." Although "She was goin'" is used very quickly in (47), the reporter adds the phrase "or something like that," at the end of the report. This shows that the emotion just mentioned is not the reported speaker's exact utterance but a paraphrase or a demonstration. This is also observed in reports of emotion which are represented as inner speech:

(48) It don't happen overnight. Sometime you can get very disgusted thinking, you know, *I can't get nothing going, nothing happening. You know, I talked to people and still, you know, everybody turning me down or this or that.*

In (48), the speaker mentions the emotion of disgust followed by the direct reporting of the content of the inner feeling, which is introduced by "thinking." This is also an exemplified emotion as we can see by "or this or that" in the end.

The fact that direct reporting style is often used to exemplify emotion is related to the Main Clause Phenomena (MCP) proposed by Banfield (1973). She points out that 'expressive elements' occur only in direct reporting discourse. With expressive elements such as these, a speaker can communicate affective aspects of meaning. Sakita (1996c) showed that when speakers report in direct style, they frequently use interjections such as "ah," "oh," and "well," that are not in the original speech (part of the experimental result is presented in 7.2.). Such affective interjections as "oh," "oh my God," and "God" accompany the reporting of emotional remarks in (46) and (47). Because such affective interjections can not be included in indirect style, this effect can only be achieved with a direct style.

7.3.2.3. Dramatization

Many linguists have supposed that reporting discourse is used for reporting speech events which existed in the past, but this is not always the case. Tannen (1988; 1989) questions the literal conception of 'reported speech.' She claims that "uttering dialogue in conversation is as much a creative act as is the creation of dialogue in fiction and drama" (1989: 101). She further proffers the term 'constructed dialogue' to replace 'reported speech,' because "the dialogue animated in the narrative was not actually spoken by the person to whom it is attributed" (1989: 110). She raises the following example, in which a speaker represents, in a form of dialogue, what she did NOT say to her father.

(49) a little girl: You can't say, "Well Daddy I didn't hear you." (1989: 111)

This dialogue is constructed rather than reported, as the speaker states explicitly, with "You can't say," that the line of dialogue was not spoken. Tannen presents examples from dialogue representing what wasn't said, dialogue as instantiation, summarizing dialogue, dialogue as inner speech or inner speech of others, dialogue constructed by a listener, dialogue including fade-out and fade-in, vague referents, or

216   *Reporting Discourse, Tense, and Cognition*

non-human speakers.[26] Her claim is based on Bakhtin's ([1975]1981: 338) observation on the nature of conversation: "every conversation is full of transmissions and interpretations of other people's words." Tannen claims (1989: 110) that the act of transforming others' words into one's own discourse is creative and enlivening.

In the following sections, I will show that reporting discourse is used to represent future events and imaginary events. In such situations, the reporters play the roles of the reported speakers. These dialogues are effective dramatizations.

7.3.2.3.1. Dramatizing imaginary and future events

People also use reporting discourse to demonstrate something that might occur in the future, or to narrate an imaginary interaction. The first example narrates an imaginary letter writing. N and H are talking on the phone about a man named Charles who lives far away. H loves him and waits for him to write her a letter, but he never does. They say that it takes him a while to write, and start the following conversation:

(50) H: khh-hh-hhe writes one word a day, hhih [hn
      N: [Yeahhh
      N: *Dea:r?* hh nex'day. *Heidi,*=
      H: = u u hhh
      N: *Ho:w?*
      H: hhhi: [nh] heh-heh,
      N: [*A:*]*re?*
      N: *You:.*=   (HG)

H says, "he writes one word a day," then N jokingly demonstrates how slowly he writes, while H is laughing all the time. N reports a sentence that she imagined Charles would write. N changes her voice slightly and speaks slowly, which makes the reporting discourse more realistic. The following excerpt is a narration of an imaginary telephone conversation. N and H imagine that Charles will make a long distance call to H:

(51) N: Three minutes yeh that's not rilly that long,=
      N: =t[uh ta:lk,
      H: [It's- hh
      N: *Hi howareyou,*=
      H: =mhhh[hhhehhh]
      N: [*Click,*]   (HG)

In this example, N says that three minutes is not much time to talk, and demonstrates how short it is by changing her voice and speaking the part "Hi how are you" very quickly, and then demonstrating the sound of the telephone being disconnected, with a low voice imitating the machinery sound. This reporting discourse enacts an imaginary future conversation. Both (50) and (51) achieve effects of irony and humor. Speakers act as actors in the imaginary conversation to dramatize and present it vividly. Sanchez (1987) considers the dramatization effect as a function of direct reporting style. Mathis (1991) asserts that zero-quotation is particularly effective at dramatization. Both of the examples above confirm these arguments. Wierzbicka (1974) points out that direct reporting discourse is characterized by its 'theatrical' nature: a reporter acts as a reported speaker when she/he utters a direct quote. The reporter plays the role of the reported speaker. The reporter intends the hearer to believe that the form, content, and nonverbal messages such as gestures and facial expressions of the reporting discourse originate from the reported speaker (Li 1986).

I would suggest that the dramatization effect is a more rhetorical version of the theatrical aspect. Li (1986) suggests that the theatrical aspect of direct reporting discourse requires two parts. First, the reporter identifies the reported speaker. Second, the reporter performs in role as the reported speaker. This means that the theatrical feature of direct reporting discourse presupposes the identification of the reported speaker, and thus the direct reporting discourse construction requires a matrix clause. However, the identification of the speaker often does not accompany the dramatization, but is a shared knowledge given by the context. So, reporting discourse with dramatization may consist only of the second part of Li's characterization of the theatrical feature: the reporter acts as the reported speaker. Zero-quotation is the ultimate example of this.[27]

Such dramatization often accompanies close interpersonal involvement between the speaker and hearer. As Bakhtin ([1952-53]1986: 68) observes, listening is active participation in communication, in that when the listener perceives and understands the meaning of speech, she/he "simultaneously takes an active, responsive attitude toward it." Reporting with dramatization is one of the cases when listeners are likely to participate more actively. Let me present examples that include cooperative reporting. When a speaker establishes reporting backgrounds of dramatization, both the speaker and the listener cooperate to build a dramatized reporting discourse. In example (52), H and N are talking on the telephone about Charles, who never writes to H. N suggests that H write a thank you note to Charles, saying, "thank you for not writing." Then they start creating the text of an imaginary letter together:

218   *Reporting Discourse, Tense, and Cognition*

(52) N: En the:n, send im a thankyou [no(h)te, hh
     H: [hehh
     H: uh [hhh
     N: [hnhhh [hh
     H: [*Thankyou fer no(h)t wri(h)ti(h)ng,*=
     N: =*Dear Charles,* hhh hh
          (0.4)
     N: *Thankyou.*hhhhuh.
     N: [hhhhhhh]
     H: [*Fer noth*] [*ing.*]
     N: [*Fer*]*ruining my li*[*fe,*   [heh]
     H: heh [heh [heh] huh,
     N: [hhhh]hh [A:n'] *now I* [*going t'commit* [*sui* [*c*-uh-huh-[huh-huh]
     H: [hehh]   [heh]   [*By th'time yih* [*git* [t h i s:,   [h h eh] *I will*
          be dead.=
     H: =*I(hh)* [*h(h)ope,*] hhh
     N: [he-he-he]=
     H: =hhh *I* [*hope you,* hhnh=
     N: [ahhhhhhh
     N: =hn=
     H: =*live* [*with a clea(h)r* [*conscience*] hn]
     N: [hhhhh hhhhhhh [*But if you*] do] *n'want that tih happen,*=
     N: =*I will hang in there. if you will c(h)a(h)ll*=
     H: =e- e- e- uh- uh- uh- uh,
     H: hh [hhh
    (N: [hn-uh=)
     H: =*I will give you: ten sec'nds after you read this le(h)tter,*   (HG)

After N's remark "then, send him a thank you note," H starts the narration by saying, "Thank you for not writing." N immediately follows this with "Dear Charles . . . Thank you . . . ." and keeps laughing without finishing the sentence. H takes a turn and finishes N's sentence with "for nothing." N proceeds to make it more ironic, by adding "for ruining my life." The rest of the letter continues with N and H taking turns. These collaboratively built up exchanges are filled with laughter. N and H do not actually intend to write a letter, but simply enjoy the irony of the idea of writing a thank you letter to Charles who did nothing for H. In this reporting discourse, both of the conversation participants, usually characterized as a speaker and a hearer, play the parts of reporters. Both of the conversation participants are actors in the drama.

The following example is a similar narration of an imaginary telephone conversation. The same two women, H and N, now suppose that Charles is calling H

(Heidi), and imagine what the phone conversation will be like. They dramatically change their voices to imitate Charles, Heidi, the telephone operator, and the sound of the telephone disconnecting, to make the imaginary conversation more realistic. They start this narration by saying that he should have something good to say because long-distance calls are expensive:

(53) H: Y'bedder'v sump'n good tuh sa:y, hhh=
    N: =hhhhh=
    H: =hhh [Li-ike   [hh [*will you*] *ma-arry me?*   [hhh]
    N: [h u h   [uh [h e h   ]   [huh]=
    H: = [hih [h e h   ] e h]
    N: [hhh[*Will y'*] *mar*]*ry me?*
    N: [*Click,*]
    H: [hhhhh]That's wor(h)th (.) fhhour dhhollahhrs,=
    H: = [hhih]
    N: [*Please*] *deposit five cen*[*ts for*] *the*   [*next*] *(.)* [*one minu(h)te?*=
    H: [eh eh]   [eh]   [k
    H: = eh eh eh=
    N: *Heidi w't's yer a:nswer w't's yer answer-*
    N: *Plea:se de* [*p o s i t*   ] *fif*[*ty ce(h)nts,*]
    H: [hhh: hhh]   [uh uh uh uh] h uh u [h
    N: [huuhh
    H: hhh hh=
    H: *Heidi ('d) bett(h)*[*er be yes*   [*or ah'll* [*shoo(h)oot-*]
    N: [*Don't take* [*so much* [*time t u h*   ] *think*=
    N: =*It's costing me money*.hh
    H: hhh: hhh: [hhh:
    N: [hhhh[hh
    H: [*This's investing in yer ri(h)ng* en=   (HG)

We observe that H and N cooperatively create the imaginary telephone conversation, playing the four roles including telephone sound effects, as in a drama. Since one of the purposes of this series of reportings is for N to hearten H with a joke, the fact that H is laughing aloud and starts being involved in the collaboration shows the success of N's encouragement, and the close 'rapport' (Bateson 1972) or solidarity established between H and N.

The dramatization observed in examples (50), (51), (52), and (53) follows the pattern:

proposition; *demonstration*

One of the speakers first states a proposition, one of them starts demonstrating, and when another finds it interesting, she/he joins it. The proposition is about something in the future or in the imagination. Even when it is not necessary to demonstrate the whole process, the speakers do the demonstration anyway. This is because the important thing is not the content but the way the communication proceeds. The speakers, as actors, dramatize the imaginary communication. Most instances of this role-playing use zero-quotation direct style. Interestingly enough, even though they do not make clear who said what, both of them understand the event, smoothly start the demonstrations, and collaboratively build up the narrations. They animate dialogues with distinct voices. Dramatization often produces irony, humor, or realism.

In (54), which is an excerpt from Tannen's (1989: 120) narrative example, the listener participates in a dramatization. A young man who works as a resident in the emergency room of a hospital tells a story to a group of his friends when he comes home. He tells a very long story that involves five participants, with repetition and dramatization. It includes numerous sequences of zero-quotation direct reporting discourse. Tannen mentions that the voices are realized in a paralinguistically distinct acoustic representation. At the end, one of the listeners participates in the dialogic part of the story:

(54) "How old are you."
"Nineteen."
"Shit. Can't call his parents."
[hysterically pleading voice] "Don't tell my parents. Please don't tell my parents. You're not gonna tell my parents, are you?"
[Listener: /?/ "We're gonna wrap you in bandages."]

(Tannen 1989: 120)

It shows that even the listener who has no access at all to the original interaction and is supposed to be listening to the story may start collaboratively playing a participatory role, once she/he is deeply involved in the reported interactions. His remark attributed to the story participant ("We're gonna wrap you in bandages") is totally in his imagination and is obviously not from the actual interactions. It demonstrates that dramatization arouses 'mutual engagement' (Merritt 1982) between a speaker and a hearer, which is an observable state of being in coordinated interaction, as distinguished from mere co-presence (Tannen 1989: 11).

7.3.2.3.2. Dramatizing archetypical events

Zero-quotation direct reporting style is also often seen in demonstration of archetypical events in supposition. When dramatizing dialogues, speakers turn into actors and create subsidiary effects of irony, humor, and realism. The following example is from a dinner-table conversation. J, a woman, tells her dog Ginger not to spill its food on the floor. Her husband D mentions that J always grumbles. He demonstrates it for their friends K and N, who are nonnative speakers of English:

(55) J: [to a dog] Ginger, would you keep your food in your bowl?
      (5.0)
      D: Joy grumbles a lot.
      (2.0)
      K: Grumbles?
      D: Yeah, *wuhrrrrrrrr wuhrrrrrrrr wuhrrrrrrrr Ginger, keep your food in your bowl.*
      K: ahhh hhh hhh
      D: *Erik, would you ask a week in advance?*
      K: ahhh hhh hhh
      N: ahhh hhhhhhh
      D: *Dave, why do you keep bothering me?* uhhhhh hhhh hhhh That's grumbling.
      K: ah grumbling hhh hhh hhh
      D: *Dave, why do you grumble at us a lot?*
      J: It's men who think somebody else is magically gonna do it.
      D: No, left to themselves men will come up with simpler solutions.
      J: The they they have thought of me that women will do it.
      D: The house is your property. If you leave it to me, it will be simplified drastically and quickly.

D demonstrates how J grumbles, by using zero-quotation direct reporting style. Without indicating whom he is impersonating with a reporting clause such as "Joy always says," he immediately starts mimicry of three typical instances of J's grumbling, with great voice changes. He can do this effectively because he already stated his proposition in his preceding utterance ("J grumbles a lot"). His main purpose seems to be to show the meaning of grumbling. For that, it is easier and often more effective to demonstrate rather than to explain it. It also involves subsidiary effects of irony and humor. He teases J, and at the same time blames her for always grumbling. He acts to make the grumbling sound as annoying as possible by exaggerating and overacting. Indeed, J reacts negatively to it, and starts defending herself.

Dramatization is a way of using the theatrical potential of direct reporting discourse, which typically assumes exact quotation and accompanies the identification of the original speaker. But, dramatization often occurs in zero-quotation form, with the background setting given in the form of a proposition beforehand or implied in context. Speakers can dramatize and act out speech events without any original discourse. I have shown instances of dramatization of imaginary events, future events, and archetypical events for this function.

7.3.3. Summary

In this section, I presented some interactional functions of reporting discourse observed in English conversation. Reporting discourse, as a form of evidentiality, is employed as a discourse strategy to support one's proposition or even to cover for one's lack of information. In the latter case, it works to keep the conversation flowing. It was also discussed as a strategy to avoid personal commitment or responsibility. As another important tactic of conversation, speakers use reporting discourse for its demonstrative effect. When it is easy to guess what the climax will be, showing how it happened is more important than simply reporting what happened. On the emotional front, after stating an emotion, speakers voice what is in their minds using direct style, to exemplify the emotion. The dramatization effect of reporting discourse was identified as a special realization of the theatrical potential of direct reporting discourse, which does not require the identification of the reported speaker, and is characterized by zero-quotation direct style, cooperative reporting, irony, humor, or realism. Tannen's point that reporting discourse is not limited to reports of what actually happened was elucidated with examples of its use in representing future or imaginary events. When used for certain purposes, reporting discourse follows certain patterns or scripts.

7.4. CORRELATIONS BETWEEN STYLE AND FUNCTION

So far, I have shown some interactional functions of reporting discourse that are frequently seen in natural conversational data. Each purpose is best met by the use of a certain style. Let me characterize how I view reporting discourse on a continuum, and then summarize how the different functions of reporting discourse correlate with reporting styles on the continuum.

7.4.1. Reporting discourse on continuum

Although reporting discourse has often been viewed and taught as a dichotomy, the boundary between direct and indirect discourse is fuzzy (Tannen 1989). There have been attempts to question whether this simple dichotomy can do justice to the complexities of reporting discourse and to suggest a third kind of reporting style. Tobler (1894) introduced a third type of speech reporting, defined as "a peculiar mingling of direct and indirect discourse." Yule (1993) modeled reporting discourse on a continuum with this third type of reporting style as an intermediate form, referring to it as 'free indirect discourse.'[28] His attempt to look at reporting discourse forms as falling along a continuum from the abstract terminal points of diegesis and mimesis is indicated in the following figure:[29]

Figure 2: Yule's Continuum

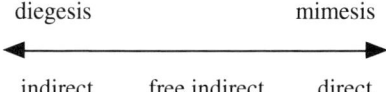

diegesis   mimesis

indirect   free indirect   direct

In my observations of differing characteristics of direct and indirect style in natural conversations (Sakita 1992) the notion of continuum proved significant also, but it needed to be elaborated to meet the reality of natural conversation phenomena. Du Bois (1986) also classifies hierarchical speech categories depending on the degree to which the speech is shaped by either the 'proximate speaker' or the 'alter prime speaker.' His speech categories range from sovereign speech, indirect speech, direct quotation, allusive quotation, mimicry, and impersonation, to trance.

In the experimental study presented in 7.2., I divided indirect style into three subcategories: indirect style using a gerund or a noun phrase, indirect style using a sentence, and description style. I treated direct style as a single category. In further examination of the experimental data, carefully comparing reporting utterances with their original utterances, as well as in exploration of the available natural English data, I developed the following continuum:[30]

Figure 3: Reporting Style Continuum

(tense alteration added)
(variation of verbs added)
Q---zero---*like*---*go*---*say*---*say that*---*tell*---Description---Summary---Gerund---One Word

224 *Reporting Discourse, Tense, and Cognition*

Styles farther to the left on the continuum are more direct and those farther to the right are more indirect. "Q" at the left end of the continuum includes quoting the original discourse by using audiotapes and videos as seen in TV or radio news. "Zero" represents reportings without any introductory phrases. Between "like" and "tell" are reportings categorized by reporting verbs or phrases. "Description" style is a reporter's paraphrase of the original speaker's utterances. It usually does not accompany reporting phrases (examples 4b; 17). Especially condensed versions may be called "Summary" style. "Gerund" includes reportings which use gerunds instead of reported clauses. "One-Word" includes reportings which condense the reported content to one word, as in the sentence, "He talked about coffee."[31]

7.4.2. Style and function along a continuum

To distribute functional features along the style continuum in Figure 3, a vast amount of further research is necessary. For the present section, let me show what styles the discourse functions discussed in 7.3. accompanied, from a limited data set. The following figure illustrates the correlations between reporting discourse functions and reporting style variations along the continuum:

Figure 4: Correlations between Reporting Styles and Functions

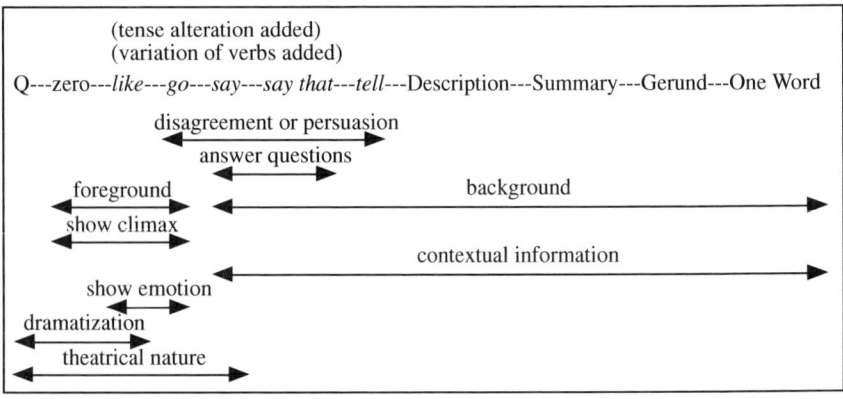

In Figure 4, stretches of arrows represent possible reporting styles associated with the reporting discourse functions or effects that I discussed in 7.3. First, the top two arrows indicate style variations for the evidential functions of reporting discourse. When reporting discourses function as evidentials, reporting phrases that indicate reported speakers are often included to assure the reliability of the reported utterances. For instance, to disagree with or to persuade others, reporting styles that have reporting phrases with "go," "say," "say that," "tell," are used. When one lacks enough information to answer questions, one may count on information borrowed by others to back up one's responses. Reporting styles that involve "say" and "say that" are often used for this purpose.

Second, foreground and background information are typically reported in contrasting styles of reporting discourse. In situations such as narrating climax or exemplifying emotion, reporting styles are chosen for their ability to 'show' rather than merely 'describe' the salient information. Climax is shown with direct reporting style variations that use zero-quotation, the reporting verb "be like," and the reporting verb "go." Emotion is also demonstrated by the use of direct reporting styles with "be like" and "go." In contrast, contextual information is presented in indirect reporting style variations.

Third, the lowest arrow shows that direct style has theatrical features and may use exact quote (Q), zero-quotation, reporting verbs "be like," "go," and "say." The second arrow from the bottom further indicates that dramatization effects often occur with "be like," or without any reporting phrases since they do not require the identification of reported speakers. Since the style-function correlation in Figure 4 is based on the observation of limited data, further research is needed to elaborate it.

7.5. CONCLUSION

Reporting discourse, an essential construction in language, has multiple functions and complex stylistic variations. This chapter has explored factors that affect reporting discourse style, taking multiple approaches. Using an experimental approach, the first study examined how structural factors affect reporting style choice. It showed that, as primitive factors, the length and structural complexity of the original discourse affect reporting style. Using a discourse analytic approach, the second study explored the discourse functions of reporting discourse in linguistic performance. In particular, it focused on how functions of reporting discourse correlate with discourse patterns and styles, in terms of three important notions: evidentiality, information grounding, and dramatization.

For human reporting behavior, many interwoven factors shape stylistic choices. In the great majority of cases, in fact, a variety of different factors affect the choice of style, so that the reporting style in each case is determined by a number of factors operating simultaneously. Those factors interact with each other differently in response to differences in contextual backgrounds and communicative purposes. To clarify these factors and grasp the whole picture of reporting discourse, further research into the transactional and interactional features of reporting discourse from different viewpoints, and with different approaches, is needed.

8

Conclusion

8.1. Summary of Chapters

The main objective of this book has been to provide systematic accounts of reporting discourse behaviors in naturally spoken English. It approached reporting discourse from a discourse perspective, paying special attention to discourse, cognition, and consciousness. It showed reporting discourse to be an integral whole formed by speakers' constant interpretations and choices at different information processing stages, with close interactions among cognitive constraint, discourse organization, contextual information, and communicative purposes.

In chapter 1, I introduced basic concepts and definitions concerning reporting discourse, narrative, and discourse analysis. In chapters 2 through 5, I explored dialogue-introducer tense-alternation phenomena, which have been among the controversial problems of reporting discourse. In chapter 2, I reviewed the previous studies on tense-alternation. After outlining general tense-alternation theories, I pointed to the fact that dialogue-introducer tense-switching is not well explained by any of the previous theories. I reexamined previous hypotheses and identified the limitations of the existing frameworks. To approach the issue of dialogue-introducer tense-alternation, the succeeding three chapters focused on different aspects of reporting, and elucidated dialogue-introducer tenses as cognitive, attitudinal, and consciousness state markers. In each chapter, I focused on a different phase of complex reporting discourse. Chapter 3 focused on cognitive backgrounds of reporting at the recollection stage; chapter 4 highlighted a reporter's perception of reported speakers' attitudinal contrast; and chapter 5 examined a reporter's consciousness flow in discourse.

In chapter 3, I illustrated a speaker's conceptualization of recalled events with the Cognitive Recollection Model, to account for frequency distributions of dialogue-introducer tense variations in discourse. The model incorporated proximity, psychological involvement, and self-identity, as key factors. I proposed that when a speaker chooses specific vantage points in recalling past interactional events, there is an inherent asymmetry between a narrator's conceptualization of the third person and of the past self. To report third-person interactions, a narrator's choice between the present or past tense depends on the degrees of ego's psychological involvement in the recalled episodes. In reporting self-involving interactions, a narrator mainly uses the past-tense form "I said" for her/his own remarks, in order to protect the ego's identity as narrator rather than as protagonist. In addition, I suggested that there is also a context for the use of "I says," as an optional choice when the narrator assumes a third-person perspective. I discussed the importance of narrator's self-identity in theories of narrative, discourse, and psychology.

In chapter 4, I explored dialogue-introducer tense as an attitudinal contrasting device with which speakers encode their interpretation of information in utterances, human relations, and the attitudes of reported speakers. Since reporting verbs in direct reporting discourse are usually neutral place markers, tense forms are useful means of weaving into stories attitudinal factors that are not expressed by verb itself. Speakers utilize tense forms in order to effectively construct narratives. By feature analyses of discourse examples, I developed generalizations of systematic contrasts that dialogue-introducers mark. I showed first, that the past tense and the present tense contrast resultative versus searching modes. Second, especially in conflict stories that involve a speaker's attitudinal contrast as a significant point of the stories, the past tense and the present tense contrast attitudes that show no intimidation versus those that denote a retreat and power balance versus its breakthrough. Third, the past tense and the present tense contrast strong versus weak attitudes, reflecting the degrees of certainty, assuredness, firmness, and emotional upset. On the whole, I concluded that the past tense introduces more assured stronger attitude than utterances introduced with the present tense. Since this attitudinal contrast of reported speakers depends on a narrator's subjective interpretation of reported events, tense realization in each story is individualistic and particular to each situation.

In chapter 5, I showed that dialogue-introducers and their tense forms function as markers for a speaker's flow of consciousness along with the development of discourse organizations. Dialogue-introducers mark the structures of discourse acts and moves, and their tense-shifts mark the flow and rest of the speaker's consciousness. By means of the Consciousness Stream Model, I illustrated correlations of discourse organization, consciousness flow, and shifts of dialogue-introducers. First, in cases of exchange such as adjacency pair and three-part exchange, the dialogue-introducer shifts from "says" to "said" when consciousness flows at initiation and rests at response, while it shifts back to "says" at an additional follow-up move. Second, dialogue-introducers mark the development of a narrative line over a series of remarks. Generally "says" marks the start of the flow, while "said" marks the rest. In the midst of the flow, "saying" and "say" characterize continuity. In an apparently chaotic discourse, there is still a synthetic coherence, and the consciousness flow and tense forms are well modulated within it. Third, dialogue-introducer tense-shifts reflect the consciousness flow in repeatedly used dialogue-introducers in the cases of pre-posing and post-posing dialogue-introducers, and at restatements: (a) In pre-posing double dialogue-introducers, the first one sets up background information, and the second one marks a subsequent flow; (b) A tense-shift from pre-posed to post-posed dialogue-introducers marks a quick change of the consciousness flow. A post-posed introducer may mark a flow when the pre-posed dialogue-introducer tense does not match the discourse act of a local clause; (c) The tenses of repeated dialogue-introducers at restatements mark suspensions and interruptions. In this chapter, I paid special attention to different directional tense-shifts, and to the use of dialogue-introducers that seem to behave irregularly in other frameworks. I showed that such forms as "I says," "he say," "I saying," and "he saying," which have been considered 'ungrammatical' or 'mistakes,' or otherwise have been totally neglected, work toward making a narrative a coherent whole with a natural consciousness flow.

In this way, chapters 3 through 5 showed the systematic nature of dialogue-introducer tense-alternation in spoken English. While previous theories have attempted simple unified accounts, this book viewed tense-alternation phenomena as manifestations of multiple factors in complex reporting processes. The three accounts that I have presented may seem redundant in some cases, so that one simple account would suffice. Indeed, I first struggled in an attempt to develop a single theory to cover the whole field of data. However, in approaching natural discourse, I have come to believe that "in the great majority of cases, a variety of different factors affect the choice of which form to use, so that marking in individual cases is determined by a number of factors operating simultaneously," as Myhill (1992: 90) suggested. My conclusive view is that my three approaches to dialogue-introducer tenses as cognitive markers, attitudinal markers, and consciousness stream markers, each points to essential phases of reporting discourse related to contextual and interactional factors in human communications.

I have shown that the three accounts of dialogue-introducer tense-alternation have some situational preferences. First, tense-alternation that reflects the cognitive recollection mode is the most basic, although it is often overridden by other factors. It often appears most clearly when a speaker reports interactional exchanges, especially with an emphasis or a focus on turn-taking. Second, tense-alternation that functions as an attitudinal contrasting marker appears when a speaker places significance in contrast, shift, or balance of reported speakers' attitudes, and in the saliency of one of the attitudes. It often appears in reporting conflict stories, authority stories, or arguments. Third, tense-shift that marks the consciousness flow along with discourse organization is often seen when a speaker emphasizes information shift or development, and incorporates evaluative points in them. It often appears when a speaker develops a series of remarks. A particular form of dialogue-introducer tense is a manifestation of one or more of these three uses, depending upon the situation. For instance, the use of "I says" may be a result of a speaker's third-person construal, or a marker of unassured attitude, or a marker of the consciousness flow, or it may even reflect combinations of such factors. When "I says" results from a speaker's third-person construal, the speaker more consistently reports the first person with "I says," whereas when it functions to mark a speaker's consciousness stream, such forms as "I says," "I say," and "I said" may be used interchangeably. Precisely how the three functions interact with each other is a significant question that is left to further research. It requires more extensive analyses of discourse data.

Chapter 6 turned to tense determination in indirect reporting discourse, and introduced discourse perspectives on the issue, touching upon the fact that tense-alternation may occur in indirect reporting discourse. In spoken English, tense in indirect reporting discourse does not behave rigidly as has been supposed by traditional views. I showed that tenses of reported verbs are often naturally determined by the reporter's perspective, citing three types of evidence. First, speakers often avoid the past perfect tense, except for its use as the absolute tense for a discourse functional necessity. Second, indirect reporting discourse has tense-alternation phenomena, in which reporting clauses behave flexibly as dialogue markers that hardly function as temporal reference points. Third, some reporting clauses behave flexibly as dialogue markers that function as hedges, evidential markers, and source markers. I also identified some factors that allow or even favor occurrences of the absolute tense in spoken discourse: pragmatic information that supports temporal order of events; linguistic restrictions; and discourse coherence.

Finally, in chapter 7, I explored macro-level style choice of reporting discourse: what determines reporting style itself, how it is related to its function, and how it is patterned in discourse. In order to clarify the interwoven factors for style choice, two studies with different approaches (quantitative and qualitative) addressed different factors. First, an experimental study showed that, as primitive factors, the structural complexities and the sentence length of the original discourse affect reporting style choice. It also demonstrated that there are a variety of ways to report the same original discourse. Second, a discourse analytic study showed how the functions of reporting discourse correlate with discourse patterns and styles. Reporting discourse functions as a discourse strategic device related to evidentiality, information grounding, and dramatization. I discussed reporting discourse as rule-governed, goal-directed and purposeful linguistic action. I finally located function-style correlations on a continuum, and suggested that for a complete picture of reporting discourse, we need further research into the transactional and interactional features of reporting discourse from different viewpoints, and with different approaches.

8.2. THEORETICAL IMPLICATIONS

At first glance ordinary language appears chaotic and filled with mistakes, repetitions, and unnecessary digressions. However, human language follows certain systems even when it is produced in natural linguistic activities. Such systematicity is not well explained by the introspective studies with which traditional linguists have attempted to determine the meanings of verbal forms only by thinking about the use of these forms, without looking at language usage or systematically taking discourse contexts into consideration. The systematic nature of language can be revealed in close analyses of actual language uses, with the use of discourse data in addition to introspection. By using a discourse analytic approach, this book has presented new perspectives and theoretical developments in the study of reporting discourse. It particularly focused on dialogue-introducer tense-alternation phenomena, and presented a new theory on this topic. Tense-alternation and tense-shift including such forms as "I says," "she say," "I saying," and "she saying" have been totally neglected in the traditional framework which looked at invented unnatural language and neglected the study of the empirical details of actual speech. Since studies in the traditional framework tended to idealize situations of language use, they simply ignored anomalous uses as performance failures, or even were blind to their existence. The present work has, in this regard, demonstrated that through extensive analyses of natural data, we can better find out what language is really like.

Because language reflects the multifaceted nature of the human mind and human activities, a full exploration of it requires multiple perspectives. This book has viewed reporting discourse as a reflection of complex systems and the nature of communication, interactional dynamics, and human cognition. Thus it approached reporting discourse by incorporating factors such as cognition, self-identity, attitude, consciousness, and psychological background, as well as conversational strategy, discourse organization, discourse rule, and narrative structure. Some of them have been outside of language study proper, but all are closely related to human reporting activities. The inclusion of all these factors was essential for the development of an integral view of reporting discourse. Throughout this study, I pursued an interdisciplinary discourse analysis, and introduced multiple perspectives for reporting discourse and narrative. Chapters 2 through 5 explored multiple factors for tense-alternation, including cognition, attitude, and consciousness. Chapter 6 added a discourse perspective to indirect reporting discourse. Chapter 7 included different approaches to reporting discourse style choice, an experiment and a conversation analysis. In chapters 3 and 7, I presented both quantitative and qualitative analyses. The present study is, of course, still far from grasping the whole picture of reporting discourse, but I believe that it certainly is a meaningful step in the further scientific research into reporting discourse.

Reporting discourse is a mirror of the operation of the human mind. Extensive analysis of reporting discourse, Voloshinov ([1929]1986) claimed, explicates fundamental issues of the operation of language, mind, and consciousness. The present study has shed light on the mode of existence of received utterances in the recipient's consciousness and its manipulation there, and the orientation processes of the recipient's subsequent speech. The realization of reporting discourse shows how a speaker perceived the speech interaction, and how she/he interpreted it, or recalled it. I have attempted to discuss these operations of reporting discourse in this book. In this sense, this study conforms to Voloshinov's claim that the form of reporting discourse is a precise and objective document of human speech reception.

The present research also has significant implications for foreign language acquisition research and pedagogy. It reveals how people naturally report in spoken English, and what it reveals is very different from what traditional grammar has presented about reporting discourse and tense. There are occasions when a non-native feels her/his English is grammatically sound, yet still lacks some essential quality that would make it natural. Sometimes it is a matter of fluency and rhythm, but in many cases it is a matter of the appropriate choice of forms and expressions that fit in each context. The present research has provided a key to resolving this imperfection of foreign language performances. Since recent foreign language pedagogy has set communication skills as its goal, it is increasingly important for teachers to know what achieves natural performance in language. For instance, the tense-alternation phenomenon, which traditional grammar has neglected, appears to be essential to the realization of natural language performance. The tense determination in indirect reporting discourse which is often free from backshifting of tenses is also very different from the treatment in grammar books. For language learners, mastering the use of reporting discourse is crucially important for successful communication in the language. However, many nonnative speakers of English, even at advanced levels, exhibit a great difficulty in learning English reporting discourse (Goodell 1987). The outcome of the present research, I hope, will contribute to the reexamination of the presentation of reporting discourse in English pedagogy.

8.3. FUTURE PERSPECTIVES

There are many questions still to be clarified in order to achieve a fuller understanding of reporting discourse. One significant point that the present research has left out is the choice of reporting verbs. As I briefly touched upon, there are varieties of reporting verbs in both direct and indirect reporting discourse. It is easy to imagine that there are wide variations of verb choices in indirect style, while in direct style, the choice is more limited to the forms such as "go," "like," zero-quotation (ø), and "say." But in both cases, the operation of verb choices is complicated, reflecting multiple factors. The elucidation of reporting verb systems is essential for the further elaboration of reporting style continuum that I presented at the end of chapter 7. It must await further extensive research.[1]

Although this study focused exclusively on spoken discourse, one of the necessary next steps is to examine written discourse as well, since how oral versions of reporting discourse, storytelling, and narrative are different from or similar to their written counterparts is a significant question. In the past, researchers who have explored tense-alternation (e.g., Wolfson 1982; Johnstone 1987) have claimed that it is genre-specific, restricting their studies to conversational performances. But since written narratives also involve the historical present tense, not all of which have been fully elucidated yet, the present theory on dialogue-introducer tense-alternation may be adapted to analyze written reporting discourse and written narratives. Additionally, even in spoken discourse, it is necessary to examine whether the present theory has a genre-specific nature. The use of tense-alternation appears not only in conversational discourse but also in interviews and news reports.

The present study has shown that tense-alternation occurs in indirect reporting discourse as well, in describing reported verb tense determination. Since my focus in chapter 6 was not exactly on tense-alternation itself, I did not explore in detail the occurrences and meanings of tense-alternation in indirect reporting discourse. But, it is indeed a significant theoretical advancement, since previous studies on tense-alternation always limited their scopes only to direct reporting style in performed stories. Further elucidation of tense-alternation in indirect reporting discourse should lead to a unified theory for direct and indirect reporting discourse situated on a continuum.

Finally, although this study has attempted to explore the operations and functions of reporting discourse with closely related issues such as cognition, consciousness, communication, and psychology, the present treatments are far from being adequate. But with such multiple perspectives, the present research has at least demonstrated a possible research direction for further studies. A true understanding of reporting discourse systems and structures is realized in inquiries into the situational or contextual information, the participants' cognitive operations, and the communicative goals, integrated with knowledge and information from other related fields. Future research into reporting discourse, I would suggest, requires more extensive analyses of such human fundamentals in broad perspectives: humanistically based interpretive work in combination with social scientific approaches.

NOTES

Notes to Chapter 1

1. Tannen (1986: 311) further acknowledges the close resemblance of constructed dialogue to fiction and plays:

> A difference is that in fiction and plays, the characters and actions are also constructed, whereas in personal narrative, they are based on actual characters and events. But even this difference is not absolute. Many works of fiction and drama are also based on real people and events, and many conversational storytellers . . . embellish and adjust characters and events.

2. Chafe (1994: 127-32) illustrates the relation of the narrative schema to the flow of consciousness. He suggests the pattern that emerges from conversational narratives by revising Labov and Waletzky (1967). He raises the following major components: initial summary (or abstract); orientation; complication; climax; denouement; and coda. There he makes clear that narratives move toward and away from a climax, something that is inexplicit in Labov (1972a).

3. According to Halliday and Hasan (1976: 1), 'text' refers to passages of sentences that "form a unified whole" and exhibit semantic cohesion.

4. Conversation analysis holds an integral view of context as knowledge, situation, and text.

5. Although Abercrombie (1965) characterizes 'monologue' as a very specialized use of spoken language with "certain distinguishing linguistic, including phonetic, peculiarities" which set it off from other uses of language, Ford (1994) shows elements of the dialogic nature of monologic texts in support of the claim that every utterance is dialogic.

6. Tannen stresses the notion of 'a linguistics of particularity' drawing upon Becker (1984; 1988). Becker (1988: 31) claims that the problem with science is that "it does not touch the personal and particular."

7. Functionalism, according to Schiffrin (1994: 22), is based on two general assumptions:

(i) Language has functions external to the linguistic system itself.
(ii) External functions influence the internal organization of the linguistic system.

8. There are, of course, other ways to define discourse. The classic definition of discourse by formalists or structuralists is "language above the sentence or above the

clause" (Stubbs 1983: 1). Narrative theorists view discourse as "the sentences in the text" (Segal 1995: 62). Lyons (1977a: 385-87) sees it as 'text-sentences' which are "context-dependent utterance-signals, tokens of which may occur in particular texts" in contrast to 'system-sentences' that are "the well-formed strings that [are] generated by the grammar" (Schiffrin 1994: 27).

9. Edwards (1997: 87-88) points out several assumptions that the traditional customs of inventing examples have generally been based upon, in contrast to the methodology of conversation analysis (CA). To me, the most problematic assumptions are the following two:

(i) that we know *what talk is like*—and that we know it well enough to invent our own examples of it, or simulations of it, and treat those synthetic objects as worthy of analysis, or as illustrations of theoretical models.

(ii) that, since somebody *could* have said it, and there is nothing obviously wrong with it, an invented example of dialogue will suffice. But recordings of talk do not closely resemble the kinds of invented examples used prior to and outside of CA, while many of CA's empirical discoveries require detailed transcripts and, though recognizable once pointed out, were not obvious before that.

10. Schiffrin (1994: 409) characterizes conversation analysis as follows:

Conversation analysis began by searching for ways to discover our ordinary, everyday procedures for constructing a sense of social and personal reality. Its main focus is the way language is shaped by context, and, in turn, the way language shapes context.

According to Edwards (1997: 108), CA is interested in talk as social practice, and therefore analyzes its "intersubjectively constituted meanings." It aims to explicate "participants' own descriptive and explanatory practices, rather than ignoring those in favor of analysts' descriptions and causal explanations."

11. The cognitive approach to narrative analysis assumes "the existence of a mind that has produced the narrative work as well as of a mind that is cognizing the narrative work" (Talmy 1995: 421). Talmy criticizes "approaches that limit their scope of attention to the confine of the narrative alone, or deny the existence of individual minds" and claims that the cognitive approach "describes a wealth of structural interrelationships that could only be observed by the adoption of a wider scope that includes the existence of both generative and interpretative mental activity."

12. For instance, they differ in immediacy, relation to context, lexical density, grammatical complexity (Halliday 1979), and degrees of integration and involvement (Chafe 1982). They have different influences on cognitive development (Greenfield 1972). There are additional differences in characterizations of speaking and writing,

in terms of permanence, transportability, tempo, spontaneity, prosody, naturalness, and situatedness (Chafe 1994).

13. Coulmas (1986: 10) suggests that since writing, which is an important cultural achievement, is closely related to spoken language, a study of reporting discourse must take into account "the possibility that writing itself influences the way how speech reporting is carried out and understood."

14. For instance, Labov and Waletzky (1967) suppose that fundamental narrative structures are found in oral versions of personal experience, the ordinary narratives of ordinary speakers. Rosen (1988) and Tannen (1989) claim that literary storytelling is a refinement of storytelling in everyday life. Tannen (1989) agrees that literary storytelling is simply an elaboration of conversational storytelling. Thus, Polanyi's (1981: 316) view that oral storytelling in conversational contexts is the primary site for understanding narrative structure is now widely shared:

> Once we understand what every competent speaker is doing when s(he) recounts the experiences in his/her life or the lives of other people, we will be in a somewhat better position to understand the transformation of the 'story' into written, fictional, and literary artifacts.

15. The term 'dialogue-introducer' is currently used interchangeably with 'reporting phrase.'

16. Wolfson (1982) raises the following performance features: direct speech; asides; repetition; expressive sounds; sound effects; motions and gestures; conversational historic present (CHP) alternating with narrative past tense.

17. Some conversational data originate from the 1984-1986 UCLA class packets collected by students and participants: Cecilia Ford (VK), Charles and Marjorie Goodwin (AD), Anne Lazaraton (AL), John Reeves (JR), Emanuel Schegloff (TG), and others (HK), (HG), (SN). They are analyzed with transcriptions and audiotapes.

Notes to Chapter 2

1. Fleischman (1990: 285) uses the term narrative present (NP) for "a spontaneous use of the PR [present] that occurs consistently in *alternation* with tense of the P [past] and is linked to a performative mode of *oral* storytelling" in contrast to the HP which is "a stylistic feature of narrative *writing* that, while it can occur in alternation with the P [past], also occurs in *sustained sequences* across descriptive and eventive clauses."

2. In contrast, in other narrative genres such as folk tales, jokes and travelogues, the historical present may occur throughout a text (Wolfson 1978: 218).

238 *Notes to Chapter 2*

3. 'Performance' is a certain type of particularly involved and dramatized oral narrative (Toolan 1988: 165). Wolfson (1982: 24) characterizes it as follows:

> When a speaker acts out a story, as if to give his audience the opportunity to experience the event and his evaluation of it, he may be said to be giving a performance.

Wolfson further explains that telling a performed story involves similar performance features to those in actual theatrical performance. It is as if a story is theatrically staged. Performance functions to "structure the experience from the point of view of the speaker and to dramatize it" (Wolfson 1978: 216). The alternation between CHP and the past tense is one of the performance features that give structure and drama to the story.

4. Table 1 is based on the categorizations established by Labov (1972a). There, it is not explicit that narratives move toward and away from a climax. Chafe (1994: 127-32) revises this point by adding 'climax' and 'denouement' to the categorizations summarized in Table 1. See also note 2 in chapter 1.

5. Schiffrin also claims that the occurrence of tense-switching is affected by the use of conjunctions and the occurrence of subject-switching, on which Myhill (1992: 72) comments:

> using the same subject and/or a coordinating conjunction is associated with general continuity in the story line, so that the continued use of the Historical Present would fit in with this, while the switch to a new subject or the use of a temporal conjunction involves a change in orientation, stepping out of the plot line which had been depicted with a sequence of fast-and-furious Historical Presents.

Silva-Corvalán (1983) and Wehr (1984) acknowledge that, in other languages also, the shift out of the present tense to the past can serve to partition a narrative into subunits.

6. Chafe points out that the immediacy conveyed by the HP is often reinforced by the use of "now," which locates the event or state at the time of the represented consciousness as well as the representing:

(i)   Well, she's petrified *now* because she knows . . .
(ii) The door's closed and locked *now* and the guy in the next apartment bangs his door.
(iii) . . . *now* what I do is, I pick up this thing . . .   (Wolfson 1982: 39-40)

7. Quirk, et al. (1985: 181) take the traditional view of the HP, that it describes the past as if it is happening now, conveying something of the dramatic immediacy of an eyewitness account. But they view the verbs of communication as very different-

ly behaving. As for the verbs of communication including verbs which refer to the receptive end of the communication process like "understand," "hear," and "learn," the sentences would also be acceptable with the simple past or present perfective:

(i) The ten o'clock news *says* that there's going to be a bad storm.
(ii) Martin *tells* me the Smiths are moving from No. 20.
(iii) I *hear* that poor Mr Simpson has gone into hospital [*sic*].

They claim that the implication of the present tense is that although the communication event took place in the past, its result—the information communicated—is still operative. Thus the following sentence suggests that although the *Book of Genesis* was written thousands of years ago, it still 'speaks' to us at the present time:

(iv) The Book of Genesis *speaks* of the terrible fate of Sodom and Gomorrah.

Leech (1987: 11) also claims that the use of the HP with verbs of communication (e.g., "tell," "write," and "say") is unique.

8. Haiman (1991) discusses the "undisputed fact" that repetition causes meaning to erode.

9. Examples from Johnstone (1987) did not originally have quotation marks nor punctuations, and were transcribed in lines of one intonation unit each (Chafe 1985a). In this book, quotation marks are added for convenience. Punctuation marks are added only when necessary.

10. For general verbs in early Romance, several researchers claimed that tense-switching functions to distinguish or individuate participants in the story world (e.g., Gilman 1961; Schøsler 1985). However, Fleischman (1990: 81) claims that such a 'participant tracking' function does not hold across texts with any meaningful frequency.

11. In some American dialects, the forms such as the following are commonly seen:

(i) I always calls him Joseph.
(ii) I likes anything salty.   (Clarke 1997: 242)

12. Goffman (1981a: 144) defines the author as the person "who has selected the sentiments that are being expressed and the words in which they are encoded."

13. Fludernik further suggests that in literature, the use of "says I" and "says he" is a standard pattern already in Shakespeare and Defoe, which she claims mimetically recreates what is believed to have been the colloquial standard of the day.

14. EJ = *The English Journal*. Tokyo: ALC Press.

Notes to Chapter 3

1. Narrative psychology is an approach largely allied to autobiographical case studies (Bruner 1990; Freeman 1993; Plummer 1995) and is mainly concerned with self, identity, or subjectivity (Sarbin 1986; Young 1987; Shotter and Gergen 1989), according to Edwards (1997: 269).

2. I do not include the reporting of the second persons in the scope of the present theory, since the reporting of the second persons is rare in my corpus. Ferrara and Bell (1995) reported that, in a study of casual reporting discourse that is introduced with "be like," out of 284 instances of reporting discourse, there was only one instance used with the second person. Schiffrin (1993: 233) claims that the form of reporting of the second person speech in the form of "you said" should often be treated differently from the other cases of reportings. She claims that the one for whom we are most likely to construct dialogue is probably not someone who is with us at the time, especially not one to whom we are directing our speech (i.e., an 'addressed recipient,' in Goffman's [1981b] term); indeed, reporting the words of an addressed recipient to that recipient (e.g., "You said . . .") seems likely to be heard as a challenge to the veracity or appropriateness of what was said. And even when we make statements about another's internal state—something that only the other is in a position to know about (Labov and Fanshel's [1977: 226-28] 'B-event')—they are heard as requests for confirmation from the one about whom the state is predicated: saying "You're hungry," for example, elicits either a confirmation or a denial of the state about whom it is assumed to hold. In my corpus, there are few instances of reporting second-person utterances. Let me raise a few instances (reporting phrases that lead the second-person utterances are italicized):

(i) H: Getting my hair cut tihmorrow,=
    N: =Oh rilly?
    H: Yea::::h,
    N: Oh fer foo:d?
    (0.4)
    H: Wha:t?
    (0.2)
    N: Cuz member *you said* you were g'nna make en appointm'n,
    H: whhhhhhhoo Oh : y a ah.=
    H: =a- Yihknow whh't I thhought *you sai:d* hh=
    N: Wha:t,
    H: f o r f oo:d, hhhhh hhhhhhh
    N: e-fhhor f(h)oo(h)d
    H: ihhhhh=
    H: =Oh fer foo:d? ehh he h heh ih (so I sz) waa::t.
    N: hhehh- eh h h u h S u :re.   (HG)

(ii) H: Din'I jus' say that?
     N: No I thought *you said* yu- he'd be married, with six kids,=
     H: =That's w't I sai:d,   (HG)

These are confirmations of previous utterances made by the interlocutor. Other instances of the reporting of second-person utterances are talking about the future and making suggestions to the interlocutor as in the following:

(iii) H: *Y'bedder'v sump'n good tuh sa:y*, hhh=
 N: =hhhhh=
 H: = hhh Li-ike hh will you ma-arry me? hhh (HG)

(iv) C: If she calls you, *you can just say*=
 V: =Yeah.
 C: in a very steady way, I think you're wrong Mom. I think I'm convinced that it's OK. bt don't- put your energy into trying to convince her,
  (VK)

3. The 'PRE-*s*' row in Table 1 includes both "she/he says" (normal case of 'third-person singular present' form) and "I says" (special case of 'third-person singular present' form).

4. According to Galbraith (1995: 21), deixis is a term "for those aspects of meaning associated with self-world orientation. Deixis is a language universal (Hockett 1963) that orients the use of language with respect to a particular time, place, and person."

5. Memory has STS (short-term store) and LTS (long-term store) that are further divided into declarative memory and procedural memory. Declarative memory is further divided into semantic memory and episodic memory. Episodic memory (Tulving 1972), or reconstructive memory (Bartlett 1932), is recalled with socio-cultural memory schemata (Bartlett 1932). The memory system has an important role in human reporting behavior, but I do not go into such details in this book.

6. 'Schema' is a pattern that includes some kind of breakdown into subchunks and relations between them (Bartlett 1932). 'Frame' is a set of expectations we associate with conventionalized situations (Tannen 1979; Chafe 1987). It is a similar notion to 'script' (Schank and Abelson 1975).

7. The notion of event is disputable. Wolfson (1982) and Schiffrin (1981) admit that definitions of event are not consistent, which leads to different views of narrative tense-alternations. Fleischman (1990: 97-100) raises variable definitions of event as follows. The simplest definition, which is in the *Oxford English Dictionary*, views an 'event' as "anything that happens or is contemplated as happening." Dorfman (1969: 5) details it as "anything that happens, an incident of some kind, particularly if some importance is attached to its occurrence." Chatman (1978: 32) again refines it to 'action' or 'happening,' to which Rimmon-Kenan (1983: 15) adds that an event is "a change from one state of affairs to another." For Polanyi (1985: 10), an event is "an occurrence in some world which is described as having an instantaneous rather than a durative or iterative character." Banfield (1982: 265) also points to the punctual, perfective nature of an event, so that it is "a discrete unit occurring in time which may be counted and, hence, which is defined by the sequential relationship with the

unit(s) which precede or follow it in the series." Fleischman acknowledges that an event is ontologically but a hermeneutic construct for converting an undifferentiated continuum of the raw data of experience, or of the imagination, into the verbal structures we use to talk about experience, namely, narratives and stories.

8. In this chapter, we do not discuss the issue of how knowledge is stored in subconscious memory, since what we are concerned with is the nature of the recall process.

9. I assume that my claim in this chapter applies basically to both reporting of story and of interactive events, because story understanding is only a special case of event understanding (e.g., Lichtenstein and Brewer 1980; Bower and Cirilo 1985). Lichtenstein and Brewer (1980) demonstrate that memories of simple event sequences presented on film show properties very similar to memories of stories. Bower and Cirilo (1985: 94) assume that stories are understood by way of the typical information patterns represented by schemata.

10. Chafe (1985b: 116) raises three types of involvement in conversation: self-involvement of the speaker, interpersonal involvement between speaker and hearer, and involvement of the speaker with what is being talked about. The last type of involvement is the one with which I am primarily concerned.

11. It may not sound new to use the stage model to view reporting discourse. Many researchers have often metaphorically equated reporting discourse to theatrical events. Some claimed that direct reporting style is of a 'theatrical nature' (Wierzbicka 1974; Li 1986) with 'dramatization effect' (Sanchez 1987). It is also related to 'showing effect' (Sakita 1992; 1995) and 'staging effect' (Yule and Mathis 1992). But such claims have almost always focused on illustrating direct reporting style, in the production stage of reporting discourse which is only one phase of the whole reporting process. Here I use the stage model to illustrate both direct and indirect reporting styles, and the focus is on the recollection process before the reporting starts.

12. Although I often representatively use the "say" verb to proceed my discussion, the argument also applies to other reporting phrases such as "she goes" and "I'm like."

13. In natural conversational discourse, such forms as "I say" or "I says" are used in some situations, as I showed in the quantitative analysis in 3.1. I will discuss the backgrounds of this usage later in this chapter, and functional reasons for it in the next chapter. Here in modeling basic cognitive patterns of recall, I postulate that there is basically no cognitive background for the use of first person with the timeless present tense.

14. Johnstone (1987) also made a similar assumption that the present tense is rarely used for the first persons although she did not clearly state it. Her account for it,

however, was totally different from mine. She explained it by claiming that the first persons are always nonauthorities in stories that involve authorities, and that nonauthorities are introduced with the past tense.

15. Indeed, there is another "I" that is embedded in the quotation, "he said, 'You talk to Terry, I'm goin' to the bathroom.'"

16. Johnstone (1987) also claims the roles of tense choices for tracking shifts in 'footing.' In her argument, tense choice is a means of distinguishing status differences of reported speakers, namely, authority and nonauthority distinctions.

17. Schiffrin (1993) defines 'identity display' as the way a particular utterance (or action) can display those social roles and statuses that are sometimes thought to be relatively stable and enduring properties of persons (e.g., one's gender, social class, ethnicity).

Schiffrin (1993) adopts the definition of 'interactive frames' by Tannen and Wallat (1993): what people think they are doing when they talk to each other. "Interactive frames are related to what they refer to as 'knowledge schemas' (a structure of knowledge about situations, actions, and actors) simply because such schemas provide expectations not only about what can happen, but about how to interpret what is said and done (Goffman 1974; Gumperz 1982; Tannen and Wallet 1993)" (p. 233).

18. Schiffrin notes that the 'speak for yourself' rule is part of Goffman's (1967a: 12) 'traffic rules of social interaction.'

19. Schiffrin explains the operation of the 'speak for yourself' rule more in greater detail. The rule gives both conversation participants a license to make their own contribution to talk, in exchange for a willingness to refrain from making another's contribution. She views this rule as an offer of mutual deference to negative face wants: i.e., it serves people's desire not to be intruded upon (Brown and Levinson 1987).

20. Haiman (1995) argues that this type of alienation from oneself is culture specific. It is not a priori a universal of human conceptualization nor of social behavior.

21. The other examples that Haiman raises include:

(i)   I like me. My best friend is me.
(ii) Apparently you don't listen to you either.
(iii) I had a little meeting with myself tonight and I talked me into it.
                                                    (Haiman 1995: 230)

Haiman claims that the failure of reflexive pronouns to occur in syntactic contexts where they should be expected is usually a sign that the individual is divided into a self and a counterpart. In (iii), for instance, the speaker represents himself as two distinct people.

22. Fleischman (1990: 84-85) also mentions the "apparent constraint on co-occurring of present tense with ego." She raises three hypothetical views on the issue. First, the present tense is avoided out of politeness not to highlight the ego. She claims that it accounts for "says I" (and also "I says" although she does not mention it), which casts ego in the grammatical person of the other, since it is acceptable to draw attention to other people's speech and actions. Second, from a cognitive standpoint, we have less need to emphasize our own words and deeds, because being our own, they are intrinsically salient in our horizon of concerns, and therefore there is less reason to textually mark the first person's words for saliency. Third, she claims that it is awkward to try to characterize ourselves. So when narrators need to self-quote, they use the past tense or to attribute the words of ego to a grammatical third person.

23. Georgakopoulou and Goutsos (1997) treat proximity as a notion related to far/near orientations, "the speaker's positioning towards the discourse and its participants":

> All discourse, narrative in particular, is capable of signaling different degrees of proximity to or distance from its message and its participants. This is an indispensable means of encoding subjectivity. (p. 142)

They claim that Chafe's (1982) involvement and detachment are a scheme for capturing the linguistic means by which different degrees of proximity are marked in discourse.

Although Georgakopoulou and Goutsos's work points out the correlation of proximity and tense-alternation, it does not go into detail.

Notes to Chapter 4

1. Chafe claims that speakers use adjectives, relative clauses, and other modifiers in "the situation of low codability, where there is less agreement and less consistency in the categorization" (1977a: 233).

2. 'Searching mode' is one's mental or physical state to search for information to satisfy one's inner desire that arises as quest, anxiety, curiosity, expectation, etc.

3. 'Turn initiator' indicates those in utterance-initial positions. Its use is not based on semantic meaning or grammatical status. "Well" is also labeled as an interjection, filler, particle, hesitator, and initiator (Svartvik 1980).

4. In Edwards' transcription, 'greater than' and 'lesser than' signs enclose speeded-up talk as in: >he said<.

5. By perlocutionary act, speakers pursue a certain effect by saying something, usually by way of pursuing an illocutionary act with some intention and purpose. Austin

(1962) subclassifies speech act into locutionary act, illocutionary act, and perlocutionary act. See also Searle (1969) and Yamanashi (1986) for subclassification of speech act.

6. The last remark may also be considered as an additional remark that is often introduced with the present tense, which I have shown in relation to example (4).

7. This transcription is segmented into intonation units. Two dots indicate a brief break in timing, three dots a full-fledged pause. I am grateful to Chafe for providing contextual information about this example and discussing it with me.

8. Even when we suppose that what is here is not the correction at the time of the report but a correction which happened in the actual utterance, the correlation between the tense form and the attitude is justified. The first utterance, "Yeah I know," sounds more like a temporary hesitation, while the speaker stiffened her attitude immediately, saying, "ah I know," with her insistence. It was her never-intimidated attitude that made the police officer step back with a surprise: ". . . oh . . ." Her weaker answer is introduced with "I says," and her insistent attitude is reflected in "I said."

9. 'Repair' is a speech activity during which speakers locate and replace a prior information unit. Because they focus on prior information, they achieve information transitions anaphorically—forcing speakers to adjust their orientation to what has been said before they respond to it in upcoming talk (Schiffrin 1987: 74).

10. Exclamation also very frequently occurs with a reporting phrase "be like." The correlation of tense-switching with verb-switching is another significant issue that I do not go into detail in this book.

11. Some readers may question some of my interpretations of the speaker attitudes presented in sections 4.2. and 4.3., giving preference to the notion of 'emotional highlight.' For them, 'step back' and 'emotional highlight' may not seem compatible. My argument, however, does not deny the traditional interpretation of the historical present tense that the speaker expresses the reported speaker's heightened emotional content, but suggests that there are manipulative uses of the two tenses in combination.

12. See Sakita (2000a; forthcoming) for further discussion of this issue.

Notes to Chapter 5

1. Chafe (1994: 137-45) claims, in discussing topic hierarchies and the status of sentences, that it is not sentences but intonation units that represent relatively stable units in the mind. He points out the variability of sentences compared to the cognitive stability of intonation units (p. 145):

The information brought together in a sentence seems not to represent any cognitively stable unit of perception, storage, or remembering. Rather, sentence boundaries appear when a speaker judges, during a particular telling, that a coherent center of interest has been verbalized at that point. There are a variety of grounds for judging such coherence, and those grounds are subject to variation in repeated verbalizations of the same subject matter.

2. Halliday and Hasan's (1976) work on cohesion highlights how linguistic features signal connection.

3. I am not concerned with dialect differences in this book, although some people have pointed out that "he say" and "I saying" are more frequent in Black English.

4. Tsui (1994: 261) claims that speech act theory overlooks the fact that what speech act is being performed cannot be determined by the linguistic form alone. I agree with her that a lot depends on the context of the situation, as well as what preceded and follows in the discourse.

5. Schiffrin (1987: 84) points out that the reason why questions constrain the next conversational slot is semantic:

> WH-questions are incomplete propositions; yes-no questions are propositions whose polarity is unspecified (e.g., Carlson 1983). Completion of the proposition is up to the recipient of the question, who either fills in the WH-information, or fixes the polarity. This semantic completion allows a speaker/hearer reorientation toward an information unit, i.e. redistribution of knowledge about a proposition.

Schiffrin (1987: 333) also raises a pragmatic reason for the question/answer constraint:

> Questions are among the linguistic means of enacting requests for information and actions, and thus impose—through their underlying appropriateness conditions (Gordon and Lakoff 1971; Labov and Fanshel 1977; . . .)—an expectation of fulfillment. Thus, both the completion of a proposition, and compliance with a request, can be enacted through the second-pair-part of an answer.

6. Chafe also raises the following five variable properties of consciousness:

(i) Conscious experiences arise from different sources.
(ii) Conscious experiences may be immediate or displaced.
(iii) Conscious experiences may be factual or fictional.
(iv) Conscious experiences are more or less interesting.
(v) Conscious experiences may be verbal or nonverbal.   (1994: 30-35)

7. Spontaneous spoken language is not usually considered planned, compared with more planned varieties of spoken and written language. But in narrating events and telling stories, spontaneous spoken language still has a rather big picture, which is a large schema or frame. It is partly reflected in the fact that when people tell a story, they usually give an abstract or an orientation first, and then go into substantial complicating actions.

8. Following Chafe (1987: 22), I use the term 'activate' in this context, meaning that a narrator temporarily lights up a certain limited amount of information in her/his mind.

9. Labov (1972b) and Chafe (1994) propose more precisely defined narrative categories: abstract; orientation; complicating actions; (embedded orientation; evaluation;) climax; denouement; and coda (see note 2 in chapter 1). Since I will not deal with whole narrative discourses but focus mostly on embedded dialogues in narratives, I will not go into detail about narrative categories here.

10. I am not saying that the story's content follows expectation. I am suggesting that an information structure follows expectation, at the story-structural level.

11. In daily conversations, we often come across the situation when a narrator's consciousness flow does not meet the listener's expectation that follows the adjacency pairs because the narrator is not focusing on the fulfillment of the pairs. The following exchange involves an expectation discrepancy between a speaker and a hearer. It is a conversation between a husband and a wife in the Japanese language. It is translated into English:

(i) K: The other day, Takashi was preparing a bath. Then Minechika came. Takashi said, "You think I'm doing something unusual, don't you?"
 T: And what did Minechika say?
 K: Oh, no, I didn't hear what he said.

Obviously, the listener T assumes that what K reports is an adjacency pair, and expects to hear both parts of the pair. But the narrator K's point is that it was funny that Takashi himself commented on his doing housework as unusual. In this case, the narrator's consciousness focuses only on the initiation move of the pair, which shapes the narrative organization as it appeared in his first turn.

12. Discourse topic: whatever a conversation, text, etc. is about. This might be identified explicitly (e.g., one speaker says, "I want to talk about x") or it might not (Matthews 1997: 380).

13. I am not claiming here any association between the 'flow and rest' of consciousness and the 'flow and stop' of sound in phonetics.

14. Johnstone (1987: 42) claims that verbs like "say" or "go" do not carry the sort of lexical meaning that other verbs do:

248 Notes to Chapter 5

They are semantically neutral place markers, indicating only that what follows is supposed to be taken as someone's exact words. Unlike verbs like "yell," "shout," "whisper," and so on, "say" and "go" do not carry any information about the exact nature of the verbal event, beyond the fact that it is verbal.

15. Tsui (1994: 220) claims that in producing an initiation move, the speaker has the choice of performing an elicitation, a requestive, a directive, or an informative.

16. The subclasses of informatives that Tsui (1994) summarizes are the following:

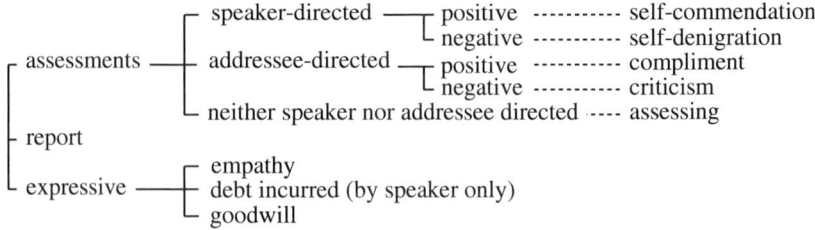

17. An 'assessment' asserts the speaker's judgment or evaluation of people, objects, events, or states of affairs (Tsui 1994: 183). Tsui further characterizes it as follows:

> Its illocutionary intent is to get the addressee to agree with the speaker's judgment or evaluation. It presupposes that the speaker believes that his/her judgment or evaluation is an accurate representation of the evaluated referent. Theoretically, a positive responding act should be realized by an agreement with the speaker's evaluation or judgment.

18. Wolfson (1979) mentions that, usually, the tense in the head clause agrees with the tense in the *when*-clause, but that such a rule is sometimes overridden by the strength of the CHP (conversational historical present) alternation rule, so that the verb in the head clause is in CHP.

19. CSAE = Corpus of Spoken American English (John W. Du Bois, University of California, Santa Barbara).

20. There are many functions of zero-introducers. For instance, they are often categorized as one of the present-tense forms, when they are used at the climax in narratives (e.g., Johnstone 1987; Sakita 1995). In (19), the narrator uses them rather for de-emphasizing who the speaker is. In a sense, the use of a zero-introducer to de-emphasize the speaker overlaps with its use as the historical present tense when the narrator is deeply psychologically involved in the narratives. By not using the dialogue-introducer, the reaction to the man's remarks by the narrated self synchronizes with the narrating self's reaction to it at the time of the narration.

21. Sakita (1996a) reported that the length and complexity of reported events affect reporting styles.

Notes to Chapter 6

1. Comrie's analytical framework is based on traditional theories of reporting discourse: a dichotomic approach (e.g., Celce-Murcia and Larsen-Freeman 1983; Comrie 1986), derivational relationships (e.g., Jespersen 1964; Jackson 1990), and wording theories (e.g., Jespersen 1931). In such frameworks, analysts examine pairs of constructions of direct and indirect reporting styles. Comrie (1986: 267-68) defines the set of pairs of constructions in the following way:

> An indirect speech construction will be said to correspond to a direct speech construction if the former carries the same message as the latter and if there is no other direct speech construction carrying the same message to which the given indirect speech construction is closer.

In contrast, I assume that direct discourse and indirect discourse are constructions independent of each other (e.g., Banfield 1982; Clark and Gerrig 1990; Mayes 1990).

2. The relative time hypothesis supposes that the tense form in the complement clause depends on the tense of the head clause, and on the temporal relation that is expressed between the complement clause and the head clause. Some linguists (e.g., Allen 1966; Huddleston 1984) supported this hypothesis. Comrie (1986) denied the possibility that this hypothesis operates in English, but admitted that it works in some other languages, for instance Russian.

The absolute deixis hypothesis treats tense as relating directly to the moment of speaking, i.e., the reporter's deictic center is the reference point, not that of the original speaker. This hypothesis has been propounded by Brecht (1974), Riddle (1978), and Heny (1982). Comrie (1986) claimed that the absolute deixis hypothesis cannot account for the use of tenses in English indirect discourse. It predicts that the indirect discourse version of (ia) is (ib), not (ic), because Dan's cooking is in the future. But it is not a correct prediction.

(i) (a) Dan will say, "I am cooking."
    (b)* Dan will say that he will be cooking.
    (c) Dan will say that he is cooking.

3. A (temporal) domain is a time interval taken up either by one situation or by a number of situations that are temporally related to each other by means of special tense forms (Declerck 1990: 515).

4. Declerck bases his idea of the choice of the absolute tense on Grice's (1975) maxims of conversation.

5. There still are some cases in which Declerck's hypothesis does not work. Huddleston (1989) raised the following examples:

(i) (a) It is time you said to her, "I am married."
 (b) It is time you told her you were married.
(ii) (a) I wish I knew the answer to the question, "Where is she?"
 (b) I wish I knew where she was.   (Huddleston 1989: 335-36)

The past tense in the head clauses in these sentences has modals rather than past-time meaning. The past-tense forms "were" in (ib) and "was" in (iib) do not express simultaneity in a past time sphere with their head clauses, because the time of saying and knowing in the head clauses is non-past. In such cases, the past tenses must be accounted for by reference to the syntactic fact that they occur in the complements of past-tense reporting verbs, not in terms of the relative time of the situations.

6. In this chapter, italicizing is used to draw attention to the tense of reported verbs. Their original verb forms are italicized as well in examples of their original discourse versions.

7. CE: *The Study of Current English*. Tokyo: Kenkyusha.

8. The spontaneous use of the simple present tense occurs with verbs expressing events, in contrast to the unrestrictive use that occurs with verbs expressing states. The instantaneous use of event verbs normally occurs only in certain easily definable contexts as in sports commentaries and in the patter or commentary of magicians and demonstrators. It may also occur as a dramatic use in the following example (i) that insists on the total enactment of the event as it is reported, in contrast to (ii) that contains a progressive verb form and is a neutral description in answer to the question "What are you doing?":

(i) I *open* the cage.
(ii) I *am opening* the cage.   (Leech 1987: 7)

It also occurs in asseverations with performative verbs:

(iii) I *beg* your pardon.
(iv) We *accept* your offer.
(v) I *deny* your charge.   (Ibid.)

9. Tense-alternation is more commonly seen in direct discourse as we saw in chapters 2-5.

10. Free indirect discourse is common in literature. The second sentence in the following is an example of free indirect discourse:

(i) He begged her to believe him when he said he could not earn. *Had* he not already *sunk* a small fortune in attempts to do so? He begged her to believe that he was a chronic emeritus. But it was not altogether a question of economy. (Samuel Beckett, *Murphy*: 18)

The formal SoT has difficulty determining what tense should be used for "had sunk" in this example since this sentence lacks a reporting clause which, the SoT claims, determines tense in reported clause. It attempts to solve this problem by considering free indirect discourse to be derived from indirect reporting discourse by deleting the head clause. CoRA claims that in this case the speaker simply relates the situations to a particular past time rather than to his own here-and-now (Declerck 1991: 176).

11. 'Absolute tense' generally refers to the present perfect, the present tense, the future tense, and the past tense. They are directly defined in relation to the moment of speech (Declerck 1990: 514). Since the past perfect is located relative to a certain point in the past, it is generally treated as a relative tense. Here I claim that speakers use the past perfect tense in an analogous way to the absolute tense. They use the past perfect from their own standpoints, not relative to the tenses in the head clauses. Speakers do not shift their deictic centers to the reportees' deictic centers as their temporal reference points.

12. Quirk et al. (1985: 1026) point out that the reporting verb may be in the present tense for communications in recent past time (i), for reports attributed to famous works or authors which have present validity (ii), or for verbs of cognition (iii):

(i) Joan tells me she's going to the airport in an hour's time.
(ii) Chaucer somewhere writes that love is blind.
(iii) Sylvia thinks Paul went to Lancaster last night.

But the present tense in (43) does not belong to any such cases.

13. Since such reporting clauses behave similarly to dialogue-introducers of direct reporting discourse, they may have analogous discourse functions, for example, as 'attitudinal contrasting devices' (see chapter 4) or as 'consciousness flow markers' (see chapter 5). This should be examined in further research.

14. The six types of comment clauses that Quirk et al. (1985: 1112) distinguish are the following:

(i) like the matrix clause of a main clause:
  There were no other applicants, *I believe*, for that job.
(ii) like an adverbial finite clause (introduced by *as*):
  I'm working the night shift, *as you know*.
(iii) like a nominal relative clause:
  What was more upsetting, we lost all our luggage.

(iv) *to*-infinitive clause as style disjunct:
I'm not sure what to do, *to be honest.*
(v) *-ing* clause as style disjunct:
I doubt, *speaking as a layman*, whether television is the right medium for that story.
(vi) *-ed* clause as style disjunct:
Stated bluntly, he had no chance of winning.

15. A 'hedge' is any linguistic device by which a speaker avoids being compromised by a statement that turns out to be wrong, a request that is not acceptable, and so on. Thus, instead of saying, "This argument is convincing," one might use a hedge and say, "As far as I can see this argument is convincing" (Matthews 1997: 160).

16. They raise the following examples:

(i) (a) John imagined that his wife was/?*is pregnant.
 (b) What John imagined was that his wife was/?is pregnant.
 (c) That John's wife was/is pregnant was said by Bill, not by John.
 (Declerck and Tanaka 1996: 293)

According to their claim, in (ia), the present tense is virtually impossible because of the strong intentional verb "imagine" and the highly private contents of the *that*-clause. However, in (ib), the present tense looks slightly better, because the *that*-clause is no longer syntactically dependent on "imagined." Its syntactic form is '*wh*-clause + *be* + *that*-clause,' and "The *that*-clause is thus on a par with the *wh*-clause, and this looser syntactic relation renders it better possible to locate the *that*-clause situation in a world that is different from the strong intentional world created by 'imagined'" (Declerck and Tanaka 1996: 293). In (ic), since "the *that*-clause is used as subject rather than as a constituent of the VP," "A subject does not syntactically depend on the verb the way an object does. (A subject is an 'external argument' of the predicate; it does not belong to the VP.)" The present tense is perfectly all right in this case. The case as (ib) with the present tense in the reported clause certainly often appears:

(ii) Well, I can see that's what people think, but <u>what we were saying was</u>, Japan *has* always *been* very slow.
 (*Active English* 1992. 9: 95 [Tokyo: ALC Press])

17. Growing numbers of cross-linguistic studies have supported that tense determination systems vary considerably across linguistic groupings.

Notes to Chapter 7

1. The mention theory claims that quotation is the mention rather than the use of an expression. It assumes that a quotation designates its object not by describing it in terms of other objects, but by picturing it. The demonstrative theory assumes that quotation is a device for pointing to utterances. The demonstrative reference is part of

the utterance, but what it points at is not. The dramaturgical theory assumes that quotations are imaginary speech performances. The speaker "does something that enables the hearer to SEE for himself what it is, that is to say, in a way, he SHOWS this content" (Wierzbicka 1974: 272). It makes no provision for the selectivity of quotations.

2. Urdang (1991: 17-18) points out that "the style manuals are explicit in their directions regarding the citing of others' writings." Accordingly, he suggests that in quotations of oral material also, "the speaker's words should never be changed."

3. Chafe pointed out to me that 'demonstration' vs. 'description' equals 'mimesis' vs. 'diegesis' which I mention later in this chapter (see note 29).

4. Banfield points out, for instance, direct quote in interrogative form cannot be directly translated into indirect speech, since the rhetorical functions of the original interrogative and the verb "ask" differ. She also points out that if the direct quote has the form of an imperative, but its rhetorical function is not that of an order, it cannot be changed into indirect speech.

5. Nakagawa (1983) presents detailed characterizations of intermediate reporting discourse style.

6. Varieties of terms for intermediate forms are: Kalepky's (1899) 'veiled speech,' Bally's (1912) 'free indirect style,' Lerch's (1919) 'quasi-direct speech,' Lorck's (1921) 'experienced speech,' Jespersen's (1924) 'dependent speech' or 'represented speech,' and Voloshinov's ([1929]1986) 'quasi-direct discourse.' See Coulmas (1986) for their detailed characterizations and definitions.

Chafe (1994) calls the intermediate form 'verbatim indirect speech' because it "combines the verbatim quality of direct speech with the tense and person characteristic of indirect speech" (p. 242). He discusses it in detail in its relation with consciousness (pp. 240-43). It is much more prevalent in certain styles of writing, although its rare occurrence in conversations is certainly interesting, as Chafe points out (p. 222). Chafe raises the following references as useful discussions of this reporting style (pp. 195-96): Weinrich (1964), Lethcoe (1969), Bronzwaer (1970), Hamburger (1973), Pascal (1977), McHale (1978), Leech and Short (1981), Banfield (1982), Ehrlich (1990), Fleischman (1990), and Fludernik (1993).

7. However, Macaulay (1987) also argues that when a quoted speech is fully integrated into a story, it is not functioning merely as a way of making it more dramatic.

8. Perridon (1996: 165-66) notes that as the boundary-line between drama and story is not always easy to draw, indirect speech may pass over into direct speech, and vice versa.

9. External evaluation means that the narrator gives a justification, why the story is worth telling, explicitly as a comment in her own role as narrator.

254 *Notes to Chapter 7*

10. Schiffrin (1987) claims that these are markers of information management, including shifts in speaker orientation.

11. The following interjections frequently appeared in direct style:

   (i)   *ah* it's about time, I really wanna have my muffin.
   (ii) *oh good*, I want the coffee now to have with my muffin.
   (iii) *well*, I wasn't feeling good either.
   (iv) *yes* but made my stomach feel better.
   (v)   *well you know* it's a good business. It has been continuing for some time.

   (Sakita 1996c)

12. It would be tautological to present one's current thought as a quote.

13. The previous studies have shown various results of gender difference for the frequency of reporting style, some of which seem to contradict each other. The difference may be attributable to the different speech norms that women and men follow in different speech situations. Sanchez (1987) found that in children's storytelling, males used more direct style than females. Whereas Ferrara and Bell (1991) discovered that, in personal experience narratives among friends and families, age and sex are correlated. Among the young, females used more direct style than males (74%: 61%), but among the old, males used more direct style than females (71%: 50%). Ely (1993) noted that in dinner-table conversations among families, females used direct style three times as often as males.

14. For instance, Tannen (1988) points out that direct style is used in conversational narratives more often than in written narratives.

15. The context was narrowly focused in order to exclude contextual variables. For example, the sentence type was restricted to statement, to avoid the results being influenced by the possibility that the sentence type is another variable which affects reporting style. Since the gender of the actors may also influence reporting style, only males were used as reportees in this study. Of course, it is possible to conduct the same experiment with females, and then compare the results to see if the reportees' gender affects the reporting styles.

16. The short utterances were added at the end after the longest and most complicated one. This is to exclude the possibility that another factor, the time shift, influences speech styles. The possible claim is that the reporters gradually shift from direct to indirect style regardless of the length or complexities of the sentences. By examining the reportings of the last remarks as well as of the others, we can see whether the reporters are influenced by either the time shift or by the length and the complexities.

17. Classifying the reportings into two styles was not hard, partly because I had grasped the actors' original discourse. It was more difficult in the observations of

conversational data in the preliminary study, since the original speeches were unknown.

18. Chafe (1994) calls the style using a gerund or a noun (examples 8, 11, 15, 23, 24) 'referred-to speech.' It is a way in which language "represents distal language simply by referring to it as a speech event, without attempting to represent the language itself" (Chafe 1994: 213). It corresponds to what Leech and Short (1981) call a 'narrative report of a speech act,' and to McHale's (1978) 'diegetic summary.' Chafe distinguishes it from indirect reporting, but I categorize it as one of indirect styles here (cf. note 31 in this chapter).

19. Dialogue grammars of Hundsnurscher and Franke apply the heuristic priority of the analysis of competence to the description of linguistic performance. In this respect, they have adopted the methodological principle from transformational grammar.

20. Sociolinguistic correlational studies (e.g., Sanchez 1987; Rimmer 1988) have pointed out inter-personal variations of reporting discourse. It is expected that the usage of reporting discourse is affected by many factors: discourse style, genre, purpose, settings of the discourse, relationship between the speakers and the hearers, gender and age. There is a perceived need for both quantitative and qualitative approaches to data (Rimmer 1988). This study, as a step of functional study of reporting discourse, focused on the narrower aspect of the variations.

21. 'Evidentiality' is also often used more broadly to include a speaker's assessment of the validity/reliability of information (Chafe: personal communication).

22. Hopper and Thompson (1980: 277) have defined the 'realis/irrealis' distinction as the opposition between indicative and such non-assertive forms as subjunctive, optative, hypothetical, imaginary, conditional, etc.

23. Chafe pointed out to me another interpretation of "You're kidding." It may not be really disagreement, but simply an expression of how surprised the person is. It is more like saying "Wow!" A narrator may be very pleased by this reaction, and may not see it as disagreement.

24. Thompson (1987) suggests clausal distinctions for narrative discourse, stressing correlations between subordination, temporal sequencing, and foregrounding.

25. This is in accordance with the direct/indirect distinction that Clark and Gerrig (1990) propose in demonstration theory, that direct quotation is demonstration, while indirect reporting discourse is description.

26. The use of reporting discourse to portray one's emotion by direct example discussed in the previous section is considered similar to Tannen's idea of the use of dialogue for instantiation.

27. We can trace such dramatization with zero-quotation reporting discourse to narrating stories, in which narrators often choose to act out a drama rather than simply to tell stories. In narrated stories, long dialogic segments are composed only of dialogues, once the scene is set.

28. See 7.1.1. and note 6 in this chapter for discussions of the 'free indirect discourse.'

29. Diegesis and mimesis are classical literary distinctions of narrative between telling and showing. According to Toolan (1988: 126), diegesis places the emphasis on a more indirect, detached teller-oriented conspectual presentation, while mimesis places the emphasis on a direct characterological representation or impersonation. Diegesis is linked to a condensed or 'edited' summarized account—with a greater overt role played by the teller who condenses or edits, while mimesis is associated with a scenic presentation. Diegesis presents 'everything that happened' in one sense, but only everything that a detached external reporter decides is worth telling. On the other hand, mimesis presents 'everything that happened' in another sense, but really only everything as it would be revealed to a witness within the scene; it is rather partial and non-comprehensive.

30. Variations of reporting verbs and their tense are omitted on the continuum.

31. The styles on the right-hand side "Gerund" and "One-Word" are categorized as 'referred-to speech' by Chafe (1994) (cf. note 18 in this chapter).

Notes to Chapter 8

1. See Sakita (2000b; 2001b) for a further exploration of this topic.

TRANSCRIPTION CONVENTIONS

The following notational conventions are used in the transcripts of the conversational examples:

(0.0)	Length of silence
:	Lengthened syllable
-	Sound cut off in a delivery
=	Two utterances are latched without a usual beat of silence
[	Onset of simultaneous talk
]	Offset of simultaneous talk
hh	Audible breath or laughter
	(hh shows exhalation; .hh shows inhalation)
?	Rising intonation
( )	Unintelligible stretch
(.)	A short beat of silence

Other features such as italicizing and underlining are noted in each chapter. In some examples from published sources, transcription symbols are simplified or slightly altered for convenience, as noted in the text. Person and place names in some cases are changed to preserve anonymity.

REFERENCES

Abercrombie, David (1965). *Studies in Phonetics and Linguistics*. Oxford University Press, London.

Ageno, Franca Brambilla (1964). *Il verbo nell'italiano antico: Ricerche di sintassi*. Riccardi Editore, Milan.

Allen, Robert Livingston (1966). *The Verb System of Present-Day American English*. Mouton, The Hague.

Almeida, Michael J. (1995). Time in narratives. In: *Deixis in Narrative: A Cognitive Science Perspective* (Judith F. Duchan, Gail A. Bruder and Lynne E. Hewitt, eds.), pp. 159-89. Lawrence Erlbaum Associates, Hillsdale, NJ.

Anderson, Lloyd B. (1986). Evidentials, paths of change, and mental maps: Typologically regular asymmetries. In: *Evidentiality: The Linguistic Coding of Epistemology* (Wallace Chafe and Johanna Nichols, eds.), pp. 273-312. Ablex, Norwood, NJ.

Aristotle ([c 325 BCE]1965). On the art of poetry. In: *Aristotle/Horacel/Longinus: Classical Literary Criticism* (T. S. Dorsch, trans.), pp. 29-75. Viking, New York.

Austin, J. L. (1962). *How to Do Things with Words*. Oxford University Press, Oxford.

Bain, Alexander (1879). *A Higher English Grammar*. Henry Holt, New York.

Bakhtin, Mikhail M. ([1975]1981). *The Dialogic Imagination*. University of Texas Press, Austin.

Bakhtin, Mikhail M. ([1952-53]1986). The problem of speech genres. In: *Speech Genres and Other Late Essays* (Caryl Emerson and Michael Holquist, eds., Vern W. McGee, trans.), pp. 60-102. University of Texas Press, Austin.

Bal, Mieke ([1980]1985). *Narratology: Introduction to the Theory of Narrative* (Christine van Boheemen, trans.). University of Toronto Press, Toronto.

Bally, Charles (1912). Le style indirect libre en français moderne. *Germanisch-Romanische Monatsschrift*, **4**, 549-56 and 597-606.

Bamgbose, Ayo (1986). Reported speech in Yoruba. In: *Direct and Indirect Speech* (Florian Coulmas, ed.), pp. 77-97. Mouton de Gruyter, Berlin.

Banfield, Ann (1973). Narrative style and the grammar of direct and indirect speech. *Foundations of Language*, **10**, 1-39.

Banfield, Ann (1982). *Unspeakable Sentences: Narration and Representation in the Language of Fiction*. Routledge & Kegan Paul, Boston.

Bartlett, Frederic C. (1932). *Remembering: A Study in Experimental and Social Psychology*. Cambridge University Press, Cambridge.

Bates, E., M. Masling and W. Kintsch (1978). Recognition memory for aspects of dialogue. *Journal of Experimental Psychology: Human Learning and Memory*, **4**, 187-97.

Bateson, Gregory (1972). *Steps to an Ecology of Mind*. Ballantine, New York.

Becker, A. L. (1984). The linguistics of particularity: Interpreting superordination in a Javanese text. In: *Proceedings of the Tenth Annual Meeting of the Berkeley Linguistics Society*, pp. 425-36. University of California, Berkeley, CA.

Becker, A. L. (1988). Language in particular: A lecture. In: *Linguistics in Context: Connecting Observation and Understanding* (Deborah Tannen, ed.), pp. 17-35. Ablex, Norwood, NJ.

Bellos, David M. (1980). The narrative absolute tense. *Language and Style*, **13** (1), 77-84.

Berry, Margaret (1981). Systemic linguistics and discourse analysis: A multi-layered approach to exchange structure. In: *Studies in Discourse Analysis* (Malcolm Coulthard and Martin Montgomery, eds.), pp. 120-45. Routledge & Kegan Paul, London.

Berry, Margaret (1987). Is teacher an unanalyzed concept? In: *New Developments in Systemic Linguistics* (M. A. K. Halliday and Robin P. Fawcett, eds.), Vol. 1. Frances Pinter, London.

Besnier, Niko (1993). Reported speech and affect on Nukulaelae atoll. In: *Responsibility and Evidence in Oral Discourse: Studies in the Social and Cultural Foundations of Language* (Jane H. Hill and Judith T. Irvine, eds.), pp. 163-81. Cambridge University Press, Cambridge.

Bloomfield, Leonard (1933). *Language*. Henry Holt, New York.

Bower, Gordon H. and Randolph K. Cirilo (1985). Cognitive psychology and text processing. In: *Handbook of Discourse Analysis*, Vol. 1: *Disciplines of Discourse* (Teun A. van Dijk, ed.), pp. 71-105. Academic Press, London.

Brazil, David C. (1995). *A Grammar of Speech*. Oxford University Press, Oxford.

Brecht, R. D. (1974). Deixis in embedded structures. *Foundations of Language*, **11**, 489-518.

Bronzwaer, W. J. M. (1970). *Tense in the Novel: An Investigation of Some Potentialities of Linguistic Criticism*. Wolters-Noordhoff, Groningen.

Brown, Goold (1880). *The Grammar of English Grammars*. William Wood, New York.

Brown, Gillian and George Yule (1983). *Discourse Analysis*. Cambridge University Press, Cambridge.

Brown, Penelope and Stephen C. Levinson (1987). *Politeness: Some Universals in Language Usage*. Cambridge University Press, Cambridge.

Bruner, Jerome (1990). *Acts of Meaning*. Harvard University Press, Cambridge, MA.

Buffin, J. M. (1925). *Remarques sur les moyens d'expression de la durée et du temps en français*. Presses Universitaires de France, Paris.

Burton, Deirdre (1981). Analyzing spoken discourse. In: *Studies in Discourse Analysis* (Malcolm Coulthard and Martin Montgomery, eds.), pp. 61-81. Routledge & Kegan Paul, London.

Bühler, C. (1982). The deictic field of language and deictic words. In: *Speech, Place, and Action: Studies in Deixis and Related Topics* (Robert J. Jarvella and Wolfgang Klein, eds.), pp. 9-30. Wiley, New York.

Carlson, Lauri (1983). *Dialogue Games: An Approach to Discourse Analysis*. Reidel, Dordrecht.

Casparis, Christian Paul (1975). *Tense without Time: The Present Tense in Narration*. Francke, Bern.

Cate, Abraham P. ten (1996). Modality of verb forms in German reported speech. In: *Reported Speech* (Theo A. J. M. Janssen and Wim van der Wurff, eds.), pp. 189-211. John Benjamins, Amsterdam.

Celce-Murcia, Marianne and Diane Larsen-Freeman (1983). *The Grammar Book: An ESL/EFL Teacher's Course*. Newbury House, Rowley.

Chafe, Wallace L. (1977a). The recall and verbalization of past experience. In: *Current Issues in Linguistic Theory* (Roger W. Cole, ed.), pp. 215-46. Indiana University Press, Bloomington.

Chafe, Wallace L. (1977b). Creativity in verbalization and its implications for the nature of stored knowledge. In: *Discourse Production and Comprehension* (Roy O. Freedle, ed.), pp. 41-55. Ablex, Norwood, NJ.

Chafe, Wallace L. (1980). *The Pear Stories: Cognitive, Cultural, and Linguistic Aspects of Narrative Production*. Ablex, Norwood, NJ.

Chafe, Wallace L. (1982). Integration and involvement in speaking, writing, and oral literature. In: *Spoken and Written Language: Exploring Orality and Literacy* (Deborah Tannen, ed.), pp. 35-53. Ablex, Norwood, NJ.

Chafe, Wallace L. (1985a). Some reasons for hesitating. In: *Perspectives on Silence* (Deborah Tannen and M. Saville-Troike, eds.), pp. 77-89. Ablex, Norwood, NJ.

Chafe, Wallace L. (1985b). Linguistic differences produced by differences between speaking and writing. In: *Literacy, Language, and Learning: The Nature and Consequences of Reading and Writing* (David R. Olson, Nancy Torrance and Angela Hildyard, eds.), pp. 105-23. Cambridge University Press, Cambridge.

Chafe, Wallace L. (1986). Evidentiality in English conversation and academic writing. In: *Evidentiality: The Linguistic Coding of Epistemology* (Wallace Chafe and Johanna Nichols, eds.), pp. 261-72. Ablex, Norwood, NJ.

Chafe, Wallace L. (1987). Cognitive constraints on information flow. In: *Coherence and Grounding in Discourse* (Russell S. Tomlin, ed.), pp. 21-51. John Benjamins, Amsterdam.

Chafe, Wallace L. (1990). Some things that narratives tell us about the mind. In: *Narrative Thought and Narrative Language* (Bruce K. Britton and Anthony D. Pellegrini, eds.), pp. 79-98. Lawrence Erlbaum Associates, Hillsdale, NJ.

Chafe, Wallace L. (1994). *Discourse, Consciousness, and Time*. University of Chicago Press, Chicago.

Chafe, Wallace L. (1996). How consciousness shapes language. *Pragmatics and Cognition*, **4** (1), 35-54.

Chafe, Wallace L. (1997). Polyphonic topic development. In: *Conversation: Cognitive, Communicative, and Social Perspectives* (T. Givón, ed.), pp. 41-53. John Benjamins, Amsterdam.

Charleston, Britta Marian (1941). *Studies on the Syntax of the English Verb*. Francke, Bern.

Chatman, Seymour (1978). *Story and Discourse: Narrative Structure in Fiction and Film*. Cornell University Press, Ithaca, NY.

Chomsky, Noam (1965). *Aspects of the Theory of Syntax*. MIT Press, Cambridge, MA.

Church, Alonzo (1964). *Introduction to Mathematical Logic*. Princeton University Press, Princeton.

Clark, Herbert H. (1973). Space, time, semantics, and the child. In: *Cognitive Development and the Acquisition of Language* (Timothy E. Moore, ed.), pp. 27-63. Academic Press, New York.

Clark, Herbert H. and Richard J. Gerrig (1990). Quotations as demonstration. *Language*, **66** (4), 764-805.

Clarke, Sandra (1997). English verbal -*s* revisited: The evidence from Newfoundland. *American Speech*, **72** (3), 227-59.

Comrie, Bernard (1986). Tense in indirect speech. *Folia Linguistica: Acta Societatis Linguisticae Europaeae*, **20** (3-4), 265-96.

Coulmas, Florian (1981). *Über Schrift*. Suhrkamp, Frankfurt.

Coulmas, Florian (1986). Reported speech: Some general issues. In: *Direct and Indirect Speech* (Florian Coulmas, ed.), pp. 1-28. Mouton de Gruyter, Berlin.

Coulthard, Malcolm and David C. Brazil (1981). Exchange structure. In: *Studies in Discourse Analysis* (Malcolm Coulthard and Martin Montgomery, eds.), pp. 82-106. Routledge & Kegan Paul, London.

Crystal, David (1966). Specification and English tenses. *Journal of Linguistics*, **2**, 1-34.

Crystal, David ([1980]1992). *A Dictionary of Linguistics and Phonetics*. 3rd ed. Blackwell, Oxford.

Curme, George O. (1931). *A Grammar of the English Language*. Heath, Boston.

Davidson, Donald (1984). Quotation. In: *Inquiries into Truth and Interpretation* (Donald Davidson, ed.), pp. 79-92. Clarendon, Oxford.

Davidson, Judy (1984). Subsequent versions of initiations, offers, requests and proposals dealing with potential or actual rejection. In: *Structures of Social Action: Studies in Conversation Analysis* (J. Maxwell Atkinson and John C. Heritage, eds.), pp. 102-28. Cambridge University Press, Cambridge.

Declerck, Renaat (1990). Sequence of tenses in English. *Folia Linguistica: Acta Societatis Linguisticae Europaeae*, **24**, 513-44.

Declerck, Renaat (1991). *Tense in English: Its Structure and Use in Discourse.* Routledge, London.

Declerck, Renaat and Kazuhiko Tanaka (1996). Constraints on tense choice in reported speech. *Studia Linguistica*, **50** (3), 283-301.

Diver, William (1963). The chronological system of the English verb. *Word*, **19**, 141-81.

Dixon, R. M. W. (1991). *A New Approach to English Grammar, on Semantic Principles.* Oxford University Press, Oxford.

Dorfman, Eugene (1969). *The Nareme in Medieval Romance Epics.* University of Toronto Press, Toronto.

Du Bois, John W. (1986). Self-evidence and ritual speech. In: *Evidentiality: The Linguistic Coding of Epistemology* (Wallace Chafe and Johanna Nichols, eds.), pp. 313-36. Ablex, Norwood, NJ.

Dumas, Bethany K. (1997). Structural autonomy and narrative success: Evidence from incomplete narratives. Paper presented at the Sixth International Conference on Narratives, Lexington, KY.

Edwards, Derek (1997). *Discourse and Cognition.* Sage, London.

Ehrlich, Susan (1990). *Point of View: A Linguistic Analysis of Literary Style.* Routledge, London.

Elias, Norbert (1982). *The Civilizing Process* (Edmund Jephcott, trans.). Pantheon, New York.

Ely, Richard (1993). Remembered voices: Reported speech in children's discourse (memory). Ph.D. dissertation. Tufts University.

Emery, Annie Crosby (1897). *The Historical Present in Early Latin.* Hancock, Ellsworth, ME.

Emmott, Catherine (1997). *Narrative Comprehension: A Discourse Perspective.* Clarendon, Oxford.

Fasold, Ralph (1990). *The Sociolinguistics of Language.* Blackwell, Oxford.

Feldman, Carol Fleisher, Jerome Bruner, Bobbie Renderer and Sally Spitzer (1990). Narrative comprehension. In: *Narrative Thought and Narrative Language* (Bruce K. Britton and Anthony D. Pellegrini, eds.), pp. 1-78. Lawrence Erlbaum Associates, Hillsdale, NJ.

Ferrara, Kathleen and Barbara Bell (1991). Variation and innovation in constructed dialogue introducers. Paper presented at the Linguistic Society of America, Chicago, January.

Ferrara, Kathleen and Barbara Bell (1995). Sociolinguistic variation and discourse function of constructed dialogue introducers: The case of *be+like*. *American Speech*, **70** (3), 265-90.

Fillmore, Charles J. (1975a). An alternative to checklist theories of meaning. In: *Proceedings of the First Annual Meeting of the Berkeley Linguistics Society*, pp. 123-31. University of California, Berkeley, CA.

Fillmore, Charles J. (1975b). *Santa Cruz Lectures on Deixis*. Indiana University Linguistics Club, Bloomington.

Flavell, J. H. (1978). Metacognitive development. In: *Structural/Process Models of Complex Human Behavior* (Joseph M. Scandura and Charles J. Brainerd, eds.). Sijihoff and Noordhoff, Alphen a. d. Riju, The Netherlands.

Flavell, J. H. (1979). Metacognition and cognitive monitoring: A new area of cognitive developmental inquiry. *American Psychologist*, **34**, 906-11.

Fleischman, Suzanne (1990). *Tense and Narrativity: From Medieval Performance to Modern Fiction*. University of Texas Press, Austin.

Fludernik, Monika (1991). The historical present tense yet again: Tense switching and narrative dynamics in oral and quasi-oral storytelling. *Text*, **11** (3), 365-98.

Fludernik, Monika (1993). *The Fictions of Language and the Languages of Fiction*. Routledge, London.

Ford, Cecilia E. (1994). Dialogic aspects of talk and writing: *Because* on the interactive-edited continuum. *Text*, **14** (4), 531-54.

Forster, E. M. ([1927]1963). *Aspects of the Novel*. Penguin, Middlesex.

Foulet, Lucien (1920). La disparition du prétérit. *Romania*, **46**, 271-313.

Franke, Wilhelm (1990). *Elementare Dialogstrukturen: Darstellung, Analyse, Diskussion*. M. Niemeyer, Tübingen.

Freeman, Mark (1993). *Rewriting the Self: History, Memory, Narrative*. Routledge, London.

Friden, G. (1948). *Studies on the Tenses of the English Verb from Chaucer to Shakespeare, with Special Reference to the Late Sixteenth Century*. Almqvist, Stockholm, Sweden.

Fónagy, Ivan (1986). Reported speech in French and Hungarian. In: *Direct and Indirect Speech* (Florian Coulmas, ed.), pp. 255-309. Mouton de Gruyter, Berlin.

Galbraith, Mary (1995). Deictic shift theory and the poetics of involvement in narrative. In: *Deixis in Narrative: A Cognitive Science Perspective* (Judith F. Duchan, Gail A. Bruder and Lynne E. Hewitt, eds.), pp. 19-59. Lawrence Erlbaum Associates, Hillsdale, NJ.

Genette, Gérard (1980). *Narrative Discourse: An Essay in Method* (Jane E. Lewin, trans.). Cornell University Press, Ithaca, NY.

Genette, Gérard (1988). *Narrative Discourse Revisited* (Jane E. Lewin, trans.). Cornell University Press, Ithaca, NY.

Georgakopoulou, Alexandra (1997). *Narrative Performances: A Study of Modern Greek Storytelling*. John Benjamins, Amsterdam.

Georgakopoulou, Alexandra and Dionysis Goutsos (1997). *Discourse Analysis: An Introduction*. Edinburgh University Press, Edinburgh.

Gergen, Kenneth J. and M. M. Gergen (1983). Narratives of the self. In: *Studies in Social Identity* (Theodore R. Sarbin and Karl E. Scheibe, eds.). Praeger, New York.

Gilman, Stephen (1961). *Tiempo y formas temporales en el 'Poema del Cid'*. Gredos, Madrid.

Goffman, Erving (1967a). On face-work: An analysis of ritual elements in social interaction. In: *Interaction Ritual: Essays on Face-to-Face Behavior* (Erving Goffman, ed.), pp. 1-49. Anchor Books, New York.

Goffman, Erving (1967b). The nature of deference and demeanor. In: *Interaction Ritual: Essays on Face-to-Face Behavior* (Erving Goffman, ed.), pp. 49-95. Anchor Books, New York.

Goffman, Erving (1967c). *Interaction Ritual: Essays on Face-to-Face Behavior*. Anchor Books, New York.

Goffman, Erving (1971). *Relations in Public*. Harper & Row, New York.

Goffman, Erving (1974). *Frame Analysis*. Harper & Row, New York.

Goffman, Erving (1976). Replies and responses. *Language in Society*, **5**, 257-313.

Goffman, Erving (1981a). Footing. In his *Forms of Talk*, pp. 124-59. University of Pennsylvania Press, Philadelphia.

Goffman, Erving (1981b). *Forms of Talk*. University of Pennsylvania Press, Philadelphia.

Goodell, Elizabeth W. (1987). Integrating theory with practice: An alternative approach to reported speech in English. *TESOL Quarterly*, **21** (2), 305-25.

Goodwin, Charles and Alessandro Duranti (1992). Rethinking context: An introduction. In: *Rethinking Context: Language as an Interactive Phenomenon* (Alessandro Duranti and Charles Goodwin, eds.), pp. 1-42. Cambridge University Press, Cambridge.

Gordon, D. and G. Lakoff (1971). Conversational postulates. In: *Papers from the Seventh Regional Meeting of the Chicago Linguistic Society*, pp. 63-84. University of Chicago, Chicago. (Reprinted in: *Syntax and Semantics,* Vol. 3: *Speech Acts* [Peter Cole and Jerry L. Morgan eds.], pp. 83-106. Academic Press, New York. 1975).

Grassi, C. (1966). Sull'aspetto verbale, con particolare riferimento al latino. In: *Problemi di sintassi latina*, pp. 93-250. La Nuova Italia, Florence.

Green, Georgia M. (1989). *Pragmatics and Natural Language Understanding*. Lawrence Erlbaum Associates, Hillsdale, NJ.

Greenfield, Patricia (1972). Oral and written language: The consequences for cognitive development in Africa, the United States, and England. *Language and Speech*, **15**, 169-78.

Grice, Paul H. (1975). Logic and conversation. In: *Syntax and Semantics,* Vol. 3: *Speech Acts* (Peter Cole and Jerry L. Morgan eds.), pp. 41-58. Academic Press, New York.

Grimes, Joseph E. (1975). *The Thread of Discourse*. Mouton, The Hague.

Gumperz, John J. (1982). *Discourse Strategies*. Cambridge University Press, Cambridge.

Haberland, Hartmut (1986). Reported speech in Danish. In: *Direct and Indirect Speech* (Florian Coulmas, ed.), pp. 219-53. Mouton de Gruyter, Berlin.

Haiman, John (1989). Alienation in grammar. *Studies in Language*, **13**, 129-70.

Haiman, John (1991). The bureaucratisation of language. In: *Linguistic Studies Presented to John Finlay* (H. C. Wolfart, ed.), pp. 45-70. Winnipeg.

Haiman, John (1995). Grammatical signs of the divided self: A study of language and culture. In: *Discourse Grammar and Typology: Papers in Honor of John W. M. Verhaar* (Werner Abraham, T. Givón and Sandra A. Thompson, eds.), pp. 213-34. John Benjamins, Amsterdam.

Halliday, M. A. K. (1979). Differences between spoken and written language: Some implications for literacy teaching. In: *Communication through Reading: Proceedings of the Fourth Australian Reading Conference* (Glenda Page, John Elkins and Barrie O'Connor, eds.), Vol. 2, pp. 37-52. Australian Reading Association, Adelaide, SA.

Halliday, M. A. K. and Ruqaiya Hasan (1976). *Cohesion in English.* Longman, London.

Hamada, Hidenori (1993). Memory-hallucination. In: *Shin Seishin-Igaku Jiten [Encyclopedia of Psychiatry]* (Masaaki Kato, ed.), p. 134. Koubundou, Tokyo.

Hamburger, Käte (1973). *The Logic of Literature* (Marilynn J. Rose, trans.). Indiana University Press, Bloomington.

Haverkate, Henk (1996). Modal patterns of direct and indirect discourse in Peninsular Spanish: An analysis within the framework of speech act typology. In: *Reported Speech* (Theo A. J. M. Janssen and Wim van der Wurff, eds.), pp. 97-119. John Benjamins, Amsterdam.

Heny, F. (1982). Tense, aspect and time adverbials: Part 2. *Linguistics and Philosophy*, 5, 109-54.

Heritage, John C. (1984). A change-of-state token and aspects of its sequential placement. In: *Structures of Social Action: Studies in Conversation Analysis* (J. Maxwell Atkinson and John C. Heritage, eds.), pp. 299-345. Cambridge University Press, Cambridge.

Heritage, John C. and J. Maxwell Atkinson (1984). Introduction. In: *Structures of Social Action: Studies in Conversation Analysis* (J. Maxwell Atkinson and John C. Heritage, eds.), pp. 1-16. Cambridge University Press, Cambridge.

Herring, Susan (1986). Marking and unmarking via the present tense in narration: The historical present redefined. ms. Berkeley, CA.

Hirschman, L. and G. Story (1981). Representing implicit and explicit time relations in narrative. In: *Proceedings of the Seventh International Joint Conference on Artificial Intelligence*, pp. 289-95. Morgan Kaufman, Los Altos, CA.

Hjelmquist, E. (1984). Memory for conversations. *Discourse Processes*, 7, 321-36.

Hochberg, J. E. (1964). *Perception.* Prentice-Hall, Englewood Cliffs, NJ.

Hockett, Charles F. (1963). The problem of universals in language. In: *Universals of Language* (Joseph H. Greenberg, ed.), pp. 1-29. MIT Press, Cambridge, MA.

Hoey, Michael P. (1979). *Signalling in Discourse*. English Language Research Group, University of Birmingham, Birmingham.

Hoey, Michael P. (1983). *On the Surface of Discourse*. George Allen & Unwin, London.

Hoffmann, J. B. and A. Szantyr (1963). *Lateinische Syntax und Stylistik*. Beck'sche, Munich.

Home, H., Lord Kames (1867). *Elements of Criticism*. Mason Brothers, New York.

Hopper, Paul J. (1979). Aspect and foregrounding in discourse. In: *Discourse and Syntax* (T. Givón, ed.), pp. 213-41. Academic Press, New York.

Hopper, Paul J. and Sandra A. Thompson (1980). Transitivity in grammar and discourse. *Language*, **56** (2), 251-99.

Hornstein, Norbert (1990). *As Time Goes by: Tense and Universal Grammar*. MIT Press, Cambridge, MA.

Huddleston, Rodney (1984). *Introduction to the Grammar of English*. Cambridge University Press, Cambridge.

Huddleston, Rodney (1989). The treatment of tense in indirect speech. *Folia Linguistica: Acta Societatis Linguisticae Europaeae*, **23** (3-4), 335-40.

Hundsnurscher, Franz (1980). Konversationsanalyse versus Dialoggrammatik. In: *Akten des VI. Internationalen Germanisten-Kongresses*, Basel, 1980, (Heinz Rupp and Hans-Gert Roloff, eds.), Part 2, pp. 89-95. Peter Lang, Bern, Frankfurt/M., Las Vegas.

Hymes, Dell (1975). Breakthrough into performance. In: *Folklore: Performance and Communication* (Dan Ben-Amos and Kenneth S. Goldstein, eds.), pp. 11-74. Mouton, The Hague.

Hymes, Dell and C. Cazden (1980). Narrative thinking and story-telling rights: A folklorist's clue to a critique of education. In: *Language in Education: Ethnolinguistic Essays* (Dell Hymes, ed.). Center for Applied Linguistics, Washington, DC.

Jackson, Howard (1990). *Grammar and Meaning: A Semantic Approach to English Grammar*. Longman, London.

Jakobson, Roman (1985). The fundamental and specific characteristics of human language. In his *Selected Writings 7: Contributions to Comparative Mythology. Studies in Linguistics and Philology, 1972-1982*, pp. 93-97. Mouton de Gruyter, Berlin.

James, William (1890). *The Principles of Psychology*, 2 vols. Henry Holt, New York. (Reprinted by Dover Publications, New York. 1950).

Janssen, Theo A. J. M. and Wim van der Wurff (1996). Introductory remarks on reported speech and thought. In: *Reported Speech* (Theo A. J. M. Janssen and Wim van der Wurff, eds.), pp. 1-12. John Benjamins, Amsterdam.

Jespersen, Otto (1924). *The Philosophy of Grammar*. George Allen & Unwin, London.

Jespersen, Otto (1929). *A Modern English Grammar: On Historical Principles*, Part 3. Winter, Heidelberg.

Jespersen, Otto (1931). *A Modern English Grammar: On Historical Principles*, Part 4. Winter, Heidelberg.

Jespersen, Otto (1964). *Essentials of English Grammar*. University of Alabama Press, Tuscaloosa, AL.

Johnston, Judith R. (1985). The discourse symptoms of developmental disorders. In: *Handbook of Discourse Analysis*, Vol. 3: *Discourse and Dialogue* (Teun A. van Dijk, ed.), pp. 79-93. Academic Press, London.

Johnstone, Barbara (1987). 'He says . . . so I said': Verb tense alternation and narrative depictions of authority in American English. *Linguistics*, **25** (1), 33-52.

Johnstone, Barbara (1990). *Stories, Community and Place: Narratives from Middle America*. Indiana University Press, Bloomington.

Joos, Martin (1964). *The English Verb*. University of Wisconsin Press, Madison, WI.

Kalepky, T. (1899). Zur französischen syntax. *Zeitschrift für Romanische Philologie*, **23**, 491-513.

Kernan, K. T. (1977). Semantic and expressive elaboration in children's narratives. In: *Child Discourse* (Susan Ervin-Tripp and Claudia Mitchell-Kernan, eds.), pp. 91-103. Academic Press, New York.

Kiparsky, Paul (1968). Tense and mood in Indo-European syntax. *Foundations of Language*, **4**, 30-57.

Kitayama, Shinobu and Hazel Rose Markus (1999). Yin and yang of the Japanese self: The cultural psychology of personality coherence. In: *The Coherence of Personality: Social-Cognitive Bases of Consistency, Variability, and Organization* (Daniel Cervone and Yuichi Shoda, eds.). Guilford, New York.

Koyazu, Takaaki (1985). Kioku to shinka, hattatsu, kaitai no shiten [Memory and perspectives in evolution, development, and dissolution]. In: *Ninchi Shinrigaku Kouza: Kioku to Chishiki [Studies in Cognitive Psychology: Memory and Knowledge]* (Takaaki Koyazu, ed.), pp. 1-34. Tokyo University Press, Tokyo.

Kristeva, Julia (1986). Word, dialogue and novel (Alice Jardine, Thomas Gora and Leon S. Roudiez, trans.). In: *The Kristeva Reader* (Toril Moi, ed.), pp. 34-61. Columbia University Press, New York.

Kuhn, Elisabeth Dorothea (1989). Gender and authority: Classroom diplomacy in Frankfurt and Berkeley. Ph.D. dissertation. University of California, Berkeley.

Labov, William (1972a). *Language in the Inner City*. University of Pennsylvania Press, Philadelphia.

Labov, William (1972b). The transformation of experience in narrative syntax. In his *Language in the Inner City*, pp. 354-96. University of Pennsylvania Press, Philadelphia.

Labov, William and David Fanshel (1977). *Therapeutic Discourse*. Academic Press, New York.

Labov, William and Joshua Waletzky (1967). Narrative analysis: Oral versions of personal experience. In: *Essays on the Verbal and Visual Arts: Proceedings of the 1966 Annual Spring Meeting of the American Ethnological Society* (June Helm, ed.), pp. 12-44. University of Washington Press, Seattle.

Langacker, Ronald W. (1990). Subjectification. *Cognitive Linguistics*, 1 (1), 5-38.

Lanser, Susan S. (1981). *The Narrative Act: Point of View in Prose Fiction*. Princeton University Press, Princeton.

Leech, Geoffrey N. (1983). *The Principles of Pragmatics*. Longman, London.

Leech, Geoffrey N. (1987). *Meaning and the English Verb*. 2nd ed. Longman, London.

Leech, Geoffrey N. and Michael H. Short (1981). *Style in Fiction: A Linguistic Introduction to English Fictional Prose*. Longman, London.

Leech, Geoffrey N. and Jan Svartvik (1975). *A Communicative Grammar of English.* Longman, London.

LeJeune, Philippe (1980). *Je est un autre.* Seuil, Paris.

Lerch, Gertraud (1919). Uneigentliche direkte Rede. Ph.D. dissertation. University of Munich.

Lethcoe, Ronald James (1969). *Narrated Speech and Consciousness.* Ph.D. dissertation. University of Wisconsin.

Levinson, Stephen C. (1983). *Pragmatics.* Cambridge University Press, Cambridge.

Li, Charles N. (1986). Direct and indirect speech: A functional study. In: *Direct and Indirect Speech* (Florian Coulmas, ed.), pp. 29-45. Mouton de Gruyter, Berlin.

Lichtenstein, E. H. and W. F. Brewer (1980). Memory for goal-directed events. *Cognitive Psychology*, 12, 412-45.

Longacre, Robert E. (1976). *An Anatomy of Speech Notions.* Peter de Ridder Press, Lisse, Belgium.

Longacre, Robert E. (1985). Sentences as combinations of clauses. In: *Language Typology and Syntactic Description*, Vol. 2: *Complex Constructions* (Timothy Shopen, ed.), pp. 235-83. Cambridge University Press, Cambridge.

Lorck, von Etienne (1921). *Die 'Erlebte Rede': Eine sprachliche Untersuchung.* Carl Winters University, Heidelberg.

Lucy, John A., ed. (1993). *Reflexive Language: Reported Speech and Metapragmatics.* Cambridge University Press, Cambridge.

Lyons, John (1977a). *Semantics.* Vol. 1. Cambridge University Press, Cambridge.

Lyons, John (1977b). *Semantics.* Vol. 2. Cambridge University Press, Cambridge.

Macaulay, Ronald K. S. (1987). Polyphonic monologues: Quoted direct speech in oral narratives. *IPrA Papers in Pragmatics*, 1 (2), 1-34.

McHale, Brian (1978). Free indirect discourse: A survey of recent accounts. *PTL: A Journal for Descriptive Poetics and Theory of Literature*, 3, 249-87.

McHale, Brian (1983). Unspeakable sentences, unnatural acts: Linguistics and poetics revisited. *Poetics Today*, 4 (1), 17-45.

McKay, K. L. (1974). Further remarks on the 'historical present' and other phenomena. *Foundations of Language*, **11**, 247-51.

McNeill, David (1992). *Hand and Mind: What Gestures Reveal about Thought*. University of Chicago Press, Chicago.

Mandler, Jean Matter (1984). *Scripts, Stories and Scenes: Aspects of Schema Theory*. Lawrence Erlbaum Associates, Hillsdale, NJ.

Mathis, Terry Dawn (1991). The form and function of constructed dialogue in reported discourse (conversation). Ph.D. dissertation. The Louisiana State University and Agricultural and Mechanical College.

Matthews, Peter (1997). *The Concise Oxford Dictionary of Linguistics*. Oxford University Press, Oxford.

Mayes, Patricia (1990). Quotation in spoken English. *Studies in Language*, **14** (2), 325-63.

Merritt, Marilyn (1982). Distributing and directing attention in primary classrooms. In: *Communicating in the Classroom* (Louise Cherry-Wilkinson, ed.), pp. 223-44. Academic Press, New York.

Minsky, Marvin (1975). A framework for representing knowledge. In: *The Psychology of Computer Vision* (Patrick H. Winston, ed.), pp. 211-77. McGraw Hill, New York.

Moerman, L. (1977). The preference for self-correction in a Tai conversational corpus. *Language*, **53**, 872-82.

Munro, Pamela (1982). On the transitivity of 'say' verbs. In: *Studies in Transitivity* (Paul Hopper and Sandra A. Thompson, eds.), pp. 301-18. Academic Press, New York.

Myhill, John (1992). *Typological Discourse Analysis: Quantitative Approaches to the Study of Linguistic Fiction*. Blackwell, Cambridge, MA.

Nakata, Osamu (1993). Ecmnesia. In: *Shin Seishin-Igaku Jiten [Encyclopedia of Psychiatry]* (Masaaki Kato, ed.), p. 71. Koubundou, Tokyo.

Nakagawa, Yukiko (1983). *Jiyuu Kansetsu Wahou [Free Indirect Speech: Its Forms and Functions in English Literature]*. Apolon, Kyoto.

Nelson, Katherine (1986). *Event Knowledge: Structure and Function in Development*. Lawrence Erlbaum Associates, Hillsdale, NJ.

Owen, Marion (1983). *Apologies and Remedial Interchanges: A Study of Language Use in Social Interaction*. Mouton, The Hague.

Paden, William D., Jr. (1977). L'emploi vicaire de présent verbal dans les plus anciens textes narratifs romans. In: *XIV Congresso internazionale di linguistica e filologia romanze*, Napoli, 1974, Vol. 4, pp. 545-57. Macchiaroli, Naples; John Benjamins, Amsterdam.

Palmer, Frank R. (1965). *A Linguistic Study of the English Verb*. Longman, London.

Parsons, Terence (1990). *Events in the Semantics of English: A Study in Subatomic Semantics*. MIT Press, Cambridge, MA.

Partee, Barbara Hall (1973). The syntax and semantics of quotation. In: *A Festschrift for Morris Halle* (Stephen R. Anderson and Paul Kiparsky, eds.), pp. 410-18. Holt, Rinehart and Winston, New York.

Pascal, Roy (1977). *The Dual Voice: Free Indirect Speech and Its Functioning in the Nineteenth Century European Novel*. Manchester University Press, Manchester.

Pavel, Thomas G. (1986). *Fictional Worlds*. Harvard University Press, Cambridge, MA.

Perridon, Harry (1996). Reported speech in Swedish. In: *Reported Speech* (Theo A. J. M. Janssen and Wim van der Wurff, eds.), pp. 165-88. John Benjamins, Amsterdam.

Philips, Susan U. (1985). Reported speech as evidence in an American trial. In: *Languages and Linguistics: The Interdependence of Theory, Data, and Application* (Deborah Tannen and James E. Alatis, eds.), pp. 154-70. Georgetown University Round Table on Languages and Linguistics, Georgetown University Press, Washington DC.

Pike, Kenneth L. (1954). *Language in Relation to a Unified Theory of the Structure of Human Behavior*. Summer Institute of Linguistics, Glendale, CA.

Plato ([c 375 BCE]1987). *The Republic* (H. D. P. Lee, trans.). Viking, New York.

Plummer, K. (1995). Life story research. In: *Rethinking Methods in Psychology* (Jonathan A. Smith, Rom Harré and Luk Van Langenhove, eds.). Sage, London.

Polanyi, Livia (1979). So what's the point? *Semiotica*, **25**, 207-41.

Polanyi, Livia (1981). Telling the same story twice. *Text*, **1** (4), 315-36.

Polanyi, Livia (1985). *Telling the American Story: A Structural and Cultural Analysis of Conversational Storytelling*. Ablex, Norwood, NJ.

Polanyi, Livia and R. Scha (1983). On the recursive structure of discourse. In: *Connectedness in Sentence, Discourse and Text* (K. Ehlich and H. van Riemsdijk, eds.), pp. 141-78. Tilburg University, Tilburg.

Polkinghorne, Donald E. (1988). *Narrative Knowing and the Human Sciences*. State University of New York Press, Albany, NY.

Pomerantz, Anita (1984). Agreeing and disagreeing with assessments: Some features of preferred/dispreferred turn shapes. In: *Structures of Social Action: Studies in Conversation Analysis* (J. Maxwell Atkinson and John C. Heritage, eds.), pp. 57-101. Cambridge University Press, Cambridge.

Prince, Gerald A. (1982). *Narratology: The Form and Function of Narrative*. Mouton, The Hague.

Psathas, George (1995). *Conversation Analysis: The Study of Talk-in-Interaction*. Sage, London.

Quine, Willard van Orman (1951). *Mathematical Logic*. Harvard University Press, Cambridge, MA.

Quine, Willard van Orman (1960). *Word and Object*. MIT Press, Cambridge, MA.

Quirk, Randolph, Sidney Greenbaum, Geoffrey Leech and Jan Svartvik (1972). *A Grammar of Contemporary English*. Longman, London.

Quirk, Randolph, Sidney Greenbaum, Geoffrey Leech and Jan Svartvik (1985). *A Comprehensive Grammar of the English Language*. Longman, London.

Rickford, John R. and Christine Théberge Rafal (1996). Preterite *had*+V-*ed* in the narratives of African-American preadolescents. *American Speech*, **71** (3), 227-54

Riddle, E. M. (1978). Sequence of tenses in English. Ph.D. dissertation. University of Illinois at Urbana-Champaign.

Riesman, David (1950). *The Lonely Crowd: A Study of the Changing American Character*. Yale University Press, New Haven.

Rimmer, Sharon Elizabeth (1988). Sociolinguistic variability in oral narrative. Ph.D. dissertation. Aston University.

Rimmon-Kenan, Shlomith (1983). *Narrative Fiction: Contemporary Poetics*. Methuen, London.

Ronconi, Alessandro (1942). Il presente storico italiano e il suo aspetto. *Lingua Nostra*, **4**, 34-36.

Rosen, Harold (1988). The autobiographical impulse. In: *Linguistics in Context: Connecting Observation and Understanding* (Deborah Tannen, ed.), pp. 69-88. Ablex, Norwood, NJ.

Sacks, Harvey (1984). Notes on methodology. In: *Structures of Social Action: Studies in Conversation Analysis* (J. Maxwell Atkinson and John C. Heritage, eds.), pp. 21-27. Cambridge University Press, Cambridge.

Sacks, Harvey, Emanuel A. Schegloff and Gail Jefferson (1974). A simplest systematics for the organization of turn-taking for conversation. *Language*, **50** (4), 696-753.

Sakita, Tomoko I. (1992). Observational study of direct and indirect reporting discourse. ms. University of Wisconsin, Madison.

Sakita, Tomoko I. (1995). Functions of reporting discourse from a discourse analytic perspective. *Papers in Linguistic Science*, **1**, 1-13.

Sakita, Tomoko I. (1996a). Style choice of reporting discourse related to sentence length and complexities. *KLS: Kansai Linguistic Society*, **16**, 89-99.

Sakita, Tomoko I. (1996b). Tense in indirect reporting discourse in spoken English. *Annual Review of English Learning and Teaching*, **1**, 83-97.

Sakita, Tomoko I. (1996c). Direct and indirect reporting discourse related to structural factors: Discourse analysis by a combination of observational and experimental research. Paper presented at the 11th World Congress of Applied Linguistics, Jyvaskyla, Finland.

Sakita, Tomoko I. (1997a). Choice of narrative dialogue forms: Subjectification and self identity. Paper presented at the Sixth International Conference on Narratives, Lexington, KY.

Sakita, Tomoko I. (1997b). Tense alternation in English conversational narratives. *Annual Review of English Learning and Teaching*, **2**, 1-14.

Sakita, Tomoko I. (1998). Reporting discourse in English: Discourse, cognition, and consciousness. Ph.D. dissertation. Kyoto University.

Sakita, Tomoko I. (1999). Manifestations of speaker attitudes in conflict stories. *Studies in Pragmatics*, **1**, 74-88.

Sakita, Tomoko I. (2000a). Tense, dialogue features, and attitudes. *KLS: Kansai Linguistic Society*, **20**, 164-74.

Sakita, Tomoko I. (2000b). *Like* in discourse: Its functions and grammaticalization. *Papers in Linguistic Science*, **6**.

Sakita, Tomoko I. (2001a). Cognition in reporting discourse: Mental representation and speaker perspectives. In: *Cognition in Language Use: Selected Papers from the 7th International Pragmatics Conference* (Enikö T. Németh, ed.), Vol. 1, pp. 375-87. International Pragmatics Association, Antwerp.

Sakita, Tomoko I. (2001b). Another semantic extension of *go*. *Doshisha Studies in Language and Culture*, **4** (2), 447-66.

Sakita, Tomoko I. (forthcoming). Dialogue internal and external features representing mental imagery of speaker attitudes. *Text*.

Sanchez, Julieta Chapellin (1987). Dramatization devices in children's oral narratives. Ph.D. dissertation. University of Pennsylvania.

Sarbin, Theodore R. (1986). *Narrative Psychology: The Storied Nature of Human Conduct*. Praeger, New York.

Saussure, Ferdinand de ([1922]1966). *Course in General Linguistics* (Wade Baskin, trans.). McGraw-Hill, New York.

Schank, Roger C. and Robert P. Abelson (1975). Scripts, plans and knowledge. In: *Advance Papers of the Fourth International Joint Conference on Artificial Intelligence*, Tbilisi, Georgia, USSR, pp. 151-57. Artificial Intelligence Lab, Cambridge, MA.

Schank, Roger C. and Robert P. Abelson (1977). *Scripts, Plans, Goals and Understanding: An Inquiry into Human Knowledge Structures*. Lawrence Erlbaum Associates, Hillsdale, NJ.

Schegloff, Emanuel A. (1972). Notes on a conversational practice: Formulating place. In: *Studies in Social Interaction* (David N. Sudnow, ed.), pp. 75-119. Free Press, New York.

Schegloff, Emanuel A. (1992). On talk and its institutional occasions. In: *Talk at Work: Interaction in Institutional Settings* (Paul Drew and John C. Heritage, eds.), pp. 110-34. Cambridge University Press, Cambridge.

Schegloff, Emanuel A., Gail Jefferson and Harvey Sacks (1977). The preference for self-correction in the organization of repair in conversation. *Language*, **53**, 361-82.

Schegloff, Emanuel A. and Harvey Sacks (1973). Opening up closings. *Semiotica*, **7** (4), 289-327.

Schiffrin, Deborah (1981). Tense variation in narrative. *Language*, **57** (1), 45-62.

Schiffrin, Deborah (1987). *Discourse Markers.* Cambridge University Press, Cambridge.

Schiffrin, Deborah (1990). The management of a co-operative self during argument: The role of opinions and stories. In: *Conflict Talk: Sociolinguistic Investigations of Arguments in Conversations* (Allen D. Grimshaw, ed.), pp. 241-59. Cambridge University Press, Cambridge.

Schiffrin, Deborah (1993). 'Speaking for another' in sociolinguistic interviews: Alignments, identities, and frames. In: *Framing in Discourse* (Deborah Tannen, ed.), pp. 231-63. Oxford University Press, New York.

Schiffrin, Deborah (1994). *Approaches to Discourse.* Blackwell, Cambridge, MA.

Scholes, Robert and Robert Kellogg (1966). *The Nature of Narrative.* Oxford University Press, New York.

Schøsler, Lene (1985). L'Emploi des temps du passé en ancien français: Etude sur quelques textes manuscrits. *Razo* (Cahiers du Centre d'Etudes Médiévales de Nice), **5**, 107-19.

Searle, John R. (1969). *Speech Acts.* Cambridge University Press, New York.

Segal, Erwin M. (1995). Narrative comprehension and the role of deictic shift theory. In: *Deixis in Narrative: A Cognitive Science Perspective* (Judith F. Duchan, Gail A. Bruder and Lynne E. Hewitt, eds.), pp. 3-17. Lawrence Erlbaum Associates, Hillsdale, NJ.

Shotter, John (1989). Social accountability and the social construction of 'you'. In: *Texts of Identity* (John Shotter and Kenneth J. Gergen, eds.), pp. 133-51. Sage, London.

Shotter, John and Kenneth J. Gergen (1989). *Texts of Identity.* Sage, London.

Silva-Corvalán, Carmen (1983). Tense and aspect in oral Spanish narrative: Context and meaning. *Language*, **59** (4), 760-80.

Sinclair, J. McH. (1988). Mirror for a text. ms. University of Birmingham.

Sinclair, J. McH. and Malcolm Coulthard (1975). *Towards an Analysis of Discourse: The English Used by Teachers and Pupils.* Oxford University Press, London.

Smith, Barbara Herrnstein (1981). Narrative versions, narrative theories. In: *On Narrative* (W. J. T. Mitchell, ed.), pp. 209-32. University of Chicago Press, Chicago.

Sprenger, Ulrike (1951). *Praesens Historicum und Praeteritum in der altisländischen Saga: Ein Beitrag zur Frage Freiprosa-Buchprosa*. Benno Schwabe, Basel.

Stein, Nancy L., Ronan S. Bernas and David J. Calicchia (1997). Conflict talk: Understanding and resolving arguments. In: *Conversation: Cognitive, Communicative, and Social Perspectives* (T. Givón, ed.), pp. 233-67. John Benjamins, Amsterdam.

Stein, Nancy L. and C. A. Miller (1990). I win - you lose: The development of argumentative thinking. In: *Informal Reasoning and Instruction* (J. Voss, D. Perkins and J. Segal, eds.), pp. 265-90. Lawrence Erlbaum Associates, Hillsdale, NJ.

Stein, Nancy L. and C. A. Miller (1993a). A theory of argumentative understanding: Relationships among position preference, judgments of goodness, memory and reasoning. *Argumentation*, 7, 183-204.

Stein, Nancy L. and C. A. Miller (1993b). The development of memory and reasoning skill in argumentative contexts: Evaluating, explaining and generating evidence. In: *Advances in Instructional Psychology* (Robert Glaser, ed.), Vol. 4, pp. 285-335. Lawrence Erlbaum Associates, Hillsdale, NJ.

Stein, Nancy L., T. Trabasso and M. D. Liwag (1994). The rashomon phenomenon: Personal frames and future-oriented appraisals in memory for emotional events. In: *The Development of Future-Oriented Processes* (Marshall M. Haith, J. Benson, R. Roberts and B. Pennington, eds.), pp. 409-36. University of Chicago Press, Chicago.

Stubbs, Michael (1983). *Discourse Analysis*. University of Chicago Press, Chicago.

Svartvik, Jan (1980). 'Well' in conversation. In: *Studies in English Linguistics for Randolph Quirk* (Sidney Greenbaum, Geoffrey Leech, and Jan Svartvik, eds.), pp. 167-77. Longman, London.

Sweet, Henry (1892). *A New English Grammar: Logical and Historical*. Clarendon, Oxford.

Talmy, Leonard (1995). Narrative structure in a cognitive framework. In: *Deixis in Narrative: A Cognitive Science Perspective* (Judith F. Duchan, Gail A. Bruder and Lynne E. Hewitt, eds.), pp. 421-60. Lawrence Erlbaum Associates, Hillsdale, NJ.

Tannen, Deborah (1979). What's in a frame?: Surface evidence for underlying expectations. In: *New Directions in Discourse Processing* (Roy O. Freedle, ed.), pp. 137-81. Ablex, Norwood, NJ.

Tannen, Deborah, ed. (1982a). *Spoken and Written Language: Exploring Orality and Literacy*. Ablex, Norwood, NJ.

Tannen, Deborah (1982b). Oral and literal strategies in spoken and written narratives. *Language*, **58** (1), 1-21.

Tannen, Deborah (1986). Introducing constructed dialogue in Greek and American conversational and literary narrative. In: *Direct and Indirect Speech* (Florian Coulmas, ed.), pp. 311-32. Mouton de Gruyter, Berlin.

Tannen, Deborah (1988). Hearing voices in conversation, fiction, and mixed genres. In: *Linguistics in Context: Connecting Observation and Understanding* (Deborah Tannen, ed.), pp. 89-113. Ablex, Norwood, NJ.

Tannen, Deborah (1989). *Talking Voices: Repetition, Dialogue, and Imagery in Conversational Discourse*. Cambridge University Press, Cambridge.

Tannen, Deborah (1993). What's in a frame?: Surface evidence for underlying expectations. In: *Framing in Discourse* (Deborah Tannen, ed.), pp. 14-56. Oxford University Press, New York.

Tannen, Deborah and Cynthia Wallat (1993). Interactive frames and knowledge schemas in interaction: Examples from a medical examination/interview. In: *Framing in Discourse* (Deborah Tannen, ed.), pp. 57-76. Oxford University Press, New York.

Thomas, Susan (1987). Reported speech in English: Form and function in a testimonial setting. Ph.D. dissertation. University of Pennsylvania.

Thompson, Sandra A. (1987). 'Subordination' and narrative event structure. In: *Coherence and Grounding in Discourse* (Russell S. Tomlin, ed.), pp. 435-54. John Benjamins, Amsterdam.

Thomson, A. J. and A. V. Martinet, eds. (1980). *A Practical English Grammar*. Oxford University Press, Oxford.

Thurgood, Graham (1981). The historical development of the Akha evidentials system. In: *Proceedings of the Seventh Annual Meeting of the Berkeley Linguistics Society*, pp. 295-302. University of California, Berkeley, CA.

Tobler, Adolf (1894). *Vermischte Beiträge zur Französischen Grammatik II*. S. Hirzel, Leipzig.

Toolan, Michael J. (1988). *Narrative: A Critical Linguistic Introduction*. Routledge, London.

Traugott, Elizabeth Closs and Mary Louise Pratt (1980). *Linguistics for Students of Literature*. Harcourt Brace Jovanovich, New York.

Trilling, Lionel (1972). *Sincerity and Authenticity.* Harvard University Press, Cambridge, MA.

Tsui, Amy B. M. (1994). *English Conversation.* Oxford University Press, Oxford.

Tuan, Yi-Fu (1982). *Segmented Worlds and Self: A Study of Group Life and Individual Consciousness.* University of Minnesota Press, Minneapolis.

Tulving, Endel (1972). Episodic and semantic memory. In: *Organization of Memory* (Endel Tulving and Wayne Donaldson, eds.), pp. 382-403. Academic Press, New York.

Twaddell, William Freeman (1960). *The English Verb Auxiliaries.* Brown University Press, Providence, RI.

Urdang, Laurence (1991). Accuracy in quotations. *Verbatim,* **17** (4), 17-18.

van Dijk, Teun A. (1985). Introduction: Levels and dimensions of discourse analysis. In: *Handbook of Discourse Analysis,* Vol. 2: *Dimensions of Discourse* (Teun A. van Dijk, ed.), pp. 1-11. Academic Press, London.

van Dijk, Teun A. and W. Kintsch (1983). *Strategies of Discourse Comprehension.* Academic Press, New York.

Visser, F. Th. (1966). *A Historical Syntax of the English Language,* Vol. 2: *Syntactical Units with One Verb.* Brill, Leiden.

Voloshinov, V. N. ([1929]1986). *Marxism and the Philosophy of Language* (Ladislav Matejka and I. R. Titunik, trans.). Harvard University Press, Cambridge, MA.

Wackernagel, Jakob (1920). *Vorlesungen über Syntax mit besonderer Berücksichtigung von Griechisch, Latein und Deutsch.* 2 vols. E. Birkhäuser, Basel.

Wade, Elizabeth and Herbert H. Clark (1993). Reproduction and demonstration in quotations. *Journal of Memory and Language,* **32,** 805-19.

Wartburg, Walther von ([1937]1971). *Evolution et structure de la langue française.* 10th ed. Francke, Bern.

Wehr, Barbara (1984). *Diskurs-Strategien im Romanischen.* Gunther Narr, Tübingen.

Weinrich, Harald (1964). *Tempus: Besprochene und Erzählte Welt.* W. Kohlhammer Verlag, Stuttgart.

Wierzbicka, Anna (1974). The semantics of direct and indirect discourse. *Papers in Linguistics,* **7** (3-4), pp. 267-307.

Wolfson, Nessa (1978). A feature of performed narrative: The conversational historical present. *Language in Society*, **7** (1), 215-37.

Wolfson, Nessa (1979). The conversational historical present alternation. *Language*, **55** (1), 168-82.

Wolfson, Nessa (1982). *CHP: The Conversational Historical Present in American English Narrative*. Foris, Dordrecht.

Yamanashi, Masa-aki (1986). *Hatsuwa Koui [Speech Acts]*. Taishukan, Tokyo.

Yamanashi, Masa-aki (1995). *Ninchi Bunpouron [The Theory of Cognitive Grammar]*. Hitsuji Shobou, Tokyo.

Yamanashi, Masa-aki (2000). *Ninchi Gengogaku Genri [The Principle of Cognitive Linguistics]*. Kuroshio, Tokyo.

Yasunaga, Hiroshi (1984). Pseudomnesia. In: *Kodansha Seishin-Igaku Daijiten [Kodansha's Comprehensive Dictionary of Psychiatry]* (Naotake Shinhuku, ed.), p. 155. Kodansha, Tokyo.

Young, Katherine (1987). *Taleworlds and Storyrealms: The Phenomenology of Narrative*. Nijhoff, Dordrecht.

Yule, George (1993). Vera Hayden's dilemma: Or, the indirection in direct speech. In: *Principles and Prediction: The Analysis of Natural Language: Papers in Honor of Gerald Sanders* (Mushira Eid and Gregory K. Iverson, eds.), pp. 233-42. John Benjamins, Amsterdam.

Yule, George and Terrie Mathis (1992). The role of staging and constructed dialogue in establishing speaker's topic. *Linguistics*, **30**, 199-215.

Zubin, David A. and Lynne E. Hewitt (1995). The deictic center: A theory of deixis in narrative. In: *Deixis in Narrative: A Cognitive Science Perspective* (Judith F. Duchan, Gail A. Bruder and Lynne E. Hewitt, eds.), pp. 129-55. Lawrence Erlbaum Associates, Hillsdale, NJ.

AUTHOR INDEX

Abelson, Robert P., 205, 241
Abercrombie, David, 235
Ageno, Franca Brambilla, 21
Allen, Robert Livingston, 249
Almeida, Michael J., 7
Anderson, Lloyd B., 206
Aristotle, 8
Atkinson, J. Maxwell, 12
Austin, J. L., 95, 121, 244

Bain, Alexander, 20
Bakhtin, Mikhail M., 2–3, 10, 216–17
Bal, Mieke, 8, 55
Bally, Charles, 188, 253
Bamgbose, Ayo, 1
Banfield, Ann, 7, 186–87, 190, 215, 241, 249, 253
Bartlett, Frederic C., 5, 52, 241
Bates, E., 204
Bateson, Gregory, 219
Becker, A. L., 2, 35, 235
Bell, Barbara, 190, 240, 254
Bellos, David M., 50
Berry, Margaret, 123
Besnier, Niko, 5, 211
Bower, Gordon H., 120, 242
Brazil, David C., 23, 123
Brecht, R. D., 249
Brewer, W. F., 242
Bronzwaer, W. J. M., 253
Brown, Gillian, 5, 10–11, 188
Brown, Goold, 20
Brown, Penelope, 243
Bruner, Jerome, 13, 43, 240
Buffin, J. M., 21
Bühler, C., 51, 69
Burton, Deirdre, 123

Carlson, Lauri, 246
Casparis, Christian Paul, 50
Cate, Abraham P. ten, 185–86
Cazden, C., 8
Celce-Murcia, Marianne, 159, 187, 249

Chafe, Wallace L., 5, 8–9, 12–14, 26, 41, 43, 51–52, 55, 57, 67, 81, 119–20, 123–25, 158, 188–90, 206, 235–39, 241–42, 244–47, 253, 255–56
Charleston, Britta Marian, 20
Chatman, Seymour, 7–8, 241
Chomsky, Noam, 12
Church, Alonzo, 186
Cirilo, Randolph K., 120, 242
Clark, Herbert H., 5, 69, 186–87, 202, 204, 249, 255
Clarke, Sandra, 239
Comrie, Bernard, 5, 159–63, 166, 181, 185, 249
Coulmas, Florian, 1, 5–6, 12, 14, 23, 181, 185–86, 237, 253
Coulthard, Malcolm, 120–23, 132
Crystal, David, 19, 22
Curme, George O., 20

Davidson, Donald, 186
Davidson, Judy, 123
Declerck, Renaat, 160, 162–67, 169, 178, 181, 249–52
Diver, William, 20
Dixon, R. M. W., 168
Dorfman, Eugene, 241
Du Bois, John W., 209–10, 223
Dumas, Bethany K., 119
Duranti, Alessandro, 12

Edwards, Derek, 13, 43, 236, 240
Ehrlich, Susan, 253
Elias, Norbert, 75
Ely, Richard, 190, 202, 254
Emery, Annie Crosby, 21
Emmott, Catherine, 7, 10, 14, 119

Fanshel, David, 240, 246
Fasold, Ralph, 11
Feldman, Carol Fleisher, 5
Ferrara, Kathleen, 190, 240, 254
Fillmore, Charles J., 52, 69

Author Index

Flavell, J. H., 44, 76
Fleischman, Suzanne, 50, 52, 79, 158, 237, 239, 241–42, 244, 253
Fludernik, Monika, 20, 28, 38, 239, 253
Fónagy, Ivan, 189
Ford, Cecilia E., 10, 235
Forster, E. M., 7
Foulet, Lucien, 21
Franke, Wilhelm, 205, 255
Freeman, Mark, 240
Friden, G., 20

Galbraith, Mary, 241
Genette, Gérard, 7–8, 57
Georgakopoulou, Alexandra, 8, 11, 23, 52, 79, 105, 158, 244
Gergen, Kenneth J., 61, 240
Gergen, M. M., 61
Gerrig, Richard J., 186–87, 249, 255
Gilman, Stephen, 239
Goffman, Erving, 24, 37, 44, 52, 71–73, 121, 123, 132, 189, 239–40, 243
Goodell, Elizabeth W., 163, 232
Goodwin, Charles, 12
Gordon, D., 246
Goutsos, Dionysis, 23, 79, 244
Grassi, C., 21
Green, Georgia M., 10
Greenfield, Patricia, 236
Grice, Paul H., 126, 202, 249
Grimes, Joseph E., 158
Gumperz, John J., 243

Haberland, Hartmut, 1
Haiman, John, 74–75, 77, 80, 190, 239, 243
Halliday, M. A. K., 10, 235–36, 246
Hamada, Hidenori, 75
Hamburger, Käte, 253
Hasan, Ruqaiya, 10, 235, 246
Haverkate, Henk, 189
Heny, F., 249
Heritage, John C., 12, 123
Herring, Susan, 22
Hewitt, Lynne E., 69, 71
Hirschman, L., 7

Hjelmquist, E., 204
Hochberg, J. E., 51
Hockett, Charles F., 72, 241
Hoey, Michael P., 10, 24
Hoffmann, J. B., 21
Home, H., Lord Kames, 20
Hopper, Paul J., 44, 70, 211, 255
Hornstein, Norbert, 41, 160
Huddleston, Rodney, 171, 249–50
Hundsnurscher, Franz, 205, 255
Hymes, Dell, 8, 24

Jackson, Howard, 185, 249
Jakobson, Roman, 2
James, William, 123–24
Janssen, Theo A. J. M., 2–3, 5, 183
Jespersen, Otto, 19–22, 159–60, 185, 187–88, 249, 253
Johnstone, Barbara, 20, 27, 29, 35–42, 76, 99, 101, 103–5, 112, 141, 158, 170, 233, 239, 242–43, 247–48
Joos, Martin, 19–21

Kalepky, T., 188, 253
Kellogg, Robert, 8
Kernan, K. T., 68
Kintsch, W., 9, 204
Kiparsky, Paul, 19, 21–22, 25
Koyazu, Takaaki, 44, 75–76
Kristeva, Julia, 2
Kuhn, Elisabeth Dorothea, 189–90, 211

Labov, William, 7–8, 10, 14, 24–25, 37, 44, 57, 68, 70, 143, 153, 189, 205, 235, 237–38, 240, 246–47
Lakoff, G., 246
Langacker, Ronald W., 53–54, 58
Lanser, Susan S., 57
Larsen-Freeman, Diane, 159, 188, 249
Leech, Geoffrey N., 10, 20, 160, 168, 239, 250, 253, 255
LeJeune, Philippe, 75
Lerch, Gertraud, 188, 253
Lethcoe, Ronald James, 253
Levinson, Stephen C., 10, 243
Li, Charles N., 57, 66, 185, 189–90, 206, 217, 242

Lichtenstein, E. H., 242
Longacre, Robert E., 158, 185
Lorck, von Etienne, 188, 253
Lucy, John A., 2
Lyons, John, 22, 236

Macaulay, Ronald K. S., 189-91, 202, 204, 253
Mandler, Jean Matter, 205
Martinet, A. V., 160
Masling, M., 204
Mathis, Terry Dawn (Mathis, Terrie), 217, 242
Matthews, Peter, 247, 252
Mayes, Patricia, 186, 189-91, 203-4, 249
McHale, Brian, 3, 7, 253, 255
McKay, K. L., 22
McNeill, David, 44, 70, 119
Merritt, Marilyn, 220
Miller, C. A., 89
Minsky, Marvin, 52
Moerman, L., 119
Munro, Pamela, 5
Myhill, John, 15, 19, 25, 42, 229, 238

Nakagawa, Yukiko, 253
Nakata, Osamu, 75
Nelson, Katherine, 205

Owen, Marion, 101

Paden, William D., Jr., 21
Palmer, Frank R., 20
Parsons, Terence, 41
Partee, Barbara Hall, 185
Pascal, Roy, 253
Pavel, Thomas G., 8
Perridon, Harry, 186, 253
Philips, Susan U., 189
Pike, Kenneth L., 10
Plato, 8
Plummer, K., 240
Polanyi, Livia, 14, 24, 37, 237, 241
Polkinghorne, Donald E., 13
Pomerantz, Anita, 101, 103

Pratt, Mary Louise, 8
Prince, Gerald A., 7
Psathas, George, 13

Quine, Willard van Orman, 186
Quirk, Randolph, 19-20, 27, 159-60, 176-78, 184, 188, 197, 238, 251

Riddle, E. M., 249
Riesman, David, 75
Rimmer, Sharon Elizabeth, 255
Rimmon-Kenan, Shlomith, 7-8, 241
Ronconi, Alessandro, 21
Rosen, Harold, 14, 237

Sacks, Harvey, 12, 121-22
Sakita, Tomoko I., 42, 105, 110, 148-49, 171, 186-87, 189-90, 215, 223, 242, 245, 248-49, 256
Sanchez, Julieta Chapellin, 190, 217, 242, 254-55
Sarbin, Theodore R., 240
Saussure, Ferdinand de, 12
Scha, R., 24
Schank, Roger C., 205, 241
Schegloff, Emanuel A., 12, 119, 122
Schiffrin, Deborah, 8, 10-12, 14, 19-20, 24-27, 37, 44, 73-74, 84, 91-92, 100, 119, 122-23, 129, 135, 170, 190, 205, 235-36, 238, 240-41, 243, 245-46, 254
Scholes, Robert, 7
Schøsler, Lene, 239
Searle, John R., 121, 245
Segal, Erwin M., 7-8, 236
Short, Michael H., 253, 255
Shotter, John, 69, 240
Silva-Corvalán, Carmen, 24, 238
Sinclair, J. McH., 24, 120-23, 132
Smith, Barbara Herrnstein, 8
Sprenger, Ulrike, 21
Stein, Nancy L., 89-90
Story, G., 7
Stubbs, Michael, 236
Svartvik, Jan, 160, 244
Sweet, Henry, 20
Szantyr, A., 21

Talmy, Leonard, 13, 236
Tanaka, Kazuhiko, 178, 252
Tannen, Deborah, 2–3, 5, 10–11, 14, 23, 44, 52, 55, 57, 67, 73, 119, 141, 186–87, 189–90, 205, 215–16, 220, 222–23, 235, 237, 241, 243, 254–55
Thomas, Susan, 190
Thompson, Sandra A., 44, 211, 255
Thomson, A. J., 160
Thurgood, Graham, 206
Tobler, Adolf, 188, 223
Toolan, Michael J., 8–10, 14, 190, 238, 256
Traugott, Elizabeth Closs, 8
Trilling, Lionel, 75
Tsui, Amy B. M., 120–23, 132, 141, 246, 248
Tuan, Yi-Fu, 75
Tulving, Endel, 241
Twaddell, William Freeman, 22

Urdang, Laurence, 186, 253

van Dijk, Teun A., 9, 13
Visser, F. Th., 21

Voloshinov, V. N., 1, 3–5, 9–12, 159, 162, 188, 191–92, 232, 253

Wackernagel, Jakob, 21
Wade, Elizabeth, 5, 186, 202, 204
Waletzky, Joshua, 7, 10, 14, 44, 68, 70, 235, 237
Wallat, Cynthia, 73, 243
Wartburg, Walther von, 21
Wehr, Barbara, 238
Weinrich, Harald, 253
Wierzbicka, Anna, 5, 74, 186, 189, 217, 242, 253
Wolfson, Nessa, 17, 19–20, 22–29, 31–32, 34–35, 41–42, 44, 79, 95, 145, 170, 233, 237–38, 241, 248
Wurff, Wim van der, 2–3, 5, 183

Yamanashi, Masa-aki, 13, 211, 245
Yasunaga, Hiroshi, 75
Young, Katherine, 240
Yule, George, 5, 10–11, 187–89, 213, 223, 242

Zubin, David A., 69, 71

Subject Index

Frequently used terms such as "tense" or "discourse" are indexed only for passages that define, subcategorize, or significantly elaborate on them.

absolute tense, 163–65, 167–70, 172, 174, 181, 251
abstract, in narrative schema, 8
act, 120–22
adjacency pair, 122–23, 126–32, 190, 247
affective element. *See* expressive element
animator, 72–73
assessment, 142–44, 248
asymmetrical construal, 64–65, 67, 69, 78–79
attitudinal contrast
   conflict vs. conflict-avoidance, 89–106
   searching vs. resultative, 82–89
   weak vs. strong, 106–16
author, 37, 71, 239
authority, 35, 37
authority story, 37, 104–5

background information, 139–41, 145–46, 150–51, 157, 190, 211–15, 225
backshifting, 161

choral dialogue, 141
CHP alternation, 23–24
clause, relationship
   main and subordinate, head and complement, reporting and reported, 170–71, 174–75, 177–79, 182
coda, in narrative schema, 8, 125
cognitive monitoring theories, 75–76
Cognitive Recollection Model (CRM), 54–67
comment clause, 176–78, 182, 251–52
complementizer *that*, 187–88
complicating action, 8, 25, 125
conditional, 154
conflict, 89–106
conflict(-based) story, 89–106
connective, 158

connectivity, 119
consciousness, 26, 51–54
   properties of, 123, 246
   stream of, 123–24
consciousness flow
   at post-posed dialogue-introducers, 151–55, 157–58
   at pre-posed dialogue-introducers, 150–51, 157–58
   at restatement, 155–56, 158
   in adjacency pair, 126–32, 156
   in discourse, 123–24
   in narrative dialogues, 124–56
   in three-part exchange, 132–33, 157
   over a series of remarks, 133–50, 157
Consciousness Stream Model (CSM), 127–28, 130–31, 133–34, 136–40, 142–46, 152–53, 155–56
construal. *See also* asymmetrical construal
   perceived events, 54
   remembered events, 54–67
      self-involving interaction, 61–67
      third-person interaction, 58–61
constructed dialogue, 2–3, 52, 73–74, 186, 205, 215–16, 235
context, 9–10
continuing applicability, 161–62
continuum, 187–88, 223–25
conversation analysis (CA), 12–13, 235–36
conversational historical present (CHP) tense, 19, 23–24
cooperative principle, 126
cooperative reporting, 110, 217–22

data, natural, 12–14
de dicto, 186
de re, 187

deixis, 203, 241
  personal, 50–51
demonstration theory, 187, 255
demonstrative theory, 186, 252–53
derivational relationship, 185, 187, 249
description style, 188, 198–99, 224
dialogic nature of language, 3–4, 10, 235
dialogue, 3–4
dialogue marker, 175–76, 181–82
dialogue-introducer, 237
  repetition, 47–50, 150–58
dialogue-introducer tense-alternation
  Outside the tense system hypothesis, 34–35
  Participant distinction hypothesis, 32–34, 44
  Relative status hypothesis, 35–41, 99
  Single speaker continuity hypothesis, 30–31
  Speech act hypothesis, 29–30
  Third-person story hypothesis, 31–32
dichotomic approach, 159, 184–85, 249
diegesis, 223, 253, 256
direct reporting discourse, 55–59, 67–68, 184–88, 213, 215, 217, 225
  function, 189–90
direct speech. *See* direct reporting discourse
directive, 135–36
discourse, 11–12, 235–36
discourse act, 120–21, 141
discourse analysis, 10–14
discourse marker, 100, 190. *See also* turn initiator
discourse organization unit, 120–23
displaced mode, 26, 52–53
distal conception style, 55, 68
distance. *See* psychological distance
divided self, 74–75
domain, temporal, 164–65, 249
dramatic present, 21
dramatization, 215–22, 256
dramatization effect, 217, 222, 225, 242
dramaturgical theory, 186, 253

ecmnesia, 75
emotional heightening. *See* psychological involvement

evaluation, 25, 37, 81, 189, 253
evaluation, in narrative schema, 8
evaluative point, 57, 67, 143, 149
event, 241–42
event verb, 168–69, 250
evidential, 206–7, 210, 224
evidentiality, 189, 206–11, 222, 255
expressive element, 190, 215
extroverted consciousness, 26, 53

figure, 71
focalization, 57
follow-up (move), 121–23, 132–33, 157
footing, 37–38, 71–73, 243
foreground information, 211–15, 225
frame, 52, 241
free direct discourse, 188
free indirect discourse, 170, 188, 223, 250–51, 253
functionalism, 11, 235

go, 27, 66, 213–14, 225

have a verb construction, 168
head act, 122
hedge, 177, 252
historical present (HP) tense
  in consciousness theory, 26–27
  syntactic hypothesis, 21–22
  traditional theory, 20–21

I says, 50, 76–78, 230. *See also says I*
immediate mode, 26, 52–53
indirect reporting discourse, 55–58, 68, 184–88, 213
  function, 190
  variation, 188, 195, 204, 223–24
indirect speech. *See* indirect reporting discourse
information flow, 119, 126
information processing of past experience, 51–54
informative, 141, 248
initiation (move), 121–23, 127, 156–57, 248
inner language, 190, 214
inner speech. *See* inner language

interdisciplinary approach, 11–13, 231–32
interjection, 190, 215, 254
intonation unit, 119, 245
introverted consciousness, 26, 53
involvement. *See* psychological involvement

like, 213–14, 225, 245

Main Clause Phenomena (MCP), 215
maxim of conversation, 126, 202, 249
memory, 51–52, 186, 202, 204–5, 241–42
mental field, 55
mental imagery, 55, 81, 117–18
mention theory, 186, 252
mimesis, 223, 253, 256
monitoring ability, 75–76
monologue, 235
move, 121–22

narrative, 7–9, 43, 52, 236–37
  categorization, 8, 25–26, 235, 247
  clause type, 24–25
  definition, 7–8
  levels, 70–71, 119
  schema, 125, 235
narrative convention, 7
narrativization, 52
neutral place marker, 27, 117, 247–48

onstage region, 54–55
orientation, 8

pair, 122–23
participation framework, 72–73
particularity, 35, 235
past perfect tense
  avoidance of, 170–72
  discourse functional use, 172–74
perceptual field, 54
performance feature, 24, 237–38
personal deixis, 50–51
person-tense distribution in discourse, 44–50
principal, 71
profile, 54
progressive, 143, 153

proximal conception style, 55, 68–69
proximity, 79, 244
psychological distance, 57, 59–61, 68–69
psychological involvement, 55–61, 63–69, 78, 189, 242

realis/irrealis, 206, 255
recollection will, 58, 73
reflexivity, 1–2
relative tense, 163–65
repair, 245
reported speech. *See* reporting discourse
reporting clause
  as dialogue marker, 174–81
reporting discourse
  cognitive processes and, 5, 13
  context and, 9–10
  continuum, 187–88, 223–25
  definition, 1–3
  duplex structure, 1–2
  function, 188–91, 206–22
  function-pattern correlation, 205–22
  interpretive processes, 51–54
  pragmatic view, 188–91
  reflexivity, 1–2
  significance, 3–5
  social dynamics and, 5
  speech reception and, 4–5, 232
  spoken and written, 14, 233, 237
  style-function correlation, 222–25
  style-structure correlation, 191–205
  terminology, 2–3, 253
  theoretical backgrounds, 184–88
  universality of, 1–2
response (move), 121–23, 127, 156–57

say
  irregular tense-alternation, 28–29
  as a special reporting verb, 27–28
says I, 39, 50, 239, 244. *See also I says*
schema, 52, 241
script, 205, 241
self-alienation, 74–75, 243
self-identity, 61–64, 69–76, 78–80
self-involving interaction, 61–67, 72–73, 76, 78, 105
self-justification, 105
self-promotion, 105

self-separation, 75–76, 79–80. *See also* self-alienation
sequence, 122
sequence of tenses (SoT). *See* tense of reported clause
speak for yourself rule, 73–74, 243
speech act, 120–21, 244–45
speech act theory, 202, 246
stage, 54
stage model, 54, 242
state verb, 168
stream of consciousness, 123–24
stream of speech, 123
summary style, 141, 148–49, 190, 224
summons, 136, 151–53
syntactic dependency, 178, 252

temporal domain, 164–65, 249
tense, 19
tense of reported clause
   absolute deixis hypothesis, 163, 249
   combination of relative and absolute tense (CoRA) hypothesis, 163–65, 181
   discourse perspective, 165–81
   in traditional English grammar, 159–62
   pragmatic view, 162–63
   relative time hypothesis, 163, 249
   sequence of tenses (SoT), 159–62, 181–82
tense-alternation theories, 20–27
   CHP alternation theory, 23–24
tense-person distribution in discourse, 44–50
text, 119, 235
theatrical nature, 217, 225, 242
third-person interaction, 58–61, 76, 78
three-part exchange, 123, 132–33
timeless present, 22–23
topic development, 124–25, 130
turn, 121
turn initiator, 85, 92, 102, 244

utterance, 121

vantage point, 53–55, 61–62, 67
verbatim assumption, 185–87, 190

when-clause, 145, 248
wording theory, 186, 202, 249

zero-introducer, 36, 148–49, 248
zero-quotation, 84, 89, 91, 213, 217, 220–22, 224–25, 256